A HUNDRED YEARS OF THE
RAF AIR DISPLAY
1920-2020

A HUNDRED YEARS OF THE RAF AIR DISPLAY
1920-2020

IAN SMITH WATSON

FONTHILL

Fonthill Media Language Policy

Fonthill Media publishes in the international English language market. One language edition is published worldwide. As there are minor differences in spelling and presentation, especially with regard to American English and British English, a policy is necessary to define which form of English to use. The Fonthill Policy is to use the form of English native to the author. Ian Smith Watson was born in Irvine, Scotland, and educated mostly in West Yorkshire; therefore, British English has been adopted in this publication.

Fonthill Media Limited
Fonthill Media LLC
www.fonthillmedia.com
office@fonthillmedia.com

First published in the United Kingdom and the United States of America 2022

British Library Cataloguing in Publication Data:
A catalogue record for this book is available from the British Library

Typeset in 10pt on 13pt Sabon
Printed and bound in England

Preface

In writing this book, I have sought to make a comprehensive effort to peel back the cover, beneath which appears the detailed workings and thinking of the Royal Air Force in what has essentially been an extensive public relations exercise. The really interesting and for some the most intriguing endeavour of this is the endeavour in question—display flying and air displays. The RAF is a professional fighting service with a record second to none; in fact, you could argue that its place in history is not just enviable but unique.

Despite being the oldest independent air force, the RAF has never laid claim to be the largest but has chalked up a record of successful operations in wartime and results during peacetime exercises, testing its reliability, building a record of which it can be justly proud. The RAF owes its creation to the rapid development and application of aerial warfare during the First World War, having been created out of the respective air arms of the two recognised armed services of the time—the navy and the army. As a military arm, entertainment is not the air force's core business; it does not even fit into the service's ethos or operational planning. So why then is the RAF seen by many through the image of the Red Arrows?

What I have attempted to do in the following pages amounts to two principal points—first is to mark the centenary of the first official RAF organised public air event; secondly to reveal just why the RAF, given its *raison d'être*, has over the last 100 years made available such substantial resources, fuel, maintenance hours, training time, and personnel to present to the public, not just in the UK but overseas, demonstrations of flying by a comprehensive range of available aircraft. To this end, I have also tried to avoid this being simply another book about aerobatics teams, but instead to ask why aerobatics teams, why flying displays at all, and why did the RAF arrive at the stage of inviting as wide a public attendance as possible onto as many stations as could be opened to the public gaze, while allocating enough aircraft to support a large-scale invasion simply to fly demonstrations at each, once a year?

Also there have been continuous changes to service policy on displays and exhibitions, often driven by changes in the nature of the changing security threat and international situation and of course the overarching denominators, politics, and public reaction through the representations of the media.

There are, of course, stories from the shop floor and details of the participants as well as the thinking and conclusions that have seen millions attend air shows for decades at which the RAF has almost invariably been represented, certainly in the UK, although with increasing sparsity.

Finally, as the informed will soon detect, there are instances of some magnitude that have pockmarked the air show scene in the UK over the decades. The crash of the DH.110 at Farnborough in 1952 did not concern the RAF specifically, but any such incidents do influence policy decisions, in this case procurement. However, such incidents at public events, although rare, can set in train reactions that can be used to argue for curtailment or suspension of display flying and can lead to a raft of safety regulations. The earlier post-war years were particularly affected by tragedy; the chief of the air staff could not expect each September to pass without at least one aircraft accident during that year's Battle of Britain 'At Home' Day.

The 1950s ended on a tragic note with the disintegration of a Vulcan over RAF Syerston in 1958. Some pivotal moments where tragedy has occurred resulting in several deaths have been touched on here. There are others, but although I have endeavoured a complete account, time and cost have dominated, and I hope that I will not be judged too harshly for any surprise omissions.

That said, I trust anyone who has purchased or otherwise gotten hold of this tome, no matter how keen or remotely interested in aviation, will find they have had an insightful exposure to just why the RAF and other military air arms have spared time and resources to place themselves on show before the public over the last 100 years.

Acknowledgements

When setting out to record the history of this rarely visited facet of the RAF's repertoire—essentially 100 years of the service's public display flying commitment—it occurred to me to seek out one or two people with an anecdotal observation, a memory or two from over the years that would provide some much-needed insight. In so doing, I was fortunate enough to connect with a handful of willing contributors.

I would like to extend a special thank you to them now for providing some personal insight and some lighter moments; they are Paul Wheatley, former RAF helicopter pilot; Ian McFadyen, former fighter and display pilot; John Treadwell, aviation enthusiast; Trevor Pearson, former RAF air traffic controller; Steve Ward, John Houlston, gliding instructor and former fighter pilot; Nick Wilcock, Julian Treadwell, Paul Wheatley, David Edward Langley, Ian Anderson, R. A. Stitchell, John Higgins, Alec Blyth, Frank Klassens, and Johan 'Hans' Engels.

No book of this nature would be whole without the inclusion of images providing some impression of the different stages through the last 100 years. Images have been kindly made available via Peter March, Lee Barton, Ben Dunnell, John Wareham, John Fisher, Hugh Alexander, Tony Hawes, Adrian Balch, eLaRef, HJ Black, Shaun Connor, Chris England, Brian Bickers, Steve Raper, David Kerfoot, Rob Finch, Mal Grosse, and Alec Blyth. Mal flew in the Hunter segment of the 1968 RAF golden jubilee flypast over Abingdon before HM Queen Elizabeth.

At this stage, I always have my fingers crossed, while typing, that I have not left anyone out; if so, your name will certainly feature as an accreditation to the photo you provided or the short trip down memory lane. As 100 years is a long period to cover, my only regret is so much of what has filled this historic reference has now disappeared from living memory, but I trust with the aid of the aforementioned and a spot of diligent research, I have put together a worthy and comprehensive account.

Finally, a special mention for George Lee, formerly of 23 Squadron, who kindly provided his proofreading services.

Contents

Glossary

A&AEE	Aircraft and Armament Experimental Establishment
AAIB	Air Accident Investigation Branch
ACAS	Assistant Chief of the Air Staff
AFB	Air Force Board
AMP	Air Member for Personnel
AMSO	Air Member for Supply and Organisation
AMTS	Air Member for Technical Services
BBMF	Battle of Britain Memorial Flight
CAS	Chief of the Air Staff
CPC	Central Participation Committee
CS (A)	Controller of Supply (Aircraft)
DCAS	Deputy Chief of the Air Staff
FCHQ	Fighter Command Headquarters
GPO	General Post Office
IAT	International Air Tattoo
KLU	Koninklijke Luchtmacht (Royal Netherlands Air Force)
MOA	Ministry of Aviation
ORB	Operational Record Book
RAFA	Royal Air Forces Association
RAFBFE	Royal Air Force Benevolent Fund Enterprise
RAFCTE	Royal Air Force Charitable Trust Enterprise
RIAT	Royal International Air Tattoo
SASO	Senior Air Staff Officer
SHAPE	Supreme Allied Powers Europe
SSAFA	Soldiers, Sailors and Airmen's Families Association
USAF	United States Air Force
USAFE	United States Air Force European Command
VCAS	Vice Chief of the Air Staff
VCIGS	Vice Chief of the Imperial General Staff

Introduction

If there is one spectator pastime/sport/endeavour (call it what you will) that is both hated and adored by the general population, it has to be flying displays. Air shows, displays, pageants, fêtes, or tattoos—the chosen descriptive vernacular means the same thing to anyone with the slightest awareness of such events. The choice of descriptive term has also been used by, for example, aviation magazines as a ratings marker as to the approximate size and prestige of the event. 'Air show' means big, and 'air display' is often regarded as something smaller, but this certainly is not a set rule of measurement. Pageants (certainly fêtes) suggest something much less; however, the one air event called an 'air fête' in the UK was the chosen reference to what was also advertised as the largest militarily organised air show in Europe.

The once annual Mildenhall Air Fête was a must for aviation enthusiasts, including many regular attendees from around the world. It ran from 1976 to 2001. There was only one fallow year, 1999, due to the demands of the Kosovan conflict at the time meaning that much of the assets that would be relied upon to make it all happen were likely to be elsewhere, as were many of those expected to staff and run the air fête. The air fête was the United States Air Force in Europe's (USAFE) centre showpiece overseas public relations exercise. It was held over the Whitsun Bank Holiday weekend each year at RAF Mildenhall in Suffolk and boasted an international gathering of air arms rivalled only by that other behemoth of a public air extravaganza, RIAT (Royal International Air Tattoo), which is usually held at the now standby US air base at Fairford in Gloucestershire and organised by the principal RAF charity, the Royal Air Force Charitable Trust, now regarded as the largest such gathering of military air arms globally. All US Air Force bases in the UK officially are RAF stations; this status is maintained by the presence of an RAF liaison officer at each.

Before either of these events arrived, RIAT debuted simply as the 'Air Tattoo', the United Kingdom had seen a variety of militarily focused air shows. The origins of such spectacular events lay in the rise of air power during the First World War and the man selected to head the RAF on its foundation on 1 April 1918. Hugh Trenchard was appointed to command the RAF in March and promptly resigned after a week due to internal political differences but returned after the war. With budgets being cut and the armed forces jealously guarding their share of the much smaller cake. The army and the navy were concerned that the impact on their funding by the Armistice of 1918 should not be further complicated by an additional demand for ever diminishing resources. Trenchard understood this all too well. The situation prompted his return as the RAF's chief of staff.

The air pageant had been introduced by Lord Trenchard in 1920 very much to achieving an end—that end being the very survival of the Royal Air Force. In part, the aim was to match the other two services' public profile through various reviews, tattoos, etc. The 1920s therefore was a decade of probation for the RAF, and while gaining prominence and credibility—essentially supporting the army in overseas theatres, particularly across the Middle East and Afghanistan—the service's image certainly was not harmed by what had become the annual air display at Hendon with more to come.

Experiences with the Hendon Pageant encouraged a move toward staging several similar events across the country, reserving one day each year.

Hugh Trenchard's initial appointment as the RAF's first ever boss lasted about a week before he relinquished the post to command the Independent Air Force on the continent. He returned almost a year later, just four months after the Armistice, to replace his predecessor, Major General Sir Frederick Sykes, an able commander. Yet Trenchard's return to the appointment was made possible due to the same personal reasons, which centred around his divergence of opinion away from that of his political overseers. His greater public profile would be needed. He felt his resumption was imperative to saving the RAF from oblivion and found little resistance to his re-appointment in March 1919.

As he returned to the office of chief of the air staff, he was taking over the controls of an developing military arm that was already in a fight for survival. It was not the fault of his predecessor, who was up against not just governmental bloody-mindedness with the strapline 'war to end all wars' now consigned to the dustbin of history, as was hoped. The new boss was perhaps a more wary old soul than your average politician and, so it would seem, your average senior naval and army staff officers, and here was where his greatest problem lay—preventing the RAF from being consigned to the dustbin before it was even a year old, never mind 100 years old.

The navy and army were not comprehensively dismissive of air power, but they simply detested the idea of a 'Cinderella' (referring to the position of the RAF in the service hierarchy) force unique in their dull grey/blue drab uniform and pale blue insignia competing for the attention of the Treasury. The sea lords and imperial general staff were quite prepared to admit the efficacy of air power, but only where it was truly effective relative to their respective arms. This would possibly mean the end of the strategic bomber, very much seen as the one identified reason that justified the existence of an independent air force.

There is no telling what would have been the outcome of the distant conflict against Nazi Germany had the RAF not existed by then. Would the Admiralty and the War

Office or the navy and army councils have been convinced to allocate funds, pre-war, to an initial purchase of 300 or more Spitfires? Would they not be more inclined to feel the need to better serve the defence of the realm with more cruisers and battleships or more armoured vehicles and the creation of more infantry battalions? All may have conspired perhaps to thwart Hitler's military ambitions by other means, but if not, what then would ensure holding off Göring's Luftwaffe to a degree sufficient to convince the *Führer* to turn his attention toward the USSR, having grown thoroughly impatient with the lack of progress of the Luftwaffe as winter encroached?

With all this still far from anyone's imagination, apart from a vague notion in the head of Sir Hugh Trenchard, making the argument for an independent air arm so shortly after the war to end all wars left little room for argument to prove the case. Innovative projects to provide the pillars of the RAF would help place the junior service firmly in a favourable and respectable light with the war-weary British public. Trenchard's various endeavours to establish the RAF, as the third military arm of the British nation, in the hearts and minds of that nation included the creation of the Staff College at Andover. There was the establishment of the RAF answer to Dartmouth Naval College and Sandhurst, the RAF College Cranwell, the first such establishment for air force officers. It was understandably a milestone achievement and an endorsement of all his efforts when the first Cranwell graduate (not to be confused with the 'Cranwell brats/Cranberries', the technical apprentices across the road) to be appointed to command the RAF as chief of the air staff was selected, thus following in the founder's footsteps—from an *ab initio* RAF recruit through to the most senior post. All previous chiefs of the air staff had originally transferred from the navy or army or first served in the Royal Flying Corps, the officer in question, Sir Dermot Boyle, hailed from Dublin and he assumed office on 1 January 1956.

Just forty-one days later, Lord Trenchard passed away, having lived just long enough to see his efforts mature. All of these initiatives held at bay attempts by the navy and army to harness aviation entirely and confine it within the limits of their respective requirements under their own service ethos. Instead, Trenchard was able to develop and establish the traditions, ethos, and training doctrines of the new service, ensuring the wider development of military aviation. This would prove vital to confronting future threats outside of those ordinarily expected to be faced by the other two services.

Trenchard further strengthened the new service with the introduction of the apprentice schemes for teenagers with the right aptitude. This was to train vital ground crew—the airframe fitters, engine technicians, armourers, and electricians—all specialising in their various disciplines applied to aircraft engineering and as would increasingly become the case, associated support equipment, communications and eventually, radar. There was one more inspired step to shore up the RAF against the sceptics, the public profile. By default, air power had tremendous appeal and glamour attached. This could be utilised in such a way that land and sea arms could not.

Military demonstrations so far had been largely limited to the confines of Olympia at Earl's Court. Aerial demonstrations are, for all the cost and sophistication, the least restricted by the need for a suitable venue because of the nature of air as a medium. Flying was not core to the other two services, but this did not stop them in later years, especially the navy, sparing resources and effort to their own air displays. The army's traditional public face was parades, displays of skill at arms, and set piece scenarios, all of which could be conducted indoors or outdoors, day or night. However, the onetime jewel in the crown of the military showpiece spectacular in Britain, the Royal Tournament, is no more, although the Edinburgh Military Tattoo continues with its annual August Bank Holiday slot on the BBC.

Parading ships has never been an easy way to present the navy to the public; invitations aboard have usually been the easiest way of introducing civilians to take a closer peak behind the scenes of the senior service. The first Hendon Air Pageant was held on 3 July 1920, and some degree of trepidation doubtless hung over those involved because of the potential for fatal accidents to occur where the public were concentrated in great numbers. In 1920, this was something quite new, and so lacked the myriad safety measures and rules that were to be developed and introduced over the subsequent 100 years. Nevertheless, responsibility for the conduct of the event weighed heavily, even in this far less litigious time.

From the very early days, it was recognised that demonstrating air power was the best way of reaching the public. Government military expansion schemes in the 1930s provided more airfields; the RAF took advantage of this, in collaboration with the Air League, introducing Empire Air Day. This new format operated alongside the Hendon pageants from 1934 to 1937. From 1938, the Hendon displays were no longer held separate; instead, for better or worse, they became another feature of Empire Day. The airfield was an ideal venue for accommodating the public and more were being built to meet the growth of the RAF particularly.

The navy's mighty and extensive Spithead reviews could not compete with the pace and noise of a flying display with the spectators concentrated in a small area and able to see everything, whether on the ground, in the air, and, at times, overhead.

The impact was there, even well before the age of 'fast jets', which was such a long way into the future and not even a concept in 1920 that anyone could envisage. Yet with rapidly developing examples of new and experimental aircraft emerging, designers were introducing improvements to new designs that enhanced performance. Even in these early days, it was routinely anticipated that significant enhancements would be forthcoming next time. The opportunity to demonstrate, in sight and sound and at close quarters, to everyone from across the social spectrum the increasing development of aviation had not been missed. Trenchard seized the opportunity; the new RAF was to be presented to the public, and if expectations were not misplaced, the air pageant would have the desired effect on both public and political support.

At the top, the buck stopped with Trenchard himself. Some 100 years later, the RAF still holds a single air show each year; however, what has transpired in between is where the story sits. The zenith of service effort was reached long ago. We have now descended the other side of the peak through the invariable litany of defence cuts, litigation, operational demands on ever more scarce resources, and plain old-fashioned red tape blinkeredness.

The nadir would seem to be now for the RAF's involvement in air displays as the centenary of the first at Hendon passed. Today's event is not quite the grand military spectacle of a century before, but the intervening years have been most interesting.

1
Lord Trenchard and the Air Pageant

Lord Trenchard was one of life's pillars, a man with an imposing and at the same time avuncular appearance who had earned the nickname 'Boom' for his resonating, low-register voice. Hugh Trenchard cut a likely image and personality for the man who would become the founding father of the RAF. His progress through life from school days to commanding the RAF was not garlanded with unimpeded success, but someone of equal character would be hard to find, even at a time when such august types seemed to be less rare than today.

Born in 1873, thirty years before the Wright Flyer first struggled into the air to the delight of brothers Orville and Wilbur, and like another great Briton of the same generation, Winston Spencer Churchill, he was not as a boy regarded as academically gifted. He also did not have the level of financial support that was a typical feature of officers of his generation, so for this reason, he stood out at Sandhurst. Hugh Trenchard still achieved, albeit the bare minimum, qualifications to get as far as Sandhurst in 1893. He was commissioned into the Royal Scots Fusiliers and gazetted to India. He excelled in sports and won the All-India Rifle Championship in 1894.

In 1896, he came across Winston Churchill for the first time while playing opposite in a polo match. He remained in India until the end of the century and earned a degree of popularity but only through his sporting prowess. His social habits were out of alignment with those of his brother officers, such as drinking. As the twentieth century arrived and brought with it the Boer War, Trenchard's battalion went to South Africa while he remained in India; this was to halt a worrying drain of officers from India to South Africa.

Trenchard eventually joined the 2nd Battalion, Royal Scots Fusiliers, in South Africa in 1900 and trained to become a mounted cavalry officer in order to meet the Boers on a more level playing field, as the Boers were accomplished horsemen.

During September and October 1900, Trenchard led his men from the 6th Fusilier Brigade in action against Boer cavalrymen, during which he was shot in the chest but still led his men to victory in this attack against a Boer position. His wound was severe and the surgeons at Krugersdorp Military Hospital expected him to die. The bullet had punctured his left lung and he had lost 6.5 pints of blood. For all the bleakness of his outlook, he was fit enough to leave hospital after just three weeks. He was repatriated by hospital ship to Southampton, where he would undergo further treatment.

Following further convalescence in Switzerland, he returned to South Africa in 1901, this time to oversee the training of the expanding mounted infantry. In October 1901, Lord Kitchener ordered the capture of the Boer government, who were in hiding. Trenchard led a team of loyal Boers, British NCOs, and mixed-race guides on this mission.

The mission was a failure, but Trenchard and his men did not disgrace themselves when engaging the Boers in close-quarter combat after his men were ambushed. He received a mention in despatches. In 1902, Trenchard led his new unit—the 23rd Mounted Infantry Regiment—in final actions against Boer cattle rustlers and Zulu raiders. In 1903, he applied to join the West African Frontier service, the same year that the Wright brothers took to the air, just about, and made history. The world officially had its first heavier-than-air flying machine.

Trenchard was posted to Nigeria as a major in December the same year. Here he was tasked with leading expeditions and surveying operations to map out 10,000 sq. miles of territory; this later became Biafra, and his efforts brought further clashes of arms, this time with Ibo tribesmen.

Those who had been defeated were hired as road builders. For his energy and service, Trenchard was awarded the DSO (distinguished service order). He remained in Africa until 1910, when he had to be repatriated again through ill health, this time a liver abscess. After recovery, he was posted to Londonderry where life was comparatively dull; he also clashed with his commanding officer, Colonel Stuart. Following a few failed attempts to get back into colonial service, Trenchard came across an old friend from Africa, Captain Eustace Lorraine, who advised him to follow in his footsteps and take up the quirky new craze for flying. This meant returning to London from Ireland, which he did, arriving on 6 July 1912.

The day before his arrival, tragedy and irony struck when Lorraine was killed in a flying accident. Undaunted, Trenchard made a start with flying lessons just the same. He started flying training at Thomas Sopwith's school at Brooklands. He was under additional pressure as well, as he was just a handful of months away from his fortieth birthday, in February. This could be problematic as forty was the cut-off point for training as an aeroplane pilot.

On top of this, he was partially blind in one eye and chose to keep this to himself as he gained his wings. Trenchard had been an attentive pupil but had struggled, having become a pilot he was admitted to the Royal Aero Club Certificate, No. 270. Training was conducted in a far-from-reassuring-looking Henry Farman biplane. To look at one of these contraptions—and there is no other way of describing them—you would be forgiven for thinking the machine would be crushed by your own body weight as soon as you climbed aboard. The next stop was the Royal Flying Corps' principal flying training unit, the Central Flying School based at Upavon. Trenchard was very much at the start of things when he was guided toward becoming a CFS examiner by the commandant, Captain (RN) Godfrey Paine.

To become an examiner, Trenchard personally devised an exam paper on flying, then sat the test, marked it himself, and awarded himself his certificate. His flying skill still left much to be desired, but he was determined to make a success of it. While classed as an instructor, he tended to spend more effort on administrative duties.

It is in this capacity that he set about laying the foundations of the future Independent Air Force. Map-reading, engine maintenance, signalling, carpentry, painting, finishing, and other practical requirements and other more pragmatic endeavours which would be paramount in running a military air arm as a significant contribution to the armed forces, independent or otherwise. He did fly some operational flying training of sorts as the observer in an aircraft involved with an army exercise in September 1912. He was to bump into Churchill one more time when Churchill was appointed as first lord of the Admiralty, at the time that Trenchard held the acting rank of lieutenant colonel.

Churchill was learning to fly himself at Eastchurch, but Trenchard arrived at the opinion that he was not a good pilot. As of August 1914, he was appointed to replace Lieutenant Colonel Frederick Sykes as commander of the military wing (as opposed to the naval wing, despite there being a Royal Naval Air Service) of the Royal Flying Corps, the military wing specifically referred to the RFC element in the UK. Sykes would later briefly replace Trenchard as chief of the air staff. The headquarters was at Farnborough, and due to the lack of enemy contact, Trenchard, of all options, applied to re-join the Royal Scots Fusiliers even at this late stage. The Royal Flying Corps was, at the outbreak of hostilities, commanded by Lieutenant General Sir David Henderson (regarded as the forgotten father of the RAF), who as head of the RFC was therefore the real first chief of the air staff, albeit of the RFC, not the RAF. He considered Trenchard to be a vital cog at home and therefore turned down his application. Trenchard indeed was playing a vital role raising new squadrons equipped with the new aircraft. In October, his old boss, General Kitchener, sent for him to move to France. Then he found that Sykes had been promoted to major-general and was to replace Henderson. This rankled a bit as the two did not get on.

By March 1916, Trenchard had been promoted to major-general and was now in command of the RFC on the Western Front. He had been asked to divert resources for a strategic bombing campaign over Germany.

His force still was not armed in any realistic sense, the principal objectives being artillery-spotting and reconnaissance in support of ground troops. The age of the dogfighter was also just seeing the red glow of dawn on the far horizon as pilots were now carrying guns aloft to open fire on enemy aircraft, which, in turn, hastened the move to design and build new types having forward-firing machine guns fitted and turret machine guns on heavier aircraft; the role of attacking enemy forces on the ground was also soon being pursued. Trenchard whole-heartedly supported tactical low-level bombing. In 1917, air raids by German Zeppelins and Gotha bombers were hitting London and other targets; the government sought to respond by creating a more solid and centralised force—an air force drawing the various air elements, essentially the RFC and RNAS (Royal Naval Air Service) together in order to focus and direct operations through a simplified command and control structure.

Trenchard was approached about conducting long-range bombing missions over Germany. He understood the logic of this but did not want to split his forces. He also had his own predictions as to the direction matters were travelling in—put more candidly, his desire to be at the forefront of a centralised air force was his overriding priority. That such an arm would be created and that it would stand independent of the navy and the army meant it would need a uniformed commander of the new service. He was thinking ahead of events, but he was right. On 29 November 1917, the new air force bill received royal assent. As well as the post of a head of the new air force, just as with the other armed services of the day, there was going be a government portfolio, the Air Ministry, so there would be an air secretary as well. Trenchard headed back to the UK on 16 December and was met on arrival by Lord Rothermere, who had in the previous few days been appointed as the new secretary of state for air. Lord Rothermere offered Major-General Trenchard the brand-new titled appointment as chief of the air staff (CAS).

All was not as it seemed. The politician, perhaps not too surprisingly, treated the offer as *quid pro quo* favour. In return, Rothermere expected Trenchard to support him in a campaign to discredit the chief of the imperial general staff, Field Marshal Sir Robert Williamson, and Sir Douglas Haig. Williamson was being a thorn in the establishment foot at the time, digging his heels in against political decisions such as subordinating the British forces in France to French command.

Whatever his opinions about Williamson, Trenchard was steadfastly loyal to Haig, so he refused the offer. His loyalties to Haig were one matter, but he would not be a party to any such political shenanigans.

However, Rothermere and his brother, Lord Northcliffe, were able to argue the case that Haig's—indeed, the army's—policy of constantly directing offensive operations on the Western Front were expending young men's lives for no justifiable gain. Trenchard supported this position, but it was put to him that the development of air power and now the new air force could deliver the offensive force with far fewer casualties, even though Trenchard argued that the RFC was suffering heavy casualties in France as well. Trenchard eventually accepted the post on the condition that he be allowed to notify Haig personally. He took up his new appointment on 18 January 1918, before the new air force was officially formed. He now headed the new Air Council and proceeded to not get on with Lord Rothermere, the consummate politician versus the rough-hewn military man.

The approach to running the new Independent Air Force pitted the two against one another. Rothermere eschewed the advice of those who were at the heart of things, who were in positions of command in the RFC and RNAS, such as Trenchard. Instead, he sought the council of those from without who claimed expertise. Rothermere was if anything keen to place resources into the RAF at the expense of the other services and urged Trenchard to make some in-roads here. As much as a defender of the new air arm as Trenchard was, he did not regard the senior arms as less than vital. On 19 March, Trenchard sent Rothermere a letter of resignation following a series of acrimonious correspondence between them.

Coinciding with this and before the official formation of the RAF matters took a turn for the worse in France, the British 5th Army had been overrun by the Germans on 21 March, an example of how the progress of the First World War, even at this late stage, did not follow that of the global conflict two decades hence. Trenchard ordered all available assets and personnel to France to try and reverse the situation. Later that month, 26 March, news came from the front that the RFC were helping to resist the German advance. On 1 April 1918, just six days later, the Royal Air Force was officially born as the third and junior principal military force of the United Kingdom and its empire. Four days later, Trenchard headed out to France to see how the situation was developing first-hand.

He returned shortly to brief Prime Minister David Lloyd George and other ministers. On 10 April, Rothermere told Trenchard that the War Cabinet had accepted his resignation and that he could return to France to command what was now the expeditionary element of the RAF, he refused as to replace Major-General Salmond, then *in situ*, would be 'damnable' under the circumstances where everyone was heavily engaged in combat. For now, Sir Frederick Sykes replaced Trenchard as CAS. Even though Rothermere had tried to persuade Trenchard to stay on he agreed only until after the official formation on 1 April.

Rothermere shortly after tendered his own resignation, he was replaced as the air secretary shortly after 25 April by Sir William Weir, who approached Trenchard with an offer to command of a new formation: 'the Independent Air Force'. This was to be a strategic arm to bomb Germany and destroy the nation's industrial capacity. Trenchard refused this as well; he wanted to see the RAF reorganised so that he could perhaps be found a new position that carried parity with Sykes. He proposed that he be given command of the operational RAF while Sykes be confined to overseeing such matters as admin, support, and training.

Trenchard might have been rather more circumspect about this idea. Without a single head of command and the RAF split into two spheres, no matter how intertwined, this state of affairs would weaken the RAF's continued existence post-war if it was already fractured. The proposal was refused along with a variety of other likely posts including one which would have given him command over joint Anglo-American air policy.

While sat in Green Park one day, Trenchard overheard the conversation of two naval officers. He heard nothing good about himself; the way they saw it, and likely others, was that he had thrown his hand in at the height of battle and deserved to be shot. He contacted Weir immediately after and accepted command of the new Independent Air Force to be based in France with its headquarters at Nancy. As expected, the new force had strategic responsibility for attacks on German industry, airfields, and other vital communications, roads, and railways, etc.

The IAF was also tasked with supporting the American Air Service (the official name of the air arm of the US Army in the First World War). The contribution of air power at the Saint-Mihiel salient and the Meuse–Argonne offensive saw allied aircraft provide vital support to artillery and infantry, and the allied offensives prevailed. The end of the war was now at hand, heavily supported by both the IAF and AAS.

With the end of the war and Armistice Day on 11 November 1918, Trenchard returned to the UK for much-needed leave. He returned to military duties in January 1919; his first task was to report to Sir William Robertson, who was now in command of the Home Front Forces.

He was appointed to what was very much an army task—to resolve a crisis at Southampton Docks where about 5,000 unruly soldiers were mutinying. They could not understand why they were being ordered to France with the war now over. However, they were needed to oversee the governance of the occupied countries until such time as normal order could be restored. This was lost on them, and when Trenchard first tried to explain, he was heckled and jeered.

He responded by arming a detachment of 250 loyal troops, issuing a copious amount of ammunition, and ordering them to accompany him to the docks. He made it clear in no uncertain terms that if the mutiny was not abandoned and the mutineers returned to following orders, then his men—with bayonets fixed—would be ordered to fire upon them. The mutineers dispersed and complied—another job well done. The end of the First World War brought with it the inevitable contraction; everything had to shrink as the chiefs of the army and naval services expected the new RAF, consequently, to be rolled up.

Their prominence diminished, everyone was going to have to accept that the party was over, and things were about to revert to the way they were. The RAF could expect to be dissolved and what useful elements worth retaining subsumed into either the navy or the army.

This is where the story of Trenchard, the founding father of the RAF, truly begins. This is not to say that Sykes was poorly motivated or at all unsuitable as he put forward proposals for, if anything, an expanded air force. To confound such a suggestion further, the posts of war secretary and air secretary had recently been combined, giving rise certainly to a buoyant mood at the Admiralty and the War Office that the expectation of disbandment of the RAF was likely.

The new minister appointed to the surviving post of secretary of state for war was Winston Churchill.

The unrealistic proposals from Sykes annoyed Churchill and prompted him to look at the possibility of reinstating Trenchard in the role of CAS as he had been impressed by the latter's handling of the Southampton incident. Trenchard was approached to see if he would accept a return to the post of CAS. Some might have regarded this a poisoned chalice. Instead, Trenchard outlined his own proposals for the future of the air force. This met with Churchill's approval, and as of 31 March 1919, Sir Hugh Trenchard took over command of the RAF once again—one day shy of the service's first birthday. Through the summer of 1919, now wearing the new uniform of the RAF with its blue grey appearance and rank insignia in the form of braid for officers around the cuff, Trenchard had to approach the matter of accepting far-reaching cuts that saw many units disbanded as the RAF was, along with the other services, placed on a peacetime footing.

The RAF shrivelled up to a mere tenth its size following Armistice. The need for independence to run through to the very core of the service needed to be established at the earliest, which was not easy when all military expenditure was still contracting. Therefore, while moves were put in place to castrate the RAF, between 1919 and 1922, Trenchard ensured an officer training college was built at Cranwell in Lincolnshire, then the RAF Staff College at Andover, which would provide training for middle-ranking officers looking to move toward air staff appointments. He had secured a year's grace to the end of 1920 initially to establish the foundations of the junior service. He was now able to turn his attention to courting the public as well as political sympathy.

Whether he convinced the army and the navy or not may have been irrelevant anyway as Churchill may not necessarily have brought an end to attempts to shut down the RAF. There was, it had to be said, endless fascination flying with the entire concept, even before Trenchard learned to fly—pioneers of the new travel dimension, flying, were attracting large crowds to see them demonstrate their prowess at controlling their flying machines. There had been the air displays at Blackpool and Doncaster.

All that was needed was a field—somewhere for planes to operate and for spectators to be accommodated. The idea at the time was not to demonstrate power and majesty in the air or perform any aerobatics or dramatic performance handling; all that was required was the pilot's ability to stay the pace and land rather than crash his beloved pride and joy without sustaining anything other than superficial damage to himself and his steed. If he and machine, in perfect harmony, could get aloft, entirely without scraping a part of the plane along the ground or constantly bouncing away to the end, then onlookers would feel they had borne witness to the phenomena that men could fly.

Trenchard had this one option left to promote the RAF in the public mindset. The circumstances were not the best. After the First World War, Great Britain was not much different to its emergence from the Second World War about twenty years later; the people had been led to believe that the war just over was the last. However, military chiefs and politicians (generally) were all aware of the ever-present likelihood of further conflict.

Between the wars, the RAF was involved in operations notably against uprisings in Mesopotamia and other parts of the empire. Beyond parades and public ceremony, the navy and the army had the like of the Royal Tournament to raise their profiles and leave the public, around London at least, with a favourable impression. The RAF could join in but not to any extent that they could be seen as anything indistinguishable from the army; prowess in the air could not transfer indoors, as big as Olympia was.

As CAS, Trenchard considered the opportunity to stage a demonstration of aerial skill not a spectacle of risk by pioneers in early simple machines, such as had been seen at Blackpool and Doncaster, finding their way and writing the rules as they went (some may consider this particularly interesting). However, Trenchard had to approach this matter from the other end. This would be a display of flying by trained professionals in machines far more robust, energetic, and of advanced design and manufacture.

He would need permission from the Air Council and the Treasury to stage any kind of display and, given the aim, to promote and project the RAF. The political battle for the RAF was joined; this would be the one opportunity to make the case for retaining the RAF as an independent arm, not through effectiveness over the battlefield, but by demonstrating such skill overhead on a summer afternoon while safely on home soil. The staging of a high-profile tournament of the air would need to seek not just the public at large, but the patronage of the establishment and of course royalty.

The principal aim was to raise proceeds for the RAF Memorial Fund, not to shove dark blue and khaki noses out of joint, and a grand affair it was to be. The choice of Hendon as the venue was as good as any in 1919–20; as it was a modern airfield of 200 acres in Colindale, it was already associated with aerial events. The first ever aerial derby was held here in 1912, which attracted in the region of 3 million people—another indication of the intrigue and popularity to be exploited by the RAF. However, Hendon was not, at the time, an RAF airfield; it actually belonged to Graham White Ltd, but as the RAF had no similarly adequate premises sufficiently close to the capital and that it was seen as something of an imperative, time being at a premium, Hendon it was. From across all London and beyond, an enormous catchment area should mean that the takings were high. If not, then it was all over. As Hendon was very accessible to the population of Greater London, it was an ideal choice as opposed to an active RAF station further away.

With Treasury permission and the Air Council on board, the first Hendon Air Pageant, presenting the RAF, took place on 3 July 1920. Some 45,000 spectators paid to enter the airfield; if the RAF could repeat this, then it could compete with the Royal Tournament.

The cost was not too extortionate by today's comparisons but would depend as always on the average working man's pay, which in 1920 was £204 15s 9d per year; today, this would be no more than marginally over £9,000.

Therefore, from the layman's point of view, £2 10s for a six-seater box and 5 shillings to park your car would respectively be about £103 and £11 today, but again, the average working man's pay was much lower. Honoured guests included HRH Prince Henry, duke of Gloucester, and Winston Churchill in his capacity as secretary of state for war and air. The flying display was billed to be sixteen items in total, of which about twelve flew.

It is perhaps worthwhile saying that the difficulties and challenges encountered in 1920 and those associated with the flying displays of today are largely unchanged and can still have an adverse effect on even the most carefully planned flying display programme. Factors such as weather, aircraft serviceability, and even minor incidents can disrupt programmes that have over the years become even more dependent on split-second timing as the performance of participating aircraft has increased. Sudden changes in operational commitments can also have an impact, bearing in mind that the participants are military aircraft and aircrew.

The published programme was heavily detailed, carrying the timings, names of crews, and a quite detailed explanation of what to expect. The aircraft representation included a formation of five Bristol F2B Fighters and another of five Sopwith Snipes, along with an air race of Avro 504Ks, which took off directly over the heads of the crowd. With the press looking for something to write about, they seized on this highlight to offer a critical observation.

The Aeroplane were there and were not unimpressed; their scribe wrote, 'The most striking feature of the whole performance was the military precision with which the events were run.' This was not all they had to say, and when the magazine's edition carrying the review of the day went on sale, it listed five separate complaints—'grouses', as *The Aeroplane* described them; they were not, as the description makes

Cover of the 1920 Hendon Aerial Pageant programme. (*Via Author*)

clear, entirely charitable. The first was to advise the air staff to move the event to Croydon as it was a much more pleasant airfield and was served by better tram and rail services and expected to have electric trains running up to the main gates within the year. They also picked up on the overflying of the crowd head on and wondered what would happen if an engine failed at such a critical moment, offering the observation that 'either it would have to land in the middle of the people, or do a flat spin and crash itself'.

Furthermore, the magazine made its concerns known about the emotional effect on those watching from just a few feet below, observing that 'Only the uninitiated or the foolhardy are completely unmoved'. The first Hendon Air Pageant was a success, and the Air Council considered it 'in every way desirable that an Aerial Pageant should be organised for 1921', with early summer being the preferred window to hold it in line with the 1920 event. They considered the pageant an essential part of Royal Air Force training and should be given permission due to its being 'entirely analogous to Naval and Military Assaults at Arms, Regattas, Regimental Sports and the like and was a necessary and important part of the training in the RAF.' This was Trenchard's comment in making the case for another in 1921.

He held the training element in high regard but also felt there was another 'subsidiary consideration in its favour'. This was the exclusion of the RAF from participating, save for a very minor role, in the Royal Tournament owing to the total unsuitability of Olympia for any air force display.

Trenchard also said he would have preferred to stage the pageant at an RAF aerodrome rather than Hendon, but nowhere suitable existed that was in easy reach of London and endowed with the extent of accommodation and stands that Hendon had. A few days after the pageant, questions were raised in parliament. On 12 July 1920, Mr Charles Jesson, MP for Waltham West, asked the secretary of state:

> What was the approximate cost of the air pageant at Hendon on Saturday, 3rd July; whether such a cost was included in the Air Force Estimates; if so, under what Vote? And whether it is necessary to obtain the sanction of the House for such demonstrations?

Winston Churchill responded:

> The pay of the Royal Air Force personnel and the running expenses of Royal Air Force machines employed at Hendon on the 3rd July are normal charges already provided for in the Estimates under the relevant Votes. I am not aware that there are any other charges to be met from public funds, though there was also a trifling expenditure of old or surplus stores which do not require replacement. The question of Parliamentary sanction does not arise.

With no real parliamentary objection raised and in the absence of a suitable RAF alternative venue to Hendon, Trenchard recommended that the next RAF air pageant should be held at the North London aerodrome again. In terms of finance, he proposed that all costs pertaining to the training elements of the pageant should be borne by the RAF. All expenditure for the organising of the event, such as the use of Hendon Aerodrome, would be taken from the gate proceeds, and what was left would go to the Royal Air Force Memorial Fund. This was the outline of how funding for the next pageant should be divided essentially.

He sought the secretary of state's approval henceforth. Given the prestige of the show, picking the dates had to be selected with care. For example, the prime ministers

Avro 504Ns in formation break, *c.* 1920. (*Peter March*)

of the Dominions had to be accommodated so a date had to be chosen that would best suit. This was the stage reached by February, with the expectations that the second Hendon Air Pageant would take place around June or July. The provisional dates selected were 2 and 3 July (Saturday and Sunday), which was not put to Trenchard until April. He was not happy about having a second day, but this was when the Dominion prime ministers would all be able to attend. He wanted to confirm whether or not the second day would be necessary but also advised the secretary of state that a decision was needed quickly so he could advise the two air officers commanding inland and coastal, such was the way the RAF in the British Isles was divided at the time. When ready, he would issue instructions that he felt necessary with regards to training.

The proposal for a second day was abandoned and the 1921 Aerial Pageant therefore took place on 2 July. The proceeds to the memorial fund amounted to £8,274 17s 2d. This was an increase of £1,545 11s 10d over the 1920 event. Trenchard now wanted arrangements for the 1922 pageant to be taken up on a firm basis immediately after the 1921 show. The sum of £1,000 should be reserved from the 1921 gate and put toward the cost of 1922. Trenchard also wanted all serving officers and other ranks to be given free admission to all enclosures, and boxes—as one would see at Ascot— be made available for members of the Air Council and such senior RAF officers as befitted their rank. AOC-in-C Inland Area suggested that funds, which he was responsible for spending, should be fixed at 10 per cent of the previous year's takings rather than retaining a sum before handing over the profits due to the fund. He also did not like the idea of reserving boxes for RAF personnel for free, except for members of the Air Council. The reason for this was logistical; a good many boxes had to be placed at the disposal of distinguished visitors such as the Admiralty, imperial general staff, and other notable figures.

One senior officer, the DTO (director of training and organisation) wanted to see some of these removed from the free list and some senior RAF officers included. Trenchard wanted to relieve AOC-in-C Inland Area of much of the responsibilities of organising the pageant by appointing an ex-RAF officer as a secretary, who would then be the permanent man dealing with the project in much the same way as was the case with the naval and military tournament. For many years, private cameras were banned from RAF displays of any kind; to provide some form of substitute in these very early days, Trenchard requested 'Photographic Lorries' to be in attendance in 1922 that would develop photos on the spot, as part of a photographic competition, and sell them to the crowd. He wanted to see men and guns being loaded onto an aircraft as had recently taken place during operations in Egypt, overseen by Sir Geoffrey Salmond; he also wanted to see more items in the 1922 programme with a definite training purpose.

The DTO objected to the seeming assumption on part of the RAF Memorial Fund that the pageant was run solely for them instead of forming part of the training programme. He also objected to holding £1,000 as a deposit toward the next pageant. To clarify his objections, he observed:

Programme
of the
Royal Air Force
Aerial Pageant,
1921.

Left: Cover of the 1921 Hendon Aerial Pageant programme. (*Via Author*)

Below: Bristol F2Bs formation flying during rehearsal for the 1921 edition of the Hendon Aerial Pageant. (*Air Historical Branch*)

The pageant was entirely an Air Ministry affair, the RAF run it and shoulder the expense then hand part of the profits to the Memorial Fund, the RAF keep the rest but recording a deposit of £1,000 made it look as if this money belonged to the Memorial Fund and they were handing it back.

He might also have objected to the introduction, back in 1921 and continuing in 1922, of a novel idea to allow members of the public to fly in participating aircraft, specifically during air races and formation flying drill. The tariff was £3 3s to be taken up in a multi-engine aircraft and £5 5s for a single-engine type. The greater cost for the latter is very much because you were more likely to end up with a more 'seat of the pants' ride. The principal aerobatics teams were equipped with Sopwith Snipes in 1920–21; for 1922–23, the older but slightly faster SE5a returned to the fore. It was back to Snipes again in 1924. The year 1927 brought a change of pace—a team of DH.60 Moths, light trainers, from the Central Flying School.

In the run-up to the 1927 pageant, a decision to move the press enclosure to the other side of the new types park (a section of the static display set aside for the latest aircraft expected to or recently entered into service), caused some alarm as it meant removing them from the 'social quarter' to a less prominent position, which it was expected would be strongly resented.

The press, as always in the case of high-profile events, was looking to make good copy, selling the display and the RAF. Bearing in mind the power of the press, when they were to find that they had been dragged away from the well-to-do in order to sit in an isolated position, resulting in a reduction of both status and vantage, the reaction was a tinge of resentment. The move would break with the precedent set back in 1920. There was a further break with precedent this year— the use of light trainers in place of front-line aircraft for the principal aerobatics team.

Avro Tutors rehearsing for the forthcoming display. (*Peter March*)

VIP enclosure at the 1925 Hendon Air Pageant, from left: HM Queen Mary, HM King George V, an unidentified gentleman, Elizabeth Bowe Lyon, Lord Trenchard (both with backs turned to camera), and the duke of York. (*Via Author*)

How it all worked back in 1925—the public enclosures at that year's edition of the Hendon Aerial Pageant. (*Via Author*)

Following the 1928 pageant, the Air Council approached the Treasury to explain that they required additional funding to entertain foreign diplomats and officers invited to the display. It was explained that the Air Council endeavoured to restrict such invitations within the narrowest limits. Yet on the occasion of the 1928 display, it had been necessary to extend invitations, for diplomatic reasons, to provide entertainment on a larger scale than normal for parties of French and Italian officers and, on a smaller scale, parties from Denmark, Norway, Sweden, and Belgium.

The prompt for this approach was a letter from the secretary of government hospitality, which made clear that the minister in charge of the fund proposed that the costs should be charged to air votes—in other words, the Air Ministry share of government expenditure. While happy to agree to this course, the Air Council were anxious that the lord commissioners of the Treasury be made aware that the limited funds the council needed to meet such a large sum were insufficient.

Therefore, permission was sought to have the entertainment allowance increased by no more than the amount outstanding. As of 1 January 1930, Marshal of the Royal Air Force Sir Hugh Trenchard relinquished the appointment of CAS. His replacement was Air Chief Marshal Sir John Salmond. By 1931, with no real expectation of what the future held, new combat aircraft designs—substantially superior to earlier types that themselves had entered service in the post-war era—were appearing at Hendon. Among the impressive new machines was the latest front-line fighter, the Hawker Fury. One the RAF's most prestigious squadrons, 43, fielded a team of three Furies this year, flying a most scintillating display of close-formation aerobatics.

Bristol Bulldogs of 3 Squadron, lined up awaiting their slot in the flying display at the 1929 Hendon Air Pageant. (*Air Historical Branch*)

In 1928, the set piece had already arrived for the airfield attack on a dummy fort. (*Air Historical Pageant*)

No. 23 Squadron's aerobatics team during rehearsals for the 1932 Hendon Air Pageant. *From left to right*: Douglas Bader, Harry Day, and Geoff Stephenson.

Early solo aerobatics with smoke. (*Air Historical Branch*)

2
Hendon to Empire Air Days

The success of the Hendon Aerial Pageant was undeniable, to such a point that the Air League of the British Empire conceived the idea of affording the opportunity for making such events far more publicly accessible. The new format that they proposed involved opening the gates of as many RAF stations as could possibly meet muster. The formality of the RAF display at Hendon would not be prominent, certainly not if a widespread number of airfields were to provide displays simultaneously. Inviting heads of other air arms, along with prime ministers and their retinues, could not possibly be a feature of all the participating stations. The name of the new nationwide air events was to be 'Empire Day' or 'Empire Air Day'.

The idea was conceived by the air league back in October 1933. The aim was to more widely promote the RAF and 'get the public inside aviation'. The new CAS, Sir Edward Ellington, said he thought 'this scheme should be tried for a year or two, to see how it goes'. He also thought charging the public was acceptable as the navy did for access to their dockyards to view ships, etc., but he did not want to charge more than a shilling, with a possible reduction for 'parties of children'.

The chief of the air staff had several other suggestions. He did not think the new air day should take place on Empire Day as it was generally a holiday and would prefer on that account to choose another day. Observing that RAF stations were scattered, he expected only local people to turn up at each through mostly local advertising but felt they would rather appreciate the privilege of being able to look over their local RAF station. The AOC-in-Cs should be consulted to find out when would be the best period to suit each; furthermore, the same should be told that there was to be no special flying. However, if formation flying was being practiced on the day, then it would be all for the better.

The first to take place was arranged for 24 May 1934, which was a Thursday. Forty RAF stations were listed to open to the public across the country. A success, the day was described as 'the greatest aerial entertainment ever staged'. In the run-up on 18 April, it was suggested by Geoffrey Mander, MP, that the government felt the public carried insufficient interest in the Royal Air Force—the rationale behind the air day.

The Hendon Air Pageant had a more formal arrangement than tends to be the case, but as can be seen, it was well attended. This is the 'Service Type Park' at the 1932 event, on 25 June. (*Air Historical Branch*)

Empire Air Day posters. (*Via Author*)

Sir Philip Sassoon, undersecretary of state for air, responded:

Arrangements are being made to open about 40 Royal Air Force stations from 2 p.m. to 7 p.m. on 24th May, to enable members of the public, on payment of a small charge for admission (the proceeds of which will be devoted to Service charities), to inspect hangars, workshops and aircraft at close quarters and to obtain an insight into the everyday life of the Royal Air Force. Visitors will have an opportunity of seeing almost every phase of the peacetime work of the Royal Air Force, and I hope that the public will take full advantage of this innovation, which is due to the initiative of the Air League of the British Empire.

No expenditure from public funds will be involved.

The Hendon display continued and was held that year on 30 June, but the Air League's proposal, while it would impact on day-to-day training and operational flying, was far better disposed, as they intended, to stimulate airmindedness and interest in the RAF and cast the net wide and far as it were. In some instances, some of the stations selected would open to the public on the day prior, charging 1s for adults and 3d for children to watch the rehearsals and get to see the RAF close up, 'that they may see at first-hand how the RAF lives, works and plays'. Parking was available for cars and coaches with charges on a sliding scale.

1934 Bulldogs in mass formation from various squadrons; the serrated markings indicate aircraft from 17 Squadron. (*Peter March*)

It certainly said something about the Air League's importance that they could influence the Air Ministry and the RAF in such a way. Empire Air Day followed along the lines of providing ground exhibits and, where possible, a programme of flying, while station commanders were permitted to invite civilian aircraft to co-operate by being given free use of the airfield and generous terms for the disposal of receipts for joy rides. Given the wider public appeal, such things as the 'Lucky Programme Number' were introduced where the winning prize may be a free flight. There was no doubt that the Air League were the overseer of these events.

RAF station commanders were to collect all funds from gate and programmes sales, then forward a profit and loss account to the Air League along with a cheque for the net profit; any amount for expenses or damage to government property was deducted before this was sent off. The league then handed the proceeds to the Air Ministry to divide between whatever charities and philanthropic causes it felt worthy; the typical recipients were the RAF Benevolent Fund and the Guild of Air Pilots Benevolent Fund.

The year 1935 marked HM King George V's silver jubilee. The RAF were facing their first such formal review. The selected date was to be 6 July, and the first venue considered was Hendon, the idea being—as with Finningley forty-two years later when HM Queen Elizabeth II reached the same milestone—to replace the air pageant with the silver anniversary review. C-in-C ADGB (in later years C-in-C Fighter Command) Air Chief Marshal Sir Robert Brooke-Popham dismissed this idea. His concerns seemed mindful of the already encroaching infrastructure around the area as he considered the impact on local residents and safety risks enough to make Hendon unsuitable for the scale and demands of the event envisaged. Anyway, there would be no proceeds to the RAF Benevolent Fund if the review usurped the pageant. Instead, Brooke-Popham suggested that his majesty should attend one airfield where a comprehensive representation of the RAF would be gathered. The flypast, should, to utilise space to the best advantage, operate from somewhere else.

An interesting list of pairings were considered—Boscombe Down and Andover. However, this would entail travelling too far for the king, whose health was deteriorating. Hendon was looked at in conjunction with Northolt, Bircham Newton with Sutton Bridge, Upper Heyford with Bicester, and the winning combination of Duxford and Mildenhall. Mildenhall would host the royal party initially, where his majesty would inspect the guard of honour, then tour the vast line-up of aircraft from a total of thirty-seven squadrons, including special reserve and auxiliary units. Once the royal party left for Duxford, the flypast and other aircraft that would perform air drills prepared to leave for same. ACM Brooke-Popham accompanied King George V while Sir Edward Ellington, CAS, accompanied HRH the prince of Wales and Air Vice-Marshal P. H. L. Playfair, AOC Western Area, accompanied the duke of York. This meant a busy summer for the RAF—Empire Day at the end of May followed by Hendon on 29 June then the silver jubilee review just a week later.

Meanwhile, interest in events surfaced in parliament again regarding the Hendon pageant in particular; radical anti-establishment politics was actually just as noisy and prevalent in this era of austerity and tweedy rectitude. Following the 1935 Hendon display, Edward Mallalieu, MP, asked the home secretary:

Bristol Bulldog fighters of 3 Squadron rehearse their contribution to the 1935 Hendon Air Pageant, by which time, the pageant was being superseded by the more public friendly and accessible, nationwide, Empire Air Days, usually held in May. (*Peter March*)

> Whether his attention had been drawn to the conduct of police at the Hendon air display in attacking harmless pacifist demonstrators, in one case destroying a camera with which one was taking a photograph of the police attack on his fellow demonstrators; and is he aware that the only disturbances were caused by persons who attempted to take from the pacifists the leaflets being distributed, which persons, together with vendors of the 'Blackshirt', the police left unmolested?

John Simon, the home secretary in Conservative Stanley Baldwin's National Government, was a Liberal like Edward Mallalieu, though the latter was of the National Liberal Party, who were in opposition. He responded:

> I have had inquiries made, and the Commissioner of Police informs me that the real facts are as follow. A procession headed by a youth carrying a large red flag was marching towards the main gate of the aerodrome. Some of the demonstrators refused to obey police directions and a few minor scuffles ensued. As for the camera incident, I understand that the camera was accidentally knocked out of the hand of a bystander (who was not known to be one of the demonstrators) by a police inspector. The inspector apologised for the accident and gave his name and station to the owner, but nothing further has been heard of the matter. Nothing was seen by the police of persons attempting to seize leaflets which were being distributed. The action of the police throughout was directed solely to prevent any breach of the peace.

The Hendon pageant continued through to 1937. Among the highlights that year was a formation aerobatics team of four Furies from 1 Squadron, like 43, also based at Tangmere.

Led by Flt Lt Teddy Donaldson, the 1 Sqn team flew a sequence of loops, rolls, and stall turns in close formation. Later in the year, they were invited to take part in an international aerobatic competition at Zurich, Switzerland. They astonished the Swiss, French, Italians, and Germans by taking to the air in desperately poor weather conditions that had forced the other teams to remain on the ground. Donaldson's team flew their full aerobatics sequence with the cloud base at 200 feet. Elsewhere at Villacoublay in France, new Gloster Gladiators of 87 Sqn flew aerobatics, with rope connected between the wingtips.

The rope idea was reprised in the 1980s by the Moroccan aerobatics team, Green March. In 1937, the British government were now struggling to get funding for one military expansion scheme after another. From 1935, planning officials toured the country looking for suitable locations to construct several new airfields; this was happening quickly, and even at this stage, new airfields were being commissioned and occupied by a steadily expanding RAF. The expansion had the effect of broadening the scope for the air day.

Close to double the number of RAF stations were involved, compared with 1934. The last year for the Hendon Air Pageant was 1937; from 1938, Hendon would host the public in May under the format overseen by the Air League.

Following the last pageant, the officer commanding the armaments group, Air Commodore Garrod, wrote to the Air Ministry to air his views that flying regulations during flying displays on Empire Air Day were not fully appreciated. He based this impression on the number of requests he had to refuse from some of his unit commanders, to relax the flying regulations. Members of his staff had also reported remarks made when visiting stations amounting to the same thing. It seemed unit commanders' temptation to introduce items of a sensational nature into their flying programmes was a strong one. Without specifying which, Garrod said there were three regulations that many wanted relaxed. While noting that the Air Ministry attached great importance to the strictest observation of flying regulations, he thought it might be worth considering these requests when writing the flying regulations for the next year's Empire Air Day.

Another senior RAF officer, AOC-in-C admin, Coastal Command, visited two RAF stations on air day—Calshot and Gosfort. While he found the efforts by personnel were beyond reproach, the public attendance was poor.

For this, he blamed poor press coverage, in print, on screen, and on the airwaves. The Coastal Command chief himself added to the same report that May was the best month for the Empire air day as it preceded Hendon and so served as an advertiser for the flagship event. The stations would share assets, but the bulk of aircraft were usually home based.

While the air staff debated the merits of the entirely unique public advantage of Empire Air Day, parliament was not unanimous in its support. This time, they had a more substantial set of questions to challenge government with.

On 28 July, Mr Frederick Montague, MP, asked the undersecretary of state for air 'whether, as the result of examination of the reports of courts of inquiry held on the

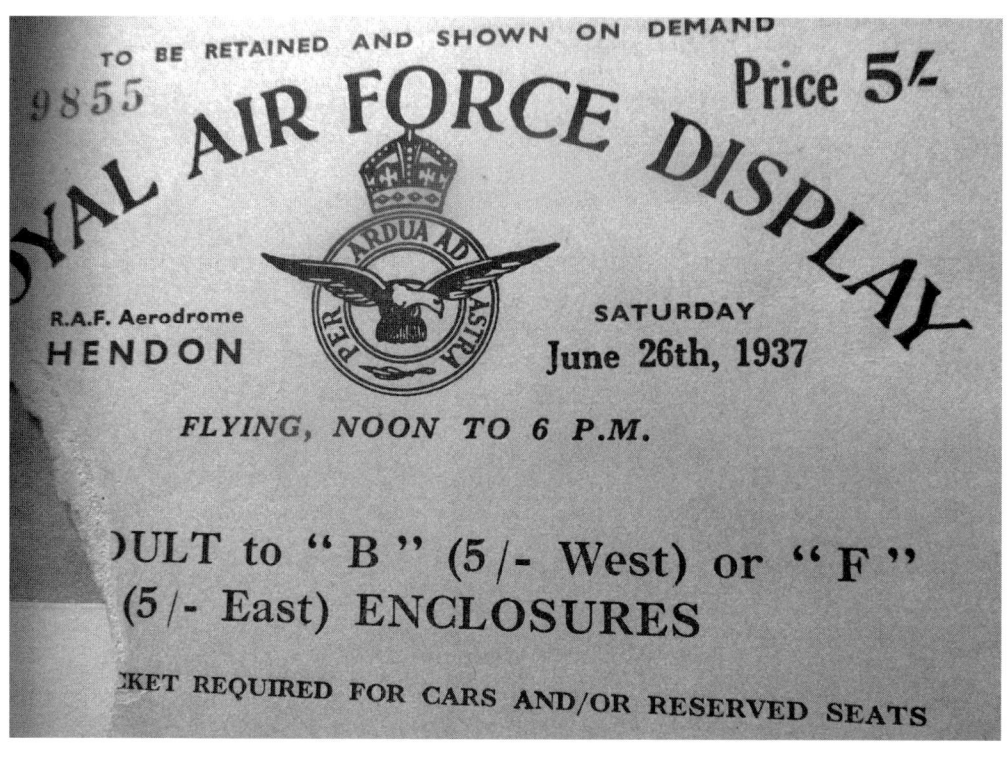

Programme
of the
Royal Air Force
Air Display
1937

Above: An original ticket, torn at lower left corner, for the final Hendon RAF Air Display. (*Author*)

Left: Final Hendon Air Pageant programme cover, 26 June 1937. (*Author*)

accidents which took place in connection with Empire Air Day displays this year, he has any further statement to make?'

Lt Col Anthony Muirhead, now undersecretary of state for air, noted:

The idea of Empire Air Day is that the public should be enabled to see the Royal Air Force at its everyday work. As many stations as possible—this year it was 53—are opened to the public on payment of a small charge for admission. At each station a programme of flying is arranged. All items of flying in the programmes are such as can be regarded as a part of normal training, and an instruction to this effect is issued to all stations. All flying in the Royal Air Force, whether on Empire Air Day or any other day, is governed by King's Regulations and Air Council Instructions which lay down the safety precautions which are always to be observed.

Under King's Regulations and Air Council Instructions aerobatics are forbidden to be carried out below 2,000 feet, except with the prior approval of an Air Officer Commanding, and even when this approval is given a definite minimum height is always to be stipulated. It has been the practice for discretion frequently to be exercised in this respect by Air Officers Commanding both at the Royal Air Force Display and on Empire Air Day, but special care is always taken, both at displays and at other times, to see that where discretion is exercised the pilots in question are adequately experienced. In May last five out of 13 Air Officers Commanding gave special authority for aerobatics below 2,000 feet.

King's Regulations and Air Council Instructions also state that a spin must be completed at a height of not less than 2,000 feet, and Air Officers Commanding possess no authority to permit a departure from this regulation.

In addition to these normal safety regulations the Air Council, on this occasion, issued the following instruction: Station Commanders are to submit their proposed programmes of flying to their Group Headquarters for approval, particularly in respect of safety arrangements. There were, however, I regret to say, two accidents in rehearsals on 28th May in which four lives were lost and three accidents in displays on 29th May, also involving the loss of four lives. As a full oral account of the facts as regards each of these accidents would involve a lengthy statement, I will, with the permission of the House, circulate the detailed particulars in the official report.

I should, however, inform the House that the Air Council think it right to state, firstly, that they can find no evidence that programmes failed to conform to the general rule that they should consist only of such exercises as pilots would carry out in their regular course of duty and training; secondly, that they can find no evidence of any case of a pilot being instructed to perform an exercise for which he was not competent; thirdly, that no accident was due to any deviation from regulations which had been authorised by the competent authority; and, fourthly, that as evidence suggesting the disregard of flying regulations has been brought to their notice in connection with certain of these accidents, they are taking all possible steps to ensure universal compliance in the future. On this latter point, however, my Noble Friend would wish me to say this. While it is clearly wrong that safety regulations should be transgressed without sufficient justification, and a strict observance is requisite, it will be appreciated that breaches of the regulations involving risk may arise out of the over-keenness and courage of those concerned.

Instead of taking reassurance, Montague instead seemed to develop an acute sense of frustration at what he felt an unsatisfactory answer, which in turn led to a heated exchange:

> May I ask whether inquiry was made as to a breach of the regulations due to over-keenness, and also whether the type of aerobatics which were undertaken was within the discretion of the commanding officer? May I ask also whether these accidents happened apart from the regulations?

Muirhead reported:

> As regards the first supplementary, that is covered by my reply that as evidence suggesting a disregard of the regulations in certain of these accidents has been brought to our notice, we are taking all possible steps to secure compliance with the regulations in the future.

Montague replied:

> That is not my point. My point is that one of the regulations gives discretion to the commanding officer, with regard to certain limits of height. Was that discretion exercised? Was an inquiry made as to how this discretion was exercised by the commanding officer and whether, in fact, aerobatics were done at an exceedingly low level or not?

Muirhead continued:

> Five out of 13 deviations from the regulations were authorised by the proper authorities. In none of the cases where such deviation was authorised did any accident take place. Evidence was given in the course of the inquiry that there was a suggestion in other cases that the flying regulations were not carried out, and we are looking into those matters. In none of the cases where deviation was properly authorised did any accident take place.
>   Following are the particulars: Odiham Accident (two airmen killed), 28 May 1937. Four Audax aircraft of No. 4 Squadron were to take off in V formation and, when in the air, to assume diamond formation. On a signal from the leader, they were to assume 'echelon right' in which the leader and the right hand aircraft retained their position, the rear aircraft of the diamond moved to third on the right, and, when this pilot had taken up his new position, the left aircraft of the diamond moved across to right rear. Each aircraft would then be at the same height, and behind and to the right of the one in front of it. The flight would then be in the correct formation preparatory to a dive on the aerodrome, a perfectly normal procedure for an Army Co-operation Squadron and one which involved no aerobatics. Several rehearsals were carried out

by the same pilots, each of whom was conversant with the movements involved and thoroughly experienced in flying these aircraft. On 28th May the exercise proceeded normally until the change of formation from diamond to echelon right.

The first part of the change was successful, but the left-hand aircraft of the diamond, in moving to its new position, came dangerously close to No. 3 in the echelon. In endeavouring to get clear, it collided with No. 3 at 5,000 feet. The two aircraft locked, separated and began to spin. Both pilots were wearing pilot type parachutes, but the two passengers, though wearing the harness, had their parachute packs detached. This was a contravention of King's Regulations, which require parachute packs to be kept attached by all occupants of an aircraft except when the wearing of them would hamper the efficient execution of duty. In this case the airmen were not called upon to act in any capacity other than passengers and had no duties to perform which necessitated detaching the packs. Regarding the spin of each aircraft subsequent to the collision, in one case the airman, in attempting to attach his parachute to his harness lost it overboard and was killed by jumping or being thrown out of the aircraft. In the other case the airman remained in the aircraft and was killed in the crash. The two pilots, after making every effort to right their respective aircraft, abandoned them at the last minute consistent with safety and landed uninjured. Martlesham Accident (one officer and one airman killed), 28 May 1937. A flight of three aircraft was detailed to participate in a display at Hanworth. The flying officer detailed to lead the flight submitted a programme on 27th May to his commanding officer who approved.

This programme consisted of formation flying, followed by individual aerobatics which were to finish up with a spin by the leader, on the conclusion of which the other aircraft were to rejoin formation. No deviation from King's Regulations was authorised. The exercise involved nothing abnormal, and the flying officer in command of the flight was an experienced and accomplished pilot of these aircraft. During a rehearsal at Martlesham on the evening of 28th May, he commenced aerobatics after formation practice. After completing a loop and a roll he began to spin from an altitude of about 1,200 feet and hit the ground still spinning. Farnborough Accident (one officer and one airman killed), 29th May 1937.

In accordance with orders issued by the officer commanding the squadron and approved by the station commander, three aircraft were to fly over the aerodrome at about 2,000 feet and then come under blank fire from an A.A. battery. One aircraft was to appear disabled, break formation and dive away. At each of the rehearsals the pilot of this aircraft executed a deliberate spin instead of a dive. This spin was not in the programme but was executed, with the approval of the officer commanding the squadron, from a height of about 2,000 feet, and at the dress rehearsal the pilot spun from this height for two or three turns. A contravention of King's Regulations, paragraph 717 (3), which states that spins will not be continued below 2,000 feet, was therefore necessarily involved.

On 29th May, the pilot spun to about 1,200 feet, recovered, at once went into a spin in the opposite direction, and was unable to pull out of the resultant dive. The pilot was fully competent in the handling of Audax aircraft and had done a large proportion of his total of over 300 hours flying in that type. Waddington Accident (one officer killed), 29th May 1937. A squadron leader from No. 2 Flying Training School, Digby, was lent to Waddington to give a display of individual aerobatics in a Fury single-seater aircraft, a type not in normal use at Waddington. Several rehearsals were carried out successfully at a minimum height of some 2,500 feet. On the 29th May, the officer in the course of his display began a slow roll at a height of some 500 feet. This was contrary to King's Regulations from which no deviation had been authorised. When in an inverted position the aircraft commenced the second half of a loop and dived into the ground. It is a matter of conjecture whether the pilot misjudged his height or lost control of his aircraft. Although this officer had only completed some six or seven hours flying on Fury aircraft, he was a highly experienced pilot with well over 3,000 hours flying to his credit. Old Sarum Accident (one officer killed), 29 May 1937. No. 16 Squadron were to carry out squadron drill at a height of about 2,000 feet followed by a dive on a ground target on the aerodrome by one flight of the formation. The exercise was simple air drill, involving a climbing turn at its conclusion. This event had been rehearsed without incident on the morning of 29 May. One pilot, in accordance with his part in the programme, pulled out of his dive and went into a steep climbing turn. This continued over the vertical the aircraft then diving into the ground. As his aircraft had plenty of speed it is not known why he attempted to recover from the vertical climb by diving, as opposed to executing the latter half of a slow roll. He had completed about three-quarters of his 500 hours total flying on Audax aircraft.

The last years of Hendon and Empire Air Day saw some interesting new aircraft, radically different from the traditional fare of the twenties and thirties—all with entirely Perspex closed cockpits, mono-wing designs, and in some cases in-line engines rather than the more familiar radials. Also, they had a retracting undercarriage. Among the strange larger yet sleeker-looking designs the punters might see were Wellingtons, Hudsons, Beauforts, Blenheims, and even the odd Hurricane and Spitfire.

The air days were not benefiting from the ever-heightening threat to peace from across the continent yet again. Having sold its soul for the promise of national redemption and international pre-eminence through the rise of the *Führer*, Adolf Hitler, Germany was rearming at a rate that had taken the country way past the limits imposed through the constraints of the Treaty of Versailles. The best argument for how this happened was quite simply a desire across Europe not to risk another needless bloody quagmire. The last Hendon Aerial Pageant was on 26 June 1937. The Air Ministry announced on 30 January 1938 that Hendon was too small an airfield for the latest type of aircraft.

Over the years since 1920, the pageants had raised more than £150,000 for the RAF charities, and over 4,000,000 visitors had poured through the gates each year. The final hurrah in 1937 brought in 186,000 people, of which 70,000 were admitted for free and 60,000 at half price. The Empire Air Days continued to be held over the next years at RAF stations across the UK. Much more emphasis at these events was based around the local station's particular role, the last one being staged on 20 May 1939.

3
Battle of Britain

The early stages of the Second World War unfolded quickly with no response from the League of Nations to Germany annexing those neighbouring chunks of other countries that Berlin determined were German. First, on 27 June 1937, the Condor Legion was sent to provide air support for General Franco's army in Spain. Then came the annexations of the Sudetenland in Czechoslovakia, all of Austria, the coercion of Romania, and various other international outrages. Britain and France had assured Poland that they would come to her aid if threatened or invaded. The German invasion of Poland came to pass on 1 September 1939. An engineered pretext was Hitler's justification, which he seemed to believe would be accepted. The SS selected suitable concentration camp inmates to play the part of Polish soldiers; they were then murdered and scattered about a German wireless station, near the Polish border. Following this, Germany invaded Poland. The Poles fought gallantly; the superlative *Wehrmacht*, in conjunction with a Soviet invasion from the east, entered Warsaw prior to the Polish surrender on 6 October 1939.

Following the Anglo-French response to declare war on Germany and the lull before the storm that became the Phoney War lasting through the Christmas that it was all supposed, again, to be over by, the next phase of Hitler's conquest came with a parachute, land, and sea assault on Norway and Denmark on 9 April 1940. This was the very first airborne assault in history. The British government was forced to find a new prime minister, narrowly surviving a vote of no confidence on 8 May.

It may sound overly sentimental and heavily patriotic to say, but had it not been Winston Churchill, the war would be over with the Third Reich victorious. Churchill had one rival to replace Chamberlain as prime minister; this was Lord Halifax, former viceroy of India and foreign secretary. Halifax simply had no confidence in himself and would have effectively handed the responsibility for the country's war conduct to Churchill anyway, thus with the agreement of the Labour Party to serve in a coalition, Churchill was received by King George VI on 10 May and accepted the Royal invitation to form a government. Hitler's next move—the subsequent invasions of the Netherlands, Belgium, and France—was the defining moment for the course of history and depended on Britain's response. While the British Expeditionary Force and other allied troops withdrew to the beaches of Dunkirk, the British government was forced to find a new prime minister.

The withdrawal of British and other allied forces from the beaches of Dunkirk were the backdrop to what was to become the moment when the RAF, very much yet to make history in the field of arms, was to justify itself. There was the tail end of the First World War and the intervening operations over Mesopotamia (Iraq), but this was to be the baptism of fire. The opening was essentially the Battle of France then Dunkirk; the impression left on the army and navy was deeply unfavourable.

It was also quite unfair. One of the reasons for the absence of RAF aircraft over the stranded soldiers at Dunkirk while the Luftwaffe appeared with alarming regularity was that the RAF were at altitude several miles further inland and over the sea, ensuring that as few German aircraft as possible got anywhere near the beaches. Still there was little faith that matters could be reversed. The Germans had advanced across Europe and succeeded with such speed that it would take an unshakeable faith to imagine they could be confronted. The evacuation from Dunkirk through the brilliant effort of all involved with Operation Dynamo had helped to save both face and the small number of soldiers desperately needed to form the nucleus of a new army. However, the future looked decidedly bleak.

The RAF were about to become the saviour not only of the nation but of civilization as we have come to recognise it. Westminster was so demoralised by the apparently unstoppable force of the *Wehrmacht* resisting further, following the evacuation of Dunkirk, that many were rationally contemplating seeking negotiations with Berlin.

There was no reason to expect victory (or global salvation) was about to be snatched from the eternal abyss. The prelude to any German landings on British soil was to be able to get across the channel in sufficient numbers to make substantial progress, quickly, once ashore. In this regard from the German perspective, the principal threat came from the Royal Navy, and it has been observed many times, by historians since, that the navy, had they been called upon in numbers, would have defeated any attempt by the Germans to cross the surrounding sea. That this would have been at a devastating cost of the navy is equally acknowledged. A German invasion would most probably have been halted if Fighter Command had failed, where that would have left Britain's ability to continue to prosecute the war elsewhere would be another matter. Yet the prize would be that any further proposed crossing would be put off indefinitely, a phrase which would actually be used in almost the same context later.

Following the withdrawal of British and other allied forces from the continent, the government could only wait and see what the *Führer*'s next move would be; after all, the Low Countries, France, Denmark, Norway, Poland, Czechoslovakia and particularly concerning, the Channel Islands were occupied. However, small and insignificant on the strategic level was the small group of islands near the French coast; they were British territory and the idea that the German war machine would be unable to find a way to make the next hop to mainland Britain was not reassuring.

The situation was critical. The service in pole position to prevent an invasion was the Royal Navy, supported by the RAF. The Battle of Britain has become a much argued over but undeniably pivotal moment in the Second World War. The Battle of Britain did not consume the level of human loss and widespread devastation, which later decisive campaigns and battles did. The outcome though was crucial to getting to such a stage where the war would be taken Germany, with the weight of resources required to run the Third Reich to ground.

Future battles, particularly fought on Soviet soil— major clashes between the Soviet and German armies such as Leningrad, Stalingrad, Kharkov, Kursk, and Sevastopol— would be where the back of Hitler's military machine would be broken. The decisive and defining campaigns with Western Forces—El Alamain, Normandy, and the Rhine Crossing—were crucial to the decisive end of the war, as was, arguably, the relentless allied bombing campaign. Perhaps most crucial of all was the Battle of the Atlantic, the one long-running campaign of the war which gave Churchill sleepless nights of worry. Considering the inestimable number of other engagements and the war in the Far East and Pacific, there is much to reflect upon.

Without the favourable outcome of the Battle of Britain, the subsequent vital military contests may never have come to pass, the consequence being the Nazi grip on Europe might well have lasted decades, perhaps while endlessly fighting the Soviet Union.

A further consequence could have seen the Americans and Japanese condemned to wage never-ending campaigns across the Pacific and the South China Sea. The eventual use of nuclear weapons may not have happened in August 1945, but would have happened sooner or later, and in a different scenario, with a different outcome for civilization, perhaps under circumstances where they may have existed also, or exclusively, in German hands. The conclusion would have been many more years or decades of genocidal misery culminating in an Armageddon of one kind or another. Could this have been the legacy of Fighter Command's failure, were it so? It is to this degree that the battle was decisive in the long term, even though the Luftwaffe, much less the rest of the Third Reich's armed forces, did not suffer an immediate decisive or irreversible defeat. That this exclusively air campaign carried so much for the outcome of civilisation and its progress is why it became the focus for the RAF above all of the service's many other wartime exploits, placing the remembrance of the Battle of Britain in a unique position of ceremony and public celebration after the war.

4
Battle of Britain 'At Home' Day

The end of the war in Europe on 8 May 1945—VE Day—was perhaps prematurely celebrated worldwide as the end of the war, rather than only to the extent of Europe (including the USSR), the Middle East, North Africa, and the South Atlantic. Across the UK and wider Europe, this was certainly the end of the war as far as its immediate impact on the lives of all and the lifting of the threat of tyranny were concerned; this was where it mattered to us—where it was directly felt. Several thousands of miles away, war continued in the Far East and the Pacific. British and Empire forces (Australia, New Zealand, India, etc.) continued alongside those of the USA and those of other allies in the region, to fight the Japanese through campaign after campaign. Whether in the fetid heat of the Burmese Jungle or amid the volcanic ash of islands like Iwo Jima and Okinawa, in the skies overhead and the surrounding seas.

Yet it would not be long as plans were afoot for a large-scale allied invasion of mainland Japan. Other plans were also afoot to render the other plans unnecessary. Within days of the VE celebrations, RAF stations and Group HQs were already receiving requests to participate in local victory celebrations by means of demonstration flights over the localities concerned. These requests were forwarded to the Air Ministry for a ruling on service policy on such activities. The policy during the war was to resist any such requests. Air Marshal Sir Norman Bottomley (VCAS) advised the air staff that it would be wise to continue this approach even though the war in Europe had now ceased. His reasons were four-fold:

a. If we gave way even for one or two large towns, we should find ourselves saddled with almost endless commitments, since it would be impracticable to discriminate between the claims of cities, towns and villages with their special associations or particular claims.

b. If these demonstrations were to be efficiently staged, they would involve considerable organisation and administrative effort, and probably some training and rehearsals. We could ill-afford this at a busy time of redeployment, disbandment and demobilisation.

c. The expenditure of petrol and machine hours would be considerable, would have no great training value and is not really justified when economy is so important to us at this stage of the war.

d. We shall have quite enough problems during the demobilisation period in maintaining a high standard of discipline, particularly a high standard of flying discipline. Natural exuberance on occasions of victory celebrations such as those proposed are apt to produce uncontrolled flying resulting in flying accidents and it is most important that we should avoid this, particularly at this stage.

The various commands were informed that invitations to take part in flying demonstrations at victory celebrations are to be 'tactfully declined'. This ruling was to be applied without any prejudice to any national celebrations or parades that may ultimately take place with inter-service co-operation. The chiefs of staff had already informed SHAEF that proposals for demonstration fights over London would require government sanction.

VJ Day marked the absolute end of the Second World War. The official line was drawn under it on 2 September 1945 when the Japanese government delegation arrived on board USS *Missouri* in Tokyo Bay in order to take their part in the ceremonial signing of the articles of surrender before so many allied servicemen, the ship's company, and senior officers from the various allied powers on board.

The wonder was that the *Missouri* remained afloat. Less than two weeks later, while the world started down the long road to come to terms with the aftermath of war, with dispossessed human beings in their millions ambling amid the ruins of largely uninhabitable cities across Europe and the Far East, the RAF afforded a war-weary British population an opportunity to enter their nearest RAF station and have a peak behind the scenes.

Back home in Britain, there was a post-war atmosphere of a chance to relax and look forward to a promising future at last, yet the UK was bankrupt. First things first, the country was in no better condition generally than much of the continent. The economy was in a most parlous state; many cities, especially London, had streets bordered either side by open wasteland where once rows of houses, tenement flats, and factories stood, now marked by strewn and piled up rubble and jagged protrusions of brick and masonry. Before any attempt could be made to resume a peacetime existence, much had to be done to regenerate economic growth. Essential services, food production, power provision, reconstruction, and a comprehensive range of other vital services had to be brought back to life before any return to peacetime normality could start to take effect.

The armed forces—largely based overseas and, in many cases, now surplus to requirements—had to be demobilised and transitioned back to desperately needed industrial productivity.

Amid this order of woe, less than two weeks following the signing of the articles of surrender on board the *Missouri*, the RAF invited the public to their nearest base to have a day/afternoon out. Many were treated to something of a flying display as well as exhibits of service equipment from aircraft to radio sets and survival dinghies—all manner of service equipment mostly pertaining to the station in question. The date was 15 September, a Saturday, and press reports from the various open stations reflected on a good day out. It was something to lift the spirits of those now recovering from all the VE/VJ Day celebrations and now turning to face what the future held.

Doubtless many felt able to relax and enjoy the day, even if within a military environment that would not have been quite everyone's cup of tea at the precise moment. The stated object of the exercise, of course, was to seize the first available opportunity to commemorate, early on, the RAF's recognisable great moment in the Battle of Britain.

It was most fortuitous that 15 September fell on the Saturday this year. This date was long since recognised as the anniversary mark of that finest hour. Quite surprisingly, there was an established institution whose members were not quite so impressed. The Air League of the British Empire, having been instrumental in the creation of the pre-war Empire Air Day, felt that if the resumption of such activities were to be allowed then Empire Air Day would be the obvious template. The club were adamant that the Empire Air Day should return, like the Battle of Britain 'At Home' day; the forerunner event was to all intents and purposes the same save for the focal point, but in whose honour was it to take place?

The former event celebrated empire, Britain's glorious past, and, for a short while, looked to the future with no expectations of significant change—a time when the globe showed more than half the land surface to be painted imperial pink, to indicate British 'Administration'. The latter focus was the moment that the RAF, essentially Fighter Command, secured the precious time vital for the British government to lay the foundation of the fight back against the National Socialist shroud across Europe—Nazi Germany. If you were to settle the argument by putting the question to a modern poll, it is a foregone certainty the latter would prevail. However, the Air League were virtually impervious to any suggestion that the British Empire was anything but a force for good. They consequently lobbied the air chiefs and the government to reconsider the establishment of what took place in September 1945 as an annual event again, but back as Empire Air Day, not the newly coined phrase, Battle of Britain 'At Home' day.

Meanwhile, the RAF approached the matter of resuming such an event but from what was arguably a more low-key approach with a heavier emphasis on reflection. The Air League embodied the spirit of the development and promotion of aviation across the spectrum from private ownership through commercial to military usage. On the other hand, the RAF looked to their laurels to find a pivotal point in history—a place at the centre of future public activities—and they already had it.

The one day that stood out in September 1945 had already received such attention, with a large-scale flypast led by the already legendary Douglas Bader, and the simultaneous opening of RAF stations across the British Isles to the public had unexpectedly set a new precedence. Yet in late 1945, nothing was established for the long term. The 'At Home' day was for the time seen as a one-off.

Meanwhile, the subject of air displays and RAF prominence in them was attracting enthusiasm from folk who could do something about. *The Daily Express* at the end of 1945 proposed holding/sponsoring an 'air pageant' in 1946; to this end, they

Aerial view of RAF Church Fenton on the first Battle of Britain 'At Home' day, 15 September 1945. (*The National Archives*)

A similar scene at RAF Upper Heyford on Battle of Britain 'At Home' day, 17 September 1949. (*Air Historical Branch*)

contacted the RAF. The undersecretary of state for air further discussed the proposal with the outgoing wartime CAS Sir Charles Portal. It was not a flat no, and a review of suitable airfields, again in the London area, was quickly carried out. Northolt, West Malling, and Blackbushe were considered by the RAF to be capable of handling 'modern aircraft'. *The Daily Express* asked if they could visit each of the three to see if they would be suitable from the point of view of hosting spectators.

On the downside, the undersecretary of state told *The Daily Express* that RAF participation would be small. The assistant chief of staff was also sure that the RAF would have to run all the flying events and be responsible for crowd control; it would therefore be on an active RAF station after all. In other words, it would be a display run entirely by the RAF for *The Daily Express*, but it would be in aid of the RAF Benevolent Fund. ACAS (Ops) requested permission to allow *The Daily Express* to visit the three airfields mentioned, on the grounds that he expected them to find the airfields unsuitable for the intended purpose; meanwhile, a decision was to come from the Air Council.

There were other requests on a smaller scale. The RAF were in the meantime warming once again to the idea of a permanent resumption of the Empire Air Day. Co-operation with *The Daily Express*' display was turned down. *The Daily Express* eventually found their airfield elsewhere, even though the pageant was delayed a while; it took place at Gatwick on 10 July 1948. It was well attended by the RAF, including a display by four de Havilland Vampires under low clouds.

There was no Empire Air Day in 1946 but a repeat of the Battle of Britain 'At Home' day on 14 September; again, an inconceivably large number of RAF stations participated. The air staff—with much more to concern themselves with in the aftermath of the war—were quite agreeable to the idea of establishing an air day at least once a year. The success of the pre-war Hendon pageants and the Empire Air Day had encouraged the air force's grandees to appreciate the pull on the public mind set that flying had and the natural stage for theatre of the air that an airfield provides.

There was the question of whether the public—adult and child alike—would be keen on military pomp. Perhaps it was not what a demob-happy country was likely to find much interest in. Celebrating the empire that was already clearly in decline could be seen as an argument to restore a sense of pride. On the other hand, following such a costly war, which we came so close to losing, which witnessed acts of conspicuous bravery and sacrifice, this was a more fitting point in history to reflect upon. More specifically, the Battle of Britain, the one turning point upon which so much depended, and which placed the RAF at the centre of the action, was surely a worthy rival, certainly to the continuing celebration of empire. The air staff were very aware that this crucial point in the war was, arguably, the RAF's great moment. It was quite clearly where the air force specifically should seek to promote itself in the public conscience.

As with any service organised public event, the final decision to make would be what to do with the proceeds. The two service charities representing the RAF were now RAFA and the RAF Benevolent Fund, the latter having initially been founded by Lord Trenchard as the RAF Memorial Fund. They were the natural beneficiaries of such proceeds. The events during the late summer and early autumn of 1940 were now firmly fixed in the public imagination. The RAF and Fighter Command, most specifically, settled on making the anniversary of the Battle of Britain a high-profile affair.

The responsibility for overseeing any future events fell to the vice chief of the air staff, as the Air Council member with whom the buck stopped. He began 1946 by suggesting that it was time the Air Council reviewed the current policy on such matters, which was, after all, still the wartime policy. A review of service participation in public events took into account the way it was back just before the war. The first post-war RAF events, which took place on 15 September 1945, could be a basis for a similar format to the Empire Air Days of the 1930s. Yet instead of celebrating the achievements of empire, the focus post-war would be the Battle of Britain; this would be more in the spirit of reflection, thanksgiving, and commemoration, with the snatching of victory from the jaws of a most dreadful likely defeat. The VCAS, Sir Douglas Evill, noted that in the pre-war years, Empire Air Day proved an excellent medium for bringing the general public into closer touch with the RAF and (most importantly) stimulating recruitment. Sir Douglas drew attention to the various additional domestic benefits for the RAF, such as 'the smartening up of stations' in preparation for the event. The work in the lead up to the Empire Air Days, apart from organisation and domestic preparation of stations, involved a great deal of air training. The prestige of the event was also a service morale booster.

What might not make clear sense is that the RAF were on a recruitment drive in 1946, at a time when large numbers of stations, at home and abroad and consequently squadrons, personnel, and equipment, were being disbanded and disposed of in accordance with the transition from a wartime to a peacetime economy.

It might seem counterintuitive, but all three of the armed forces had to maintain the continuity of recruitment, especially given the likely public perception that recruitment was the last thing the forces were drumming up amidst the process of widespread demobilisation. Another of the VCAS's points was the imperative that everything possible should be done to bring potential recruits into contact with the RAF, in which circumstances the Empire Air Day should be re-established as a permanent annual commitment.

Little mention was made of the large number of RAF stations that opened to the public 15 September 1945; estimates (and they are only estimates now) vary from 93 to 100. There were, of course, many other examples of fortitude and endeavour through the war. There were many other air operations that were vital or more intense in terms of scale and sacrifice, but again, this was in support of wider-scale military operations, such as those in the Western Desert, Normandy, and the support of the Chindits.

The Battle of Britain was unique in that it was a straightforward air-to-air campaign, with a start and an end, the moment Hitler's forces—his air force, hitherto knowing nothing but victory—suffered defeat.

Sir Douglas Evill's report focused on the effort made for the official flypast over London that day in 1945, when they had many fighter squadrons to draw from, which were at full strength and fully trained. The first formal event of 1946 would be the Victory Flypast in May. This was to include six squadrons from the BAFO (British Air Forces of Occupation) and three from the Fleet Air Arm to make up twenty squadrons.

After this, there would be further decline, and the feeling was, with some certainty, that there would not be sufficient aircraft to mount a worthwhile flypast for the Battle of Britain celebrations in September. Under the circumstances, Sir Douglas suggested abandoning any idea of a mass flypast and reviewing the idea the next year. The heavy volume of requests for the year included a wide spectrum from Victory Day to National Savings Week, and it was suggested that they consider each on merit as they came in; any decision to contribute should be based on available resources and the demands of training at the time. Many requests came from small civic events, some being sent directly to the Air Ministry and others being received at command and group level.

At the start of 1946, the RAF appointed a senior officer to establish the framework of future proceedings and thus tradition. Air Marshal Sir Richard Peck ACAS (Gen.) was assigned the task. He was shortly due for retirement in April followed by appointment as governor of the BBC. Peck recommended, with a good degree of emphasis on ceremony rather than spectacular entertainment, that the week within which 15 September fell would be 'Battle of Britain week', so one day that week would be Battle of Britain day. That day, a colour-hoisting ceremony on all RAF stations would take place, as well as parades and flypasts of aircraft, with the principal flypast over London. The Saturday would be the day when the taxpayers got to see where that bit handed to the junior service went, becoming established as 'At Home' day.

The Air Council approach to selecting participating 'At Home' stations was to draw up a list of as many RAF stations as could be mustered. The respective COs would be directed to open their gates to the general public. RAF stations, as so referred to in this context, meant anywhere the RAF ensign unfurled from a flagpole. A good number of the stations involved were not at all suitable, substantial flying displays and the presentation of interesting ground exhibits notwithstanding; to invite the general public everywhere might be counterproductive. Providing the chance to see some flying might just attract folk to see behind the scenes of a maintenance unit or supply depot, strangely the RAF's top brass did not seem to grasp this early on. The public's general expectations would become clearer with time. From here on in throughout the book, I have chosen mostly to refer to the Battle of Britain displays simply as 'At Homes' with inverted commas to clarify and for ease of reference to the event; this was the standard reference used in correspondence and minutes at official level.

The Air League still pressed for the Empire Day, in more practical terms. All this would really amount to would be a change of title and, of course, a re-scheduling of the day presumably back to May, which might be preferable to September.

The criteria limiting the selection of stations to open was quite narrow. The only factors that were accepted to justify a station being excluded from opening were operational, security, or construction work. Simply being only weeks away from closing—a prevalent situation in the earlier post-war years—was not seen as a sufficient excuse for not spending about six months minimum beforehand preparing the unit for hosting a sizeable public event. Some station commanders who received notification that their unit would be one of that year's 'At Homes' were moved to pass more rational suggestions back up the line. Some did not have airfields, some were dockyards (flying boat stations), and some were just simply too small and in a number of cases were surrounded by too much infrastructure in order to address the one factor —aeroplanes and flying—likely at all to have punters crossing the road to see if they could get in for free.

Of the many requests pouring into the Air Ministry and the RAF for aircraft to take part in various events, there had been three exceptions to the rule since the end of hostilities— the celebration of the Battle of Britain on 15 September 1945 and two more flypasts. The two flypasts included one over Guernsey on 9 May 1946 with another one on 8 June. These were a part of part of victory celebrations, which would involve seventeen RAF and three FAA Squadrons. As well as *The Daily Express'* endeavour to restart the air pageant under the newspaper's banner, other requests were received for RAF flying participation in national and civic events and displays. The Air League's Southampton branch wanted the RAF to take part in a Victory Air Pageant on 22 June, while the corporation of Birmingham was pressing for something to support a similar event.

To follow a policy of turning down such requests now was expected to have an adverse effect on the junior service—in other words, bad publicity, especially where recruitment was concerned. The decision not to take part in such events taken in May 1945 immediately after VE Day, even though the feeling was that they could meet a number of requests if on a small scale, was already out of date. Home-based operational commands—i.e. bomber, fighter, and coastal—had since been consulted and agreed that on occasions, flying at such events could be authorised. The circumstances were such that there was a considered case for relaxation of the policy. From April 1946, all requests for flying participation had to be forwarded to the Air Ministry. Each request would be considered on its merits. If the air staff determined that the request could be properly organised and controlled, then flying of a nature that justifiably enabled it to be regarded as a part of service training as far as practicably possible would be arranged. This was subject to the appropriate C-in-C being prepared to make the necessary arrangements.

It would be explained in each case, however, that participation would only be possible on a very small scale. The reason for this was largely driven by the process of the RAF reorganising into a peacetime air force together with the ongoing policing commitments in contested territories. The next step was to set up a standing committee to co-ordinate all requests for RAF involvement in any events.

The head of the new committee was expected to be the director of operations, who would have on board representatives of the rank of group captain typically from various air staff appointments—AMP (air member for personnel), AMT (air member for training), and AMSO (air member for supply and organisation). The new committee's function would be to advise, after consultation with air members and commands concerned, whether any such requests could or should be met. The committee would also take into consideration any financial implications should the participation fall outside the usual sphere of training.

Meanwhile, the new outfit's remit was outlined by four principal policy positions regarding public displays:

1. Empire Air Day to be revived and run as in the years prior to 1940, in accordance with manning and training commitments.

2. Battle of Britain celebrations to be abandoned in 1946, but subject to reconsideration in 1947.
3. Requests for air participation in national celebrations (e.g. Victory Day) to be referred to the standing committee of the Air Council.
4. Requests to be considered by a standing committee under the air staff, and each one decided on its merits, in consultation with AMP, AMSO, AMT, and commands concerned.

Subject to these measures being approved, they would need to be acquainted with the Admiralty and the War Office, who conformed with Air Council procedures. Despite these points in the mission statement, there was no Empire Day in 1946, but another 'At Home' day was held on 14 September. The date that Empire Air Day would have been held sat quite close to 8 June and the victory celebrations; the demands of both so close together could not be accommodated. This seems to have decided Air Council thinking in favour of planning for Battle of Britain week being fully recognised instead. From the outset, the overall trend in terms of the number of 'At Home' stations were endlessly downward as the impact of future defence cuts led to an ever-diminishing air force, but the standard and extent of flying continued to improve.

About ninety-four RAF stations allowed the public across the threshold this time. The standard of display flying at the time would have been difficult to judge and the level of effort to produce a flying and a static display was all over the place, so to speak. There were no recognised aerobatics teams and no gauge of what was publicly popular. Display flying regulations in place were those from immediately before the war and likely did not take into account the performance and handling of aircraft currently in service.

In 1947, there were considerations given toward a large-scale air display the following year, though there were various reasons put forward for why that could not be. The 'At Homes' were more firmly established and occurred, albeit on a single day, across the country, meaning everyone had the chance to attend. The aim was still very much to present the workings of the individual station, so you were lucky if your local venue was an operational airfield where the home-based units would be pre-eminent. Yet the experience would be much different for the parents who found themselves dragging the kids around a technical training school, having them pay attention while a chief technician, in a brown dust coat, explains the workings of a CRT (Cathode Ray tube). Younger visitors, again essentially schoolboys, were far more attracted by the chance to watch or do something exiting.

They would queue, as indeed they did, for a chance to do something that none of today's youngsters under any degree of expert supervision would be invited to do and have a go on the station rifle range to loose off a few rounds of .303 at the targets down in front of the butts. Occasionally, there would be the chance to have a go at firing 20-mm shells from the cockpit of a fighter aircraft, in a safe direction of course. This was not the resumption of the Hendon Pageant that was being pursued.

As 1947 moved to 1948, nothing was done regarding the revival of the air display. With the amount of effort expended each year on the 'At Home' day, it seemed likely to impair such effort by introducing a further extravaganza. The new Central Participation Committee had been further requested to look at holding an event in 1949.

In early 1949, the Air Council approached the Participation Committee with thoughts of holding an RAF review in 1950, after there had been consideration given to the holding of such an event in 1949. On this occasion, it was scuppered by the Participation Committee, who did not expand on their reasons for discouraging the 1949 review, but their recommendations were accepted. The idea of the review was not intended as a replacement format to the Battle of Britain day celebrations, but as an additional project. The Participation Committee made several recommendations as to what form the review might take.

Interestingly, 1950 marked the thirtieth anniversary of the first Hendon Pageant, but no mention of this was used in conjunction with this new request from on high. As of May 1949, the vice-chief of the air staff called upon the committee to address three requirements—the appointment of an organisation with an executive committee that should have a full-time appointed chairman and secretary; secondly planning for financial arrangements; and thirdly, a venue. The chief of the air staff fully agreed with the appointment of full-time appointments to handle the review; memories of organising the Hendon and Empire air displays pre-war had placed a great deal of burden on the shoulders of ADGB (Air Defence of Great Britain) within which officers had to be found to oversee everything.

The then AMSO, AMP, and CS (A) had all shared experience of organising Hendon. For a start, the Participation Committee had put forward a figure of £5,000 to £7,000 as the kind of cost for organising the event. CS (A) felt that the true cost would be nearer £20,000. The money was expected to come from the RAF Benevolent Fund.

The secretary of state for air was concerned that such an amount or any amount of funds being taken from a charity would meet with legal difficulties, believing that this matter should be approached very carefully. AMP, Air Chief Marshal Sir Leslie Hollinghurst, thought that the review should be financed from public funds, thinking it would be quite wrong to risk Benevolent Fund money on what was essentially an official requirement. The air staff were more concerned about the RAF making rationed efforts to support civilian-organised air events such as *The Daily Express*-sponsored air pageant at Gatwick. Perhaps in light of this, support for the idea of a 'first-class RAF display' was now unanimous.

All seemed agreed that the idea of any such event in 1949 had become a missed opportunity. Air Marshal Sir Victor Goddard claimed there was substantial public demand for such an event:

> He constantly heard enquiries on the subject. A good display would be a colourful National event and attract widespread support. It might interfere with training in one way but the results in improved morale and greater self-respect in the service would more than compensate for that.

On this point, the CAS, Sir Arthur Tedder, agreed about the likely improvement in service moral and tone; he also saw no reason why service participation should not continue at local events, meaning civilian-organised displays. He also remarked on the supposed technical difficulties attendant in mounting displays with modern aircraft, saying they were not in the least insuperable and unlike the Hendon air pageants, here the problems would in some respects be simpler—as an example, there should not be as large a concentration of ground personnel at the display airfield. He was also particularly pleasantly surprised at the effort made at the Battle of Britain 'At Home' stations each September.

Sir Leslie Holllinghurst also noted that the navy held a navy week each year with various ships in various ports; they also held full fleet reviews at infrequent intervals. The RAF was also expected to contribute to a combined service event in 1951 in support of the exhibition planned that year, so an air display as a preliminary run in 1950 would not be such a bad idea. As there was no flagship air display in 1949, the recommendation was for plans to be put in place straight away for an RAF review on a large scale in 1950. They concluded in January 1949 that in view of the RAF's current state both regarding manpower and equipment, the dislocation and interruption to training that would be caused would have such a serious effect on efficiency that a display should not be attempted that year.

The air staff accepted this would be an unjustifiable risk. The 'At Home' day still took place and was set for 17 September. The committee considered individual cases in which decisions were required as to whether they should be opened. At one station in Scotland, Abbotsinch, the airfield was shared with the navy. They had communicated their willingness to hold a joint 'At Home' day, dividing the proceeds.

5

The Air Display 1950–52

Just twenty-five days into January 1950, Air Commodore DHF Barnett chaired a meeting of the RAF Participation Committee. Present were representative members of the Royal Aero Club, Air League of the British Empire, and the Association of British Aero Clubs. Air Commodore Barnett started by asking for the fullest information available regarding requests for RAF participation for displays and attendance at other public events. The three club and league representatives had already furnished Barnet with a list of events that they were particularly interested in, together with their 'recommendations' for RAF participation. Non-flying wise, there were growing requests for physical training displays. The committee settled this easily—one RAF and (recalling the culture and mannerisms of the era) one WRAF team.

Two police dog display teams were authorised as well. The matter of foreign displays and what the RAF could contribute to them was considered. The committee were advised that the Luxembourg Air Display was scheduled for 4 June. Air Commodore Barnett told the committee that restrictions on overseas events would be more strictly curtailed relative to the home effort. The reason for the lion's share being distributed internally was for recruitment's sake; this was the predominant consideration. Requests were certainly to be expected from the Western Union (a reference to the forerunner of NATO and still in 1950s so referred to by some) countries but approval could only be for events of major significance and then only to the extent of a small, but impressive, demonstration.

Barnett even less wanted to issue a circular to be sent to various air attachés, as suggested by Pearson, listing the number of foreign displays that could be accommodated for concern that this would simply generate more applications for participants. A general principal for the year ahead was arrived at—the two major commitments were the RAF Display and Battle of Britain week. However, the RAF should not enter any other large-scale flying display in 1950.

The air display was set, provisionally, for 14 and 15 July and Battle of Britain week was 11–17 September. Both events were expected to absorb the resources of all commands. A second *Daily Express* pageant had been supported by the RAF in 1949; this would not be repeated in 1950. Another feature that was tried in 1949 was 'RAF Weeks'; this, too, would not return as they were essentially recruitment rallies, and the secretary of state had decided they should not be held in 1950. The reason for this was the disappointing return for a hefty effort. As far as ground displays went, apart from the Royal Tournament and the Royal Bath and West Country Show, contributions should be small and short, equipment displays mostly, taking place where there were recruiting opportunities.

As expected, a copious number of requests to take part in flying displays throughout 1950 soon started to arrive, but with the two in-house events consuming much of the surplus for the year, there was not much left to go around. The original title for the proposed display in 1950 was the RAF Review. The VCAS recommended that it should be changed simply to 'RAF Display' because the term 'Review' was associated with formal parades before his majesty. This simple title change meant having the project referred to the Treasury to secure approval for funding, which had been given originally on the basis that the event was to be a royal review. A further complication was *The Daily Express'* plan to sponsor another air pageant, which was seen as in direct competition; the CAS expected that the RAF could contribute to the air pageant as well. As for the venue, three airfields were under consideration—Northolt, North Weald, and Farnborough.

Northolt carried very little favour as it was certainly smaller than the favourite, Farnborough. North Weald was thrown into the mix as it was thought it offered greater advantages. Bearing in mind that this display represented the resumption of the Hendon Air Pageant, Farnborough was an odd choice of venue, not that the air display should have been resurrected at Hendon, but because it was not an RAF airfield (but then neither was Hendon originally). This point was raised, but Sir Arthur Tedder thought this detail to be unimportant as Farnborough was ideal in many respects. This was endorsed by the secretary of state, Arthur Henderson, another person who thought Farnborough was an excellent choice.

As of 15 December 1949, Farnborough was the venue of choice for the first post-war official RAF air display, subject to confirmation. This is not to be confused with the already substantive and world-renowned SBAC Exhibition and Flying Display, which took place over the first week of September. This was the aviation industry event otherwise known as the Farnborough Airshow or simply 'Farnborough' and was still to be held during the usual period in 1950.

This placed a gap of just two months between two huge air shows. If the two events were to be held again, both at Farnborough, in 1951, then the advice was that they should be held as close to one another as possible so as to minimise the disruption to the work of the RAE (Royal Aircraft Establishment). More pragmatically, the staging of both events at Farnborough aerodrome each year would present something of a logistics headache. The air secretary suggested that 'holding the "Review" and the SBAC show on succeeding dates would have to be studied'.

One suggestion, should the problem have ever arisen, was for the RAF display to tag onto the end of the SBAC show week and effectively replace the last of the SBAC public days, but there was more to be gained in terms of attendance if the display was held in the middle of summer, therefore 1 July was chosen as the provisional date.

The RAF Benevolent Fund would have financial responsibility, but the Air Ministry would approve all arrangements. Lord Trenchard was approached to write a message to be printed in the official programme, which naturally he did. Then the committee chose not to include Trenchard's message as the forward; the entire endeavour was to be seen as a wholly service effort. The committee were also keen to avoid any suggestion that the RAF Benevolent Fund was in fact responsible for the display. An advertisement along with Trenchard's message was nevertheless to be included. There were, not surprisingly, more changes afoot. The display was a grand affair—a kind of RAF version of Royal Ascot and Royal Tournament merged.

Royalty, specifically HM King George VI, was to be invited to attend. As the king was unable to attend on 1 July, alternative dates were looked at and the event now extended to two days—Friday and Saturday, 14 and 15 July were confirmed then changed again to 7 and 8 July. At a third meeting of the Participation Committee in January 1950, it was confirmed that the king would attend on the first day; this posed a fresh dilemma—what about the Saturday? In responding to the original invitation, the palace had suggested the duke and duchess of Gloucester attend, in place of the king. This answered the question easily enough as the duke was the senior air chief marshal and the duchess was air chief commandant of the WRAF (Women's Royal Air Force; before expectations of social normality in British society changed, female personnel in the Armed Forces were segregated on paper); indeed, it would seem inappropriate to invite any other members of the royal family if the Gloucesters had not already been offered the opportunity to turn the invite down. The presence of royals on both days was of course seen as a boost to publicity and increased attendance.

Air Council members' guests would also be invited to the VIP enclosure; the only concern here was the possibility that VIP guests invited on the second day may feel slightly offended that they were not asked along on the day that the king attended, and a certain amount of tact would need to be exercised. On more practical grounds, contracts needed arranging for fencing, tents, stands, seating, refreshments, sanitary arrangements, a public address system, the printing of programmes, and so on. Such arrangements had to be in hand by the end of March and contracts approved. The running of the spectators' enclosure was expected to fall to the Benevolent Fund, but at the start of the year, no decision had been made. The alternative was that the Air Ministry departments would take up responsibility instead, requiring a temporary increase in the establishment of those departments involved.

A decision would be required by 15 February. A repeat of the 1948 Cooper Trophy was planned initially as part of the programme of events but had been shelved; instead, a series of individual aerobatics or a quick response take-off by twelve Avro Lincolns were now considered as alternatives. Invitations were sent out later in the year to various NATO and other west European countries' air force chiefs and other senior air staff officers. Twelve USAF generals were invited direct from the United States as well senior officers from the European command. Varying numbers of senior officers were invited from Belgium, Denmark, France, Holland, Canada, Luxembourg, Norway, Portugal, Spain, Sweden, Switzerland, and Italy.

The front cover of the so far only post-war 'official' RAF Air Display, held at Farnborough on 7 and 8 July 1950. Even with the far greater effort invested in Battle of Britain displays and other events, this was the one occasion the RAF regarded as 'The Air Display'. (*Via Author*)

Army and naval chiefs were also invited. Luxembourg did not have an air force, but it was felt they should not be left out and their military chief of staff, Colonel Jacoby, was also invited. As for timings, the air display was to have a larger flying programme, not surprisingly, than the Battle of Britain 'At Homes'; it would also differ in so far as there would be admission charges. The 'At Homes' were running flying programmes that at best lasted three hours or so. The Farnborough display would begin at 10.30 a.m. Tickets were sold essentially according to the enclosure, either 10s or 3s, half price for children. The arrangements for parking allowed private cars 10s, motorcycles 2s and 6d (half a crown), and 6d for bicycles. Coaches were not allowed on the airfield and were to be parked on the ground opposite Blenheim barracks, similar to parking arrangements for the present-day SBAC shows. Service dress regulations for participating personnel were strictly applied.

The service dress code required was as follows—for all those assigned duties in the royal and special enclosures, including officers, warrant officers, NCOs, airmen, and airwomen: No. 1 home dress uniform (this being the tunic with polished buttons worn with cloth waste belt). For head dress, officers were to wear service dress cap and gloves; berets or field service caps were to be worn by other ranks. Warrant officers, as with commissioned officers, were to wear gloves. The same apparel was chosen for the Cranwell flight cadets and apprentices, who both had to wear service dress caps and, additionally, Blanco-whitened webbing belts. For all serving elsewhere and not involved with flying or ground events, they had to wear No. 2 working dress (battle dress tunic) with beret or field service cap. Apprentices and boy entrants wore service dress and beret. Service dress remained optional for officers, NCOs, and airmen. Airwomen were given the option of service dress and service dress caps. Officers and other ranks of the Princess Mary's Royal Air Force Nursing Service were requested to wear service dress in all respects.

Those personnel involved with events were to wear the appropriate issue clothing—i.e., overalls, flying suits, etc. However, if they wanted to enter any of the enclosures, No. 2 working dress or, if preferred, No. 1 home dress was to be worn. Royal Observer Corps staff were similarly assigned orders—home dress for officers and working dress for observers. Air Training Corps their standard uniform.

The SBAC Exhibition Hall was made available for displaying all manner of technical materials and various types of equipment for operations and aircrew survival. Gymnastic teams, marching bands, and police dog demonstrations filled much of the morning; they were followed by a rare contribution—a display of mortar firing by the RAF Regiment.

The *pièce de résistance* of course was the flying. This was planned to include a comprehensive range exclusively supplied by the RAF apart from a set-piece flypast that included USAF and RCAF formations and a formation of six Meteors from the Belgian Air Force. Some experimental and vintage military aircraft also took part. The flying display was truly impressive, including all the usual ingredients—formation aerobatics with Meteors of 263 Squadron and Vampires of 54 Squadron, the latter trailing smoke.

Taking centre stage, among others at the Farnborough 'Air Display' that year, was the very first RAF aerobatics team of jets—de Havilland Vampires from 54 Squadron. (*Adrian Balch*)

There was a close-circuit air race flown by Meteors, Vampires, and Spitfires of the Royal Auxiliary Air Force on the first day. On the 8th, guests saw Auxiliary Vampires and Spitfires formation flying drills.

Set-piece demonstrations included twelve Vampires firing live rockets at a mock fort while twelve Meteors scrambled to intercept incoming raids of Mosquitos and Hornets on each day. New types were seen including the new jet-bomber, the English Electric Canberra, and what was billed as the RAF's new high-altitude interceptor, the de Havilland Venom. The programme—like those of the Hendon pageants—provided lengthy meticulous detail of what to expect; not just the flying but everything taking place through the day was itemised and began with the exhibition opening at 9 a.m. then the first activity, marching bands, at 10.30 a.m. A massed physical training display preceded the interval at 2 p.m. during which a Spitfire PR19 and a Mosquito PR34 were tasked with photographing sections of the crowd, then landing for collection, rapid development, and enlargement of images to be displayed in the exhibition hall.

Flying finished with the final segment of the flypast at 5.15 p.m. with the airfield closing to the public at 7 p.m. After the event, all was hailed a success; a display debrief was planned for 18 July, commonly referred to in more recent times as the 'wash up'. A preliminary report carried the reactions of the commanders in chief; they all agreed it was an outstanding success. The report's authors noted their surprise, somewhat, that all the commanders reported comparatively little disruption to training. AOC-in-C Technical Training command claimed that in fact it was of some benefit to administrative training with new staff gaining experience in the organisation of the display. Fighter Command reported that the event provided beneficial experience for the auxiliary squadron crews.

Most felt that it should become an annual event with one or two suggesting perhaps it should alternate biannually with the SBAC show. There was unanimous approval for Farnborough as the choice of location for holding further air displays, if held in the London area. This point was qualified by the further suggestion that if it was to continue as an annual event then it should alternate with a location in the Midlands.

The date aroused some outside interest as well; the army's Aldershot Military Tattoo was being revived in 1951 and was planned to be staged 26 to 30 June with a dress rehearsal on 23 June. Saturday 30 June was the date the Central Participation Committee had suggested for the air display. Considering the news about the tattoo, the committee moved the date to 7 July corresponding with the 1950 event. The Aldershot Military Tattoo followed a similar format to the more familiar Edinburgh Military Tattoo and likewise would be held at night, exclusively in this case.

So, in the Aldershot case, traffic for the tattoo would be restricted to the evening, thus it would not clash with air display traffic during the day. This might have been too simplistic as an answer to the problem. There was concern that the police and RAC would not be too favourably disposed to the idea. Attendance at both events would likely suffer just the same with the view that even the most dedicated enthusiast would not be likely to attend both on the same day. The inevitable congestion arising as tattoo traffic started to arrive while display traffic was vacating would, even in this earlier era of lighter road traffic, be a migraine rather than a headache.

Asking the Benevolent Fund to take on the responsibility for the spectators' enclosure again looked promising as they were reporting the expectation of having made a small profit from 1950.

A chiefs of staff committee meeting on 18 August reviewed the matter of military displays generally; Air Chief Marshal Sir Arthur Sanders, DCAS, representing the CAS, told those gathered that the Air Ministry had been considering the general policy regarding holding displays such as the one recently held and was now going through preliminary planning for being repeated in 1951. Of primary consideration was the commitments that not just the RAF but all three services faced and the demands upon manpower. Any military displays in 1951 would be restricted by operational demands; of particular concern was the conflict in Korea. Sanders suggested that a common policy approach should be adopted by all three services. The air staff, after a short discussion, put the proposal on the back-burner for a while. Nine days later, a further meeting of the Air Council standing committee came to some conclusions.

Sir Arthur revealed that the secretary of state had heard from the minister for supply in the meantime. The minister reported that the RAE (Royal Aircraft Establishment), the outfit carrying out work at Farnborough to develop and test new aircraft and associated equipment, had lost about 5 per cent of working time as a result of the 1950 display. Sir Arthur informed the council that he had impressed upon the C-in-Cs the need for a common policy for displays by all the armed services in 1951.

By September 1950, the RAF chiefs had agreed in principle to make a proposition for a coordinated joint services approach to holding displays. Agreement was not quite unanimous; the army council were not interested in anything of the sort, not in 1951. They had the Aldershot Military Tattoo, which they claimed to be already committed to. Interestingly, the army were asked if they felt it possible to arrange a tattoo that was of real value in terms of operational training and at the same time appeal to the public. There was no answer immediately forthcoming. The DCAS suggested that the RAF should proceed with a decision on the 1951 air display without waiting for the War Office to decide what they wanted to do.

There was also a suggestion that if a display was held in 1951, the public would form the highly critical opinion that the RAF were misemployed. The air secretary said he disagreed with this notion but also said that if the display were to go ahead in 1951, on other grounds, he would be prepared to publicly defend it. He posed two points: 1. Did we want the RAF to hold a display in 1951, the year when the Festival of Britain was being celebrated? 2. Could we afford the diversion of effort in the current international situation?

The question of the efficacy of holding an air display on a similar scale in 1951 was to be put to the other service chiefs of staff again by the DCAS. Then he would report back at the next Air Council standing committee meeting. The undersecretary of state for defence advised that an early decision was needed if they were to proceed with the event in 1951. A further response from the minister of supply was not encouraging; he was 'disturbed at the prospect of further interruption at RAE and was not, on the whole, in favour of lending Farnborough for next year's display'. That said, he had not made up his mind decisively.

The CAS, Sir John Slessor, felt that holding the display in 1951 under the present circumstances was doubtful. National service continued and the public might be on the lookout for any indication of misemployment of service personnel. 'It would be difficult to justify retaining men, at the expense of industry, and then employing them on camp chores for the display.' He was not alone as the AMSO and AMP both agreed. The VCAS thought the display did not interfere with some elements of training, but it did hamper training for war and that energies should be devoted toward exercising with the armed forces of the Western Union (NATO). Sir Victor Goddard (AMTS) thought differently; he did not disagree but could see the various benefits of staging a good display—for example, increased public interest and the pride imbued in the service.

Others felt that the 1950 display had addressed these points sufficiently. The deputy undersecretary thought a decision need not be made so soon. There was no doubt that the public would be showing an increased interest in the RAF and related developments in the year ahead. They might well not understand why a decision not to hold the display would be taken so early, certainly as the army were pressing ahead with their tattoo at Aldershot in 1951, meaning it may look odd with the RAF out of step. The deputy chief of the air staff was requested to contact the vice chief of the imperial general staff informally. The decision to hold the Aldershot Military Tattoo had been taken at Army Council level and it was unlikely, not surprisingly, that the army would be prepared to change their plans to make way for the RAF display. A study was underway to see if both events could take place a week apart. If that were the case, the RAF display would be held on 6 and 7 July.

The principal problem was accommodation for additional support personnel. Given the location, there were other civilian public events—such as Wimbledon, Henley, and Royal Ascot—all taking place over the same period. The secretary of state suggested early June or consider holding it in the Midlands, if not in 1951 then certainly 1952. As for the DCAS's meeting with the VCIGS, he had been informed that the general was surprised that the army council had not consulted with the Air Ministry before taking their decision. They did agree that a week between the two events would cause a degree of overlap and that a minimum of three weeks or even a month to separate them was more realistic. Reviewing the 1950 display, it was revealed that there was some disparity in figures, which overall were smaller than expected anyway—25,000 attended on the Friday while 75,000 turned up on the Saturday. In addition, 30,000 tickets were sold for the rehearsal day.

Feedback had also been received from the organisers of the Festival of Britain. Their reaction was favourable saying they would be glad to see the RAF display take place in 1951, it would add to the list of attractions, and they would be willing to give it publicity at home and abroad. The Command C-in-Cs, with one exception, were in favour of Farnborough as the chosen location again. The London area offered the best chance of attracting overseas visitors and was the only airfield in the region, 'free of Handicaps'. The minister of supply therefore was to be approached to see if Farnborough could be utilised again for staging the display. Any vacillation over whether to press on regardless or not was soon answered.

The minister of supply, George Strauss, clarified his position in response to a letter from Mr Arthur Henderson, the air secretary, on 2 August. He made it clear that were it a simple matter of supporting the RAF, 'we should be only too glad to accede to your wish.' Strauss went on, however, to detail the effects of the 1950 display on the work at Farnborough, pointing out the loss of a full 5 per cent of flying activity consequently. The point was put more subjectively this time with the impact on the progress of the establishment's scientists and technicians. The loss of valuable work was considered quite serious, and at the time of Strauss' letter, the RAE were still trying to make a quantitative assessment of the full impact. Most blunt of all was the assertion that the length of time taken to develop new equipment was frequently criticised and by the Air Ministry in particular. Strauss drew attention to the international situation as a good example of what compelled his department to work to reduce the amount of time taken to procure new equipment, but the air display simply worked in the opposite direction.

The benefits of another kind from the display were not overlooked, but the minister had made it clear that he was not supportive of holding the RAF display in 1951 at Farnborough, bearing in mind that the SBAC staff had their own display to press ahead with in September and again each following September. The international situation was held up by the air secretary as the reason why there would be no RAF display in 1951. As for the far more widespread demand of resources for Battle of Britain 'At Homes', they would go ahead each September immediately following the Farnborough International air show, which at the time placed a very high demand on service aircraft.

6
1953–57

The year 1953 was a particularly demanding year for the RAF. There was the queen's coronation, Farnborough, the Battle of Britain Flypast, and the 'At Homes'. By July, the director of ops, Air Commodore Cross, was able to propose a provisional composition for the flypast in September, having consulted the various commands and the Ministry of Supply. The Battle of Britain flypast was going to be impressive and was expected to consist of the following:

1 × Hurricane
6 × Meteor Wings (Fighter Command)
1 × Sabre Wing (RCAF Fighter Command)
48 × Canberras (Bomber Command)
1 × Vulcan (M o S)
1 × Victor (M o S)
1 × Hunter (M o S)
1 × Swift (Fighter Command or M o S)

The flypast was then increased; the settled line-up was that this would be an all-jet flypast save for the Spitfire and Hurricane leading line abreast. This was the first time a Spitfire was leading; the previous Battle of Britain flypasts were led by a solitary Hurricane. The line-up this year would also include contributions from the Royal Navy, Royal Canadian Air Force, and the United States Air Force.

Royal Air Force:
  1 Hurricane
  1 Spitfire
  144 Meteors
  48 Canberras
Royal Canadian Air Force:
  24 F-86s

Royal Navy:
    12 Seahawks
United States Air Force:
    24 F-86s

Six rehearsals were flown from 4 to 14 September with the actual flypast over London on Tuesday the 15th. Earlier in the year, the deputy chief of the air staff placed a new proposal before the Participation Committee for their perusal and consideration. This was for a NATO air display. During the summer, the Belgians held such an event at Brussels airport. The Participation Committee were now, on top of everything else, looking into the sponsoring of a NATO air display in the coronation year at such short notice as well. They agreed that the holding of such a display would be most desirable, if it could be made self-supporting, and that the ministerial decision against service reviews during the coronation year would not preclude a display of this nature. For a start, the committee expected that, politically, it would offset criticism on the continent that 'we are only prepared to pay lip service to the European Defence Community' plus it would offer an excellent opportunity to take up the lead set by the Belgians.

The French had already approached USAF General Lauris Norstad, the air deputy to SACEUR, requesting his support for a similar display in Paris the following year. The USAF general had given a non-committal answer apparently in order to give the RAF first call on NATO resources. If the British were going to host such an event, it would now be in 1954; the general asked for firm plans to be in place before him at the next national chiefs of air staff meeting in October. The Central Participation Committee were keen not to lose time and end up being forced by circumstances to follow the lead set by other NATO European countries with reduced opportunity to establish proper prestige and position. In addition to the political advantages to be gained, the committee noted that a display organised along these lines—unlike the 'At Homes'—would involve a minimum disruption to training and the ongoing re-equipment programme. The much lower impact on RAF training and operations would be a consequence of a much smaller RAF contribution.

The bulk of participants would be from the other NATO air arms who would also aim to provide the more impressive aircraft and display teams from within their respective units.

On the other hand, they were not looking to put together a series of formation aerobatics teams; this is how the Brussels display shaped up. Instead, the RAF—should they organise a similar display—would look to encourage each air force to provide a 'special display item' to put together a more varied flying programme. The chief concern, of course, was funding. The Belgians sent over an estimate of the costs of the Brussels display; they charged admission, in contrast to the Battle of Britain displays that were free of charge to visitors, save for parking, which had set tariffs. The Belgian display had an attendance of 41,000, clearing a profit of £1,500. The RAF had attended this event but had insisted the Belgians pay the expenses of all RAF units taking part, including fuel.

They only had to pay for the food supplies and accommodation of all the other NATO units taking part. Now the Participation Committee were worried they would have to return the favour. They were, on the other hand, quite certain that if they charged admission for a similar display in the UK, they would make a profit. The committee also thought about planning the event to coincide with a major air exercise in which the NATO units could be invited to participate. This way some of the costs could be offset by the exercise. Once again as with the RAF display in 1950, Farnborough was the favoured location. The Hampshire airfield was deemed the most suitable location for attracting the largest 'paying' audience possible.

As the year being looked at was 1953, the coronation year, dates were few, but Friday and Saturday 3 and 4 July were free. Despite the vagaries of British weather, meteorological records for this period showed that this, even taking the fact it was early July into account, was the period when the best weather could be expected. There was also the ever-present matter of protocol—in other words, especially given the year and the occasion, the question of whether HM Queen Elizabeth II would be able to attend one of the two days in question.

These were the points recommended and that all arrangements, including spectator accommodation, should be the responsibility of the Air Ministry, at the expense of public funds. Any profits would be offset against authorised funding. The Brussels balance sheet listed a figure for attendance of 150,000, of which 41,000 paid. Again, endeavours to put on the display were later shelved.

On Saturday 19 September, sixty-nine RAF stations and one RCAF station (North Luffenham) were approved to be opened to the public, with flying displays, ground demonstrations, and static exhibits. As was the standard practice now, the proceeds would be divided between the RAF Benevolent Fund and the Royal Air Forces Association. In 1952, seventy-six RAF stations had opened on 20 September, and the aggregate attendance was measured at 966,000. The proceeds came to £20,942; this well exceeded the previous highest figure of £7,000. Given the primary practical purpose of the 'At Home' day, recruitment stalls would be prominent at each station. The commands this year were requested to select stations to open, which would be 'especially suitable for visits by Members of the Air Council'. Among the highlights this year that some—indeed, most—stations were expecting to see in the air were either a Canadian or USAF F-86 Sabre; most programmes also billed the American jet display as performing a planned supersonic dive. This was just a year on from the DH.110 tragedy at Farnborough. Also due to appear was a prototype of the Avro Vulcan, bearing in mind that only three years earlier the best and most up-to-date bombers operated by the RAF were the B-29 Superfortress and the Avro Lincoln, with prop engines and in the case of the latter, a tail-dragging derivative of the Lancaster. The future was going to be revealed to the public in the form of a delta-winged, out-of-this world-looking, aluminium triangle with four jet engines buried in the wing chords. This really was the shape of things to come; H. G. Wells himself would not have believed such machines might possibly exist.

Once again, a variety of aerobatics and formation flying drill teams of Meteors and Vampires, took centre stage. These were the hot-ships *de jour* but the F-86 from the United States now entering RAF service presented a faster swept-wing design. This was an era of rapid developments in aviation in the UK as well. Fast coming around the corner were the Swift and Hunter—the second generation of jet fighters. Another big Delta came from the UK's aircraft designers, a fighter no less, in the form of the Gloster Javelin. All these new designs were indications of very healthy order books for the RAF and rapidly developing performance with each step ahead and all thanks to the Cold War. For the navy, there was a list of prototype aircraft in the pipeline. There was the aforementioned DH.110, which would become the Sea Vixen; from Supermarine the N.113, which became the Scimitar; and just a few years away, the Blackburn NA39, which would become the Buccaneer.

British aviation was at a peak in both military and commercial terms, though it certainly would not last. A common and certainly unwelcome feature at the 'At Home' days of the era was the number of accidents, now and again fatal, but in the early 1950s, at least one fatality was expected each September. The year 1953 had its fair share for sure. A Meteor performing aerobatics over RAF Coningsby crashed, killing the pilot, Fg Off. Patrick Ward, while another met with tragedy at another station. Two others were injured. Just up the road at Binbrook, a Tiger Moth came in far too heavily. Other less serious incidents occurred elsewhere. A more tragic day than 18 September 1949 would be hard to find, when a series of fatal accidents occurred involving no fewer than three Mosquitos, each of which came down with fatal consequences at three different airfields. The worst resulted in ten civilian deaths, including a small child.

Altogether this day, there were seventeen deaths due to flying display accidents, five in all. The previous day had two accidents in rehearsal, one proving fatal.

Such incidents were arguably few when the amount of flying is considered the overall risk factor, taking everything into account. Yet such a number of incidents would be too high for any present-day parameters. Yet it is undeniably the case that the press, in the 1950s, seemed far less keen to dramatise such incidents. Then again communication technology, being what it was, limited the ability to influence the public mindset in quite the same perpetual manner afforded with online technology today. Many people would have never heard of such incidents which less than sixty years later would be displayed with graphics every time anyone logged on or saw a rolling news programme on wall-mounted screen in a coffee shop or bar. In 1949, it was not much more than local news. Apart from anything else, in an early post-war world, an accident was tragic but nothing to turn everything upside down over. Therefore, the media comment was not too politically charged about air show accidents; they still used dramatic descriptions but did not thump the tub, making comparisons with gladiatorial arenas. Today, with twenty-four-hour rolling news in every coffee shop, pub, hotel foyer, office workplace, and departure lounge, the chances of missing out on something with a dramatic 'Breaking News' message below is possible only if you purposely shut yourself off from the outside world by becoming a hermit in unspoiled hinterland.

Nevertheless, fatalities at both Farnborough and a number of 'At Homes' persisted from 1945 through to very much the end of the 1950s. After 1958, you could almost mark this as the last year where an RAF event of any kind witnessed a fatality.

That year in particular, a Vulcan disintegrated over RAF Syerston. Over the intervening years, the RAF concentrated on bringing the number down; it was said at the time that if just two fatalities occurred on 'At Home' day, the CAS would feel congratulations to all taking part were in order. Times have certainly changed. Safety records aside, there was the problem of finding the required surplus to spread around; each year from 1953, fewer stations were obliged to participate each time. The common perception today is that back then, an 'anything goes' culture prevailed in flying displays. Actually, rules were quite uncompromising. There was greater latitude for squadrons to allocate time to form aerobatics teams, which were nothing if not prolific; there would usually be about two pilots on a squadron with an approved solo display sequence.

The RAF still had not reached the stage of teams with household names and international acclaim, such as the Black Arrows, the Blue Diamonds, and the Red Arrows. Yet aerobatics teams were to be found in almost every fighter and ground attack squadron and every flying training school that flew a suitably aerobatic type. An air staff instruction was issued in August 1953 regulating the authorisation and execution of formation aerobatics for both demonstrations and training. The new rules made clear that only the AOC Group could authorise formation aerobatics for demonstration purposes. The regulations also set a limit for the number of active aerobatics teams in Fighter Command—one per group. However, this did not actually restrict each group to a single unit team.

The AOC had it within his remit to rotate the aerobatics team duty within the squadrons. The stipulation was that this should not happen at anything less than an interval of six months. When ready, the picked team would face a test. This is where the AOC would have to witness the team's practiced routine that they proposed to put before the public or have it witnessed by a personal representative. The test itself was not a simple fly-off; it was a repeat of the routine two or three times within narrow time limits, height, and positioning. This still was not a hard and fast rule as the AOC was at liberty to set the test parameters, but the repeated sequence within these imposed goal posts was believed to be the best format going by experience. All aerobatics manoeuvres by demonstration teams were to be completed not lower than 1,500 feet above ground level. This could be lowered for certain occasions subject to agreement with the command AOC.

Formation aerobatics for training purposes had heavier restrictions, with all manoeuvres to be complete above 7,000 feet and no more than three aircraft in the formation. The same height restriction was applied to work up sorties flown by demonstration teams hoping to be considered for the AOC's selection.

Authorisation for practices at lower level would be passed from the AOC-in-C Command to C-in-C Group to the station commander. Solo aerobatics pilots faced a much simpler method of selection; OC Flying Wing was considered a senior enough authority and often delegated the selection to the squadron commander. Up to 1953, synchronised aerobatics had been permitted involving pairs in close formation. The introduction of faster, heavier, and more complex aircraft had prompted the RAF to discontinue synchronised aerobatics for the present. The tightening of display team selection would mean reduced scope and the number of 'At Home' day stations continued to be steadily scaled back. There was a degree of opinion that they were not scaling back enough; to spread the effort across the summer seemed a more realistic option, which was gaining support.

At the end of 1953, Air Marshal Sir Victor Groom sent a letter to Air Marshal Sir Tom Pike at the Air Ministry. Sir Victor Groom was the air officer commanding technical training command, and as such, he was expected to approve a list of those RAF stations within his command to hold 'At Homes'. His command, as the title may suggest, was not one that had within its jurisdiction a number of stations that were suitable or would be of significant public interest. Yet he was expected to propose a list of stations for that very purpose to the Participation Committee. At the opposite end of the spectrum, the operational commands. Bomber, fighter, and coastal all had a distinct advantage for really showing off the RAF in a manner that would be fitting.

Groom's letter about Battle of Britain 'At Home' days, not surprisingly, questioned certain points affecting the policy of 'At Homes' and made certain recommendations. By the middle of May the following year, he sent a second letter, having received no reply to the first. However, he had been in touch with the VCAS, Air Chief Marshal Sir Ronald Ivelaw-Chapman, and was assured that the letter was being considered by the Air Council and they were aware that other commanders-in-chief held similar views. In the meantime, Groom had received a letter at the start of the month instructing him that the policy on 'At Home' day arrangements would be carried out as in previous years.

Air Marshal Groom's second letter was fuelled by the recent instruction, convinced that his and others' recommendations had been ignored. He registered his 'disbelief in the way C-in-Cs are considered to be of such little importance that they should be ignored completely in this way and I can only assume that in the handover between you and Ivelaw-Chapman, this subject must have got lost'.

Groom's real concerns were that the 'At Homes' were doing a lot of harm within his command and insisted he had a right to ask for the Air Council's reaction to the letter he had sent in December. He certainly was not alone; the SASO at Flying Training Command had also been in touch with Sir Thomas Pike, ACAS (policy), prompted by one of his group commanders, Air Vice-Marshal Frank Long, who was described as leading the 'Anti-Fairground' movement and that he was by no means alone with thoughts in this direction. Raising money was regarded as a poor principle and should not be the main aim of the exercise, but this seemed more and more to be 'gauged by the magnitude of receipts' and that this approach was responsible for the degradation of the original high motives behind the occasion.

Air Vice-Marshal Edward Addison was therefore looking for a general directive to pass on to his group commanders, instructions that would make clear that gate receipts were not the key measure of success and that sideshows should be limited to those calculated to amuse children while providing some further attraction should the weather be bad.

Air Vice-Marshal Addison also advised that the list of his proposed stations to hold an 'At Home' day in 1954 would be much shorter than the previous year. The reason for this was the contraction of Flying Training Command over the previous year, this likely having been a political response to the end of the Korean Conflict, allowing for a degree of run down. Secondly, several flying training schools were either working on introducing a new training schedule based on the Piston Provost to de Havilland Vampire (the latter introduced jet training into the syllabus) scheme, or because they were running down.

For all the demands on resources to meet requirements concentrated on a single date was, on the other hand, accepted. The selection of RAF stations to hold 'At Homes' was not in the view of the Air Council or the Air Ministry based on any hard and fast rule; temporary as well as permanent stations could be open.

The stated criteria were certainly far from black and white: 'the maximum number of well-kept and efficient stations capable of presenting interesting programmes should continue to be opened regardless of their function and construction'. The official view was that some stations of a non-permanent construction—i.e. fields of Nissen huts— offered some of the most interesting and attractive 'At Home' day programmes.

The air staff's point was that flying displays by the service's more impressive aircraft was just as incidental as revenue collection and that Joe Public could be lured to head out on a Saturday in September each year just as easily to ponder the workings and functions of a radio fitter training school just as they would a front-line operational station with the latest high-performance aircraft in abundance; by this stage, this meant the new English Electric Canberra, the swept-wing Sabres and Swifts, and, by September 1954, the first of the V bombers—the Vickers Valiant and the Hawker Hunter.

That is not to say that flying was not arranged in some cases; it was arranged for all but with quite a degree of variation, and this was the point of those commanders whose stations did not lend themselves to hosting aeroplanes at close quarters. They

The day following the public 'At Home' at Biggin Hill, Battle of Britain Sunday, 19 September 1954, including the investiture of a Spitfire and Hurricane, with a flypast by the home-based Meteors. Biggin Hill remained a frontline fighter station still, yet radical political thinking was shortly to change matters. (*Air Historical Branch*)

could also expect to be low in priority for available aircraft aloft. It seems an unlikely contradiction, but the air staff view ran contrary to this. The public associated the RAF with aeroplanes and that was what they expected to be foremost.

It was up to the command and group commanders to recommend the best of their stations to open, and while careful consideration was given to their views regarding those stations not recommended, the reason for leaving a station closed had to be convincing. Unless some insurmountable situation could be put forward for a station not to open, the air staff directed otherwise. Victor Groom's point, however, was that he did not have much to pick and choose from if the public's mood was properly understood. Some commanders suggested holding the 'At Homes' on separate dates through the year, which would likely make resources more easily available for each and allow the wider population a chance to attend one or, should they so desire, more than one through the year. The Air Council claimed they had considered this point on more than one occasion, but each time reached for the strictures of the 1945 decision, when the dates of Battle of Britain week were originally set. The conclusion invariably was that the RAF would stand to lose rather than gain from the dissociation of 'At Home' day from Battle of Britain week.

The 'At Homes' had become a traditional part of the week's celebrations and the date had become widely known outside the service. Another consideration was the number of additional attractions were kept to a minimum and September, from this point of view, was an excellent month with so few other significant public functions taking place. To reinforce the case, in 1953, over 1 million people attended—a fact regarded as a first-class advertisement. There was even a fear that opening stations on other dates would confuse the public. It was accepted that a greater flying effort would be likely at a smaller number of stations spread over the summer, culminating in September, but this would be to no avail if it was at the expense of established tradition and there was no other anniversary with which the 'At Homes' could be linked. As Air Marshal Pike said, 'Battle of Britain week, including the 'At Home' day, is the envy of the other two services, as for once each year we regularly steal the limelight'.

In the run up to the 1955 September celebrations, the Air Council directed the Participation Committee to examine the possibility of inviting other NATO air arms to participate. This essentially amounted to the continued exploration of the possibility of holding a NATO air display, the project that had been abandoned in 1952. The very idea was not so straightforward and easy to comprehend in 1955 as it was just a few years later. The committee remained vexed by the idea as the RAF events should celebrate and commemorate the Battle of Britain. The 'At Home' day was a national celebration of a historic battle ingrained in the service ethos. To invite NATO air forces from overseas may shift the focus to celebrating an international defence body geared toward meeting future threats.

Yet a somewhat clearer concern—although hardly an insurmountable one—was the worry that countries in NATO that remained neutral during the Battle of Britain or did not take an active part may well actually be embarrassed. Italy was an example; also, Germany had not yet re-established its post-war armed forces and was still in some respects a country under allied occupation, although now with its own democratically elected government, and by international agreement, the new *Bundeswehr* was in the early stages of being formed. However, even with the new Luftwaffe coming around the corner, inviting them just fifteen years or a little more after the commemorated battle in question left their participation out of the question. Also, any sense of awkwardness about inviting the Germans would likely be mutually felt. However, it was more problematic with a new West German Air Force being formed and joining NATO, meaning it may look tactless to invite others and not the Germans.

The committee also worried about whether a foreign air force would wish to send their premier aerobatics team, should they have one, to an event heavily focused on celebrating a British wartime operation. Such a short time after the war, there was also the awkward-to-predict question of members of the public in the UK; spurred on by the press, they may well feel particularly aggrieved, especially bereaved parents. Interestingly, the RAF felt that the nationalist sentiment of the time was sufficiently high as to imagine the presence of any outsiders at a Battle of Britain display would be quite controversial. Indeed, they already were confronted with resentment of all foreign participants.

The Royal Canadian and US Air Forces had been included in Battle of Britain flypasts over London before, and this drew criticism, more so against the Americans, presumably because it was not their campaign; as for the Canadians, it very much was so as they took part along with other nationalities, a few of which were now behind the Iron Curtain. Americans also flew in the Battle of Britain, albeit in RAF uniform, so they too were entitled to representation; they were all volunteers, so they had gone out of their way to serve. However, the feeling was that any significant participation by foreign air arms in any Battle of Britain flypasts would not be well received, especially if the aircraft of an ex-enemy were included, again thinking particularly of the Germans; this was not yet a possibility but soon would be. Arising from these points were others of a more practical nature. The Participation Committee were further concerned about putting together the right kind of publicity for the participating aircraft of a foreign air arm.

Expensive advertising was seen as the only way, and the publicity afforded to displays by any NATO air forces would encroach upon the space made available by the press for RAF activities on their own big day. On the formal side of things, the question of whether members of the royal family should be invited to one or more of the 'At Homes' had to be carefully approached. There were more questions regarding protocol, the invitation of air attachés, etc., from a NATO air force which was flying at one of the displays, and the provision of suitable hosts from the RAF. Then finally, to determine the financial arrangements, a formula would need to be in place to cover expenses, participation fees, and what would be agreeable to all parties, including the Battle of Britain charities and the Treasury.

On the other hand, it could not be denied that the inclusion of foreign air forces at RAF 'At Homes' would, official flypasts notwithstanding, provide some form of additional attraction—an exotic feature at least for some of them. This all seemed to move matters forward with a sense that the format of the 'At Home' day was developing. However, it also started to attract criticism, from within. Increasingly,

Battle of Britain 'At Home' Day, even by the time this image was recorded, was an ever-diminishing exercise as the number of stations required to be open to the public had peaked at the start. This is a typical image of youngsters queueing to get to grips with the flight controls of one of the RAF's charges, even if just a trainer such as this Piston Provost T1, at Biggin Hill on 17 September 1955. (*Air Historical Branch*)

All ages are catered for, including the very young with novelty train rides at Biggin Hill on 17 September 1955. (*Air Historical Branch*)

Foreign participation at RAF displays was initially limited to the air arms of the USA and Canada. These USAF F-86s formed an aerobatics team, the Skyblazers, drawn from pilots and aircraft of the Chaumont-based 492nd Tactical Fighter Squadron; they were regular visitors to the UK air show circuit. (*Adrian Balch*)

more station commanders believed commemorating the Battle of Britain would deteriorate as time went on anyway.

They were quite aware that the times they were a changing and that if tradition was too closely adhered to and a stuffy even curmudgeonly reaction toward our modern allies prevailed, then this would not do with a view to the future and the quite desperate need to engender public support and interest in NATO and the future with demonstrations of solidarity between the UK and its western allies. This approach did not appear to reach too far as the Central Participation Committee inclined toward the belief that demonstrations by foreign air arms—NATO or otherwise—were not conducive to maintaining the spirit of commemorating the Battle of Britain, but on balance, they accepted that the idea on its own was worth pursuing through the pursuit of alternative means—perhaps a separate event with a different aim. The Air Council had the final say over whether NATO air forces should be invited to take part in the forthcoming Battle of Britain displays, scheduled for 17 September 1955.

Should the council disagree with the CPC, then the latter had the framework of an arrangement to accommodate the Air Council's wishes. This involved selecting one of the 'At Home' stations, rather than several, to hold a NATO display. This way, they could arrange for dignitaries and representatives from the NATO air forces involved to attend the selected station rather than run the risk of offending. The option that could perhaps better derive advantages was the original 1952 proposal and have a separate NATO air day altogether, arranged for another date, separate from the 'At Home' day. However, if maximum publicity was the aim, this could best be achieved by holding a number of NATO displays at selected 'At Homes' in different parts of the country. The advantages here were that the RAF could compete at each, where the RAF could mount a comparable performance to the visiting air force but on the other hand might be overshadowed if they had to compete with as many as half a dozen foreign star aerobatics teams at one event, should that situation ever arise.

The CPC were worried that quantity would outshine quality. Also, by inviting NATO display teams to just a single 'At Home' might receive criticism for detracting from the success at other stations. Therefore, on this point, the number of NATO displays, should that be the course taken, should not be so many that anything less than a first-class display should result at each. They suggested a provisional number of six such displays.

In 1954, an attempt was made to improve the standard of flying; six of the open stations were selected for preferential treatment. The basis for selection was the geographical location and the prominence of each to a sizeable catchment area. The picked six were Biggin Hill, Thornaby, Castle Bromwich, Turnhouse, St Athan, and Horsham St Faith.

At the time inclusion of NATO displays were being considered, the results of the 1954 experiment were being reviewed; depending on what the upshot was, the committee might recommend following a similar format for the proposed NATO displays in 1955. Next there had to be a centre for Air Council guests; the very idea was not thought too productive by the committee, who took the impression that each display was supposed to be comparable, so picking one out was to deviate from the principle of equality. For example, if a Dutch display team were allocated to one display, away from the flagship event, then Dutch guests would have to be entertained either away from the flagship venue or away from where their star team were performing. The standing arrangement for the 'At Homes' was suggested as the best model for the NATO displays—the detailed arrangements for the display programme, spectators' accommodation, and general administration would be the responsibility of the respective station commanders. Overall matters concerning policy would be directed by the Air Ministry, whose instructions and directives would be passed down through the channels of the respective command.

As was the case with Battle of Britain week arrangements, a central co-ordinating authority would need to be established. The CPC, not at all surprisingly, believed itself to be the best suited outfit for the job—perhaps the one and only.

The protocol would need to be dealt with and carefully co-ordinated with respective stations, arrangements for the invitations, arrival, reception, and accommodation of the invited NATO air arms and invitations to special guests from home and national publicity. The Air Council had clearly indicated their wish to host distinguished guests, although just what the form would be depended on how the Air Council decided they would like to proceed; everything to this point was a proposal or a suggestion.

What would be especially tricky and advisedly placed before the council to consider was the old chestnut of invitations to members of the royal family. There was precedent for this as the first two NATO air displays held on the continent were attended by the king of Belgium and the queen of the Netherlands respectively. The events in Belgium and Holland had been singular, but if the RAF were going to press ahead with six or even more RAF stations simultaneously hosting a specific NATO show, which one, remembering that neither should take priority over the other, should receive HM Queen Elizabeth II and how would this affect the other five? No single event could warrant the royal patronage, so it could be argued.

There was some chance of a get-out clause here, despite being held separately from the 'At Home' day as the NATO Air Day was still expected to be in September. This being the case, the royal family would be on holiday at Balmoral and therefore would not be expecting any public engagements. However, if in exceptional circumstances the royals were able to attend some of the displays, this could appear quite tactless if they were at an event where the Belgians were displaying, but none were at the station hosting the Dutch Air Force contribution. There was also the equal division of senior RAF officers to act as hosts for visiting air attachés.

Financing these events would likely not be as straightforward as with the Battle of Britain events as the latter were still financed in the very same manner set out in 1945, as was now Air Council policy. To wit, the public should be admitted free of charge, no expenses arising from the 'At Home' days should be charged to public funds, and all the proceeds from the sale of programmes, car park charges, and so forth should go straight to RAF charities.

The introduction of the NATO air displays as well would, on whatever scale, bring substantial charges for fuel, oil, messing, and transport for the visiting air forces. In order to avoid any offset of funds to charities, it would be necessary to obtain Treasury permission to charge these costs to public funds. This would leave funds allocated for the charities accrued at those stations hosting NATO displays open to the suggestion, at least, that any public expenditure accrued should be compensated from the proceeds of these events. Naturally then, funds for the RAF Benevolent Fund and RAFA would be severely depleted.

The committee could offer no overall opinion on how to proceed but strongly recommended the following:

a. That there should be no departure from the principle that the public should not be charged for admission to 'At Homes'.

b. That the RAF charities which customarily benefit from the proceeds of 'At Homes' should not suffer from the diversion of all or part of these proceeds to meet the expenses arising out of the NATO Air Displays.

INITIAL ACTION:

If the Air Council decide that NATO Displays are to be held in association with Battle of Britain Week 1955, the Participation Committee recommend that the following action should be taken,

a. Immediate steps should be taken to notify the NATO authorities, through SHAPE, of the proposal in order that any other NATO countries who may be considering similar displays will have warning of our intentions.

b. At a later date, and after consultation with SHAPE invitations should be sent in the name of the RAF to the individual NATO Air Forces asking if they will participate in the displays. (This procedure conforms with that adopted by the Belgian Air Force in 1952, when the original invitation to the RAF was sent by General Leboutte to CAS)

c. Early in the new year and after reviewing the results of RAF 'At Home' Day, 1954, the RAF Participation Committee should initiate the necessary action for the organisation of the Displays.

The VCAS, Air Marshal Ivelaw-Chapman, was the overseeing air staff officer. He told the council that there was too little time left to proceed with such a project in either 1955 or 1956, especially as, with further defence cuts and major re-structuring within some Commands, the RAF would be experiencing too much turbulence to either consider a purely RAF air display like the one in 1950 or a NATO event if the highest standard of planning and execution was to be achieved. The VCAS was perhaps not the most enthusiastic proponent of air displays. His own feelings were that the era of precision flying within sight of crowds on the ground was coming to an end because modern aircraft were too fast and were designed to operate at great heights, plus because modern operational techniques did not call for formation flying of the traditional kind.

The year 1955 came and went. No NATO displays took place, and the number of RAF stations open to let the taxpayer see where the money went had reduced significantly from 1954—from fifty-eight to forty-six.

On the upside, the RAF was bringing into service the next generation of front-line aircraft, which brought a considerable impact. With only a year since the first Hawker Hunter aircraft was delivered to a squadron, two formation aerobatics teams were up and running.

As preparations for the 1956 'At Homes' were made, RAF Gaydon received a lot of publicity; it was the first active V bomber station and so was subject to a good deal of exposure. It raised a question over why it was not going to be open the following year—simply put, the training schedule converting the new Valiant crews consumed the time of the home-based OCU. Two more Bomber Command stations—Marham and Honington—had both been recommended but the DDIS had them deleted from the list. Fighter Command had asked that Wymeswold and Newton not be open, the latter because it only had a grass airfield that Hunters could not operate from. However, the Participation Committee were keen to open Newton as the last time it was, in 1954, it had drawn an astonishing 50,000 visitors. Both these stations covered the Nottingham/Derby area, so the command was under pressure to reconsider.

With many new aircraft in service, the level of RAF participation in the SBAC show was to be on a greater scale than the norm and the Battle of Britain flypast was to be substantial. One more attempt at reviving the 1950 display for 1957 was dismissed yet again. The Air Council reached a decision in July concerning the proposed official RAF Display for 1957. Ivelaw-Chapman said there were three main reasons that a major air display could not go ahead in 1957. First there was the affect that the scale of effort required would have on other commitments. Bomber Command would be affected particularly as they were due to commence intensive operational training in preparation for the Strategic Air Command bombing competition. This would be compromised of preparing for a large service-representative display at the same time, which would require a degree of effort to ensure a good impression was made. This

No. 74 Sqn Meteor aerobatics team at the top of a loop. The famous 'Tigers' were one of the last Meteor day fighter squadrons to re-equip with the Hawker Hunter and therefore likely the last to mount an aerobatics team with the old first-generation jets. (*Air Historical Branch*)

naturally carried greater weight in terms of international prestige. He also returned to his considered view that modern aircraft were unsuitable for displays such as that staged at Farnborough in 1950.

Therefore, the programme would need to be padded out with paradrops and set pieces. He even went as far to suggest that the evolution of military aircraft made it questionable as to whether it was worthwhile. The third reason was that the existence of the annual Battle of Britain 'At Homes' held at RAF stations up and down the country and RAF participation in displays organised by other bodies were already far more effective at placing the RAF and its capabilities in public view as they attracted vast audiences across the country. By contrast, the RAF air display in 1950 covered just two days and secured an attendance of 102,000, all confined to a single airfield in the south of England.

A particular concern that raised objections was the air staff being keen to show off their latest, most visible and noticeable acquisition, the new V bombers. This might appear to be a counter-intuitive train of thought. The V Force—certainly the Valiant and, to a lesser degree, the Vulcan—were growing in number, but enough Victors were yet to be delivered in order to allow a worthwhile contribution to take part in any grand public presentation. By the date of any official service display, the V Force, undergoing intense training in the run-up, would not be ready to do justice to any such prestigious public presentation.

The wider impact on normal levels of training, the high cost of manpower (apart from aircrew), the lengthy period of preparation, and the financial costs all seemed unnecessary anyway with the SBAC show taking place over the first week in September, which included three full public days. SBAC Farnborough and the Battle of Britain 'At Homes' were opportunity enough to reach a wide-enough margin of the public and likely would be just in time to give some truly impressive displays by the V Force. The one drawback about the RAF's contributions to Farnborough each year was control over the presentation of their assets. As guests, they could not dictate the same degree of control over the conduct of the SBAC show as they could their own. The RAF's participation at Farnborough in 1955 had taken place at the suggestion of the RAF; they approached the SBAC organisers and had been welcomed as expected.

However, they were given short notice regarding the necessary arrangements, so for 1956, they had to get in touch early on. Despite the bad timing, the service contribution was grand, with the Hawker Hunter scarcely a year in service; an aerobatics team from 54 Squadron demonstrated precision aerobatics with four of them, while sixty-four more from eight out of the so far fifteen squadrons formed on the Hunter, to flypast in four consignments of sixteen each.

Additionally, in order to advertise the junior service's shiny new (as a certain US president might use words to describe) arsenal, twelve Vickers Valiants, in six pairs, each pair from a different squadron. This would mean a substantial increase in service participation at Farnborough, and the presence of so many V-Force aircraft would be a prestigious move. Looking to 1956 and bearing in mind the desire to present the V Force in the best light, Sir Ronald Ivelaw-Chapman suggested that Valiants should not be sent to Farnborough this time after their 1955 appearance.

Instead, the maximum number of Vulcans should be sent. This raised a question from the secretary of state; he was told that the indications early in the year was that eight Vulcans should be delivered to the RAF in May–June—'should' being the operative word as there was no certainty that this was going to happen. Avro would certainly welcome the opportunity to show off their ability to produce aircraft on time, but they would not be keen if just a relatively small number of aircraft were available as this would suggest a failure to meet their delivery targets. The programme for the 1956 Farnborough SBAC show was already filling up as early as January. The amount of time made available for the RAF was no more than twenty minutes and what items were approved would need to be carefully scheduled and rehearsal times allocated.

There was some difference of opinion over whether the RAF should assign another Hunter aerobatics team. There were two teams in 1955 from 54 Squadron (Black Knights) and 43 Squadron (Fighting Cocks). Ivelaw-Chapman thought even as early as 1956, with the Hawker Hunter only two years old operationally, that this would suggest to the press that the RAF was not making any more progress with new fighter types; his immediate subordinate, Air Marshal Thomas Pike, regarded the Hunter team as one of the most impressive features.

Pike later became AOC-in-C Fighter Command and then CAS. In both posts, he was influential in the creation of the premier aerobatic teams of the era, first with Hunters then Lightnings. Pike was a great supporter of the aerobatics team concept and is largely responsible for the pre-Red Arrows super teams, such as the Black Arrows and the Firebirds. The politicians—Mr Nigel Birch, the air secretary, and Christopher Soames, the undersecretary—were both sold on the prestige of the new V bombers.

They were mindful of the importance of the 'Nuclear Deterrent' and its positive appeal to both press and public alike: 'RAF participation without a display of "V" bombers would rebound to our discredit'. Plus, after a lacklustre display by a Valiant at Farnborough in 1955, they were assured that a far better-rehearsed display could be made ready for 1956. Still if eight Vulcans could be delivered to the RAF anywhere up to the end of June, then it should be possible to work up an adequate display for September. If the jets were delivered any later than June, there was the risk of repeating the Valiant demo in 1955, which would again draw criticism. Time for familiarisation and rehearsal were critical factors.

Looking forward to the year ahead, the RAF would try to take advantage of the reduced output of prototypes at Farnborough and try to negotiate a larger share of the flying programme. The annual Battle of Britain flypast was causing more concern each year, mostly because of the growing number of heavier, higher-performance aircraft. Large formations of such aircraft over built-up areas were a risk to be managed. Therefore, it had been agreed in 1955 that the 1956 flypast over the capital would be smaller. The CPC had recommended that it should consist of about thirty–forty Hunters and that the RN and USAF should not be invited to take part that year.

This was not approved as the CAS, Sir Dermot Boyle, wanted the RN and USAF to continue to be invited to take part unless they chose not to. Battle of Britain 'At Home' day in 1956 fell, most appropriately, on 15 September. Forty-five RAF stations were approved to swing their gates open this year—just one down on the previous year, perhaps the smallest yearly contraction yet. There were other more worrying concerns: adequate measures to safeguard the public were a subject of greater consideration than normal, even though nothing out of the ordinary had arisen in 1955, beyond what was expected.

What brought this to prominence was the 1955 attendance report. Biggin Hill, Castle Bromwich, Thornaby, Horsham St Faith, and Hendon reported the following respective attendance figures—275,000, 145,000, 110,000, 61,000, and 50,000. These numbers gave rise to concerns that the present rope and post barriers augmented by police patrols were no longer adequate and better crowd control measures were going to be needed. The council were not even sure if they would be liable if any claims from the public were made arising from an incident, which could be blamed on the failure of RAF station personnel to respond and exercise effective crowd control over visitors. They accepted a moral responsibility certainly. The proposed barrier to replace the rope and post was a semi-static tubular steel fencing that did not need to be fixed to the ground and could be erected and dismantled easily. Many public corporations used this type of barrier, but no government department or branch of the armed forces had any. If they purchased the barriers outright from the supplier, it would cost £1 per foot. There was a possibility of hiring it at 1s 6d a foot (7p in modern money) if stocks were available. They calculated a need for 16,000 feet of fencing for the five stations mentioned—4,000 feet for Biggin Hill and 3,000 feet for each of the others. The RAF would likely have to purchase rather than rent as stocks were never too great. The £16,000 minimum expenditure if bought outright could not be met from the non-public funds of the stations concerned.

As it was still the case that no charge for admission was made to the public entering each station, it would not be right to take money from the proceeds meant for the Benevolent Fund and RAFA. The council were advised that unless the cost of adequate fencing could be charged to public funds, they may have to cancel the Battle of Britain 'At Home' days at the more popular stations, 'in order to protect the public from danger'. For now, the free admission per head continued.

Ivelaw-Chapman recommended continuing with the existing format of 'At Homes' and participation at other events and that they should maintain and perhaps increase the effort and level of involvement. To try and redress the issue of the specific 'air display', he recommended doubling the RAF allocation of the SBAC flying display time from fifteen to thirty minutes by the time of the 1958 SBAC show. Sir Dermot Boyle generally agreed but felt he was wrong to suggest the RAF could no longer mount interesting displays with the latest aircraft types.

He suggested that a future display concept could include Transport Command aiding the army. Two more suggestions from Ivelaw-Chapman included 'putting the whole air force on parade in a programme lasting two hours. Another was to set aside one whole day of the SBAC show as the 'RAF Day'. The parliamentary undersecretary, Christopher Soames, queried what he had in mind and how this related to an increased participation length of thirty minutes. Supposedly, the idea was to hog the limelight for just one day of the SBAC show.

> Presumably the SBAC would also be functioning the same day in which case they might not altogether welcome our putting up a special tent or taking over the President's tent for the purpose of acting as host to the officially invited guests.

Neither was it clear how this would affect the RAF contribution to the other days of the SBAC. Again, if there was to be a larger level contribution made on 'RAF Day' then would this be at the expense of the RAF contribution to all the other days? This would likely have a negative effect on raising the service's public profile if the bulk of RAF flying was seen just on one day by a small portion of those attending overall.

The CAS naturally liked the suggestion of increasing the amount of time afforded the RAF at Farnborough from fifteen to thirty minutes, especially given the reduction in new aircraft types which was now noticeable. SBAC might therefore welcome an increased share of RAF participation. However, the idea of a day set aside during the week to devote to the RAF was out of the question. Again, the scale of effort and the amount of training involved would be 'uneconomic'.

Away from Farnborough, the RAF went ahead with Battle of Britain activities as normal despite the funding dilemma in respect of public safety at some airfields. There was at least one complaint arising but not with regards to any health and safety concerns. One member of the public who visited Biggin Hill for the 1956 'At Home' left with a bee in his bonnet, so to speak. In fact, he was so annoyed that after getting home, he put pen to paper and sent in his thoughts and recommendations for the future off to the RAF, with just a smattering of good-natured sarcasm:

Dear Sir, or Your Highness or whatever,

Congratulations on the first-class display, under abominable flying conditions, at Biggin Hill on the immortal Fifteenth.

But a loud rude noise for the cretinous lack of organisation at Brown Park [an airfield car park zone] at least and probably the others too. Somebody ought to be kicked in the pants. I know service life all too well, alas, to have any illusions about this. There will of course be the usual unhurried exchange of gentle correspondence and the mists of Old Boyism will then settle over the whole affair.

Courteous and efficient airmen were there in shoals to pack us in. They followed orders. The orders it would seem of a drooling moron with the Brains of mentally deficient maggot.

I should have thought that the first arrivals—of whom I had the misfortune to be one (but never again!)—could have been directed near the sole entrance-exit and that the build-up could have proceeded from that point onwards. Thus, the first in would have been the first out. But no; the organisers' ability to think no further ahead than the blindingly obvious resulted in the reverse being true. With the result that the half-past-five dilletantes were happily away by six, while those of us who take the fifteenth seriously and thus arrived early were still hopelessly jammed at the far end of the field at well after 7 pm. So much for cretinism number one.

Flat spin number two was apparent in the magical absence of those airmen who, having thus well and truly (and quite inequitably) packed us in (at five bob a time!), could not be spared to help sort us out. Could not be spared? My enquiry of the officer in charge at the control tent by the field's exit (surrounded by a good half-dozen uniformed bodies) elicited the delightful response that his airmen had to go get their tea. The flapping noise still coming from the back end of Brown Park an hour-and-a-half later was the stomachs of several hundred motorists and their families whacking against their spines.

I was a brown job. Thank God we've still got an Army.

I should be delighted, free, gratis and for nothing, to teach your Traffic Control people 'elementary traffic control.'

The above letter was addressed to the 'The Number-One man, Air Ministry, London, WC2' from a Mr Haines, whose address was given as Kensington W10, on 21 September 1956. The station commander at RAF Biggin Hill, Group Captain J Barraclough, was subsequently, or consequently, approached to explain the arrangements and answer the gentleman's concerns. He did bear in mind that by this stage, Biggin Hill had been staging an annual 'At Home' day for ten years. Not surprisingly, the station had a growing number of cars pitching up each year, which had shaped the parking arrangements such as they were by 1956 and how they remained at many an air show for years to come.

Biggin Hill is not particularly big; it is much smaller than many of the others staging 'At Homes' at that time. Yet the airfield's location and significance with the Battle of Britain gave it a level of prestige not attracted elsewhere, and certainly during the era in question, the Biggin Hill 'At Home' was the most heavily attended. As Grp Capt.

Barraclough said in his reply, extensive previous experience of holding such events at Biggin Hill, specifically, had resulted in close co-operation between the station, the Metropolitan Police, and the Royal Automobile Club. The CO took the clear inference from the angry chap's letter that he felt he should have been positioned toward the rear of the airfield near the entrance/exit as he felt his early arrival was due the reward of a quick exit. Anyone who has ever parked up at an air display with on airfield parking—increasingly rare in the twenty-first century—would never have experienced such an arrangement. As the Biggin Hill CO explained, 'Such a system of parking was considered and discarded' because of the following:

1. A large proportion of the motorists attending remain in their cars to watch the display and picnic. In the past bitter complaints have been received by motorists who considered that they did not get the forward position and good view in the car park that their early arrival merited.

2. Experience has shown that in the car and coach parks it is important to avoid any sort of blockage or delay near the entrance. If this is not done the hold up of traffic repercusses all the way back along the Bromley and Westerham roads. An inverse system of parking would inevitably produce this affect.

3. Regarding the observation that the car park attendants were not in evidence when the public departed. This was as planned and at the specific request of the Police and the RAC.

Barraclough also went on to point out that the complainant may not have been aware that there were seven car parks in use and all of them feeding on to the tortuous Bromley–Westerham road. As a result, the police requested that they be given sole control of the rate of exit from these parks, which was done as quickly as circumstances allowed and 140 civilian police operating under radio control could arrange.

At the time, Biggin Hill typically handled about 250,000 spectators and several thousand cars. Importantly, the experience was of early arrivals wishing to be parked near the display boundary so they could utilise their cars as grandstands and picnic areas. Then there was the advice and influence of the Met and the RAC, seen as the experts in dealing with heavy volumes of traffic. There had been very few complaints—proof most spectators were satisfied.

Among the various reports sent into the Participation Committee from the commands, the indications were that the experiences of station personnel involved with the 1956 'At Home' day, pointed to further shortcomings with the current format. Technical Training Command, as the title might suggest, had something to say; the report made it clear that the flying display is the main draw of the 'At Home' and unless an attractive flying display is publicised and carried out, attendance at tech training stations would continue to fall. Stating directly that whatever the noble and comprehensive aims of 'At Home' day, by showing all aspects of the work of the RAF, commands like tech training were suffering because their 'stations are handicapped by their non-flying roles, the limited size of their airfields, or, as in the case of Kirkham, no airfield facilities at all'.

They relied upon other commands for their flying programmes as they had no real resources to fall back on to fill the gaps caused by inadequate allocation or last-minute cancellations. 'Invariably the net result, as was the case of Debden this year, is a laudable attempt to keep the public amused with a few Chipmunks and Varsities'. Furthermore, the officer responding on behalf of TTC recorded:

> This Command wishes to record its appreciation of the assistance afforded by other Commands, but it is felt that this assistance is inadequate. It is respectfully emphasised that adequate and reliable support from operational Commands, in the provision of modern aircraft, must be given, and weather permitting, promises fulfilled, if we are to maintain the public interest on 'At Home' stations of this Command.

The letter containing these observations was addressed directly to the undersecretary of state, Air Ministry. The overall attendance recorded for 1956 by TTC was 102,000; the largest part of this was 46,644 at St Athan, which had 'Selected Station' status and therefore received some priority regarding flying display aircraft. The weather here was also co-operative, uniquely so as it was bad at other stations. The chairman of the CPC agreed with this and other points raised along the same lines. The public expected to see a flying display, at least as good, if not better, than the one they saw the year before, especially with further improved high-performance aircraft accruing onto the RAF's inventory year in year out.

This was being borne out year after year by public discrimination in favour of flying stations, where there was every expectation of a first-class show against the non-flying ones. This matter was addressed for 1957; the number of stations open was reduced again from forty-five to thirty-seven; Gibraltar held an event as well. HQ Fighter Command would take on the responsibility this time as central co-ordinator and allocator for all resources, static and flying.

The year 1957 brought the first of what might be described as the international aerobatic teams. The outfit which can be regarded as the true antecedent of the Red Arrows made their debut in 1957. The Black Arrows, formed from within 111 Fighter Squadron based at RAF North Weald, were newly equipped with the more potent Hawker Hunter Mk 6. This new model of the RAF's star high-performance aircraft possessed more robust energy with the uprated 200 series Rolls-Royce Avon turbojet developing an extra 2,500 lb of thrust over the earlier engine. The more prestigious aerobatics teams of 1956—the Fighting Cocks and the Black Knights—had operated formations of four aircraft with no particular display colour scheme other than squadron markings. The 43 Sqn team did have their jets fitted with smoke generators. The Black Arrows brought a radical development; the team operated nine of the Hunter F6 aircraft painted in a wraparound semi-gloss black and with smoke generators.

They were selected quite late on to represent the RAF at the 1957 Farnborough show usurping the 43 Sqn team, which took centre stage in 1956. The future of the RAF looked most promising by the end of 1956 as the V Force was building and the new Gloster Javelin all-weather fighter was operational.

Even more exciting, a list of new impressive and quite radical aircraft projects was on the blocks and all at various stages of development and procurement. Among these were a long-range supersonic strike aircraft with a global reach, a supersonic high-altitude all-weather interceptor, mixed power plant designs with rocket and jet propulsion, and a new generation of long-range strategic transport aircraft. Only the USA rivalled, or rather bettered, Britain for recognition as the most ambitious and prolific aircraft designer and manufacturer as far as the western hemisphere was concerned, but the story going into 1957 was predictable in its unpredictability.

As April arrived, the defence minister, Duncan Sandys, announced to the Commons in Westminster his proposal to essentially eradicate the need for any manned fighters, whatever the capabilities. The brave new vision taking over was the age of the 'unmanned' missile. How much of an impact this had on the availability of stations and other resources by September is difficult to identify or whether it had any impact on the number of 'At Home' stations in 1957. The full impact of this radical change in defence policy took time. Across Fighter Command and RAFG particularly, squadrons began to disband, and RAF stations closed. The process began in 1957 but continued until 1961. In Germany, this usually meant handing over old, commandeered airfields of the Luftwaffe. Now they were transferred back to the newly reformed Luftwaffe, quite ceremoniously. In the case of the UK, those fighter stations that were not found a new lease of life in a different role—usually flying training—closed. Some found a short-term future by housing the very missile squadrons that some fighter units were to convert to.

Despite the flux, the RAF made its most prolific contribution to this year's SBAC show, and an impressive showing it was. Afterwards, Sir Dermot Boyle regarded the RAF's image to not have been best served at Farnborough in 1957; he complained that the publicity for the RAF representation had been poor. No. 111 Sqn had put on an unparalleled display, not least because of the team's size and striking appearance of their aircraft. Sir Dermot never saw any photos of the nine-ship loop or the V bomber formation on the one day that it appeared. The RAF items listed for Farnborough in 1957 took up sixteen minutes of the flying programme.

This was a quite reasonable length of time given the much higher tempo largely due to the much smaller gaps between aircraft displays. Provisionally, the sixteen minutes were to consist of two flypast formations—one consisting of twenty-four Hunters and another of twenty-four Javelins, all from Fighter Command. The aerobatics team from 111 Squadron formed part of the Hunter formation and were to break away then complete a five-minute aerobatics sequence. This was ultimately subject to clearance by Fighter Command. Further, twelve Canberras from RAFG were to flypast. They would fly directly from their bases in Germany, the duration of the flypast was expected to be three minutes.

From flying training, a display by a team of Hunting Provost Piston-engined trainers. The Bomber Command segment involved low-level flypasts by one of each of the three V types—Valiant, Vulcan, and Victor—combined with a contrail height overflight by a mixed formation of more V bombers (Valiants) and Canberras *en masse* contrailing, timed at three minutes.

Before Farnborough got underway, adverse reports were printed in the *Sunday Express* and *Daily Express* on 1 and 2 September, complaining about the reduced number of aircraft planned for the Battle of Britain flypast this year to just three aircraft. The Participation Committee chose not to respond to the articles, bearing in mind they had no idea what the makeup of future Battle of Britain flypasts would look like. Such uncertainty made a concise response unwise. A significant number of aircraft prototypes were offered to the RAF for the 'At Home', and the Gloster Javelin—the latest cutting-edge fighter—along with all three V bombers and some new higher performance USAF types—F-100s and F-101s—promised to make 1957 the most impressive year yet.

7
1958–65

The contribution to the Farnborough Airshow in 1957 would be difficult to improve upon. The year 1958 was difficult for the RAF following the announcement by Duncan Sandys, proposing to end the era of manned fighters. On the other hand, the V Force continued to expand, and despite the continued cuts, the 1958 'At Home' day brought a reduction of only four stations. As far as the latter was concerned, the most significant casualty was Biggin Hill.

The station was to be relinquished by Fighter Command, and as no other commands had any use for the airfield, it was to be abandoned operationally. The RAF remained present through the movement in and out of various small support units such as the London University Air Squadron and 1 Air Experience Flight, up until February 1959. The last operational squadron, 41, left with their Hunters at the end of January 1958. The airfield slipped away from RAF control gradually. Civilian flying had already started to move in during 1956 from the old London Croydon Airport; this then continued. The next development, seemingly to hang onto some form of official RAF presence, was to find a home for the aircrew selection centre, but this did not begin until April 1962.

The airfield was, from 1959, fully under civilian control. It would not be needed by the RAF for any other primary flying purpose. This was a shame given Biggin Hill's historic status in addition to being on the outskirts of the Greater London area. Perhaps the most sizeable public market from the point of any public outdoor event, surely this would make it a special case?

There was nothing that could retain Biggin Hill as an active RAF airfield. Therefore, continuing to hold the annual 'At Home' was justified based on the airfield's synonymous history and prestige. And of course, the large levels of attendance. However, it was not expected to last. Whether it should have remained operational as a point defence interceptor base for the capital would perhaps have been an easier argument to make, had anyone been able to properly predict the outcome of Duncan Sandys' plan for the air defence of the British Isles.

The RAF's new nuclear deterrent carrying V Force represented by a Valiant and Vulcan here at RAF Binbrook's 1958 'At Home'. (*The National Archives*)

The manned fighter had so far proved vital to air defence because it could be scrambled to intercept, shadow, and identify, then, if necessary and upon receipt of an order, engage and destroy. By the end of the 1960s, when the UK interceptor force had been reduced to just five squadrons of short-legged if superlative performing Lightnings, interceptions of long-range Soviet reconnaissance bombers were routine. Most of these intercepts were carried out by fighters from the RAF base at Leuchars in Scotland, occurring almost daily. The notion that the ground-launched guided missile could address this task was clearly not thought of by Sandys and co. Yet within the confines of finite resources, it placed Biggin Hill well outside any favourable argument for either being retained or for the return of the fighters. The operational focus had in this post-war (now Cold War) era centred somewhere else—the east coast of Scotland.

Yet why not training units? It is possible that the growth in commercial aviation around the capital limited the scope for this idea. For all the obstacles, Biggin Hill in civilian hands has continued to host a reasonably sized air show each year to this day, but the recent disruption caused by COVID-19 seems to have put a halt to any further events for the present.

Another possible explanation for the loss of Biggin to operational flying however may be explained by a serious incident involving the home-based Meteor fighters in 1951. This had prompted concerns over the efficacy of retaining 'the Bump' as an operational station; with military aircraft getting heavier and faster, the growing level of infrastructure in the local area could not be ignored. Yet defence cuts rather than health and safety considerations were the primary reason for Biggin Hill becoming a civilian airfield, even though it retained an RAF presence and therefore, officially, remained an RAF station for the rest of the Cold War.

As the 1960s approached, formation aerobatics teams drawn from operational units were rapidly declining. Flying Training Command continued to mount a sizeable number. These are Vampire T11s from one of several training school teams, *c.* 1960. (*Adrian Balch*)

Just the same, Biggin was too highly thought of by the Air Council to simply to be dispensed with. At the time, to look at choosing somewhere else just did not seem right. The last 'At Home' to be held here then, while the station was operational, was 1957. Already established for obvious reasons, the display held here in 1957 was quite impressive with several premier military aerobatics teams including the then newly established Black Arrows and a USAF European Command representative team of supersonic F-100 Super Sabres—the Skyblazers.

With the airfield still to all intents and purposes in the hands of the RAF in 1958, Biggin Hill was to hold another display. There should not have been too much of a logistical nightmare, but if another was to be held here, it had to be comparable to the last one. If the manpower could be organised, then certainly the CPC and Fighter Command HQ between them could ensure the standard of flying and ground displays would not be found wanting. As the last RAF units with any active aircraft moved out and Croydon airport effectively moved in, the airfield, for now, still officially under RAF control, set about organising another display. It was not expected to be a problem but there was considerable commercial flying at Biggin now.

Staging another Battle of Britain display under RAF organisation would perhaps need a degree of consultation if not negotiation. The RAF felt that if there were to be 'At Homes' at all during Battle of Britain week, then the opening of RAF Biggin Hill could not be dispensed with.

In order to stage the 1959 display, the agreement of Surrey Aviation had to be obtained. To kick off, the Ground Officer Selection Centre, the only source of service personnel, had a very limited number of personnel. Ten officers and 219 other ranks were attached to Biggin to help with the event. Of this number, two officers and six airmen were attached for three months. The rest were at the station from a month to a single day.

Aircraft servicing equipment, barracks equipment and forty-four vehicles were loaned. The air traffic telecommunications equipment which ordinarily would have been removed when military flying ceased was fortunately still installed. The GPO indeed, were awaiting a decision on future 'At Homes' before recovering the equipment. The arrangements arrived at for the 1959 display would need to be repeated for 1960, which was a significant Battle of Britain anniversary. The importance of this station could not be understated. Its synonymous history with the Battle of Britain alone ensured priority status among all stations when allocating resources each year. Apart from its clear link to the battle itself, the annual 'At Home' here, on the edge of Greater London, invariably attracted the highest attendance figures of all. In recent years, during the operational era, attendances varied between 200,000 and 275,000. In 1959, the figure dropped to 170,000.

It was a significant drop but still a fantastic number by anyone's standards. Furthermore, the display had previously attracted the BBC to televise the best parts of the day. They had already indicated that while they would be happy to do so again, if held at Biggin Hill, they could not confirm televising a display at any other station should one not take place at the famous Kent station. From the RAF perspective, it was important that the people of London and the Home Counties 'should be able to visit an impressive "At Home"'.

At the same event, Vulcan B1, XA902, from 230 Operational Conversion Unit, based at Waddington, makes a slow pass down Farnborough's main runway. (*Air Historical Branch*)

Right: Although not the famous twenty-two aircraft 'Pterodactyl' loop, this is the same formation, flown by just 16 Hunters of 111 Sqn's Black Arrows aeros team. They were led by Sqn Ldr Peter Latham over Farnborough once again, September 1959. (*Air Historical Branch*)

Below: A week later, another Vulcan from 230 OCU is parked up at Biggin Hill while the Black Arrows do their stuff and punters squeeze past the safety barrier, in time-honoured fashion, before the RAF police shepherd them back again. (*Air Historical Branch*)

Sir Edmund Huddleston, now VCAS, concluded in a feasibility report:

> The holding of an 'At Home' day at Biggin Hill is so important to the success of Battle of Britain week and the prestige of the Royal Air Force that this station should continue as long as possible to be opened to the public, despite the special arrangements made necessary by reason of the station's present non-flying role. I also invite the standing committee to note that the long-term plans for Biggin Hill may make it impracticable to hold 'At Home' days at the station after 1963.

In the run up to the twentieth anniversary of the battle, the RAF's chief publicity officer, in view of the importance of commemorating and celebrating the twentieth anniversary, further supported the belief that if there were 'At Homes' on Battle of Britain week then the opening of Biggin Hill seemed indispensable: 'to deprive Londoners of the opportunity of seeing the RAF "At Home" would seem unthinkable.'

At the start of 1959, the wash-up (post-event debrief and report) from the previous year had to accept that resources and stations to act as venues were going to continue to be at an increased premium. By June, a proposed list of recommended RAF stations to open to the public had been received by the Participation Committee, and even though the RAF was now at its smallest since the end of the war, the list of stations that the various command C-in-Cs recommended to hold such a demanding event represented a monumental exercise in every aspect of service discipline:

Bomber Command
Bassingbourn
Cottesmore
Gaydon
Honington
Lindholme
Marham
Upwood
Waddington

Fighter Command
Acklington
Chivenor
Coltishall
Leconfield
Leuchars
Middleton St. George
Turnhouse
Wattisham

Coastal Command
Aldergrove
St Mawgan

Transport Command
Benson
Colerne

Flying Training Command
Biggin Hill
Syerston
Valley

Technical Training Command
Cosford
Felixstowe
Halton
Jurby
St. Athan

Maintenance Command
Andover

Signals Command
Norton

Tangmere

Overseas
Gibraltar Sea Front

Equally sizeable was the list of stations not recommended for various reasons. Biggin Hill was to open come Hell, high water, or plague. Both the BBC and ITV had also indicated their wish to televise the event here. Horsham St Faith, St. Athan, Cosford, and Gaydon were also treated as 'special cases'; they had each been open in 1958 under such recommendations, and it was expected that they should be afforded such status again. Turnhouse was another, selected because of its proximity to Edinburgh. Fighter Command had decided against recommending it for 1959 as by September, it was likely, under the circumstances of the day, that the airfield would be in the hands of the Ministry of Transport and Civil Aviation Authority. RAF Leeming, which had been open in 1958, was not recommended this time because of its proximity to Middleton St George, which was itself closer to population centres such as Durham and Middlesbrough and so it was requested that the special status afforded Leeming in 1958 should be extended to Middleton St George in 1959.

During 1959, the commands found it difficult, due to a shortage in flying hours, to provide aircraft for participation in air displays elsewhere. The Participation Committee therefore recommended to the Air Council that they should continue to participate in those air displays that were most rewarding in terms of prestige and publicity. Yet the number of events that they took part in should be smaller overall. An overall programme was prepared at the start of the year, which provided for a considerable reduction in the scale of RAF participation.

However, unexpected requests for RAF aircraft were received. Some of these were for events of such importance—for political and other reasons where RAF participation was essential. It was the norm for the committee to meet later to address the all-important issues of what everyone was going to see wherever they turned up. This aspect was proving to be problematic for those stations which while RAF stations were not airfields. This was specifically where Maintenance and Technical Training Commands were at a considerable disadvantage. Any locations that could suitably host the kind of event that stood a good chance of attracting the public in droves was an extra special headache for them. Maintenance command could only make one station available—Andover.

Signals Command had more options and recommended that in addition to Tangmere (a recent acquisition from Fighter Command), Norton could be opened. The latter was the location of the RAF's No. 3 Ground Radio Servicing School and not in possession of an airfield, but the station had been open in previous years and had been very successful, perhaps largely due to having Sheffield on the doorstep.

The list of rejections—that is, suggestions to remain closed—was as long. AOC-in-C Coastal Command had initially recommended that Kinloss near Inverness should open then had to write a further reply explaining that the officer commanding 18

Group, his immediate subordinate, had advised that the decision was complicated by the hosting of a similar event at the nearby Royal Naval Air Station at Lossiemouth, which planned to be open on 18 July, just two months before.

They were worried that Lossiemouth would steal the thunder of the RAF event. Both the RAF and RN station commanders felt there was insufficient public support to make both events a success so close to one another and over such a short space of time. It was suggested by the two that Kinloss could open in 1960 while Lossiemouth, by agreement, would not stage an air day that year. The Kinloss CO was also keen to avoid sparing precious time and resources to arranging an 'At Home' day, the reason being cited that they had a particularly intense training programme that year—a consequence of being the base for the MOTU (Maritime Operational Training Unit). Coastal Command also requested that St Mawgan should be kept out of the programme for 1959.

On 25 May 1959, a meeting was hosted by the Central Participation Committee involving representation from the various commands and other elements likely to contribute including the Ministry of Supply, the Admiralty, the MTCA (Ministry of Transport and Civil Aviation), and the United States Air Force.

On 9 September, the Participation Committee were contacted by the police in Beverley, East Yorkshire, to advise that rumours had come to their attention that the Direct-Action Committee against Nuclear War and the Committee for Nuclear Disarmament may organise a demonstration on the day—19 September 1959—at RAF Leconfield. The chief concern was that they may enter as normal punters (this was done successfully by left-wing demonstrators at the American air base at Ramstein in 1983) and then assemble to hold a demonstration from within. The RAF rightly judged that this would be embarrassing, not to mention the unfavourable impact on the *bona fide* members of the public attending the air show.

The RAF police and Air Ministry police had experience dealing with demonstrators at the Thor missile sites and RAF stations generally, but this situation raised somewhat different questions. There had never been such an incident at an 'At Home' day before.

If the threat materialised, the situation would be more difficult to handle, but it was different to the normal threat posed by the anti-nuclear bodies at Thor and V bomber bases. The approach was to be ready to manage any such demonstration within; the aim was to control the demonstration while ensuring the day remained a success—in effect, crowd control. An emphasis was to be placed on the use of Air Ministry and civil police. However, kid gloves the approach, there were clear political implications which the RAF were keenly aware of.

Altogether, thirty-two stations, including Gibraltar, were open this year as the number of stations continued to contract. Among the highlights was the first chance to see the English Electric Lightning outside of the Farnborough SBAC show. The standard brochure, *the Battle of Britain Souvenir Book*, this year was general to most stations, topped and tailed to provide specific details of the station in question.

As of 19 October 1959, there still had not been a decision made on whether Biggin would be open in 1960, but one would need to be made soon so that an early start could be made on all aspects of publicity. The station commander had his work cut out as it was and would also need to know, at the earliest convenience, that his station was to hold an 'At Home'.

As well as the usual arrangements, he had to approach Surrey Aviation to give notice and seek agreement for the RAF to commandeer the airfield to cover the requisite period and arrange to have a detachment of a larger than usual number of RAF personnel than would normally be the case anywhere else; this would increase gradually from about three months out, just as had been the case for 1959. Television coverage was considered particularly important.

An early decision was also required because although the much of the RAF flying control apparatus still remained intact. It was in danger of being removed by the GPO, who were labouring under the understanding that more 'At Homes' were unlikely. An instruction to leave it all alone was needed, or they would lose the teleprinters and telephones that would be imperative, all subject to the Air Council's decision. Despite what the BBC had implied and just how much prestige sat with Biggin Hill, the director of operations was already suggesting looking for an alternative venue. The nearest station that would be suitable was West Malling, but again faith was lacking in any expectation of this station managing to attract anything like the crowds pouring into Biggin each September.

The director of operations offered to assemble a report containing all the 'pros and cons' to present to VCAS, who would then present the report to the Air Council. Before any such decision was made either way, however, the GPO had to be held off from recovering all the airfield comms equipment, without which holding another service organised air show of any kind at Biggin Hill would be quite out of the question. The air staff asked them to be patient a bit longer and resist the temptation to descend on the airfield and proceed to unplug and unscrew things until they had decided. The year 1960 continued the pattern of diminishing returns and another cut in open stations was going to be unavoidable, certainly as more Fighter Squadrons disbanded to reform on the Bloodhound missile or disappear.

On the upside, 1960 saw a couple of operational debuts, that of the English Electric Lightning, the first Mk 2 Vulcan, and the heavy and cumbersome but impressive Javelin, which had gone as far in development as it would.

Up until now, appearances by truly supersonic types came from the United States Air Force. The USAF at overseas locations, particularly, tended to restrict their public flying efforts to flypasts, whatever the performance of the aircraft they had in theatre. The USAF European command did still operate an official aerobatics team, the Skyblazers, equipped with the F-100C Super Sabre. This was in stark contrast to the RAF approach, which took a far more liberal and imaginative attitude to display flying and still approved a wide selection of both aerobatics teams and individual aerobatics as well as formation flying drill, performance handling and operational role demonstrations. There is no doubt about it—the RAF stood out among the world's air forces in the field of aerial demonstrations.

Neither the USAF or any other air arm, even back in the USA, ever attempted to emulate the unique approach of the RAF to their approach characterised by the pre-war Empire Air Days and now the post-war 'At Home' day. The format in question came in for some mild and just criticism following the 1960 display season.

Left: In its element, a scene which has characterised the Cold War/post-war RAF's public image. Four Lightnings of 74 Sqn, only weeks after the squadron formed, at the 1960 Farnborough air show, demonstrate the Lightning's high performance, rotating near vertical before reaching the end of the runway on take-off. (*AHB*)

Below: From 1956, the USAF Skyblazers aeros team had transferred back to the original control of the 36th Tactical Fighter Wing, based at Bitburg in West Germany and re-equipped with the truly supersonic F-100C Super Sabre. They continued to be regular attendees of selected RAF 'At Homes' until the inevitable cutbacks brought the curtain down on them after 1961. (*Adrian Balch*)

The Battle of Britain office at RAF Aldergrove, in their post-display report, highlighted three points, all of which particularly affected them given their location in Northern Ireland and the operational requirements of their command at this time of year.

Apart from the overarching concern that September simply was not the right time for holding displays in this part of the country, the two specific reasons compounding this were first; that it was too close to the well-established Farnborough SBAC show which at the time occupied typically the first week of September and rounded off with three public days. Secondly, the operational commands were usually starting a round of autumn exercises and most pertinently concerning Aldergrove. As the weather had already deteriorated considerably by September in Ireland, most of the holidaymakers had gone home, leaving a much-reduced market in this area. Aldergrove was in a rural quiet part of the world, even by the standards of most other RAF stations.

In 1960, Farnborough was the RIAT of the day, and whatever the RAF 'At Homes' could provide in the week or two following, it would require a particularly grand effort to avoid being eclipsed by the Hampshire airfield's cutting-edge fare. Farnborough had first hosted RAF participation in 1955 and since 1957 was now a prominent publicity platform for the RAF and other services each year. Here the public had better chance to see aircraft recently introduced to service, making Farnborough the principal stage for British wares in the aviation market.

Watching new aircraft in service hands, rather than those of a company test and development crew, was expected to increase the chance of potential sales to the overseas market. The year 1960 saw a slight increase in the number of events participated in over 1959. Nineteen displays were attended in the UK in 1959, twenty in 1960; overseas, the figures were thirty-five in 1959 and thirty-eight in 1960. These figures did not include 'At Homes' and USAF armed forces days or displays attended by a single helicopter. A considerable saving of effort was achieved though, by concentrating as many of the displays attended on one or two dates. If two displays were to take place simultaneously, even if organised entirely separately, the RAF could widen their presence by attending both. The 1960 Farnborough, courtesy of the RAF, saw quite a spectacle with V bomber scrambles each day to start the flying programme rotating each time between Valiants, Vulcans, and Victors.

The Black Arrows were prominent as the RAF's first truly pre-eminent aerobatics team with the full sixteen-ship Hunter aerobatics display, but what really raised the stakes in terms of never-been-seen before spectacle was the rotation take-off by four Lightnings from 74 Squadron, each following the other into a vertical climb over the end of the runway.

Meanwhile, further questions were raised over what was now called the 'silly season'—an in-house reference to September often used by squadron commanders. No one was suggesting that the RAF's great moment—the Battle of Britain—should not be honoured, but that the 'At Homes' could be spread out across July and August while still retaining a synonymous connection with the period covering the campaign.

Separating 'At Home' day from Battle of Britain week had become an old chestnut especially with station commanders. Many recorded their reservations about the wisdom of such a rigid process. In both cases, the Participation Committee had explained that the wider public perception and understanding of the battle, its link with 'At Homes', and

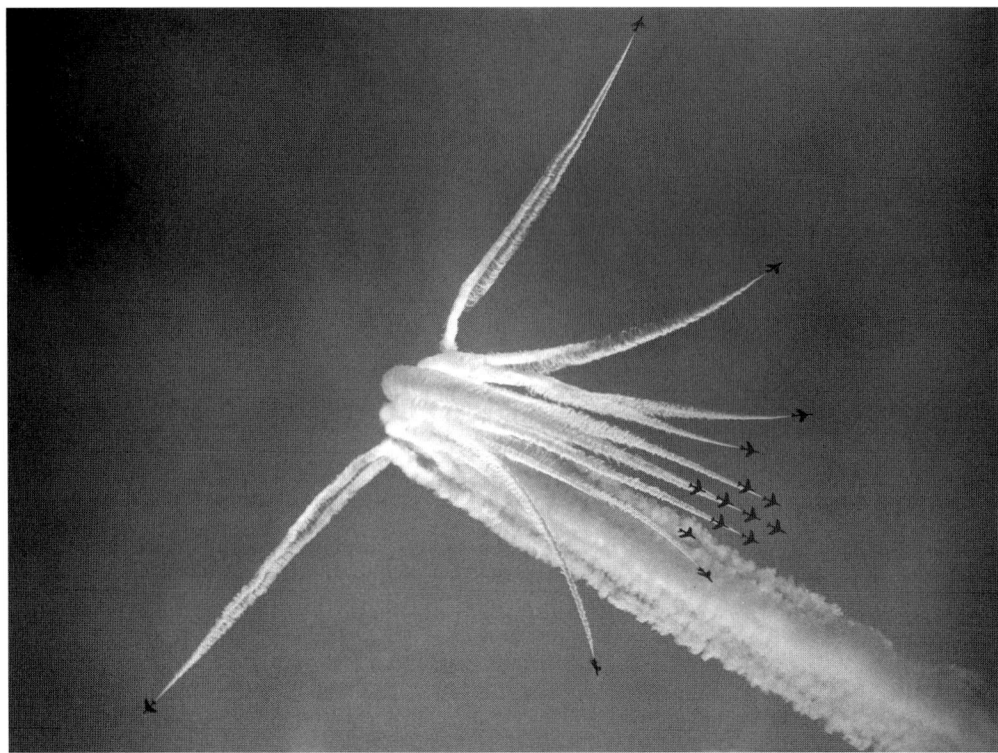

As iconic an image as any of the RAF on display, the 1959 Black Arrows 'bomb burst' manoeuvre overhead the Farnborough crowd. (*Air Historical Branch*)

Contrasting types and roles, by 1960, when this image was taken at RAF Bassingbourn, every station 'At Home' event endeavoured to provide as comprehensive a line up as possible of the RAF's inventory. (*The National Archives*)

the special significance that maximum publicity could only be gained by retaining the link. The established order was set in Queen's Regulation QR 159(3). This ruling was arrived at following a review conducted by Air Marshal Sir Richard Peck, known during the war as the voice of the Air Ministry; from 1946 to 1949, he was also a governor at the BBC. Peck's recommendations were now enshrined in military law, meaning it was in 'QRs'—a reference often heard in service life whenever a legal matter cropped up. Despite the Participation Committee's attachment to tradition, they also recognised the strain on resources and recommended no more than twenty stations should open in 1960, but the Air Council ordered that twenty-five be open. This was honoured and so 1960 drew an attendance of 727,019 visitors compared with 1,051,950 in 1959, perhaps a consequence of twenty-five instead of thirty-two open stations.

Fighter Command's flying display co-ordinators reported that most of the service flying displays in 1960 were from non-operational units and that standards had suffered as a result. Compounding this, as some aircraft flew several displays consecutively at different stations through the afternoon, there were delays, impacting on safety standards.

After 1960, Fighter Command recommended that no more than eight stations should open simultaneously and that they should be selected according to their location; they specifically recommended Biggin Hill (or Manston) due proximity to London and the south-east of England; Honington (or Wattisham) to represent East Anglia; Gaydon representing the Midlands; Finningley also representing the Midlands; Middleton St George representing the north of England; Leuchars representing Scotland; Aldergrove representing Northern Ireland; and St Athan representing South Wales.

In addition, however, HQFC later recommended adding the following to increase the list to fifteen stations as they all sat near large population centres and had previously attracted large attendance figures: Benson, Bassingbourn, Colerne, Cosford, Cottesmore, Tangmere, and Waddington.

Station commanders needed to be told in good time that they were on the list. Such was the fluidity of the situation that some COs would not necessarily expect their base to be open on an annual basis and would not prepare a year in advance; some were notified a mere six months away. Biggin Hill again posed a problem due to the civilianisation of the airfield. Each year, they needed a period for negotiation with Surrey Aviation Ltd. This was not simple formality; Surrey had to be compensated after the 1959 and 1960 events due to the level of disruption in their own routine flying programme. The airfield would also need £2,000 of repair work carried out on the subsidiary runways to allow the parking of aircraft.

Of course, Biggin Hill was to be included again for 1961, but the long-term future did not look at all promising. The year 1962 was a possibility but factors of a classified nature were expected to prohibit the station being used for service-organised displays thereafter. Having had twenty-five open in 1960, eight would have a dreadful impact on the service image, therefore the CPC agreed with fighter command's recommendation that it would be feasible to open fifteen stations together with Biggin Hill under current arrangements. Attendance figures for 'At Home' stations on 17 September 1960, compared with the attendance figures over the previous two years in respect of those from 1960 open in those years, are as follows:

Stn	Cmd	1958	1959	1960
Acklington	Ftr	28,000	32,000	7,500
Aldergrove	Ctl	15,000	11,700	10,000
Bassingbourn	Bmr	16,000	25,000	15,000
Benson	Tpt	22,000	15,000	14,000
Biggin Hill	Fg Trg	260,000	170,000	180,000
Chivenor	Ftr	15,000	10,000	10,000
Colerne	Tpt	28,000	29,000	17,000
Coltishall	Ftr	-	20,000	27,000
Cosford	Tch Trg	30,000	42,000	20,000
Cottesmore	Bmr	60,000	46,000	24,200
Finningley	Bmr	-	-	65,000
Gaydon	Bmr	105,000	115,000	80,500
Halton	Tch Trg	10,000	10,000	11,523
Jurby	Tch Trg	7,000	5,200	2,500
Kinloss	Ctl	-	-	9,000
Leconfield	Ftr	-	20,000	21,000
Leuchars	Ftr	37,000	33,000	24,000
Norton	Sgl	25,000	29,000	20,737
St. Athan	Tch Trg	38,000	34,500	27,559
Shawbury	Fg Trg	-	-	29,000
Tangmere	Sgl	-	30,000	28,000
Valley	Ftr	23,000	12,750	12,500
Waddington	Bmr	40,000	25,000	21,000
Waterbeach	Ftr	12,000	-	20,000
Wattisham	Ftr	20,000	25,500	30,000
1960 TOTAL				727,019

Bmr = Bomber, Ftr = Fighter, Ctl = Coastal, Tpt = Transport, Sgl = Signal, Fg Trg = Flying Training, and Tch Trg = Technical Training.

Of all the stations listed above, a handful were open for the last time, certainly under the Battle of Britain format. Most if not all of those had a relatively small gate and several did not have a substantial airfield, another factor that cropped up in the post-1960 report.

The last national service recruits had been called up in December 1960; consequently, the abundance of available manpower made possible through conscription was about to end. National service was an unwelcome imposition on young men with no intention or inclination to serve and, in some ways, a burden that the armed forces could now happily abandon.

There was something rather more positive that had taken place over the same period as national service. Since 1946, the RAF had sponsored an exhibition on Horse Guards Parade with static aircraft; this exhibit was open for all of Battle of Britain week. From 1957, the display was embellished with a marquee and a further display in the Air Ministry Whitehall building.

When the air secretary approached the prime minister, Harold McMillan, about continuing the Horse Guards Parade exhibition, McMillan agreed it should but was concerned that the Battle of Britain exhibit was the only one of its kind to be held and that its being staged year on year would become increasingly anachronistic. He suggested 1960, the twentieth anniversary, would be as good a point as any to call it a day.

The foreign secretary, Alec Douglas-Home, went further in his critique of the exhibition, he saw no point, it 'was not in tune with our present policies'. The air secretary agreed, so 1960 presented a timely opportunity to announce a change. There was no Horse Guards Battle of Britain exhibition in 1961.

Therefore, the CPC were to be invited to consider an alternative venue with one further suggestion, the powers did not like the reference to the Battle of Britain. The CPC might wish to consider calling it the 'Royal Air Force Exhibition' instead. As for the 'At Home' day, there was further criticism—that of all things, this had become a series of flying displays and all mounted in a short space of time (clearly alluding to them all being held simultaneously) and so close to the Farnborough SBAC show. The recommendation was to review the 'primary aims' of 'At Home' days before deciding on the number of stations to be open in 1961.

The Battle of Britain exhibition on Horse Guards Parade, September 1961. Even the then Conservative prime minister, Harold McMillan, felt the exhibition was becoming anachronistic. (*Peter March*)

At command level, Fighter and Signals Commands had respectively made a point about the format in 1956 and 1959. The VCAS at the time had written to AOC-in-C Signals Command:

So much has already gone into establishing the existing celebration in the week of the year which has such special significance, we are convinced that our efforts are most likely to receive maximum recognition from the Press and the Public at that time.

Cosford, which had a not entirely small attendance, was now considered inadequate; the small airfield could not accommodate much in terms of visiting aircraft and was ironically confronted by attendance as a problem with increased numbers of cars. The secretary of state observed that the list of stations proposed still left large populous areas of the country without an RAF station to attend on the day, he specifically referred to the north-west of England and Scotland. To compensate in some way, he suggested holding as many Battle of Britain Sunday parades through major towns as possible.

The armed forces were now entering an era whereby they faced more critical observations and searching questions as to how they continued to justify their existence, not from the public domain so much, but they were under the parliamentary spotlight almost continuously. The new CAS, Sir Thomas Pike, had warned station commanders to be wary of official parliamentary visits to RAF commands and stations.

He felt past visits 'had been a serious disappointment'. Station commanders received informal visits by MPs, for example, who were not entirely aware of current Air Ministry thinking and philosophy, and as a result, the CO might find himself responding to questions of policy posed by a possible hostile critic. The air secretary, Julien Amery, instructed that in future, station commanding officers were not to discuss policy, and as a further safeguard, were to issue invitations to MPs in such a way which effectively placed with the Air Ministry the right to refuse any request for a visit, without embarrassment, if it seemed 'inconvenient or undesirable'.

The standard of flying displays and the perceived deterioration of some was another air staff concern. There remained several stations—for example, Halton, Jurby, and Norton—that were essentially non-flying. Hitherto, this challenge had been met but depended on a heavier amount of fly-through touring aircraft as very little could operate from these stations. These stations had all been open in 1960. Norton was like Cosford—an unsuitable location seemingly, but it enjoyed a high attendance despite the noted restrictions.

Despite non-primary flying stations still holding their own, the all-important matter of allocating flying resources at each faced an unfair disadvantage, and the feeling was that for all the gate success, these stations were too inadequate to do justice in terms of service presentation. More suggestions appeared suggesting the move of some 'At Homes' to different dates, though this was promptly dismissed. This time, the argument from on high was moving to several dates was only likely to multiply the already serious complications with the present arrangements in terms of air traffic control.

With the likely loss of the smaller locations, other more suitable replacements were reviewed for suitability. Leconfield, which had opened in the previous two years, was dismissed. The station was losing one of its three operational squadrons prior to converting to Lightnings; this did not place it in a difficult situation, but the cuts had an impact in the overall balance and level of commitment. This in turn can impact on each squadron and station in terms of flexibility. The contraction of the RAF had mostly flattened out by 1961. The RAF in Germany were just completing a very far-reaching re-structure started in 1957; no fewer than seven stations were relinquished—more than half the total.

Given that twenty open stations in 1960 was considered insufficient by the air staff, the number settled on for 1961 was sixteen—a figure that had been revised up. Among things to look forward to by the tax-paying families and enthusiasts was a greater chance to see the new English Electric Lightnings, which were now fully operational and their numbers were growing.

The CPC wanted the new superlative fighter to be prominent in 1961, attending as many displays, both in the UK and overseas, as could be managed. Naturally, the new jets would be confined to events with a minimum level of prestige. There was also a belief that such an aircraft was best shown in formation rather than solo. For all the cuts, these were exciting times. There was also the new Blue Steel missile-carrying Vulcan and Victor Mk 2 aircraft bringing a further impact on the sight and sound at air displays.

For the 'At Homes', there was a scant number of Lightnings from which to find sufficient to cover as many airfields as possible; seventeen were made available. This included the 74 Sqn Tigers aerobatics team, while each RAF operator and the MOA supplied eight jets, mostly for slow and fast runs with a couple available for individual aerobatics. This effort stretched to fourteen out of the sixteen stations to cover.

The situation in 1961 was typical of the era—still a substantial proportion of aircraft being provided, yet a tight number to spread over sixteen locations. About nine Hunters and ten Javelins were made available for individual demonstrations and aerobatics from Fighter Command, in addition to touring formations and two Hunter aeros teams. This level of effort, across the service, still stretched resources to make each event worthwhile and represent the RAF in a befitting manner.

With the rate of closures and units disbanding, a much welcome settled period of consolidation beckoned. The V Force in 1962 reached its short-lived peak. By the time of the Cuban Missile Crisis that October, twenty-two squadrons were at various stages of availability for operations from fully operational and declared to forming on type. For the Fighter Command squadrons, it was a different story; the squadrons' orbat (order of battle, referring to a military organisation's available resources and their formation) had experienced the reverse—from about thirty-four squadrons in 1957 down to ten, three with the new Lightnings, two with Hunters still (two more Hunter squadrons had recently been transferred to Transport Command's control as an in-house tactical support wing).

Five more squadrons continued for now with the Gloster Javelin, all later marks (8 and 9), but these would be reduced further from the end of September. The RAF's first 'premier' aerobatics team, 111 Sqn's Black Arrows, ended their reign after four years due to the RAF's re-equipment and re-structure schedules. In 1961, they handed the mantle to 92 Sqn's Blue Diamonds. They continued to hog the limelight in 1962 under the leadership of Sqn Ldr Brian Mercer. The Blue Diamonds flew a maximum formation aerobatics sequence with eighteen Hawker Hunters. Despite the RAF traditionally fielding several aerobatics teams, before 1957, they had no premier nationally representative team like the Red Arrows or the Black Arrows. Other countries—including France, Italy, and the USA—had a single full-time aerobatics team, established shortly after the war, and have endured through to the present. For example, the US Navy vied alongside the US Air Force with their own demonstration team, the Blue Angels, while the USAF European Command maintained a representative team until 1961.

The Black Arrows, in preparation for the peak of demand in September, flew a standard full team of sixteen jets, then split into five- and nine-ship teams to spread out and reach as many displays as possible. This was an overly complex arrangement, requiring the pilots to learn aerobatics sequences with varying numbers of aircraft, to be performed across a single afternoon at separate locations; it must have made some demand on pilot fatigue. Nevertheless, these displays all came to pass without incident.

The Blue Diamonds did likewise and in 1962 managed to provide aerobatics displays variously with either nine or eighteen aircraft, therefore being seen at four locations in one afternoon without tiring the pilots too much. No. 74 Sqn provided their seven-ship Lightning team 'The Tigers'. A large diamond formation of twenty-five aircraft comprising the Hunters and Lightnings of both teams was flown over Farnborough. What was yet to be announced was that this would be the last annual Farnborough SBAC show; the next one would be in 1964.

Another milestone for 1962 was the appearance, for the first time, at the official RAF 'see how we spend our share of your taxes' day, of a not inconsiderable line up of aircraft from various NATO European air forces. The CAS in 1962 had extended an invitation to his counterparts in Belgium, Denmark, France, the Netherlands, and Norway to participate. The invitations had been well received, and the overseas displays were very greatly appreciated.

The air staff had been prompted by the circumstances to review the policy of allowing other NATO air arms to take part. Sir Thomas Pike summed up the change of heart:

> Apart from the need to augment our own dwindling resources, the opportunity offered to these air forces to join us in our 'At Home' day would seem to be an important corollary to our own appearance in these countries.

The invitations were to go out to respective air attachés again.

Among those sent over from the continent were aerobatics teams from the Netherlands (Whisky Four with T-33s), Belgium (Diables Rouge with Hunters), Denmark (Formations of F-86Ks and Hunters), and France (Fouga Magisters). A handful of aircraft from these and other air arms were placed in the static parks at various airfields for close inspection. This brought some one-off opportunities, especially at RAF Benson, which had a French Air Force Vautour nuclear strike aircraft on display.

After 1960, with 111 Squadron re-equipping with Lightnings, Fighter Command transferred the task of representing the RAF with an aerobatics team internationally to 92 Squadron, who formed their Blue Diamonds. A section of the team is seen here at altitude. (*Adrian Balch*)

Above left: At the same event, a veteran trainer, the Avro Tutor, with relaxing mechanic, is watching a formation of 74 Sqn's Lightnings overfly the crowd line. The display was held to celebrate the fiftieth anniversary of the formation of the Royal Flying Corps and was attended by HRH Prince Philip. (*Air Historical Branch*)

Above right: The year 1962 brought European NATO Air Force participation at most RAF 'At Home' days. The Dutch aerobatics team, Whiskey Four, displayed at RAF Leuchars in Fife. (*KLU Archives, via Netherlands Embassy*)

Away from aerobatics teams and noisy jets, air transport is an indispensable asset. This is a tactical demonstration involving a Benson-based Armstrong-Whitworth Argosy, off-loading supplies to ground troops during a display at RAF Upavon, 16 June 1962. (*Peter March*)

Above left: Battle of Britain 'At Home' Day at Biggin Hill, 15 September 1962. By this stage, the airfield here had to be borrowed by the RAF from the commercial occupants, each year for the requisite period, to stage the annual display. (*Air Historical Branch*)

Above right: 1962 brought overseas attendance at RAF 'At Homes' in force. This French Vautour and Paris 760, from the French Air Force, at RAF Benson, will have made an unusual adornment to the more familiar UK/US/Canadian military fare. (*Peter March*)

Then October came and quite suddenly; the world stood closer to Armageddon than at any time before or since, during peacetime. As the Cuban Missile Crisis unfolded, testing the mettle of US President John F. Kennedy, V Force air and ground crews were ferried to various pre-selected airfields across the British Isles while other crews flew four-strong formations of armed Vulcans and Victors to each in preparation for 'MAD' (mutually assured destruction). Following this tense period, where Armageddon was thwarted at the last second by skilful negotiation at various levels between Washington and Moscow, the RAF's primary nuclear deterrent and the required air defence screen went into further contraction. The UK-based missile squadrons, aimed at replacing the manned fighter and bomber, were also now mostly to disband and quickly. From a total of twelve squadrons in 1963, by the end of 1964, one Bloodhound missile unit remained on UK soil.

The year 1963 was the last that the RAF approved official aerobatics teams to be formed from operational units, and it certainly brought matters to a head. There was not much left to choose from within Fighter Command—three Javelin squadrons remained along with five more squadrons either operational with or working up to operational declaration with the Lightning. There were also two operational conversion units, one for Lightnings and one with Hunters to support the remaining Hunter squadrons now all assigned to the ground attack and reconnaissance roles.

The Hunter OCU worked up a team of five aircraft—the Black Dragons. From the Lightning force, three of the five squadrons were operational in the early part of the year,

Despite, or rather because of, the public notoriety of the Black Arrows and Blue Diamonds, other contemporary aeros teams went unnoticed, one being the 'Black Dragons' of 229 OCU who had a busy day on 14 September 1963 with four displays booked through the day. They disbanded shortly afterwards. (*Air Historical Branch*)

while the OCU on the other hand was quite busy. No. 74 Sqn had the team aerobatics commitment with the Lightning for 1961 and 1962, and the air staff were not keen to inflict another year of high fatigue consumption on the basic Mk 1s operated by 74 Sqn. In any case, their jets were soon to be handed over to the OCU and other specialist units yet to be formed. This left only two squadrons, 56 and 111, both based at Wattisham; they had the later Mk 1As but an establishment of just twelve aircraft each.

Of the two squadrons, 111 had no pilots on strength with current experience of formation aerobatics, while 56 had six to form a nucleus to build on. No. 111 Sqn started its conversion to Lightnings after 56 was further restricted as its pilots had not received any substantial air-to-air refuelling training yet. The plan for the aerobatics team was to start a prolonged work-up period as early as possible; this had been the case in 1961 when 92 Sqn took over the premier aerobatics team role from 111. If all went according to plan, a team of nine aircraft would be ready to go to Paris in June. So, on balance, AOC-in-C Fighter Command, Air Marshal Sir Douglas Morris, told the air staff, that he would have to give the prize to 56 Squadron.

It was not an easy choice, and the air staff were told that a crash in-flight refuelling programme would need to begin for 111 so they could take over the overseas commitment from 56. This had the further impact of necessitating the next squadron due to form on Lightnings, 19, to have their schedule for reforming brought forward to March/April time, so they could be of some assistance to 111. Air Marshal Morris also made clear his command's ability to reinforce overseas theatres would be diminished. As the premier team, 56, would have to have nine aircraft in order to make any kind of display worthwhile, so the thinking went. The Firebirds, the chosen moniker, now in a very non-operational mindset, had their jets painted with crimson down the spine of their aircraft, the entire fin, wing, and tail leading edges, while their famous red and white chequerboards ran through the nose roundels; it made for a striking appearance for sure. The design was selected from a few proposals received. Their new role effectively took the whole squadron out of the line for the duration of their tour.

Nine aircraft formed just the standard 'full' team in the display sequence and as they were Lightnings, consumed a copious amount of fuel. Overall, the scale of RAF public participation in 1963 was about the same as the previous year in the UK but slightly less overseas. Paris was the big event this year. Held at Le Bourget, being overseas, the air salon would be more demanding this time as the Firebirds would be flying the flag over foreign soil and in a truly international atmosphere, with comparisons to be made with the leading aerobatics teams of other air arms. In 1963, this included the USAF Thunderbirds in their F-100s, the Patrouille de France (Mystere IV), and a team from the Hellenic Air Force with North American Sabres (Hellenic Flame).

The salon was to take place on 6 to 16 June, and the RAF made a generous contribution—Mk 2 Victor and Vulcan (with Blue Steel) for the static park at the weekend—while concentrating the bulk of the flying effort on the Sunday. A Victor B2 flew direct from the UK and a Vulcan (Blue Steel) that included a rapid engine start followed by take-off. The V bombers flew on the Saturday as well, with the intended *pièce de résistance*, 56's Lightnings; they were to present a co-ordinated sixteen minutes of formation and solo aerobatics. This, however, was restricted to Sunday only as the

Right: The first Lightning squadron, 74, formed this nine-ship aeros team for 1961, with their kerosene-guzzling, heavy and powerful new supersonic mounts, breaking into the Farnborough circuit in September 1961. (*Air Historical Branch*)

Below: No. 92 Squadron's Blue Diamonds execute their bomb burst manoeuvre during rehearsals. (*Air Historical Branch*)

Salon organisers wanted no military formations flying on Saturday; the reason why was not given. The Vulcan and Victor were permitted to fly on the Saturday also.

There were other British items, from manufacturers, at the show—a Buccaneer, P1127, VC-10, Hunter Mk 66, Folland Gnat, an assortment of military helicopters: Wessex, Belvedere, Whirlwind, Scout, and many more. Bristol Aircraft Ltd also exhibited a Bloodhound missile (having reached the peak of deployment, now being mostly withdrawn) requiring a retinue of two RAF officers and four NCOs. No aircraft were displayed by the navy or army this year. The original service contribution was to have been larger, as approval had been given for a Jet Provost solo aerobatics display and a flypast by a Spitfire and Hurricane.

Norwich Aero Club organised a display to be held at RAF Swanton Morley and had requested RAF participation on Saturday and Sunday, 8 and 9 June; this was politely declined by the director of operations under the policy of not allocating flying participation to an event for more than just a day, except for shows of exceptional importance, i.e., Farnborough and Paris. This did not stop the Norwich flying committee in their tracks; instead, the chairman of their flying display committee contacted the director of operations, Air Commodore Reginald Burwell, to ask him to reconsider. Further, Mr Burton of the Norfolk and Norwich Aero Club had phoned the CPC and another club official had contacted the local MP, Mr Geoffrey Rippon, then minister of works. The RAF had offered a single helicopter display to Norwich, for the Saturday only; the chairman of the Norwich Committee drew attention to his letter:

> The participants (other than the helicopter) are prepared to give a display on the Sunday.
>   We have checked with the units concerned and I am afraid that they have too readily agreed to give the displays.

In response, Air Commodore Burwell urged that the RAF should now officially offer something for the Sunday and suggested a Spitfire, Hurricane, and Jet Provost as well as the Saturday, all subject to the usual financial and insurance conditions.

Also, the organiser was to be made aware that this exceptional consideration was not considered a new precedent. The secretary of state for air normally had to give his clearance for flying displays on Sundays; the undersecretary of state could oversee proceedings, providing there were no previous recorded complaints from the Swanton Morley area. RAF participation would also be timed to avoid religious services. Burwell finally ordered that all commands have drawn to their attention, 'the embarrassment that can be caused by participants exceeding the scale of participation authorised by the Department'. The chairman of the Participation Committee had set out the policy for proposed RAF participation in public displays in 1963. The secretary of state had told one and all that it was important for the RAF to put up a good showing at air displays in this country, particularly on Battle of Britain open day, and wanted to be kept in touch with developments.

Prominent among the CPC chairman's recommendations was the Firebirds aerobatics team in 1963, and their focus on firstly Paris; depending on Fighter Command's training programme, the full team would be available for the Battle of

Whirlwind HC2 tactical support helicopters demonstrating abseiling at Benson, *c.* 1962. (*Air Historical Branch*)

A standard feature of RAF 'At Homes' in the 1960s and 1970s was the SAR demo. This Westland Whirlwind HAR10 is the salvation of a young airman in peril on the grass verge of the runway at RAF Finningley, 14 September 1963. (*John Wharam*)

C-124 Globemaster II of the US Military Air Transport Service sits in Finningley's static park alongside the station museum's Japanese Ki 100, 14 September 1963. (*John Wharam*)

Britain displays. It was the intention in any case to keep at least a part of the nine-ship aeros team available for then.

The chairman regarded the Paris air show of 1963 as lacking the impact of the Farnborough show. Attendance on 'At Home' days had improved—the attendance figures in 1961 were 845,000; with the same number of stations in 1962, attendance was 912,000. For 14 September 1963, just fifteen stations were selected. Fighter Command had recommended a substantial reduction as there would be still fewer aircraft available in 1963. The CPC disagreed; looking at the gate figures and the direction they were moving in did not justify a heavy reduction. The evidence of the past two years confirmed the soundness of the Air Council's policy.

There were problems to address for 1963. The populous areas of the north and West Midlands were poorly served and providing for these regions was difficult. The only two RAF stations that were within reasonable proximity were Cosford and Ternhill. Cosford's severe airfield limitations had been established while Ternhill was seen as comparable. The latter had been open the previous year and had attracted 35,000 visitors. Technical Training Command had been reluctant to open Cosford in 1963, meaning Flying Training were approached to open Ternhill, who were also encountering difficulties. Yet if the Salop base could open, all main areas of population would be covered.

Biggin Hill was in the process of transferring ownership to the Ministry of Aviation; the ultimate date of transfer was not known as of March, but a suitable safeguard in the transfer agreement was to be included, which would ensure the continued practice of the standing arrangement.

Avro Vulcan B1A, southern route tourer, making a low pass over Biggin Hill on 12 September 1963 during rehearsals for the forthcoming Battle of Britain displays. (*Air Historical Branch*)

Next up, the Central Flying School aerobatics team, the Red Pelicans, and their dayglo red Jet Provosts, run in over 'The Bump'. (*Air Historical Branch*)

The RAF still fielded Bofors gun display teams in 1963, which was now seen as rather anachronistic and suitable only for tattoos and the like, so a decision was taken to discontinue it. The high mark of the Paris show in 1963 was claimed to be a scramble of V bombers, while the display by the Firebirds was reportedly not fully appreciated by the general public here.

On the Saturday, the overcast skies appeared more stratocumulus than cumulonimbus, so they performed a formation loop that disappeared straight into cloud while their senior line manager, Air Marshal Douglas 'Zulu' Morris, looked on, apparently less than impressed. Still, he reported back to the VCAS that the 'Firebirds' had rendered an impeccable performance but had failed to impress the public at large:

> Particularly in comparison with noisy and more superficially impressive performances by aircraft of other countries.
>
> It was not possible to mount a Lightning aerobatics team of size large enough to be a spectacular success and it had to be recognised that, for such aircraft, the era of formation aerobatics was over.

Further analysis concluded that the public, during the Hunter era, had developed a taste for large formations performing extremely tight aerobatics. The Lightning formation of just nine was deemed beyond the layman's comprehension and could only be appreciated by an expert.

Officially, the short list of public appearances was the real reason why the Participation Committee were instructed to review the intention to form an official Lightning aerobatics team for 1964. The problems in providing a Lightning formation aerobatics team outweighed the advantages. The Air Council accepted the recommendation even though it meant the committee would struggle more to provide an impressive flagship aeros team in 1964, which also was a Farnborough year. The recommendation was that for 1964, involvement in displays should go as far as possible to be of operational training value and that 'an even more determined effort should be made to an extent compatible with the overriding requirements of operations and training'.

It was hoped this would now go some way to relieving the strain on the slender resources available. So despite the favourable impact on recruitment and keeping the junior service in the public eye, choices of what to send where in future would need to be more selective. The following points were collated, ending the commitment of anymore operational squadrons for formation aerobatics:

1. The loss of a Fighter Squadron from the front line for about one third of the year. Even in emergency it would take three weeks to bring the squadron up to an operational standard. This will be made more serious in 1964 by the disbandment of 41 Squadron, and the conversion of two squadrons to Lightning mark 3s, which is expected to screen them both from overseas reinforcement for six months.
2. The consumption of over one-third of the fatigue life of the aircraft, during the course of the display season.

Right: The last official Fighter Command aerobatics team, 56 Squadron's 'The Firebirds'. Two of the team's Lightnings are seen here in a display take-off, each following one another into a steep climb off RAF Wattisham's main runway. (*Air Historical Branch*)

Below: The Firebirds, likely during early rehearsals over the home stead at RAF Wattisham. The bare state of the trees indicate spring is yet to come. (*Air Historical Branch*)

3. Acceptance of the risks inherent in formation aerobatics, which in 1963 cost a severely injured pilot, one Lightning destroyed and another damaged category 2.
4. Excessive technical effort, to maintain the very high level of serviceability required.
5. A loss in overall flying hours.

As 1964 approached, each of the Home Commands were asked for proposals for what they might be able to do with the knowledge that Farnborough would be back that September. Coastal Command offered a static Mk 3 Shackleton, resplendent with a variety of weapons and equipment pertaining to its principal roles from anti-submarine warfare to trooping. Bomber Command pleaded poverty, claiming that the cancellation of Skybolt (the nuclear armed missile, which was to be carried under the wings of the Vulcan) meant that a new training programme had to be embarked on following a decision to operate the force at low level; this, in turn, had meant a considerable curtailment in Bomber Command's participation this year, particularly flying due to the time, fuel, and crews needed.

> In the low-level role, the greatest possible restraint must be exercised during our training flying in order that the aircraft will have sufficient fatigue life to ensure their useful operational employment up to 1970. Every aircraft is fitted with a 'g' meter and the fatigue life of the aircraft is recorded after every flight.
>
> We are no longer able to do display flying involving measures not normally employed in daily flying training.

Therefore, Bomber Command's contribution to Farnborough was limited to a single Vulcan B2 and a Victor B2, each fitted with Blue Steel and each sat in the static area. If necessary, a take-off and landing would have to do for display flying purposes. These restrictions were to apply to all display flying requests as preserving fatigue life was of paramount importance. When reviewing the RAF's contribution to air displays and other public events in 1964, at home and abroad, the overall effort included thirty displays, described as eighteen major and twelve minor events, in the UK and, surprisingly perhaps, thirty-eight events overseas. For the first time, the RAF's top two aerobatics teams of the year came from Flying Training Command. The Red Pelicans, of the CFS and the Yellow Jacks from 4 FTS appeared disproportionately; the former got to fourteen events while the latter to just four.

This did not include 'At Home' displays. On top of this, RAF helicopters flew at no fewer than forty-seven ground-based events across the British Isles, mostly demonstrating SAR drills. As for the ground displays, three main contributors existed—the RAF police dog display team, the Queen's Colour Squadron, and the RAF PT display team. Financial arrangements for RAF displays at the likes of the SBAC show and other trade affairs had been overseen by the Treasury since 1 February 1928.

The amount of effort involved in preparing for and taking part in public events by aerobatics teams was seen in earlier times as valuable training. This culture endured all the way until 1963–64. The training syllabus of fighter pilots related to formation aerobatics. The arrival of Javelins and Lightnings further distanced operational

Set piece air–land battle demonstration at Farnborough in September 1964 with Wessex and Argosy landing troops on the field. (*Peter March*)

Another Argosy, from 114 Squadron, taking part in the same demonstration. Note representative aircraft of three RAF display teams in the background—a Jet Provost (Red Pelicans), Gnats (Yellow Jacks), and a Lightning from the lesser known 92 Sqn display team authorised after the decision to end frontline aerobatic teams. (*Air Historical Branch*)

training from the realm of aerobatics; the new radar-equipped all-weather heavier, noisier beasts meant far more focus on pinging the target on radar before shooting it down. By the early 1960s in any case, Flying Training Command was already providing the bigger share of aerobatics teams.

The CFS and other training units were able to find sufficient flying instructors on the Jet Provost and a smaller number instructing on the Vampire and Meteor, to provide several teams. Again, the mounts were less demanding in terms of fuel and maintenance and the nature of flying instruction still shared a fair amount in common with the demands of formation aerobatics. On the other hand, the consumption of flying hours, fuel and personnel, etc., had grown significantly overall. A review of the 1964 teams concluded that the Jet Provost was already too old to represent the RAF as a display team aircraft if the aims of the RAF, in public events, had not altered. Entering service at the time was the smaller, lighter, more powerful, and more appropriate-looking Folland Gnat.

The Gnat was seen as a worthy successor to adequately meet this requirement. The logistics plan of the day was to prepare for attrition and wastage, this meant that a large enough number of Gnats would be available to provide for (according to 1964 estimates)

The Fleet Air Arm made a significant foray into display flying and aerobatics while they had the resources to do so. This is the 1962 RN Sea Vixen aerobatics team, 'Fred's Five', drawn from 766 Headquarters Training Squadron based at RNAS Yeovilton. (*Via author*)

The Yellow Jacks of 4 FTS at their home base, RAF Valley. This aeros team represented the answer to the embargo on operational aerobatics teams. Operating the new Folland Gnat, this aircraft comprised simplicity and low-cost combined with a sporty appearance and high-performance limits, seen during rehearsals on 28 August 1964. (*Air Historical Branch*)

The Yellow Jacks of 4 Flying Training School and the Red Pelicans of the Central Flying School, the two principal RAF aerobatics teams, from Flying Training Command, seen splitting formation over Farnborough, September 1964. (*Air Historical Branch*)

an aerobatics team of six. So, a new aerobatics team equipped with the Gnat was to be established, the funding for which was set at £100,000 *per annum*. The arguments making the case for aerobatics teams were still easily made despite the growing divergence between operational flying and the activities of display teams. Aerobatics teams raised flying standards generally. Pilots regarded selection for an official aerobatics team as the hallmark of their flying career. Furthermore, the continued opportunity to apply to join 'the team' was in inducement to maintain the highest standards of airmanship. Another accepted theory was that the practice of placing former team members throughout the RAF would spread high standards through influence.

The amount of publicity gained by an official team would outweigh the cost of direct expenditure on publicity. The usual belief maintained that aerobatics teams are a great recruitment tool, attracting the kind of young men the RAF needed, if the service was going to maintain its combat capability. All these points were seen as particularly pertinent for the UK where RAF airfields were spread across the more inaccessible and remote parts of the country, away from population centres, which meant the RAF as a service was largely far removed from the routine public gaze, unlike the army, which could only rely on the more traditional means of making an impression on the public mind set.

A further argument to make the case for a representative aerobatics team was that the air forces of France, Italy, Belgium, Holland, and the United States all fielded national aerobatics teams. In the case of the US, equally prominent teams, representing both the air force and the navy, had been running for several years. Similar continuity was also the case with the French and Italian teams. The idea that the RAF would not field a comparable aerobatics team at an international air show overseas would not do much to promote prestige and reputation, not only of the RAF but the United Kingdom. Recently, in 2018, various rumours have circulated about the RAF aerobatics team replacing their current Hawk jets. The suggestion that the aircraft flown must be British-built is much more of a challenge now than it was in 1964. Additionally, the existence of a national team in the climate of 1964, with operational squadrons still seen as the best material source but the least desirable for the operational impact and cost, would cut down on the calls for the gap to be plugged by taking a squadron out of the front line.

To conclude, the cost was outweighed by the advantages of fielding a national team as opposed to several comparable teams. For the next twelve years, the RAF still allowed aerobatics teams to form among other training units which ensured that there was always something available, particularly to meet the still copious if ever dwindling surge in demand each September. Aside from the aerobatics teams, flying drill formation from both training and operational units continued to operate on a supply and demand footing subject to availability. The drill teams were mostly active in the run up to Battle of Britain week at a time when the 'At Homes' still reached double figures.

They were easier to draw on; they required much less of a work-up, so could begin preparation at short notice (about a month), increasing the range of available aircraft. Indeed, such formations used to carry the unofficial title 'Battle of Britain Four' after the standard formation size. The principal difference between aerobatics and drill

Westland Wessex of 72 Sqn during air–land battle set piece at Finningley, 19 September 1964. The mock fort is shortly going to be destroyed by Hunters and a Vulcan. (*John Wharam*)

A Royal Navy Sea Vixen IFR pair at Finningley, 19 September 1964. Role demonstrations again were far more commonplace in times when assets and personnel to spare were a by-product of healthier defence spending. (*John Wharam*)

formations was that the latter maintained tight formations through turns and climbs while conducting various formation changes usually complete with a spectacular break/flypast, perhaps an airfield beat up culminating in a steep energy climb or a formation break over the crowd line—nothing wrong with that *circa* 1964.

In time for the 1964 season, the new team, the Yellowjacks (equipped with Gnats), were flown by instructors of No. 4 Flying Training School based at RAF Valley in Anglesey. Flt Lt Lee Jones, an experienced formation aerobatics team pilot, later related in an interview for a documentary about the Red Arrows how he was approached in the gents at RAF Hornchurch by Air Commodore Bird-Wilson, then commandant of the Central Flying School. He was asked if he would like to form an aerobatics team flying the new Gnat advanced jet trainer. As the team's name suggests, the five Folland Gnat T1 aircraft had a wraparound lemon-yellow scheme with service markings and, as with their predecessors, smoke generators releasing white smoke. The Yellowjacks had their debut, not at Farnborough or any Battle of Britain event, but at the Royal Naval Air Station, Culdrose in Cornwall, in July. The most prominent among the existing Flying Training Command aeros teams were the CFS's Red Pelicans, whose Jet Provosts were dayglo red and were equipped to release coloured smoke.

Fighter Command supposedly now out of the aerobatics team business formed a semi-aerobatics/drill team from Lightnings of 92 Squadron, which operated in 1963 and 1964. All three teams ensured the RAF presence at Farnborough was far from lacklustre after the Golden years of 1955 to 1962. The Gnats and Jet Provosts formed together for a colourful combined flypast. There were some more official changes during 1964; the armed forces and respective government structures changed to a more centralised structure.

On 1 April, the three government ministerial departments responsible for each of the armed services—the Admiralty, the War Office, and the Air Ministry—were disbanded. All that remained was the Ministry of Defence. Therefore, the Navy Council became the Navy Board, the Army Council the Army Board, and the Air Council became the Air Force Board, all under the umbrella of the new Defence Council.

Twelve RAF stations opened to the public on 19 September this year, three down on 1963. Middleton St George was to be abandoned and turned into Teesside Airport. Aldergrove was no longer considered suitable for reasons provided previously concerning the weather. Another casualty was Tangmere, being run down with the disbandment or relocation of flying units. Bomber Command's original concern about the availability of aircraft for Farnborough did not extend to Battle of Britain activities with more than twenty aircraft assigned to flying displays.

On 11 January 1965, the MOD proposed to allocate £103,000 to fund a representative aerobatics team for the forthcoming display season subject to air votes in the defence budget, this was needed for approval allowing additional funds to be included in the RAF share for the year 1965–66. This funding broke down as £99,000 for aircraft operating costs and £4,000 for the modification of one Folland Gnat. A formal letter was issued to the Treasury with a note that referred to previous Treasury authority from 1 February 1928. Prior to this date, the Air Ministry had apparently obtained authority back in 1924, to provide RAF aircraft for up to four air displays

During the 1950s and '60s the USAF was quite heavily represented at RAF 'At Home' days, usually with touring formations. These four F-100D Super Sabres are overhead RAF Finningley, with various other stations across the northern half of the country along the route. (*John Wharam*)

Avro Vulcan B Mk 2, in anti-flash white scheme at Finningley, 19 September 1964. This year the new Green/Grey scheme was introduced. (*John Wharam*)

Another formation to fill up the flying programmes and provide a broad representation of service aircraft—three Canberra T4s of the College of Air warfare, based at RAF Manby seen over Finningley, 19 September 1964. (*John Wharam*)

a year. This limit had been increased in 1928 to six displays and that the Treasury had endorsed the Air Council's policy to that end. The Air Council accordingly made aircraft available for air displays on the following conditions:

a. The display was likely to stimulate recruitment

b. A display organised by a local aero club was likely to lead to an increase in the reserve of civil pilots.

c. The flying undertaken must be in the interests of training.

d. The exchequer must be reimbursed expenditure incurred additional to that met on normal flying training missions.

e. The exchequer must be relieved of liability for risks above those incurred under normal training conditions.

Toward the end of the 1930s when the armed forces were pursuing a much greater recruitment drive, displays by the RAF were, under the 1928 limits, seen as too limited. Another Air Ministry proposal to lift restrictions further was issued on 8 April 1938. The prevailing situation and the expansion plans in place demanded a much greater effort toward advertising a career in the junior service. With little time left to be effective, the Treasury approved the proposal on 12 December. In 1965, the MOD noted that the earlier restrictions had not since been re-imposed.

Based on a report from 1958, the Treasury understood that altogether the RAF attempted to contribute to twelve events across the UK outside of Farnborough and the 'At Homes'. Referred to as the 'hardy annuals', these included RAFA and SSAFA organised events, in the main at North Weald, Plymouth, Coventry, Exeter, and Wolverhampton. In addition, there were the overseas commitments, particularly Paris and other events in Belgium, the Netherlands, and various Scandinavian countries, from which requests were invariably received. The Treasury was aware that there had been considerably greater activity by the air force in this field of endeavour since 1938.

In 1960, overseas participation had been reviewed regarding trade shows. An interdepartmental agreement was reached on 20 June and endorsed by the Air Ministry nine days later. The agreement, after considerable negotiations, concluded that *inter alia*, the host governments would now meet the extra costs over and above those that would normally be incurred on a training mission. The RAF would also be provided with an indemnity against third-party claims, but as far as 'air displays' were concerned, the agreement amounted to a re-statement of the 1928 understanding. The Treasury was under the impression that Hunters along with Jet Provosts were used for displays in 1964 that were no longer suitable. In fact, no Hunters were used for formation aerobatics specifically during that year, other displays yes, solo aerobatics, formation drills and role demonstrations heavily engaged several Hunters. They correctly understood that 'Gnats of Flying Training Command' would be used in 1965, but at least the bean counters were happy that aircraft from within the existing establishment were to be used and from within Flying Training Command. With no new aircraft to be purchased specifically to meet the display team requirement, they were content but with one reservation. This time funding was limited to £99,000; anything else was to come from outside the usual resources, otherwise the Jet Provost and Gnat teams in 1964 were to be self-funding.

RAF operational requirements did not allow for aircraft and crews to be earmarked for displays. The resources for the Gnat team in 1965 though would be made available from Flying Training Command. Funds formerly made available for training would be spent on seven months of display practice and presentation of the rehearsed display. Therefore, why had the extra £99,000 been approved? The Treasury now thought that there should be a corresponding cut in training costs or a near reduction. Maybe the RAF were working on presenting a more refined display team in 1965 than had been seen before and that the £99,000 was likely to be consumed in more elaborate preparation. However, this had not been specifically stated.

The five Gnats of the 1964 team, the Yellowjacks, were still available and converted for display flying—that is they still had their smoke generators fitted and were painted yellow. A sixth Gnat was to have a smoke generator fitted for the new team at a cost of £4,000. The Treasury understood the efficacy of RAF flying displays but still fretted that in the year 1965–66, the £99,000 additional expenditure would be hard to refuse thereafter. The 1964 team had counted its displays as training. Yet the likes of the SBAC show at Farnborough, where they had displayed, and other event organisers who had seen the team, had not contributed to any of the costs incurred. This included display practices and fuel; this raised a query and an eyebrow at the Treasury. Yet event organisers should be expected to contribute to costs incurred above that of routine training, such as travelling costs and accommodation of personnel.

The Air Department of the MOD told the Treasury that they had no intention of recouping the expenses over and above the administrative extras. Their reason was that the organisers, including Farnborough, would not be able to meet any further costs. If the air department pressed them for reimbursement, then the RAF would not

Having long since become an international household name, the Red Arrows are seen here in their debut display season over Church Fenton for the 1965 SSAFA Air Display. (*John Wharam*)

be getting invited back to those events again and clearly the RAF would not like this to happen. Overall, the Treasury was ready to accept the RAF's case, as they alleged, that the display team(s) carried merit beyond being a useful tool of recruitment. Yet there was another matter they felt should be pressed at the time—a need to query a similar request in 1966–67. A typical outsider opinion was held by the Treasury. They could not quite understand why the RAF could not continue with a Jet Provost team funded from existing resources. The bean counters failed to grasp the simple matter of prestige. The RAF needed, within the existing limits, to find an aircraft for a display team which was new, sleek, and relatively sophisticated. This was going to be difficult now that Hunters and Lightnings would no longer do. HQ Flying Training Command provided an assessment of the level of back up required to support Gnat and/or Jet Provost teams. The facilities required were as follows:

	A/C	Pilots	G/Crew	Flying Hours
Gnat (five aircraft formation)	9	6	50	1,250
Gnat (nine aircraft formation)	15	11	86	2,500*
Jet Provost (six aircraft formation)	9	7	37	1,500

*Includes an element for additional practice for the complicated manoeuvres.
Such facilities could be found within the command but would be required for no fewer than nine months in the calendar year. The fifteen aircraft format could not be

met from within the existing resources and could only be achieved by reducing the establishment of the training schools. Through the summer of 1964, helicopters from Coastal, Transport and Flying Training Commands flew forty-seven demonstrations at public events. The previous year, 1963, they managed fifty-three—a significant spike on the year before, 1962, when only forty-four displays were achieved. The number in 1964 were determined to be the maximum possible while remaining consistent with operational and training commitments. The CPC accepted the position of the commands that this number should be the maximum for 1965. The rules governing RAF helicopter displays allowed them to continue to give public demonstrations within the constraints of availability and distance, the detailed parameters of which were laid down in 1959.

Helicopter Displays Requested and Approved over the Preceding Four Years to 1965

	1961	1962	1963	1964
Requests received	84	91	135	128
Requests approved and displays given	28	44	53	47

Requests for RAF ground display teams were roughly similar between 1963 and 1964—315 to 307. The RAF had a physical training display team that appeared at the Royal Tournament in 1963; they then gave three performances before the public in August before heading off to Australia in mid-September to take part in the Sydney Military Tattoo. They also took part in the Royal British Legion Festival of Remembrance in November. The two police dog display teams remained, as ever, very popular and carried out twenty-seven displays in 1964 in addition to the Bath and Edinburgh Military Tattoos. This was the highest number since 1961.

Even at that, due to training, the dog teams could only get to Bath and Edinburgh during July and August. The RAF regiment's special drill flight, the Queen's Colour Squadron, gave only ten displays compared with seventeen in 1963, but overall, the total of RAF ground team display was up from thirty-two in 1963 to forty-seven. For 1965, the physical training display at the Royal Tournament was to be provided by one of the other services and for the Festival of Remembrance. Given the transient nature of service display teams, at least by and large, the PT display team was not to be re-formed in 1965.

On 20 August 1965, the MOD received an official enquiry from the Imperial Iranian Air Force wanting to know what the RAF might send over if they received an official invite to the Imperial Iranian Air Force Day in Mehrabad, Tehran. The display was to take place on 17 October and after consideration the MOD concluded that the UK would make a substantial contribution. Treasury assistance would need to be sought again, even though such funding was not likely to find sympathy.

The MOD felt this was a special case with a good deal at stake claiming we had a 'strong interest' in convincing the Shah, the Imperial Iranian Air Force, and the Iranian people generally that British support for them through CENTO was genuine and affective. Also, there was the concern that staging and overflying rights currently extended by Tehran would be placed in jeopardy if their air show was snubbed. Such access rights had long been of high value, especially since the Sudanese government had recently imposed a ban on overfly rights in respect of British military aircraft.

The opportunity to attend the IIAF was one not to be missed. The maintenance of goodwill with Iran was nothing new; recently, a detachment to the Far East of a CENTO-assigned RAF Canberra squadron had been extended (originally known as the Baghdad Pact, the Central Treaty Organisation (CENTO) included Iran, Iraq, Turkey, Pakistan, and the United Kingdom. It was disbanded in 1979 when some member countries were overthrown by, or otherwise found themselves ruled by, authoritarian regimes not necessarily sympathetically inclined toward Western Democratic interests). This meant it was removed from the RAF contribution to the CENTO orbat for a period. Again, a goodwill gesture was considered appropriate at the time. Also, as the only non-regional member, the UK's absence from the display would be rather conspicuous and likely arouse adverse comment. The RAF participated in the 1964 Iranian air display when they sent three Javelins and a Vulcan. This had been a rather lacklustre contribution as the Iranians considered this someway behind their own F-86 demonstration. Therefore, in 1965, the planned contribution was to be three V bombers, the Falcons free fall team, and four Lightnings, supported by a Victor tanker. This was fully supported by the Foreign Office, which enthusiastically pointed out that the previous year the event was held at Shiraz, while this year it would be held at an airbase near Tehran that should carry greater political prestige.

The cost of providing this level of participation was substantially offset. The V bombers were deploying in lieu of one of their overseas exercises and would involve no extra cost. The Lightnings and tanker would already be in Cyprus on exercise and the flight to Tehran was seen as valuable training, of course. The foreign currency cost was expected not to exceed £3,000 for what was to be billed as a training flight for the tanker and fighters. The parachute display team would likely fly out in an Argosy; this too would incur costs of about £3,000, of which £700 would be in foreign currency.

The most prestigious event for the RAF since the end of the war, save for the queen's coronation, was the twenty-fifth anniversary of the Battle of Britain. With a few changes to display flying disciplines and the authorisation of RAF aerobatics and other display teams, the Air Force Board had its work cut out presenting the RAF in a stellar light on the most significant anniversary of the Battle of Britain so far reached.

Fighter Command formation aerobatics teams were now a thing of the past, other than 111 Squadron, based at RAF Wattisham, who were approached regarding the formation of a 'display team'. I make the point of placing the term in inverted commas because the resultant display was a more comprehensive formation drill rather than aerobatics—therefore, not officially an aerobatics team, but not a flypast or two either.

No. 111's Black Diamonds flew a quite scintillating display of formation changes and tight turns with nine of their Lightnings. These were the Mk 3 version; of all Lightning variants, this was the 'Hot Ship'—as light as possible with a small ventral tank and the removal of the gun armament (the Lightning F3 was intended to carry missiles alone, the misplaced perception, a variation on Sandys thinking on manned

Avro Vulcan B Mk 2 in green and grey, Finningley, 18 September 1965. (*John Wharam*)

Four Vulcans on QRA scramble. We never saw this for real; perhaps this explains some why we are still here. However, this was a dramatic set piece demonstration at some of the RAF's 'At Homes' in the 1960s and '70s. (*AHB*)

fighters, was that guns on fighter aircraft were now as relevant as swordsmanship to the infantry), all of which made the Mk 3 the most robust engine and airframe combination in the RAF to this point. They would not be the only Lightning formation to hand on 'At Home' day either. Another five or more formation drill teams would be made available to ensure a fair degree of balance.

Solo aerobatics were a different matter. There appears to have been no actual limit on these. Some were slightly shorter performance handling displays, like the formation drills, which were easier and cheaper to produce with less demand on operations and training. As far as Flying Training Command was concerned, a lot more was possible still, especially with genuine aerobatics teams. As well as the long list of Jet Provost teams, there was the new team flying seven nippy little Folland Gnat advanced jet trainers from the CFS. Like the Red Pelicans, the new outfit gave their mounts a wraparound glossy red coat; not only that, they were permitted to fit their little jets with smoke generators and to use different chemical mixes to produce different coloured smoke and by the end of the 1965 display season were already internationally acclaimed.

The Red Arrows were born. Their public debut was at the other, civilian, Biggin Hill event that year—the Air Fair. As for the broader picture, the proposals for 1965 were very much on a similar scale to what took place in 1964 but with certain additional events being organised given the significance of the year. Among the extras were a Battle of Britain exhibition in Scotland and a Thanksgiving service in Westminster Abbey together with a special parade of the Queen's Colour Squadron and a flypast on Battle of Britain day.

The Red Arrows photographed when they were but a month old, seen here descending from a loop over Church Fenton for the SSAFA Air Display, 7 June 1965. (*John Wharam*)

What was being considered as of December 1964 was holding the service in the morning and having it televised. As for the 'At Homes', thirteen stations, again including Biggin Hill, were proposed with some relative minor changes over the previous year.

Gaydon would not be selected to open as it was in the process of being transferred from Bomber to Flying Training Command and would by September be on care and maintenance. To address this, Cottesmore (also Bomber Command) had been selected as an alternative.

The exhibition in Edinburgh was expected to benefit by being held so close to the festival. There was a suggestion, late on, to invite a member of the royal family. This was not going to be possible as the programme for royal visits had already been established and it was too late to make any additions. The colour parade, which was to be attended by the queen, could not take place in London either as she would be at Balmoral. Logistically thinking, another suggestion was to parade the colour in London anyway, before the lord mayor. Putting on a parade at Balmoral was also considered and dismissed for reasons not given but likely to do with logistics. Altogether, the AFB had five specific points to address and make a formal decision over:

a. The number of RAF stations to open to the public on 'At Home' day, 18 September.

b. The holding of an 'At Home' day at Biggin Hill specifically.

c. The mounting of the Battle of Britain week Exhibition in Scotland.

d. The annual Thanksgiving Service in Westminster Abbey.

e. Further Proposals.

Reflecting on 1964, there had been eleven stations open together with Biggin Hill; the total attendance at all twelve stations was estimated at 680,000. This is compared with 980,000 in 1963, when fifteen stations were open. That three stations fewer were open was not blamed for the drop in numbers but rather the cold and blustery weather conditions during the day. Apparently, this only scuppered the bulk of the free fall parachute display teams. HQ Fighter Command's wash-up report claimed 'At Home' day 1964 was otherwise very successful.

HQFC also reported that even though they struggled to put together sufficient flying display items for 1964, given the significance of 1965, the number of stations open in September should not be reduced; instead, the commands should make more aircraft available. The Anniversary Committee were happy to agree to this, and apart from the change from Gaydon to Cottesmore, retained the same stations as the previous year, these had been selected according to geographical coverage and attendance levels. Abingdon and Benson sat close to one another and continued to be open on a Buggins' turn rotation—1964 was Benson's turn, while in 1965, it would be Abingdon's personnel pitching marquees, clearing out hangars ready for turning into exhibition halls, indoor markets, and arenas, and laying out miles of rope and metal barriers. The stations chosen to open were all pre-agreed with the respective command air officers.

As was now the routine, other NATO Air Forces as well as the USAF, the Royal Navy, and the MOA were to be approached and invited to participate in any aspects they could accommodate. It was accepted now that the flying displays and static displays would scarcely be practicable, and it was hoped that they would be forthcoming on a scale suitable to the occasion. The latter of these organisations was ultimately responsible for vetoing Biggin Hill or not. The AFB had sent a letter thanking them for the very successful display there in 1964 and the MOA had indicated that it was almost certainly the case that 'the Bump' would be available again in 1965. The AFB noted that thereafter, the airfield's availability for September 1966 was less certain. The committee recommended that costs incurred, particular to Biggin Hill, for additional personnel diverted from other stations and transportation, all amounted to relatively high administration costs. These should be met for what might well be the last opportunity to mount a display here. They also recommended inviting a member of the royal family to attend on this occasion.

The Battle of Britain exhibition, which had routinely been held in Whitehall, previously had been discontinued, replaced by a similar exhibition in Glasgow for 1963 and 1964. Despite resources being stretched, the air officer Scotland and Northern Ireland reported that the 1964 Glasgow event had been successful and was in fact better than the one held in 1963. Edinburgh being the chosen city for the 1965 exhibition was still subject to a suitable ground being found. A more ambitious project to mark the twenty-fifth anniversary was the provision of a flypast on Wednesday 15 September—Battle of Britain day itself. This would amount to a reversal of the decision to discontinue the flypast over London on the 15th back in 1961. This time, the committee sought permission for both the flypast and a ceremonial parade in front of Buckingham Palace simultaneously, the former to coincide with the end of the latter.

The holding of several 'At Home' displays on the following Saturday was expected to be the last time that so many would be held simultaneously, if only because of the over stretch now noticeable on resources. There was, on the other hand, a degree of strong feeling from the director of organisation, Air Commodore Norman Kearon, that any number of displays should continue to be held under the banner of the Battle of Britain and that maximum effort should be called for to that end. He considered that this was the only medium left to the RAF by which to make its impact on the public and to impress its image for the future on the younger generation. There was sympathy with this view naturally, but pragmatism dictated a less than rose-tinted future.

The opposite argument was that pursuing the current practice and continuing to do so would inevitably meet with diminishing resources coupled with operational commitments to such a degree as to result in such an inadequate turn out that the service image would suffer significantly—quite the opposite of the aim of the exercise. The new government were pursuing far-reaching defence cuts, and operational commitments were not lessening if matters in the South Arabian Peninsula and the recently declared state of Malaysia were anything to go by, where admittedly the RAF units involved were based in the region. Yet other commands—especially Transport, Coastal, and Bomber— were continuously called upon to supply long-range transport aircraft, maritime patrol aircraft, and high-altitude reconnaissance jets. Back home, a severely reduced interceptor fighter force was entering a new stage of the Cold War, meaning an increase in live QRA scrambles to intercept long-range Soviet bomber-reconnaissance patrols that were often transiting or conducting training sorties which now demonstrated sufficient reach to challenge UK airspace, essentially just south of the Arctic region.

If this pattern continued after 1965, the upshot would be a situation whereby the RAF could only manage a small number of embarrassingly small displays that would attract nothing but disappointment, and possible criticism, from the public. The officer responsible for overseeing the organisation of static and flying displays for the 1964 'At Homes', Squadron Leader Gill, told the CPC how difficult this was. With the resources available then and now, providing flying and static aircraft for twelve stations from St Mawgan in Cornwall all the way to Leuchars in Fife, HQ Fighter Command, were on average, able to arrange only about two hours of flying out of every three-hour programme typically arranged at each station.

At HQFC's disposal for flying displays was a total of 440 aircraft: 305 from the RAF (including 143 from Flying Training Command) and 135 from the Royal Navy, the US Air Force, European NATO Air Arms, the Ministry of Aviation, and various civilian firms (i.e., A&AEE, RAE, BOAC, Shuttleworth, and the Redhill Flying Club). Air Commodore Kearon asked if perhaps a larger RAF effort could be called for, but the Participation Committee chairman recalled that in March 1964, the VCAS had written a personal letter on these lines to the various Command C-in-Cs so one could only assume that the 1964 displays had indeed benefited from maximum effort across the RAF. Another officer and committee member, Air Commodore John Whickam, director of manning, also sympathised with Kearon's traditionalist view but made a point that would far more suit modern sentiment. He felt that 'the image of the RAF could best be achieved by looking to the future instead of continually looking back to the Battle of Britain'. He did not suggest putting this up as a bar to future proceedings, but he did bring to everyone's attention the cost in manpower, mostly imported, amounting to 2,600 individual working days in staging the last Biggin Hill display alone.

A civilian member of the committee also supported Kearon's point but made the most radical suggestion. As the Battle of Britain took place, as officially recognised, from 10 July to 31 October 1940 (dates inclusive), logic would suggest that the 'At Home' displays could be spread across that period and still fall within the anniversary period, therefore still preserving Battle of Britain Day and Week for other events—if only these men could see into the future about fifty-five years. The secretary also viewed the twenty-fifth anniversary as the opportune time to change the pattern of doing things, especially as it was likely that 1965 would be the last time that Biggin Hill could be relied on as a venue.

He also added to the view that the RAF's public image would not suffer if shorn of its Battle of Britain label. RAF aircraft flew and participated at air shows organised by other air arms and organisations across the UK and overseas, specifically the USAF, Royal Navy, RAFA, SSAFA, and others. What is more, a growing number of RAF stations, no longer selected by their commands to open in September, were, under the direction of their respective station commanders, organising their own open/air days through the summer. It now seemed all the more reason for the committee to re-think the future.

Four F-104G Starfighters from 331 Sqn, Royal Norwegian Air Force, making a very rare appearance over Finningley, 18 September 1965. The team operated from Lakenheath and took in two other 'At Home' stations along the way. (*John Wharam*)

Two Belgian AF F-84Fs from 1 Sqn 'Stingers' on the flightline at Leuchars, 18 September 1965. This was a solo display mount and spare; the display itself was described at the time by *Air-Britain* historians as having been inflicted on the crowd on account of the high-speed low-level passes. (*R. A. Stitchell*)

A rare solo demonstration by a Javelin, Finningley, 1965. (*John Wharam*)

The deputy director of public prosecutions (DDPR), Mr Gunhill, was asked to put together a suggested programme of Battle of Britain dates for 'At Homes' to be held across the summer from 1965 onwards to be presented as a separate report to the AFB. The committee did turn down a proposal for a Drumhead service on the cliffs near Dover, complete with a flypast by a Spitfire and a Hurricane. Due to the likelihood of poor weather, particularly heavy winds in such an exposed position, a reception at Lancaster House for former Battle of Britain aircrew was also under active consideration by the permanent undersecretary, to be held on 17 September. Somebody else suggested inviting Iron Curtain countries to participate this year, but this was turned down as it had been the previous year due to the inevitable political sensitivities.

Sqn Ldr Gill recommended that for 1965, more posters and larger ones be produced. During the 1964 run up, many people living in North London were unaware that there was an air display taking place close by, referring to RAF Benson in Oxfordshire and the nearest such event to people living in this area.

At the start of the year, the CPC had the usual list of requests from various authorities and event organisers, including the Paris 1965 Air Salon. This was being dealt with as a separate issue, but all commands were asked to give priority consideration to the problem of providing 'suitable' display items for the twenty-sixth salon, scheduled to take place from 11 to 20 June 1965 at Le Bourget. Late in 1964, Bomber Command, as in the previous year, advised that they would be unable to provide any V bombers for air displays in 1965. This though did not include the Battle of Britain 'At Homes', but it did mean they would have very little to offer the Paris Air Show. At the time this was being considered, the RAF did not have a formed ready 'impressive' aerobatics team that they believed would be worthy of Paris; they were intending to send the 111 Sqn display team with their Lightnings.

The CPC believed that even an aerobatics team of Gnats would not impress the organisers of the salon, who, in 1963, turned down the offer of both a Folland Gnat solo aerobatics display and the Red Pelicans. The RAF also needed to liaise with the MOA and SBAC beforehand to ensure there was no duplication of aircraft regarding what each was planning to send. This situation arose in 1963, resulting in some embarrassment caused by the RAF and the British aircraft industry, each wishing to display similar aircraft which resulted in the organisers, at a late stage, refusing to accept either offer. Requests for RAF aircraft in 1964 had been the same as previous years. With co-operation between the commands, it was possible for the RAF to attend thirty air displays in the UK and thirty-eight overseas.

In 1963, these figures were thirty-seven and twenty-nine respectively, again not including the 'At Homes' or single displays by helicopters. There was in addition, in 1964, to a request from the Royal Australian Air Force who were planning two events in early September—at Wagga on 12 September and Laverton on Sunday 19 September. Each such request was to be dealt with, following the usual practice, on consideration of individual merit. Of special consideration this year was the new Folland Gnat-equipped formation aerobatics team, the Red Arrows, which was to be utilised to the maximum. Apart from the team's possible appearance in Paris in June and which 'At Home' stations they should attend, there were ten more UK display venues and six abroad.

The aircraft to be made available for the 1965 Battle of Britain displays was extensive enough, even if no records were broken. The English Electric Lightning, in service with just six squadrons, was to be called upon to a considerable degree. Each of the 'At Home' stations this year would see a Lightning or Lightnings flying in some display format or other. Considering the review, which was forced by the cost of running a Lightning formation aerobatics team each year, 1965 was going to see more of the supersonic monsters than ever before. No fewer than five solo aerobatics pilots were authorised, one each from 23, 74, 92, 111 Squadrons and at least one instructor from the OCU together with an early example from the A&AEE. Each of the RAF units worked up formation drill teams, and two aircraft were to open the flying at Leuchars with a scramble followed by a return with a tanker. In the case of the OCU, the largest single operator of Lightnings, two teams were prepared—one of four jets and one of nine. Each operational squadron put together a formation of four in addition to 111's more firmly established team. No. 56 Squadron were the only Lightning unit not contributing to the flying; they were away on an overseas deployment until 17 September.

This did not deter the CO from offering his squadron's services. He offered a four-ship to any takers. There was one possible station, St Mawgan. This though was out of reasonable range from the homestead at Wattisham and would require the team to stay overnight. They were already committed to a ten-aircraft flypast, together with 111, on the Sunday followed by preparation for an ADEX deployment to Malta. The logistics of it all would have left very little give in the arrangement. The next most heavily in demand type were Hunters, almost all, being provided by 229 OCU based at Chivenor. A further four from the AFDS and a single aircraft each from the A&AEE and the Wattisham Ops Flight. The OCU admittedly had a sizeable number of aircraft on strength most split into two reserve squadrons, 63 and 234. Between

First flown on 19 March 1950, Canberra VX181, the prototype for the PR3 reconnaissance version is seen here. This aircraft was particularly unique; it made the record flight from Heathrow to Darwin; twenty-two hours and 21.8 seconds to cover 8,608 miles on 27 January 1953. Twelve years later, on 18 September 1965, it is seen over Finningley. (*John Wharam*)

VX181 again, this time closer at RAF Gaydon, 17 September 1966, for what may have been its last public outing. (*Adrian Balch*)

them, they contributed eight jets to take part in a large tactical set piece at Biggin Hill, two touring four-ship formations and at least two solo aircraft.

No. 231 OCU made four Canberra solo display crews available, each incorporating a demonstration of the LABS (low-altitude bombing system) technique with a solo aerobatics sequence. Each instructor crew was required to practice a set four-minute display including a barrel roll, slow-speed flypast, max. rate and minimum radius turns, and the all-important LABS manoeuvre. The latter involves a straight approach at speed followed by a rotation of the nose. The aircraft continues to rotate into a looping manoeuvre; in the inverted descent, the pilot rolls out having reversed direction. No fewer than twelve Vulcans took part in quick reaction alert scramble demonstrations at Cottesmore, Finningley, and Waddington. Four more Vulcans toured individually as did two Victor tankers splitting the country in half.

The now sparse number of UK-based Javelin all-weather fighters, still flown by the OCU at Leuchars, were also very busy with two solo aircraft and a four-ship formation. Argosy and Comet tourers came from Transport Command, again tasked with covering everything between them. Coastal Command made a similar effort with their Shackletons and made available enough SAR Whirlwind helicopters to demonstrate rescuing downed aircrew from the sea, or rather the airfield grass. Flying Training Command provided more aircraft overall with at least six Jet Provost aerobatics teams, numerous solo aircraft (such as Gnats, Jet Provosts, and Chipmunks), and the new leading service aerobatics team—the Red Arrows.

The Red Arrows, due to the obvious logistics reasons, were restricted to two venues—Biggin Hill and Ternhill. Other north and south touring formations of Varsities, Canberras, Jet Provosts, and Gnats also helped fill in any gaps. The Royal Navy made a significant contribution, as always, with their own aerobatics team—the Rough Diamonds—flying Hunters from 738 Naval Air Squadron. The fleet also contributed three solo Scimitars and three Buccaneers. A pair of Sea Vixens demonstrated air-to-air refuelling over some locations. If this did not provide a sizeable frame for the flying display at each station, there was also the overseas and civilian flying contingents. The Belgian and French national aerobatics teams paid homage given the occasion.

This was also the first time, as far as planning went, that some 'At Home' stations were to see two modern high-performance fighters from outside the UK in the air—the F-104 Starfighter and the F-4 Phantom II. The former came from the Belgian Air Force solo demonstration and a formation of four from 331 Squadron of the Royal Norwegian Air Force and from Denmark, a formation of F-100s. The United States Air Force had confirmed two large touring formations of F-100s, F-101s, and F-4s; unfortunately, they cancelled the day before based on the expectation that the weather would not be quite up to the mark. As it turned out, the weather largely proved to be kind.

Just reading through this overview shows a staggering level of effort not just from the RAF, but the surplus provided by other air arms. Outside of the military effort, civilian aircraft from tiny Turbulents and Stampes to a VC-10 from BOAC and a de Havilland Comet auto-land test bed aircraft from the Royal Aircraft Establishment turned up. Finally, from the A&AEE experimental and research crowd came a Canberra and Hunter.

The crowd at RAF Acklington, 18 September 1965. Four Lightnings break formation overhead. Formation drill teams continued after the operational aerobatics team ban, to provide enough interesting flying items to go around the still large number of simultaneously open stations. (*The National Archives*)

Another Lightning four-ship from 19 Sqn over Finningley, just days before they were due to re-deploy, permanently to Germany. Such major commitment did not absolve them from their Battle of Britain day commitment. (*John Wharam*)

Indoor attractions were necessary if the weather was atrocious; RAF Ternhill's station commander, Group Captain E. W. Deacon, is trying his hand—before the punters pitch up—at a 'test your driving skills' simulator. (*The National Archives*)

Hangars are ideal indoor exhibition halls. The time taken to clear them out, fill with all manner of displays and stand for one day, then take down again involves a great deal of free labour. Ternhill, 18 September 1965. (*The National Archives*)

Early photo of a Mk 2 Buccaneer strike aircraft, in naval colour scheme. This aircraft belonged to the Blackburn company, based at Holme-on-Spalding Moor, seen over Finningley, 18 September 1965. (*John Wharam*)

There had been larger efforts in years gone by but relative to the tight resources of 1965, this was impressive and all for free, except for parking.

The static line-ups were no less well served, and each station made every attempt to cater for other interests of all from fun fairs to feature films and hangared exhibitions of associated equipment, bands, and drill demonstrations.

Display flying regulations often vary depending on whether the airfield in use is under civilian or military control. This is often compounded, more from a civilian position, if commercial air activity is prevalent where arrival and departure routes have been established overhead or nearby. This problem has understandably become far more of a headache for air show organisers in the present. In 1965, there was still some coordination required to avoid a near miss or worse, and the following categorisations applied.

Those airfields least conflicted were designated section regulations as follows, Allocated a display area of 6-nm radius centred on the aerodrome up to FL 120: Acklington, Coltishall, Cottesmore, Leuchars, St Mawgan, Ternhill, and Waddington.

Special regulations were applicable to other airfields as follows:

Abingdon—as in section 1 above but excluding that portion contained in Airway Green 1 and the Harwell restricted area.

Biggin Hill—the display area was race-track shape, with the major axis 031 degrees/211 degrees magnetic, aligned through Biggin Hill and bounded at each end by semicircles of radius of 3nm centred 1 mile SW (51 degrees 18' 30" N 00 degrees

Warbirds in the 1960s were as rare as pools wins before the various restoration projects. This Spitfire XIV belonged to Rolls-Royce based at Hucknall, on the civil register; as seen here on 18 September 1965, it was a regular at the Finningley 'At Home' displays. (*John Wharam*)

01' 10" E) and 3 miles NE (51 degrees 21' 40" N 00 degrees 04' 40" E) of Biggin Hill. The display area could extend up to FL 80.)

Colerne—as in section 1 above by arrangement with RAF Lyneham but excluding the portion in Airway Green 1.

Finningley—as in section 1 above but excluding that portion contained in Airway Blue 1 where the maximum height was to be FL 60 unless cleared higher by Northern ATCC.

St Athan—the Western sector of a 6-nm radius circle, centred on the aerodrome, between 160 degrees and 360 degrees True, up to FL 50 unless cleared higher by ATC liaison with Cardiff Rhoose.

[Where the abbreviation FL 120, for example is expressed, this means 'Flight Level 12,000 feet'. The number expressed is always a multiplication by 100.]

Britain was still moving through the post-Suez era. This meant steady decline, over the next five years, of units based in the Far and Middle East. Some would be disbanded, while others would return to the UK or, more likely, Germany. Britain's defence policy forged a shift in emphasis away from the old outposts of empire to address the worries of the Cold War and the need to prioritise military strength in Europe. This then did not mean a sharp decline in the size of the RAF's UK base, but there was some reduction (re-structuring to use the favoured board room term) in certain areas. The year 1965 was a watershed; the scale of effort for the twenty-fifth anniversary would never see this peak again, although the fiftieth anniversary in 1990 came very close.

Imagination has resulted in some unlikely one-off set piece displays. The Daleks seen here at Finningley in 1965, at the height of their TV popularity, were built in the station workshops especially for the day. They caused quite a stir as children scattered across the airfield at one point, especially as the actor William Hartnell obligingly turned up. (*John Wharam*)

William Hartnell, as Doctor Who, having been rescued from the Daleks by various aircraft including Chipmunks, a Whirlwind, Hunters, and a Vulcan. (*John Wharam*)

8
1966–73

The year 1966 was another Farnborough year and the service holding forth this year was the navy. RAF participation did not extend to much at all. The Red Arrows made their debut appearance at the SBAC under the leadership of the late great Ray Hannah.

This was the first year the Red Arrows flew with a formation of nine aircraft. The team went through a significant turnover of pilots between the 1965 and 1966 display seasons. Ray Hannah was promoted to squadron leader and took over from Flt Lt Lee Jones who left along with Flg Off Peter Hay and Flt Lts Gerry Ranscombe, Bill Loverseed, Brian Nice, and Eric Tilsley, while Flt Lts Frank Hoare, Tim Nelson, Pete Evans, Roy Booth, Derek Bell, Bill Langworthy, and Doug McGregor all joined. Aside from Ray Hannah, Henry Prince, who moved from being synchro 2 to synchro lead, was the only other original team member to stay for a second year.

Their first Farnborough brought quite an impact. The 1965 line-up had already made a remarkable impression (hence the expansion in 1966) under Lee Jones' adept leadership; now with Ray Hannah at the helm, they were fast reaching the reputation that has followed them ever since. Apart from the aerobatics team, the Falcons free fall team jumped from a 114 Sqn Argosy.

Yet this year was certainly noted for the prominence of the 'Dark Blue' service and the HMS Hermes Air Group with Sea Vixens, virtually the entire squadron, from 892 NAS, six Buccaneers from 809, five Wessex from 826, and three Gannets from 849.

There were in-service RAF types taking part in other hands. A Lightning flew, but a Mk 53 in Royal Saudi Air Force markings. A Jet Provost T4 (XR669) from A&AEE flew but in civilian hands. Also seen for the last time was Avro Vulcan B1, XA903, the flying testbed for the Olympus 22R Turbojet which was to have powered the TSR2 and would power Concorde.

The year 1966 was also a first for Farnborough—foreign aircraft were permitted to take part. They were allowed, provided the participants were powered by a British engine or at least utilised a major British component part of the aircraft. To that end,

The Red Arrows in their second year, Biggin Hill, 17 September 1966. (*The National Archives*)

two Fiat G-91T/1s—one for flying and one for the static display—came over from Italy along with two MB-326s, again one flying and one static. One other overseas visitor was a home bred Hawker Hunter FGA9 from the Royal Jordanian Air Force. Other than that, a healthy line up of vintage aircraft including Spitfire AB910, Hurricane LF363, Mosquito RR299, and a variety of First World War types.

As 1965 was expected to mark the end of an era, the air staff began to review, at the earliest convenience, the circumstances of their ability to pursue the original philosophy on service run 'At Homes'. Sir Brian Burnett, who was now VCAS, told the air staff, with a sense of the inevitable that for 1966, his proposals for celebrating the Battle of Britain would be on a smaller scale than in 1965. The twenty-fifth anniversary, it had been made clear at the time, was regarded as a special effort given its significance, and as had also been suggested at the time, the scale of future events may not necessarily be the same.

To put on twelve events in 1965 had proved very difficult. As 1966 was a Farnborough year, there would be the usual demand for a substantial contribution here, placing additional pressure on the CPC. As the navy were prominent at the SBAC show this time, the RAF could expect the pressure to be eased a bit. Just nine RAF stations would be open on 17 September 1966. Again, perhaps not all that surprising, Biggin Hill passed muster and would be included. There would be a Battle of Britain exhibition again; having been staged in Scotland for the previous three years, thoughts turned to picking somewhere in England or Wales this time, Liverpool being the city of choice.

Although Biggin was to host an 'At Home', the CPC continued to draw attention to it not being an active RAF flying station, therefore holding a major event of the standard which had been achieved so far was an administrative and logistical strain. That said, it was also noticed that any effort was worth it given the regular level of attendance.

This was to be the leanest year yet, certainly noticeably contracted by the level of effort achieved in 1964. There were no Fighter Command aerobatics teams in 1966, but some formation drill demonstrations would still be provided. There were two unexpected problems that popped up at short notice. First the mark 3 Lightning Interceptors, at the time accounting for four out of five air defence fighter squadrons, were grounded due to a fin/rudder stabiliser fault. Some aircraft appear to have been modified in short order, especially given the crucial lack of air defence cover at the time, some flew at a couple of displays, but a few planned flying slots were cancelled.

The second predicament affected RAF Acklington's display, which had to be cancelled a day before due to an outbreak of foot and mouth in the area. This left eight stations to go ahead. This year, the open stations were now quite clearly representative of defined regions, Leuchars had Scotland and tenuously Northern Ireland; Acklington, the Borders and north of England; Finningley, the north of England and East Midlands; Gaydon, the West Midlands; Benson, south central England; Coltishall, East Anglia; Biggin Hill, the south-east and London; St Athan, Wales; and St Mawgan, the West Country.

The weather was fine everywhere on the day except at Leuchars, which sat under a blanket of low cloud all day. This was a pity for both of the more northerly stations, which were billing the last appearance at a public event, of the Gloster Javelin.

On the point of disbanding, 228 OCU put up the final Javelin formation to be seen in public in the country. They were to have flown at Acklington as well, led by the CO, Sqn Ldr George Beaton, in his own unique natural metal finished aircraft bearing his initials on the fin—'GHB'. The team got airborne in miserable conditions at Leuchars and put on a spirited performance along with a solo aircraft. Due to the problems with the Mk 3 Lightnings, Flt Lt Dave Liggett of 74 Squadron flew his solo aerobatics display in a Mk 1 of the TFF (Target Facilities Flight) both at the home stead and at Finningley. Another type or rather mark of aircraft about to bow out of service was the Vulcan Mk 1A. The squadrons based at Waddington were equally as generous as 228 OCU, sending one aircraft each from 44 and 50 Squadrons to Leuchars and St Mawgan as touring aircraft and four from 101 to Finningley to conduct the only V bomber scramble of the day. Very much reduced from the force of twenty-two squadrons just four years earlier, the V Force were still prominent in the public eye and this year including some unexpected pluses. The two remaining Victor nuclear deterrent squadrons provided three Blue Steel-armed aircraft to display over all locations; two of the aircraft, from 100 Sqn, followed the same route from opposite ends affording those gathered at Benson, Gaydon, St Athan, and St Mawgan two chances to see the largest of the V types. A single example from 139 Squadron made its way from Biggin Hill to Leuchars. Three Canberras from RAF Germany—a rare surprise—from 14, 17, and 80 Squadrons made the trip across the channel, while the future RAF was represented with two P1127 Kestrels (prototype Harriers), one sent to Biggin Hill and the other to Coltishall. Compared with 1965, this was still a lacklustre year.

The RN contribution was light after the heavy commitment to Farnborough—just two Buccaneers from 736 NAS—while two pairs of Sea Vixens from 766 NAS demonstrated air-to-air refuelling over most stations. The navy also made the usual

Literally the final appearance at any public event in the UK of the Gloster Javelin all-weather fighter in RAF hands. Four FAW9s of 228 OCU break to land following their display in marginal weather conditions over the Homestead, RAF Leuchars, 17 September 1966. (*Via Adrian Balch*)

One of two Hawker P1127 Kestrels taking part in 'At Homes' on 17 September 1966, this one seen at Coltishall while the other one headed to Biggin Hill. (*Alec Blyth*)

provision of Fairy Gannets available. From the early 1960s to the early 1970s, Gannets were a standard filler at many military displays, an ugly and squat but, not surprisingly, indispensable aircraft for anti-submarine warfare and airborne early warning for the Fleet at Sea. Having failed to present the F-4 Phantom in 1965, the US Air Force succeeded this time with their now customary series of flypasts, the iconic fighter presented in formations of four from the 81st TFW and the 10th TRW.

Other NATO air arms, notably Belgium and Holland, provided their national aerobatics teams—Les Diables Rouge (Fouga Magisters) and Whisky Four (T-33s). The Dutch Air Force also sent two F-104 Starfighters to Leuchars from 322 Sqn (African Greys) based at Leeuwarden.

The Royal Danish Air Force were represented again by a formation of F-100s, deployed to Finningley. Ultimately, the RAF had a new toy of sorts to show off—the latest version (Mk 6) of the Lightning. The recently reformed 5 Sqn at Binbrook provided a touring formation of four while 74 at Leuchars placed their single example, so far received, on hangar display.

The tactical role in the RAF at this point was mostly concentrated overseas. Only two squadrons of Hunter FGA9 close-support aircraft remained based in the UK, at West Raynham, where they probably escaped the cuts five years earlier by being re-assigned from Fighter Command to 38 Group Transport Command. The air cargo branch were themselves expecting the arrival of the Lockheed C-130K Hercules to replace the currently heavily worked Argosies and Beverlies.

These aircraft and crews were in a similar situation to the RAF's transport element in the early twenty-first century, ferrying both the army and RAF back and forth to Aden during the emergency. The Aden crisis continued to a highly publicised crescendo in 1967. Adding to this the constant supply of men and materials to Hong Kong, Singapore, Cyprus, and Malta, HM Forces had their work cut.

More on the upside, the RAF were expecting Santa to bring three new much advanced combat types—the F-4 Phantom and the F-111K from the USA along with the fully developed P-1127 Kestrel, the Harrier, to replace the now dated Hunters. Yet the one principal role that many have always regarded as the RAF's *raison d'être*, the task of strategic bombing, was facing the end; the V Force's days were numbered due to the transfer of the primary nuclear deterrent to the Royal Navy's soon-to-be fully deployed force of four Polaris submarines.

It was not all good news for the navy. Their much-looked-forward-to CVA-01 class carriers were due to be cancelled and, along with them, the remaining carriers and all fixed-wing flying. That was the government's plan as of September 1966. As the display season ended for the year, the now revered Red Arrows were placed under review. They had achieved a growing reputation since their first public display at the Biggin Hill Air Fair in May 1965. A working party to conduct the review was drawn from those service staff concerned. They were, as of 10 October 1966, able to present their study findings to the air staff. One recommendation was that until new aircraft became available, the team were to continue, and with the Folland Gnat.

The DCAS, Sir Reginald Emson, explained that despite the need for fatigue modifications between 1967 and 1970, there would be sufficient Gnats to maintain

A very early appearance at an RAF display by an F-4 Phantom II in typical Vietnam-era tan with forest and grass green camouflage. This is an F-4C from the Bentwaters-based 81st TFW, in the static park at Finningley, 17 September 1966. (*John Wharam*)

Four of the first F-4 Phantoms to appear at Battle of Britain displays. These USAF RF-4Cs are from 10 TRW, Alconbury, overhead Coltishall, 17 September 1966. (*Alec Blyth*)

Central Flying School Whirlwind in standard training colour scheme of the era, not entirely appropriate for the role demonstration it involved in, re-supply during a troop assault landing. Gaydon, 17 September 1966. (*Adrian Balch*)

Another CFS helicopter wing contribution at the same event, a Bell Sioux light utility and training chopper. (*Adrian Balch*)

No air show would be complete without expensive pleasure flights; even for RAF and other military run affairs, this is always provided by an outside contractor. The warrant officer here appears to have his work cut out for the day escorting customers to and from the Hiller utility copter at Gaydon, 1966. (*HJ Black*)

the training role that would be supplemented by Hunters and, until 1968, by Vampires. This would also cater for a double output expected from Cranwell from 1968. The increased officer output was due to an earlier planned reduction in academic and basic officer training. There would, however, be no surplus of aircraft to form an aerobatics team. To withdraw the same number of Gnats to form another team in 1967 had been calculated to cost the training of twenty-six pilots during the period.

The RAF were still prepared to weigh the benefit gained from the prestige and public image impact of running an aerobatics team against the demands for training all the new pilots required. The investigating working party and the DCAS, despite the store placed by maintenance of the public profile in 1966, gave priority to training. They were further urged to do so by the need to have their current aircraft withdrawn, after 1967, for modifications. There was one alternative that was to use the Hunter in place of the Gnat to form the team but finding enough airframes in 1967 and beyond would be quite unlikely.

The AFB refused to look at further alternatives, short of returning to front-line units to provide an aerobatics team; there were not any. Despite the situation and the pending loss of the team, there was a possible solution that was to reduce the number of aircraft from the current ten to eight, should they be retained.

Indeed, senior RAF officers were prepared to make every economy in order the keep 'the Reds' going. AOC-in-C Bomber Command, ACM Sir Wallace Kyle, had been approached with the idea of having his pilots conduct advanced training on Varsities in place of Gnats, which he agreed to. So much store was placed by continuing the team that the air staff were also ready to consider some adjustments to the number of training hours. Whatever the conclusions, nothing could be implemented until Treasury approval had been received. The upshot was that there was no suitable type for the Red Arrows, or an alternative, to use as a mount, other than the Folland Gnat

Many RAF stations concluded 'At Home' day with a 'Sunset Ceremony'. RAF Leuchars maintained this tradition through to the final one on 7 September 2013. Usually, the pipe band beat the retreat from before the CO's dais for his salute accompanied usually by a fast past by one of the home-based fighters. This was the 1966 pipe band marching on to the aircraft pan in front of the old control tower for the salute and finale. (*The National Archives*)

and that subject to the team being reduced from an establishment of ten to eight aircraft, being accepted, then they could continue for another year.

A detailed costing of the proposal to keep the Red Arrows going, in reduced size, for the next year was to be placed before the Treasury for approval. As 1967 began, the RAF conducted its customary review of its previous efforts in terms of public displays. It may seem counterintuitive, given the perennial contraction of the RAF and the other services, but looking back, 1966 had seen a record level of RAF participation in public events; again, this did not include the Battle of Britain displays, which were always the subject of a separate report. The year 1967 was to be no different; the AFB imposed no limits, so taking part in flying displays and public events to the maximum extent was authorised. This was subject to operational interests, but even here, the air staff were happy if it would prove possible to rearrange operational and training flying tasks to enable display commitments to be met, so long as it did not place undue strain on resources.

The planned number of displays at events in the UK in 1967 would treble—from thirty in 1964 to ninety-one this year—with overseas events increasing from thirty-eight to fifty-eight. The Red Arrows gave seventy-three displays in 1967 compared with eighty-four in 1966. They had been reduced to seven aircraft again and with some technical difficulties; this meant four of their displays at the end of the season were flown with just three aircraft. Suitable requests for the Red Arrows were honoured as far as possible including appearances on the continent, taking in Belgium, Germany, Italy, and Paris. The organisers of the Paris Air Salon had never restricted themselves strictly to French designs, allowing for a regular international attendance. The homemade stuff appearing at the salon in 1967 included a proposed new type in the developing Mirage series; this version was dubbed the Super Mirage F2. Due to the international open invitation, a much more impressive show was possible than what was mustered for the last Farnborough.

Indeed, the main body of content came from overseas air arms. A showcase of military aerobatics teams were at the Paris air salon in 1967, including the Red Arrows, with Ray Hannah still at the helm. The Patrouille de France took centre stage, operating the Fouga Magister. From elsewhere came the US Navy's Blue Angels flying Grumman F-11F Tigers (perhaps not a familiar fighter type to some), the USAF Thunderbirds flying F-100D Super Sabres, and the Italian Air Force's Il Frecce Tricolori with their Fiat G-91s. Yet it was the new military aircraft that should have shaken the SBAC organisers, two F-111As, the very aircraft promised by the government following the cancellation of the TSR2. The F-111 should certainly have been pitching up at Farnborough seeing as it was the RAF and not the *l'Armee de l'Air* that were making plans for its introduction into service.

The US Navy were there in force with both F-4B and F-4N Phantom II while the USAFE were represented by an Alconbury-based 10th TRW RF-4C Phantom II. Many other countries, including the UK, were yet to start operating their own F-4s. US Forces had a growing heavy number deployed, especially with the demands of Vietnam.

The US fielded the most prominent range of new military types at Paris this year—F-5A, A-7A, A-4F, E-2 Hawkeye, P-3 Orion, and so on. The widening space between American military aircraft procurement and that of the UK left no further room for serious comparison, but despite the RAF relying on older aircraft to a larger degree, they still held their own with some new acquisitions. The Red Arrows headed up a respectable UK military contingent. The RAF at least had the new strategic transport—the Short Belfast—to show off. An example from 53 Squadron stood out in the static park—a Lightning F6 from 5 Squadron, Vulcan B2, Victor B2, VC-10, Andover, Dominie T1, and what was likely the very first public outing of a production Harrier GR1, XV279. The navy were well represented with aircraft from the HMS Eagle Air Group represented by a Buccaneer, two Sea Vixens, and a Wasp helicopter. Joining the Red Arrows in the flying was a solo Lightning from 23 Squadron based at Leuchars.

This year's principal opportunity for the public to see what their taxes paid for aviation wise featured the new transport types. As well as the Hercules and Andover that would be widely seen, the heavier Belfast and VC-10 made more limited appearances. What had been Transport Command was now re-branded as Air Support Command. There was no merger, which was the usual cause of retitling; however, this was coming.

The weather for this year's 'At Homes', always a prominent factor, split the country into three. Those stations on the extreme west and east of the country—Coltishall and St Mawgan—enjoyed good weather. Everyone in between had variations from blustery to low cloud and mist. Rain was never far away, and two formations travelling from Coltishall to and from Lyneham did not risk it. This included four F-104s from the Danish Air Force and four of Coltishall's Lightnings; the latter were to have deployed to Lyneham earlier but remained home. The Dutch national aerobatics team, Whisky Four, originally formed by instructors of the KLU Flight Training School based at Woensdrecht back in 1956, had operated T-33 Shooting Stars until 1967. Now they were disbanding as the T-33s were in greater demand for the day job. An operational KLU squadron, 314 'The Redskins', were instead selected to carry the torch forward, forming a team with their more robust F-84Fs.

They had a planned appearance at Leuchars, then tragedy struck. One pilot, Lt Schuur, was killed during rehearsals. This came only two years after the death of Captains Liem and Sommer, again during rehearsals following a collision. Enough was enough for the KLU; the team disbanded, never to reform. However, what some today might find an odd decision given the circumstances, a team of Starfighters—the 'Dutch Masters'—were sent from the F-104 TCA (Training and Conversion Unit) based at Leeuwarden.

A serious accident involving one of the only two Lightning solo pilots, Flt Lt Al Turley of 23 Sqn, had left him seriously injured following a crash in a light aircraft. As a result, another pilot was tasked to take over, this time from the newly forming 11 Squadron.

The pilot was Flying Officer Richard Rhodes. As his junior rank indicates, he would not necessarily be the most experienced Lightning pilot but was described as more familiar with the type than most of his new squadron mates. He was given very little time to work up a display before being tasked with the first of the remaining public displays of the year. The new squadron were also tasked with providing the home four-ship team.

The pilots in the formation had just two appointments—Battle of Britain displays at Acklington and Leuchars. Despite the lack of depth of Lightning experience, they had even less time to work up a display than Fg Off. Rhodes. That they all managed to get through the day without incident and in marginal flying conditions was truly

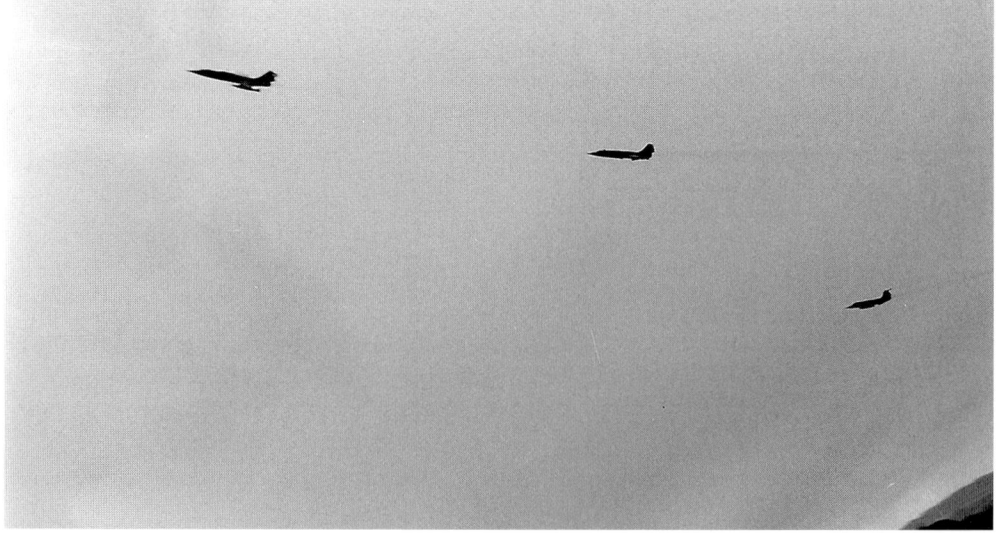

Through the 1960s, the demand for aircraft at several 'At Home' stations being harder to meet was addressed by inviting more overseas, essentially NATO Air Forces contributions. These are Dutch F-104 Starfighters in a high-performance break over Leuchars, 16 September 1967. (*eLaReF*)

Competing with the home-based team are four Lightnings of 11 Sqn. This unit was still getting to grips with the Lightning and most of the pilots had only recently completed conversion to the supersonic beast and had precious little time to form the display team seen here. (*eLaReF*)

Also based at Leuchars, 23 Sqn sent their solo display maestro, Flt Lt Al Turley, to Le Bourget for the 1967 Paris Air Salon. Al is seen alongside the squadron's junior engineering officer, George Lee, together with the display ground crew in white overalls especially for the occasion, the air force equivalent of a Formula One pit crew.

commendable. The Red Arrows were assigned to display again at Biggin Hill while one more station, Abingdon, was honoured with their presence.

One of the key features of the flying at Abingdon was the swansong of the Blackburn Beverley heavy transport and the debut of its lightweight muscular replacement, the Hawker Siddley Andover. The particularly bad weather and the constant prioritising of Biggin Hill when FCHQ detailed the available resources again raised the question of wisdom in the 'At Home' format. Two station commanders chose this year to record their frustration at the flaws in concentrating tight resources across so many locations on a single day. While understanding the significance of September with the anniversary of the Battle of Britain, they failed to understand why events were not spread across the period of the campaign—for example, starting from 10 July and continuing forward to September—as had been suggested in the run up to the 1965 bash.

In their wash-up reports, the station commanders for Acklington and Finningley each drew attention to what seemed a poor way to present the RAF given the assets and what was judged to be the greater hit-and-miss situation with the weather so late in the year. Group Captain Terry Gledhill, a veteran of Operation Grapple (nuclear tests), had only recently taken over as CO at RAF Finningley; Gledhill's post-'At Home' day report detailed the outcome of the flying at Finningley, which made bleak reading. The report described the flying display length as three hours and thirty-five minutes, including gliders at the start and a set-piece role demonstration as a finale. The length would not seem impressive to modern enthusiasts with plenty of current experience of the recent displays at Waddington and RIAT, but what differs quite strikingly is the time window between the end of one display slot and the start of the next.

The window has grown from a minute in the 1960s to ten minutes not being untypical now with many more aircraft operating locally, rather than flying through, which has resulted in far longer flying display timetables over the years. The planned Finningley display was unbroken and planned to run from 1.25 to 5 p.m. Remembering the responsibility of what Gledhill referred to as the 'Co-ordination Authority', meaning the FCHQ project team, they were responsible for organising about one hour and thirty-seven minutes of the flying. One hour and twenty-five minutes' worth was organised by RAF Finningley. This was very much how the form took shape everywhere and sat at the heart of the reservations voiced by other station commanders.

There were still too many stations naturally facing difficulty in negotiating resources against such competition for the same date together with correspondingly fewer aircraft. The flying time total at Finningley left a balance of thirty-three minutes; this was accounted for as the one-minute intervals between each display. Two of the home-based Vulcans were assigned as static displays, two more were sent to Leuchars and St Mawgan for the same purpose, while two more were assigned to the local flying display with one acting as spare—altogether, six aircraft from the OCU's unit establishment total of eleven, maintenance demands not-withstanding.

Under the circumstances, timekeeping was described as good with three individual aircraft –a Canberra, a Victor, and a Navy Gannet—all turning up appreciably early. That was about all the good news. The bad news included a list of cancellations and at least one missed slot; a formation of USAF F-100s never arrived but were confirmed

Above: 'The Nerve Centre'—Air Traffic Control—the principal means of managing airspace activity and no less vital during an air show. This image of the inside of the ATC Tower at RAF Gaydon, together with the following shot and caption, appeared in a special colour supplement produced by the *Coventry Evening Standard* to promote the 1967 Battle of Britain 'At Home' at Gaydon. (*Coventry Evening Standard*)

Right: Planning the flying programme, Sqn Ldr T. H. Watson and Flt Lt J. C. Elmer. The Battle of Britain office, at each station, was responsible for coordinating and securing additional resources to that provided by Fighter Command HQ. (*Coventry Evening Standard*)

The final details of timing the display are worked out in the Battle of Britain project office at Gaydon. Squadron Leader T. H. Watson, the project officer (right), discusses a detail with Flight Lieut. J. C. Elmer. Behind the display lies months of planning. The station's own men have been reinforced with nearly 50 airmen from other camps. They erect 1,400 yards of tubular crush barrier, use nearly ten miles of rope in marking off the spectators' enclosures and car parks, and generally cope with at least 80,000 people and 10,000 cars.

to have got airborne. The Canberra had to make an unscheduled landing to refuel which had been notified in advance by ops at RAF Bassingbourn, the operating base, but caused no problems. The other two early arrivals had, it was assumed, to curtail displays elsewhere. On top of this, there were nine cancellations:

Time	Event	Reason	Organiser
2.06 p.m.	Lightnings	WX at Binbrook	HQFC
2.11 p.m.	Stampe/Turbulent	WX at Bases	Finningley
2.24 p.m.	Bristol F2 Fighter	U/S and WX	Finningley
3.06 p.m.	Super Mystere	Local WX	HQFC
3.23 p.m.	Sky Divers	Local WX	Finningley
3.28 p.m.	Sea Vixen	Cancelled early	HQFC
3.51 p.m.	Dominie T1	Never Broke Cloud	HQFC
3.57 p.m.	Vulcan	Local WX	Finningley
4.11 p.m.	Hercules	Ops Commitments	HQFC

In addition, the display by the Canberra had to be severely curtailed while a further display by a de Havilland Vampire barely broke cloud. Another Canberra, a PR3, was tasked with flying over the airfield to photograph the crowds and car parks for assessments on attendance. Again, owing to low cloud and poor visibility, the results were less than satisfactory. The Gannet, a Britannia, and a Shackleton were all confined to a single pass each.

The weather forecast had not been too bad, but the clearer weather failed to move in, leaving the airfield under full stratus cover at 600 feet with visibility at 3,000 yards in haze throughout the afternoon. The allocation of aircraft was a roundly appreciated problem but with new aircraft just in service, which were conspicuous by their absence.

The report recommended that VC-10, Belfast, and Nimrod to be available in 1968 but most ambitious of all, 'that Harriers be allocated for individual display work, preferably one per station'. Two more points were made; one likely to ruffle a few feathers was the question of the date. Gledhill's report further stated, 'With this year's depressing weather in mind, it is thought that consideration might be given to an earlier date for the "At Home" displays?' With emphasis on the weather in September, the end of summer being cold, damp, and cloudy, the report claimed this was hardly conducive to a large 'Gate'. What still seemed to be lost on the Air Force Board, as Gledhill pointed out what had been advanced before, was that the public made their way to an RAF station holding an 'At Home' day to see an air display. They were not too inspired about the Battle of Britain, even now in 1967—only twenty-two years after the war.

This was another inescapable fact about modern British society as in all other western countries; the younger generations were more minded, for the greater part, toward a less sympathetic empathy with any kind of military ceremony, no matter the occasion—whether the Royal Tournament, Edinburgh Military Tattoo or the RAF 'At Homes'. Therefore, nothing could be taken for granted.

Grp Capt. Gledhill recorded his sympathies with the overall aims: 'Public relations were never more important than today. They might be much improved by the introduction of a more professional organisation for the handling of Station air days.'

The recommendations to spread the number of 'At Homes' across the summer seemed the most logical alternative. 'Any Saturday from mid-June onwards would be suitable for any "At Home" display which could still be associated with the Battle of Britain, together, of course, with the likelihood that the weather would be more conducive to enjoyment and success'. During 1968, it was expected that the public would have the opportunity to visit any one of several other RAF stations holding open days independent of the official Battle of Britain stations in September and the service's golden jubilee.

Of the latter, both ceremonial and public days were to be held at Abingdon in June. The consequent risk from this, combined with numerous air days taking place in the run up together with Farnborough, meant the new year looked quite full, but would the Battle of Britain weekend lose its impact? With 1968 in mind, Grp Capt. Gledhill recommended this year holding the more significant displays much earlier than mid-September. His final point was on behalf of the display controllers; major air events such as the subject in hand meant participation by many unfamiliar aircraft and crews, the capabilities of which were unknown, and as was very much the case in 1967, when conditions were poor, display controllers needed to be familiar with display flying minimums for all aircraft involved. The authority for this is usually the operators at the bases from which the display aircraft hail.

Some stations were good enough to issue written instructions covering the display flying, permissible sequences, and limits, but frequently, it was necessary to enquire on the phone at a late stage. Most stations sent out pro forma to participating units, seeking information on a variety of matters. Gledhill recommended a 'suitable certificate of operating limitations' that should be included with the operating proforma and that the 'At Home' day operation order should lay down the requirement for an operating authority's certificate authorising display sequences. This should include appropriate weather minimum restrictions, including maximum acceptable wind conditions and downwind components.

Finningley was not the only station to have a bad 'At Home' 1967. Acklington's wash-up report was even more critical, again regarding two key points—the weather and aircraft participation.

For the first time at Acklington (and, as it would prove, the last), a vehicle and pedestrian census was conducted on the day. This recorded an attendance figure of 34,628, significantly down on the 60,000 to 70,000 estimated figures for the 1965 'At Home' day, but no more than an estimate just the same. The event, as the CO, Group Captain Sutton, mentioned in his opening sentence, 'was undoubtedly affected by the deteriorating weather experienced during the day'. Here, a modified flying programme had to be hastily arranged, but despite all, the attendance level was considered to be good under the circumstances. The morning had begun with low cloud, which showed promise by clearing to give a visibility of 10 nm with complete cloud cover remaining at 2,500 feet. At 2.30 p.m., shortly after the flying display began, rain started to fall and became heavy before clearing at 3.15 p.m.

This brought a marked deterioration in visibility with lowering clouds that persisted. As far as external organisation went, all was in place. British Rail had provided special services to Acklington rail station and United Automobile Services laid on a shuttle service from there to the RAF base. The RAC put up signs on all roads leading to RAF Acklington. As was the custom at most air shows of the day, car parking was accommodated on as much of the grass side of the crowd line, which was dry in the morning, and the aprons in front of the hangars.

Despite a vehicle identification system for VIP cars, introduced for speedier entry and distribution, by mid-afternoon, queues 3 miles long had developed on some approach roads. A total of 5,209 cars, thirty coaches, and 200 motorcycles were eventually admitted. Considering the overall attendance level for 1965, the number of cars parked on the base then came to 3,374, with just three coaches and 112 motorcycles. This was quite an eye-opener showing how the ratio of private vehicles and coach hire to overall head count had moved.

Crowd barriers had been hired for £555 in 1965. The following year, rope and metal spike barriers had been loaned from the army's Northern Command for free. The static display comprised sixteen visiting aircraft, all but two of which were in position by Friday. The two late arrivals, a Gnat and a Hunter, arrived after the public had been admitted on Saturday morning. Of these aircraft, only eleven had been allocated by the Battle of Britain project team at Fighter Command HQ, the remainder by local arrangement or, as Grp Capt. Sutton put it, on a self-help basis.

Positioning the two late aircraft for the static park caused some difficulty as the active airfield side was separated from the static park by two of the car parks. Further at the end of the display when the public began to leave, static aircraft looking to depart were delayed because of litter on the taxiway. The priority though was still to get the public safely off the station. As at Finningley and other stations, the centrepiece of the open day—the flying—was severely curtailed by the same limitations of low cloud, worsening rain, and poor visibility. Here, the free fall team, the Black Knights (23rd SAS Reserve Regiment), got airborne for their slot in the expectation of the cloud clearing but to no avail. The station project team had organised a set piece involving a launch of sixteen Jet Provosts to fly a Balboa then split for an airfield attack. This was limited to just four Jet Provosts and a Wessex helicopter working in conjunction with an RAF regiment attack on a dummy fort.

For all the problems, only four other items of flying had to be cancelled—a Hercules, withdrawn at short notice for operational reasons, a Hawker Hurricane due to serviceability, and a Tiger Moth and Spitfire, both due to weather *en route*, which prevented flight using visual rules that both aircraft were restricted to. This wrecked the plan to open the flying and close it with the two iconic fighters from the Battle of Britain. Apart from these disappointments, the otherwise full flying display went ahead with participating aircraft, modifying their display sequences to suit the conditions. Excellent radar control and good timekeeping by formation leaders and captains ensured that with just a few minor adjustments, the flying was continuous.

The thrust of the report was critical of the organisation of the 'At Home' day in terms of policy and execution. Just as with the Finningley CO, Sutton complained that the allocation of resources was both incompatible and inadequate for the event, especially given the degree of widespread publicity, upon which the public were understood to have placed high expectations.

The 'At Home' was compared unfavourably with other recent events in the area, particularly a comparatively minor display organised by the Sunderland Flying Club, which secured the participation of the Red Arrows and other star attractions. The Sunderland display was attended by broadly the same people who visited Acklington, 'who could fail to be dismayed by the scarcity of interesting features at what should be a superior display, laid on by a superior organisation'.

Furthermore, the report pointed out that the number of 'At Homes' were not contracting as fast as the level of resources made available; increasingly, it was seen that more interesting aircraft were fewer as well as the number of display teams. Acklington had also previously made recommendations that the RAF stations selected to be 'At Home' stations should be spread across separate dates, therefore allowing a wider level of public attendance and the better opportunity at each to see the RAF and other air arms better represented and the 'few really good items' still available. Grp Capt. Sutton went on to outline the terms of reference for 'At Home' day unit project officers regarding the correct procedure for 'self-help' items from various outside sources; this was nearly always needed to fill in the gaps and indeed expand the number of flying and static aircraft allocated by the FCHQ team.

The procedure was deemed to be inadequate. Firm advice in a signal sent out from FCHQ to the various commands had simply stated: 'Normal mutual liaison and loan between stations not precluded but this Headquarters must be informed of such arrangements.' The rather stern tone of the instruction had left some external agencies under the impression that any such local arrangements were precluded.

One final problem was that Chrisair Aviation Services, which had been contracted to provide pleasure flights, failed to send any aircraft. Therefore, revenue from this activity was lost. There was no financial penalty otherwise, but resources assigned to assisting with pleasure flights could have been directed elsewhere. Grp Capt. Sutton made four principal recommendations:

> Stagger 'At Home' days: stations should be grouped geographically, and the dates for each display should be staggered, to ensure maximum coverage of the few star items, i.e. the Red Arrows.
>
> Provision of instructions to flying display organisers: there should be more detailed instructions available to display organisers for the purpose of arranging 'self-help' flying display items.
>
> Civilian passenger flights: action should be taken to warn display organisers of the problems that have arisen in the planning of civilian passenger flights.
>
> Publicity: window displays, printed slips and rubber stamps should continue to be used for publicising 'At Home' Day. Centrally produced posters should give notice of intended fees for parking.

The points raised by various station commanders in 1967 did not appear to have had much effect in 1968. This was a particularly significant year—the fiftieth anniversary of the foundation of the Royal Air Force. So, it was going to be busy as Farnborough too was looking forward to an impressive show. The Phantom and Harrier were planned to appear, and to celebrate the half century, HM Queen Elizabeth II was to review her air force; this was to be at RAF Abingdon in June. A number of 'Open Days' were to supplement the September displays.

There was a conscious sense that the best use of all resources be made available in order to maintain and promote recruitment and, as the mission statement stated, 'maintain the prestige of the RAF in the current climate of defence retrenchment'. Therefore, a continuation of the policy of maximum participation was the way forward. Participation (in public events) was the best recruitment tool still, and while the RAF appreciated the boost to RAF and national prestige through appearances at events overseas, they were mindful of the fact that it was UK audiences that provided the pool of recruitment.

So major and minor events in the UK would be prioritised; major events overseas would be accommodated with what was left available. The Red Arrows had been subject to a review and had been cleared to continue for another year; despite their popularity, they still did not exist based on an institution in quite the way they have since the 1970s. The free fall team, the Falcons, was cleared to continue for just the next two years. Part of the reason for their continuation was that 1968 would see other resources stretched to the limit. The elements that would be most hampered by training and operational commitments would be helicopter units. Whatever the forecast operational commitments in 1968, this year has gone down in history as the one whole calendar year in which not a single British serviceman or woman was deployed on any level of war footing.

A limit on helicopter displays was dismissed as unnecessary, but some decrease might be unavoidable. On a finer level, Technical Training Command urged that the RAF Physical Training Team should be retitled the RAF Gymnastic Display Team as this would be more in keeping with the nature of the display given. The Red Arrows, voluntary aerobatics teams, the various Jet Provost teams, and solo displays should be made available as far as possible to the maximum possible extent. As far as the Battle of Britain celebrations were concerned, the likelihood of having nine stations selected again was slender. Bearing in mind the bad weather in 1967, when just two stations escaped the band of low cloud and mist as a result of being on the east and west extremities of the country, any impressive displays managed elsewhere was given much acclaim and afforded to the organisers' efforts. As Abingdon was hosting the golden jubilee celebrations, the 'At Home' task for this area would pass back to Benson; regardless of how often the task was now being rotated between the two, it might be affected by works services on the runways at Benson this year. Also, St Mawgan was about to undergo similar airfield work. This reduced the total number of available airfields to six.

The continuing question over Biggin Hill had been answered by high attendance figures—200,000 in 1966. However, this dropped all the way down to 60,000 in 1967 where the weather had been particularly severe, resulting in a severely limited flying programme. The airfield's availability now was as much in the hands of the Board of Trade, who had already indicated that as far as they were concerned, Biggin Hill would be available as an 'At Home' venue once again in 1968. With the availability of Benson

F-100 at St Mawgan 1967 parked up for public inspection. (*Chris England*)

RF-101, again at St Mawgan, 16 September 1967. The weather appears fair, but most of the 'At Home' stations sat under low cloud and mist; only the east and west extremes sat outside the grey cloud bank stretching up and down the country. (*Chris England*)

and St Mawgan also confirmed (works services expected not withstanding), the AFB were able to approve a list of eight stations. Unusually, Farnborough was to be held the week forward from Battle of Britain—15 to 22 September. Once again, the commands were invited to put forward proposals for what they could send down to the Hampshire drome.

Strike Command, recently formed from the amalgamation of Bomber and Fighter Commands, offered to send a Victor K1A and a Vulcan B2 for static display. They also would provide four Vulcans for a scramble each day; the scramble would be followed by an airfield attack by two of the V bombers with pyrotechnics. A flypast by the Lancaster with a Spitfire and a Hurricane representing the past was followed by a Victor with two Lightnings to represent the 'new'. In addition came a solo aerobatics display by a Lightning and a complete Bloodhound missile section to be included in the static park. Flying Training Command would send the Red Arrows to give a 16.5-minute display each day. A Folland Gnat solo display would also be provided and the Tomahawks CFS helicopter display team. This was not all—a '50' formation made up of Jet Provosts would flypast and one of the Jet Provost formation aerobatics teams would be included; the 'Macaws' from Manby were nominated while a Dominie, a Gnat, and a Jet Provost would be in the static display.

Coastal Command would demonstrate their current and future roles with a suitable display in the static park, an SAR demonstration by a Whirlwind HAR 10, and, yet to enter service, an HS Nimrod MR1 from Hawker Siddeley. Air Support Command were very heavily committed but were willing, if heavily pressed, to supply both a tactical display involving a parachute drop and stores, with Hunters flying close air support, and a second display with one of the brand-new Short Belfast's disgorging its load to then be retrieved by helicopters—an ambitious contribution given the constraints.

That was not all. The Falcons free fall team would jump from an Argosy. In the static park, they would have a C-130 Hercules, an Andover, and (subject to space availability) a VC-10. They would also provide the support aircraft for the Red Arrows.

Other aircraft just entering or about to enter RAF service would be represented; the McDonnell Douglas Phantom, however, would be presented by the Royal Navy in the form of a formation flypast and a static exhibit. The VCAS, Sir Peter Fletcher, did not want the navy to steal the show with the newest fighter and 'considered that, if possible, we should also try to display our Phantoms in the air and on the ground'. Unfortunately, the later and slower rate of delivery of F-4 Phantoms to the RAF was expected to limit the junior service, despite this being the occasion of their fiftieth birthday bash, to an aircraft for the static display only. An update on firmer delivery dates and a period of crew familiarisation would need to be more clearly understood before a decision was taken, but Sir Peter wanted to leave the matter open over whether a flypast might yet be mounted. This was the position as of 5 June 1968.

Otherwise, he was satisfied that these proposals were the best that could be offered and recommended the board offer what was outlined to the SBAC organisers. A total of 114 displays were attended in the UK by the RAF in 1968, reflecting another significant increase from ninety-one in 1967. This even allowed for twenty-eight further events connected with the fiftieth anniversary celebrations. These figures, as always, were counted separately from the Battle of Britain displays and the golden jubilee display at Abingdon. The Red Arrows gave ninety-eight displays, including thirty-five 'domestic' bookings for VIPs and the press. All UK commands and RAF Germany gave displays, with Lightning and Hunter solo aerobatics being among the more popular non-team items.

In the twenty-first century, it has become common currency to describe solo display aircraft as teams, though this is somewhat misleading. The egalitarian spirit behind this is justifiable enough as the intent is to refer to all involved behind the scenes, but the thinking behind this development also overstates and misrepresents what is on offer. For example, when a football team is described, it is the team players alone that are being presented; the fitness coach, kit manager, and analyst are never counted in the line-up. These people are all vital components but are not part of the presentation. The same is true of a rock band; only the band members on stage appear in the advertised billing. This is not to ignore anyone's efforts but to manage public expectations.

Of a more formal nature, the Battle of Britain thanksgiving service at Westminster Abbey was to go ahead on Sunday 21 September. In 1967, this service had filled the abbey; in 1968, additional seating was made available and, despite the weather, was filled to capacity again.

The gymnastics team performed at the Royal Tournament. A one-off rather theatrical display by the RAF at the tournament was a demonstration of basic training set back in 1918 where serving personnel of the day got used to drilling with Lee-Enfields, bayonets like swords, puttees, and button up to the collar serge tunics. My own brother-in-law was, perhaps reluctantly, one of the poor erks on parade nineteen canteen style. Most popular of all the ground displays once again were the police dog display teams—ninety-nine displays in 1968 were given by the RAF's canine wing.

The only relative disappointment was the effort made for Farnborough. A handful of the items aimed at being representative were able to make it; the V Force display fell by the wayside along with the RAF Lightning solo, replaced by the Lightning F53 in RSAF markings again. The '50' formation made up of twenty Jet Provosts flew as did the Red Arrows, the BBMF, and the tanker, with fighters flypast, consisting of Victor and two Lightnings and the Falcons. Everything else suggested by VCAS fell short. This only exemplified the heavier contribution from the Fleet Air Arm; this was quite impressive and included the 700P Flight Phantom four-ship and two navy aerobatics teams, Phoenix Five (Buccaneers), and Simon's Circus (six Sea Vixens). On top of this, the navy provided a large-scale tactical display involving eleven Wessex of 845 and 707 Naval Air Squadrons as well as more Phantoms, Buccaneers, and Sea Vixens. There was at least some representation of the RAF's future—a formation of four production Harrier GR1s.

The golden jubilee display at Abingdon proved impressive even if the scale of programmed items was comparatively limited. No fewer than twenty-eight Lightnings from various squadrons (four from 23 Squadron beat up the airfield behind the main formation before climbing to contrail height, or that was the plan certainly) and twelve Hunters, an early demonstration of the Harrier GR1 provided by HSA, a large formation of V bombers (twenty-four Vulcans and Victors), and the Royal Cypher formation—'E II R'—was flown by thirty-one Jet Provosts. Altogether, the ceremony on the ground was more central to the occasion than the flying.

As seen here, the weather is always at least one elephant in the room for air shows—a Hunter T7 from 229 OCU based at Chivenor, seen here at RAF Benson, 14 September 1968. (*Ian Anderson*)

Although hampered by the weather over Benson, September 1968, the Red Arrows, seen here at a time when they could operate perhaps with greater latitude, break formation, not clear whether alongside or over the crowd, and in marginal weather. (*Ian Anderson*)

Often air shows with a military lean have a more impressive line-up in the static park. This F-100D Super Sabre of the USAF is seen here at St Mawgan, 14 September 1968. Note the exposed metal casing around the engine as a result of high temperatures. (*Chris England*)

This big fighter is a reconnaissance version of the McDonnell Douglas F-101 Voodoo, bomber escort fighter, seen at St Mawgan, 14 September 1968. (*Chris England*)

Queen Elizabeth and Prince Philip toured the airfield in an open-top vehicle around the impressive static display containing aircraft from the First World War—the Sopwith Camel through to a battery of Bloodhound missiles, Lightning, Harrier, Vulcan, and the recently retired in the form of the Javelin and Valiant. The year finished with a maximum effort at the Battle of Britain stations, eight in all and the last time it would be this many. If one thing stood out, among a variety of golden jubilee anniversary specials, it was a Diamond formation of 16 Lightnings, made up entirely of aircraft drawn from the OCU at Coltishall. The weather, on the other hand, provided blustery conditions almost everywhere.

On 10 February 1969, a meeting of the Air Force Board endorsed guidelines for future participation designed to reduce the number of displays given by the RAF and to ensure that only worthwhile participation was undertaken.

With recruitment still the main aim, priority was to be given again to participation at UK-based public events. Overseas participation would be undertaken when in the interests of the RAF. A new record was set in 1968 for the level of service contributions; the figures had all steadily risen from an overall 157 events in 1966 to 196 in 1968. The figure for 1968 was higher essentially due to the further twenty displays attended in connection with the fiftieth anniversary and eight flypasts also marking the golden jubilee.

A wide range of various public functions and displays were reached, and the coordination of displays was greatly improved in so far as duplication of effort was avoided. The credit for this was due to the setting up of the air display co-ordination team at 11 Group HQ; this cell was set up to replace the Battle of Britain project team at the now disbanded Fighter Command headquarters.

With the end of the 1960s and the RAF now re-equipping with Harrier, Buccaneer and Phantom, in terms of scope for public display, the RAF was embarking on an era where they would be able to publicly field a renewed variety of impressive wares. All the new stuff would be at various stages of work up toward operational capability; the Phantom would be the most advanced along the path to IOC by September 1969. Not just Strike and Air Support Commands and RAF Germany were having their inventories overhauled, but the maritime component were getting a 'makeover', to borrow a modern term.

There was the new HS Nimrod MR1, a four-jet Maritime ASW type, derived from the de Havilland Comet (the first commercial Jetliner), for what was so recently Coastal Command, now 18 Group within Strike Command. The greatest effort to get any examples of the newcomers before the taxpayers on 20 September 1969 was made with the Harrier. The OCU for the VSTOL fighter received its first aircraft in May. More jump jets arrived at Wittering through the summer. Three Harriers were delivered on 19 September, bringing the total on strength to eleven. Of these, two had been grounded with category 3 damage since 11 September; one aircraft had a fuel leak repaired that day only to be stricken with an engine fire, while another suffered a heavy landing. Another aircraft had been at category 2 status all month and another, category 4. This left seven Harriers available to the OCU for training; five of these were assigned display duties on 20 September:

XV747 assigned static at Leuchars
XV750 assigned flying at Leuchars and Finningley

The provision of locally based display teams during the Lightning/Phantom era was a regular feature of the Leuchars air show. The 23 Sqn four-ship taxi in after their slot in the 1968 'At Home'. (*eLaReF*)

The twelve Hunter pilots from 229 OCU selected to take part in the service's fiftieth anniversary flypast over Abingdon, 14–15 June 1968. *Back row, left to right*: Ron Etheridge, Mal Grosse, Rod Dean, Jock Kennedy, Tony McKeon, Bill Armstrong, Syd Morris, Dick Wharmby, and Pete Jennings. *Kneeling, left to right*: Sam Toyne, Nigel Price, and Duncan Allison

Return to base, USAF RF-4C Phantom II taxiing past a Dutch F-104 to return home to Alconbury after the Leuchars 1968 'At Home' day. (*eLaReF*)

1969 brought a first as every effort w as made to ensure each 'At Home' station saw a flying Harrier. This engaged every available serviceable airframe, including these two at Leuchars. (*eLaReF*)

Diamond 16 Lightning formation, a feature of the Coltishall 'At Home' day from 1968 to 1970. (*Air Historical Branch*)

XV755 assigned flying at Biggin Hill & Coltishall (also an airfield attack at latter)
XV756 assigned static & flying at St Athan
XV757 assigned flying at Benson & Gaydon

Even by the standards of the time this was an astonishing level of declared surplus, indeed, all they had available. On the other hand, the new Nimrod, which first flew at St Mawgan and Finningley in 1968, would not be available. Likewise, the aircraft it was to replace, the Avro Shackleton, would be absent from any public events in 1969. HQ 18 Group had asked that their Shackletons be excused public displays in the future due to 'operational commitments', and VCAS had agreed.

The public attendance at the 1968 'At Home' day was counted at 299,000, significantly down on the 405,000 in 1967, which was lower still than 1966 when eight stations were open; the figure then was 607,000, when apart from Leuchars the weather was largely fine. The key factor of not just the weather conditions but the forecast from the night before up to early morning has always made up the minds of a large chunk of would-be air show attendees apart from the hardy enthusiasts who keep the faith.

With 1968 being the Golden Anniversary year, the Air Force Board had encouraged the Commands to open as many stations as possible just to get eight. Even taking this into account, the AFB considered the public attendance in 1968 to be 'very creditable' under the circumstances. The on-and-off weather conditions everywhere had inevitably resulted in some curtailed flying programmes to varying degrees, which was seen as responsible for why more did not venture out. These outcomes further fuelled the concerns among senior officers over why they persisted with the worsening headache induced by doing everything on one day.

In 1969, the agreed spread of effort was to open seven. The bad weather over the previous two years concentrated minds, but on balance, the Participation Committee had concluded that sticking with tradition would be better served in 1969. The film *Battle of Britain*, produced by Harry Saltzman, was going on public release during the week 14 to 21 September for which the VCAS wanted to fully exploit the opportunity for publicity purposes. He may have been a tad out of touch with the times as many of the film's critics at the time judged that epic war movies, however just, were simply not reaching younger audiences due to the shifting culture and attitudes.

There were the other problems applied with a degree of permanence. The year 1969 brought further rationalisation; apart from Coastal Command being reduced to a single Operational Group and subsumed into Strike Command, there were no stations available in the south-west to provide the usual balance across the country. Ordinarily, St Mawgan would fill this role but was busy preparing the Nimrod for operational service and undergoing the airfield maintenance that had been expected in 1968 as well as the construction of a purpose-built maintenance hangar for the new aircraft.

RAF Chivenor near Barnstaple was looked at but was heavily committed with a surge in training courses for pilots assigned to the Hunter aircraft. Yet they managed to hold their own open day at the end of August, which was very well supported by home-based aircraft and attracted a large line up from various NATO arms

A view of the Gaydon static line, 20 September 1969. This was the last service-organised 'At Home' day at the Warwickshire station before 2 Air Navigation School left for Finningley, along with various other air training units, leaving the airfield on care and maintenance until 1975. Today, it is the Rover and Jaguar test track. (*Warwickshire County Records*)

Ground attack demo of Hunters at Gaydon, 20 September 1969. (*Warwickshire County Records*)

that overshadowed the seven in September. There was more to come in terms of contraction.

The changes afoot this time were going to impact more heavily on the RAF than at any time since the end of the 1950s. The year 1969 would be the last time that RAF Gaydon would be 'At Home'. The station was to lose 2 ANS (No. 2 Air Navigation School) at the end of the year; 2 ANS together with 1 ANS, at Stradishall, 5 FTS at Oakington, and the AE & AEO School at Topcliffe were all to be amalgamated, like a large bowl of punch with all manner of ingredients. More still, the Jet Provosts of 6 FTS were to move from Acklington.

This process would take place over the next two years or so, and all would be headed by 6 FTS and moved eventually to Finningley, which would see the Vulcan OCU and 1 GP DU move from there to Scampton. Technical and Flying Training Commands were merged to become Training Command. The aforementioned stations losing based units with no new role were due for care and maintenance status followed in time by closure and sale or transfer to the army or the local council. Reflecting on how to proceed, there were other concerns. Biggin Hill had recorded its lowest ever attendance in 1968—just 25,000, undoubtedly again thanks to the weather—and for the first time had recorded the smallest gate of all the stations.

The CPC conducted a critical examination of policies and procedures. Improvements in administration had been devised, which were supposed to speed up the process for requesting participation. Counterintuitively, they were also convinced of the need to reduce the growing volume of RAF displays at non-service events; the biggest increase had been at minor events. So, guidelines were to be introduced to reduce this and ensure that participation was approved only if it was deemed worthwhile from either a publicity or recruiting point of view. The new guidelines would be flexible to avoid missed opportunities. The biggest headache was overseas participation, which appeared to attract the lowest priority, certainly regarding UK-based assets.

The common problems were uncertainty in securing air transport with attendant financial liabilities. So, from 1969 onwards, transport would need to be firmly committed; this then would enable overseas display organisers to be given realistic estimates of costs. If such costs were acceptable, it would avoid any last-minute haggling and possible cancellation. The CPC also noted that requests for helicopter and ground displays were increasing annually. Here again to apply some form of rationalisation, the CPC were going to introduce further guidelines to ensure unsuitable requests were filtered out. These were less stringent than those for fixed-wing aircraft displays.

Flying displays for locally organised minor events fostered much local goodwill; such participation under the current difficulties would see many such events falling outside these new parameters. To offset this as best as possible, station commanders (subject to the command's approval) could be given limited powers to provide displays at nearby small events from their station's resources. An example would be the provision of flypasts that hitherto had to be sanctioned at MOD level, but there certainly was no suggestion of applying such delegated powers to the likes of aerobatics displays or performance demonstrations.

Good weather at Biggin Hill, 20 September 1969, with one of a handful of Harriers made available for flying displays this day. 1969 was the first time that the new VSTOL jet appeared in public other than at the trade shows and the golden jubilee show in 1968. (*David Kerfoot*)

This Royal Navy 803 Sqn Buccaneer (XV867) is just taxiing in after completing a rare four public displays across Wales and southern England, finishing here at Biggin Hill on 20 September 1969. Note the Red Arrows appear to be holding one of their traditional pre-display wing-top briefings. (*David Kerfoot*)

Another first—when the Phantom entered service, only 43 Squadron routinely held the solo display commitment; the first picked crew were Sqn Ldr John Owen and Flt Lt Nick Thurston, seen here at Chivenor, July 1970. (*Adrian Balch*)

There would be no financial liability as this level of participation would be confined to the local area, and any necessary advice on indemnification and insurance could be obtained from the MOD. This approach was also in keeping with the move toward more decentralisation and would of course assist with local recruitment. Coordination of flying displays during 1968 had prompted the need for project officers to handle this task.

Staff at the different commands were dealing with participation as an unestablished commitment and, as the level had increased, trying to cope was now interfering with primary tasks. Local project officers already existed for the 'At Homes' where each command detached an officer, usually a squadron leader, to FCHQ for a period of nine months each year. The committee asked the Air Force Board to approve extending this requirement for all RAF flying participation, which now meant sending a project officer to 11 Group HQ as they were now the representation of FCHQ under Strike Command.

With one dedicated coordinator, aircraft from all commands would be dealt with by a central source, same as for the 'At Homes'. Bearing in mind that 1970 was also a Battle of Britain anniversary year with some significance, being the thirtieth, one former CAS, Sir Thomas Pike, contacted the incumbent officer, Sir John Grandy, with the suggestion that it may be worthwhile reversing the trend of reduction. This had been discussed at the end of the 1969 display season. All concerned were contacted to sound their opinion, and the response was not enthusiastic. There was no dissenting opinion from within the AFB either.

There was a simple problem—resources. Each command allocated an annual slice of their flying quota for display flying. As things stood, what each were making allowance for fell short of the demand. The operational penalties of increasing the quota allocated to displays was far too great. Re-equipment, described by Grandy

Bristol Britannia long-range transport over Gaydon, 20 September 1969—as comprehensive a cross-section of aircraft was made available until quite recently. (*Warwickshire County Records*)

as an extensive programme, was part of the problem. The work-up training involved was not to be disrupted any more than was absolutely necessary. In 1969, the seven 'At Homes' presented a false picture; the number of RAF stations holding locally organised open days through the summer was increasing more or less in line with the decrease in the official 'At Homes'. Grandy thought they would struggle to maintain just seven displays in September 1970.

The open days outside the 'silly season' relied upon their own resources and assistance from elsewhere depending on what was available at the time. There was an additional concern that prompted Sir Thomas Pike's approach; funding was being sought for the new RAF museum to be built on the site of the old RAF station and original venue for the Air Pageant at Hendon. Since the Air Council decision back in 1946, the proceeds of the 'At Home' days had been split evenly between two RAF charities—the Royal Air Force Association and the RAF Benevolent Fund. This remained unchanged with a small review in 1968 to look at whether some of the funds from same might go toward the recently launched appeal fund for the museum.

The AFB had had concerns that increased prominence of the two main charities in the Golden anniversary year might detract from the museum appeal fund, and they were determined that the latter should get off to a good start. The resolve was that the proceeds from the other open days, especially in connection with the jubilee celebrations, should go entirely to the museum appeal. This then would allow the two main charities to continue to share the output from the Battle of Britain 'At Homes' as always.

By June 1970, the museum appeal fund was in financial difficulty. The eventual cost was expected to reach £700,000; by 1972 the fund would, on forecast, be £200,000 short. Thereafter, the project would continue to suffer a cash deficit until the money needed to pay for the building had been received along with the funds due under covenant. This was very much the RAF's responsibility, and if the building was to be completed, at all, then it would depend on the maximum possible effort to assist

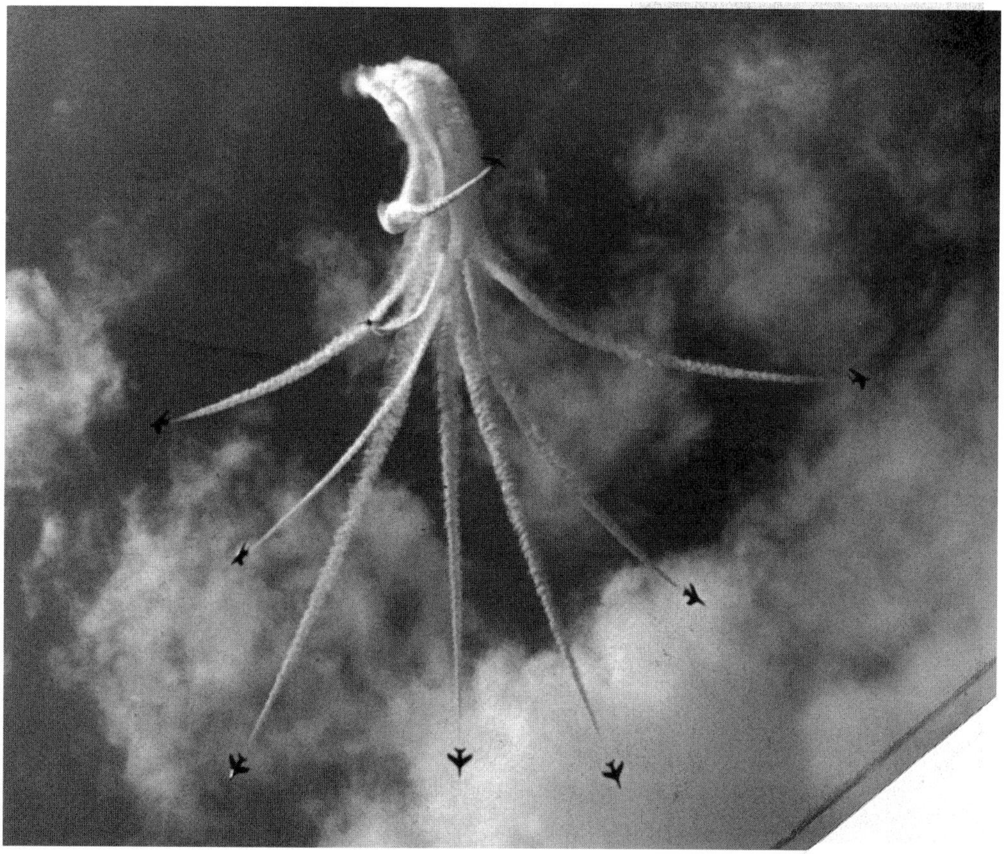

The Red Arrows, led by Sqn Ldr Den Hazell, bomb burst overhead No
RAF Horsham St Faith, July 1970. (*Alec Blyth*)

from the RAF. If the appeal target was not met, then the shortfall would need to be underwritten by the RAF Central Fund. Therefore, two years on, the circumstances had changed and the original suggestion of diverting proceeds from the Battle of Britain 'At Homes' was now re-proposed by CAS. They would start with the 'At Homes' being held on 19 September 1970. The funds would be split three ways between the two charities and the appeal fund. The permanent secretary (RAF) asked the question—was the museum a charity?

In 1970, requests for participation at public events by RAF aircraft could not be provided on the scale required to meet the demand, a problem growing with each passing year. The CPC 's earlier guidelines allowed some requests to be ruled out. The 'At Home' policy no longer pursued the ambition to simply open as many stations as possible on Battle of Britain week but still regarded all at once on one day as the best way to both reach the wider public and minimise cost and commitment.

Opening any number of stations, no matter how few at a time, spread through the summer, was placing continued strain on the accepted quota system and consequently impacted on the protected levels of operational training and into the bargain detracted from the many civilian-organised displays each summer, which also depended on as high a level of RAF aircraft demonstrations as they could possibly get.

Therefore, there was not much enthusiasm for encouraging station commanders to go down this road as any significant increase in station open days would likely have a consequential disruption to the RAF's primary task and could increase the demand for aircraft resulting in the expected disadvantage impacting on civilian-organised events.

One crucial issue with opening more than seven or eight RAF stations (as urged by Sir Thomas Pike), simultaneously again, was the level of support required in terms of ground equipment. Personnel often needed to be drafted in from other stations as well as finding stations in a position to hold such an event. Those that now held their own open days were able to call on the CPC to assist but were allowed to allocate the proceeds to whichever charities they wanted to, only the 'At Homes' were directed by DCI (defence council instruction) to make their proceeds available to the RAFA, RAFBF, and the museum appeal fund. Due to the mix of benefits and penalties of the independent open days, policy was to leave the staging of these events to respective station commanders who were the instigating authority.

The year 1970 marked the thirtieth anniversary of the Battle of Britain, and while the scale of the effort was not going to be quite at the 1965 mark, there was going to be a larger scale of available aircraft than recent years. Aerobatics teams were still quite plentiful—six with Jet Provosts, one flying a pair of Chipmunks, and the Red Arrows. Squadron air drill formations had become far less frequent and mostly only to take part in local displays rather than tour about.

The RAF's impressive line-up of transport aircraft—Hercules, Britannia, Belfast, and VC-10—could be expected. The new Nimrod maritime patrol jet was restricted to appearing aloft at the home base: St Mawgan. The Vulcan was made available to all stations open as standard.

Overseas participants were as healthy as ever, Belgian and French national aerobatics teams with a Canadian CF-104 squadron sending a formation from Baden-Soellingen in West Germany and a formation of Danish F-100s. The RAF found the time and funding for no fewer than five Lightning aerobatics pilots and three on the Harrier. Prolific numbers of solo display aircraft of such sophistication and formidable types were becoming far fewer. There were solo examples of the new F-4 Phantom, one each from the RAF and the navy. The Buccaneer, always seen in navy hands before, was represented by two solo aircraft of 12 Squadron RAF. A single aircraft came from the RN this year. The exceptional numbers of popular Lightnings and Harriers giving solo displays this year were likely authorised in view of the anniversary.

In the future, fast jet solo demonstrations would remain representative, but the days of one or more per squadron were ending. The Red Arrows were assigned their customary limit of two Battle of Britain displays, but this year at venues outside the south-east of England. Thus 1970 saw their debut appearances at Finningley and Coltishall. Benson and Biggin Hill this year hosted the French Air Force's Patrouille de France as their headline aerobatics team.

A hair-raising Belgian team of two Starfighters—the Slivers, which had first displayed at Coltishall in 1969—went to Leuchars while the premier Belgian team, Diables Rouge, covered St Athan and St Mawgan. The Slivers were drawn from the Belgian Air Force's Beauvechain-based 350 (Ambiorix) Squadron. They lasted from 1968 to 1975. Their display sequence commenced with an arrival low and fast, very fast, from crowd rear in full reheat. Once they had shattered everyone's nerves, they split left and right, then spent the next close to ten minutes or so charging up and down the display line opposite one another rolling off the top of a near vertical climb at either end to return and pass again. The team consisted of the same two pilots throughout—Steve Nuyts and Palmer de Vlieger. Steve was promoted and Palmer retired in 1975.

No other pilots could be drawn from the Belgian F-104 Force to take up the cudgels and keep the faith. The last known appearance of the Slivers in the UK was at the Scottish International Airshow on 14 June 1975; the following weekend, they flew their last ever public display at the Florennes air show in Belgium.

While significant in 1970, the Royal Navy's contribution was hereafter going to be more hit and miss as the impact of the roll up of the Fleet Air Arm was now about to be felt far more keenly. The Sea Vixen was to retire in 1972. The Buccaneer and Phantom were being cut to a single operational unit each, meaning seldom appearances in future. Coltishall once again mounted its unique party piece—the launch of sixteen-plus of the OCU's Lightnings to return over the station in big diamond before running in to break and recover.

When recovering the formation this time, one of the Lightnings popped a tyre and blocked the runway for a while as other Lightnings turned onto the base-leg to land and had to pick up power to go around. More formations held to wait their turn to enter. This had a knock-on effect; apart from other Lightnings having to disperse to the designated diversionary airfields amid this, one aircraft had to be abandoned, resulting in serious injury and the loss of one aircraft. To put matters more in perspective, the RAF's Lightning Force lost four pilots, two ground crew, and seven aircraft from 4 March to 19 September 1970, meaning the diamond 16 formation was not repeated the following year.

Above left: The Red Arrows are recorded over Coltishall during rehearsal for local television in support of the 1970 'At Home'. (*Air Historical Branch*)

Above right: Rehearsal over Biggin Hill for 1970 edition of the 'At Home' Lightning makes a fast pass. (*Air Historical Branch*)

Farnborough occupied the preceding week once again. The RAF pulled out the stops for the shop window display this year. Given the recent re-equipment programme now taking effect, a substantial role demonstration was arranged by HQ 38 Group, which included eight Harriers and nine Phantoms from 1 and 6 Squadrons respectively with eleven Hercules. Two Lightning solo demos were sent—one from 23 Sqn and one from the OCU, which alternated through the week. Nos 43 and 12 Squadrons provided Phantom and Buccaneer demos respectively, the latter alternating between two available crews. The Nimrod MR1, an in-service example, flew up from St Mawgan.

The year 1971 began with tragedy. The worst accident on record to involve the Red Arrows happened on 20 January during a rehearsal flight. Four pilots, two, Ed Perreaux and John Haddock were flying as the 'synchro pair' and collided, both were killed and so were the two new pilots assigned to join the team, who were in the rear cockpits of the two aircraft involved. These two pilots were John Lewis and Colin Armstrong.

They had already changed the team leader after Sqn Ldr Dennis Hazell broke his leg following ejection from a Gnat the previous November. The original team pilot, Sqn Ldr Bill Loverseed, took over as Red 1. Following the tragedy in January 1971, the Red Arrows were cleared to continue but reduced back to a formation of seven aircraft.

Late 1970 and early 1971 saw two young civilian air traffic controllers looking to find an airfield somewhere suitable to stage an air show initially in support of RAFA (Royal Air Forces Association). Paul Bowen and Tim Prince obtained permission to organise their display at North Weald in May. Being 1971, this meant no Farnborough although that would have little impact on this small-time endeavour. Just what the two young men had in mind was not to rival anything like Farnborough, an international event to which Captains of Aviation Industry and foreign military attachés attended, but they did want it to be more than a typical largely civilian affair, as entertaining as that would be.

Their debut event, known simply as Air Tattoo 1971, put together a relatively small but most impressive show case of aerobatics teams and some quite rare contributions from in and outside NATO. The outside bit coming from the Austrian Air Force in the form of a team of SAAB J-105s. They also managed to get Danish Drakens, Dutch and Norwegian F-5s, USAF F-4s, and the French Patrouille de France. Paul and Tim together with Battle of Britain veteran and friend of Douglas Bader, Sir Dennis Crowley-Milling, had an immediate success on their hands with this new format, growing to become, arguably, the largest military air show on the planet but essentially civilian run.

Today it is the Royal International Air Tattoo and is usually held at RAF Fairford in Gloucestershire. The Air Tattoo was sufficient a success to be held again in 1972 and introduced a new competitive edge, of sorts, to the size and scope of air displays. No one would want to encourage one-upmanship within such a sphere of endeavour. However, in 1972, Rod Dean, a name synonymous with display flying since, as a young flying officer, won the first 'Embassy' Trophy for his individual aerobatics display in a Hawker Hunter from 79 Squadron/229 OCU. The Embassy Trophy was an interesting new idea—a trophy for the best display.

The trophy has been awarded at IAT/RIATs since with a change in the honoured title from time to time, later becoming the Super King Trophy; today, it is named after the late co-founder, Paul Bowen. The IAT organisers, the RAF Benevolent Fund Enterprise, over the years introduced a variety of other display trophies, such as the 'As the Crow Flies' Trophy, Steedman Sword, and Sir Douglas Bader Trophy. Each is awarded for the best in set category. There is also a trophy that is awarded for the best overall flying demonstration by an overseas participant. As for the ongoing status of the RAF policy on public displays and demonstrations, the review process continued; for the third year running, the number of RAF stations to stage 'At Homes', confirmed for 1971, was to be seven again—a figure that the AFB seemed to have settled on after years of near relentless decline. The picked seven themselves remained largely constant—Abingdon, Biggin Hill, Coltishall, Finningley, Leuchars, St Athan, and St Mawgan, all as well positioned across the country as was possible given the circumstances, to achieve a balanced spread.

Yet they would have to share a much-reduced surplus of aircraft compared with the previous two years. The Fleet Air Arm up to now had always made a generous effort to fill in the gaps; this time, they had little to bring to the party—a solo Phantom and Hunter and down at St Mawgan, the rotary winged replacement for the Gannet, a Sea King ASW 1.

The Sea Vixen, on the point of withdrawal from service, was absent; Navy Buccaneers were also absent. The Wattisham TFF provided the RAF's sole Lightning display for 1971. TFFs (target facilities flights) were formed in 1966, located at Leuchars, Binbrook, and Wattisham; they flew early model Lightnings as high-speed, high-altitude targets and provided air-to-air combat training. The sole solo Lightning this year was flown by Flt Lt Russ Pengelly, who built a reputation as perhaps the finest Lightning aerobatics display 'jockey' of all, with his stupendous vertical climbs; he later joined BAE at Warton and showed off the MRCA/Tornado in very much the same manner until his untimely death on a test flight from Warton over the Irish Sea on 12 June 1979. In 1971, he was sent to the Paris Air Show at Le Bourget. With what was now a venerable type, and the earliest mark to boot, heading to Paris signalled a desire by the RAF to place before an international audience—a truly unrivalled and scintillating spectacle. Would overseas orders for 'Frightnings' this late in the jet's operational history follow? Selecting such an old banger to represent the junior service at such a prestigious trade event said it all about both the machine and Russ's skill with the it.

The scant surplus of assets this year pushed the Participation Committee to bend over backwards to secure ever more aircraft from other NATO sources, which they succeeded in. Early on, RAF Coltishall reported back that the impressive Diamond 16 Lightning flypast had been cancelled owing to it consuming too much time on maintenance, costs, and flying hours to stage again. It is also very likely that this decision was deeply influenced by the incident in 1970.

The year 1971 also provided the British public with their last opportunity to see USAF operated F-100s, from the 493rd TFS/48th TFW Lakenheath, and conversely, a look at something rare—the Swedish built SAAB J-35 Draken of the Royal Danish Air Force, last seen at North Weald from 725 Sqn; this time, five aircraft from 729 Sqn, operating the reconnaissance version, deployed to St Mawgan. It must be said, the contributions from NATO partner air arms, arranged through the CPC, were quite generous. A single VC-10 flew a tour of all seven Battle of Britain displays through the afternoon. The captain, Sqn Ldr Brian Burdett, advertised through the *St Andrews Courier* to request any film of his display taken at any one of the 'At Homes' in September 1971.

The report on 1971 appeared the following February, which carried the verdict that the approach of the last few years concentrating on what were considered worthwhile events when allocating resources, was recommended to continue into 1972. The chairman of the CPC also made fresh recommendations for Battle of Britain week.

Initially, the Royal Navy operated handful of Phantoms. They sanctioned a solo aerobatics crew from 767 NAS, for 1970–71, seen here departing the main runway at Abingdon, 18 September 1971. (*Adrian Balch*)

Buccaneer Mk 2 from 237 OCU over Abingdon, 18 September 1971. (*Adrian Balch*)

No. 43 Sqn Phantom in Hangar at Leuchars, 1971. Of all operational units, this and other Leuchars-based squadrons, during the Cold War, were overly committed both in terms of display and operational commitments. (*eLaReF*)

Hangar static at Coltishall, 18 September 1971. The Bristol Sycamore HT14 is by now a museum piece. (*Alec Blyth*)

The flightline at Coltishall, 18 September 1971. Hunters of 79 Sqn/229 OCU, a JP from the Poachers aeros team, and a Spitfire and Hurricane of the then home-based BBMF are shown. The resident Lightnings remained earthbound this year following the near disaster during the 1970 event, but apart from that prompt, the effort to put up a formation for the day encroached on training and maintenance more than usual. (*Alec Blyth*)

Audience guidelines and a quota system for the allocation of aircraft had made sure that a satisfactory level of flying participation had been achieved going back to 1970 while avoiding disruption of operational and training commitments.

The ration of 2:1 of displays by UK-based aircraft at UK displays over those overseas had been a result of prioritisation to favour recruitment. This was carried on in 1971 with greater emphasis on UK displays. In 1968, the RAF managed ninety-four flying displays in the UK with eighty-two overseas. In 1971, the share was 132 in the UK compared to seventy-four overseas. After the Red Arrows' fatal accident at the start of the year and the ramifications had reached their conclusion, the team resumed training and managed to carry out sixty-seven public displays; this included nineteen for the press and VIP functions.

In 1970, they had managed to complete eighty-nine displays, but to put the Arrows' effort in perspective, the 'volunteer' teams of Jet Provosts—the Linton Blades, the Red Pelicans, the Macaws, the Poachers, and the Gemini Pair—flew a total of sixty-two public events. There were fewer specific RAF displays authorised each year, yet there was a significant year-on-year increase in the spread to accommodate requests. There were other hidden factors as well, largely concerning the 'At Homes' and open days, where local units filled in, usually putting together a unique contribution. The CPC never included these often quite substantial efforts in their own assessments. The greater workload was, however, carried by established display teams; the Falcons jumped from forty-two displays in 1970 to seventy-eight in 1971. The gate tally for the seven 'At Homes' in 1971 was 573,000; this was 100,000 up on 1970, which is interesting as 1970 (being the Battle of Britain's thirtieth) enjoyed a greater effort from all of HM Forces. The weather was not necessarily a deciding factor either as both years were lucky all round in this respect.

Therefore, six plus Biggin Hill would be the order of things again for 1972. The same line up of stations was approved with Wattisham replacing Coltishall as the latter had works services taking place, but this meant the regional balance remained the same.

The star item for 1972 visitors to several air shows was the chance to see Concorde for the first time. Various events managed to secure a couple of passes. Five of the seven 'At Homes' secured a couple of flypasts a piece, the Battle of Britain Office at Abingdon went without an item or two to be sure of Concorde flying through while at Wattisham a very rare formation display' by four USAF F-4s was reduced to a more standard single flypast in order to make room.

All seven stations witnessed another first as two USAF F-111Es toured from either end of the country with a series of slow and fast passes. On the downside, the Fleet Air Arm were, save for displays by Gannets and Sea Kings, conspicuous by their absence, while the RAF's own Buccaneers were also missing save for a single example from the OCU taking part in a quite protracted Strike Command set piece at Finningley. This was also the last year that as many as seven stations would be open on the same day; unexpected circumstances forced an unprecedented change in the strict format for 1973 while St Mawgan was no longer required.

Instead, the station commander at the Cornish base was quite happy to stage a comprehensive air day but on terms that better suited the local area. Thus, the first RAF St Mawgan International Air Day was held on Wednesday 8 August at the height of the holiday season and in the middle of the week when the tourist trade was at its most dense. The weekends tended to see the changeover with one bunch of punters leaving the sunny south-west while the next lot were only just arriving and not quite settled in before deciding where and what to do first.

The perennial question hanging over Biggin Hill cropped up again, having received approval to hold another 'At Home' in 1972; many years had passed now with each one in turn expected to be the ultimate gathering. The AFB had placed the Biggin Hill display under another review after 1971 determined to reach a final decision as to whether the effort required was worth it. The popularity of the RAF air show at Biggin Hill continued unabated even with the civilian-organised air fair earlier in the year, which one might expect would impact on attendances. HQ Training Command were responsible for the RAF element at Biggin Hill (still officially an RAF station due to the presence of the Officer and Aircrew Selection Centre) and therefore were primarily responsible for the direct management of the 'At Home' day.

Despite Biggin Hill being classed as an 'inactive' station, HQTC were still confident in reporting that the problems arising from staging the display were successfully overcome, albeit at the expense of a considerable deployment of unestablished personnel each time. More importantly, no undue organisational difficulties arose, but the RAF got on well with the local civilian operators at the aerodrome.

Apart from this, the CPC were unable to suggest a suitable alternative location where it would be easier to mount a comparable display. The department of trade and industry, together with Bromley Council, the latter were to become the new owners of the airfield, further endorsed HQTC's recommendation that Biggin Hill host a Battle of Britain display again in 1973.

9
1973–79

Since 1969, the RAF's front line had been re-equipping squadrons in the UK and Germany and withdrawing and disbanding units from the Far East. There were further economies to be absorbed with ongoing restructure, redeployments, and ever-diminishing resources. With changes happening at a fast tempo, the immediate years were going to see a mix of good and bad for defence planners.

The RAF were shortly to see a large chunk of the transport fleet disbanded while on the other hand the Jaguar was on the point of entering service. As far as the public forum and the display scene went, the Air Tattoo that had been held at North Weald over the previous two years had in that time outgrown the Essex aerodrome. Tim Prince and Paul Bowen had been looking around much of the south of England for a new airfield to accommodate what was now the International Air Tattoo. They looked over a few places with little confidence until they turned up at Greenham Common, a USAF base. In these days of lesser concerns about access security, save for the odd KGB spy or (specifically for British forces) the IRA, gaining entry even to an American military establishment, providing there was no sensitive material to hand, was relatively pain-free. Paul and Tim were directed to the base commander, who was mowing his lawn. A convivial conversation took place, and Greenham Common, a large airfield developed after the war to accommodate long-range bombers and tankers in times of tension, was now the venue for the 1973 IAT.

The RAF Benevolent Fund principally supported the new air show, now in its third year, and already presenting the largest and most diverse gathering of military hardware from across Europe along with extensive support from the USAF, who were of course hosting proceedings. Absent from the 'At Homes' until the early 1990s, perhaps due to the Battle of Britain focus, the Federal German Armed Forces turned up with a substantial list of wares. F-104s from both the Luftwaffe and *Marineflieger* were billed to fly along with other firsts—a French Navy F-8E Crusader and Neptune P2. This just scratched the surface, making IAT, if not widely recognised publicly, the pre-eminent air show in the UK, even perhaps Europe.

Left: Additional formations from operational units had all but disappeared by 1975. Fewer events and therefore better availability of officially assigned displays negated the need for them to fill in. These four Phantoms from 228 OCU had a full afternoon schedule ahead covering five stations, seen on 15 September 1973. (*Air Historical Branch*)

Below: The Red Arrows synchro pair over Abingdon, 15 September 1973. This photo is proof that tales about how much more game display flying was in earlier times are not entirely exaggerated. (*Air Historical Branch*)

The air staff faced a quite unexpected problem concerning Battle of Britain week in 1973. For the first time, events wholly unconnected were about to force a compromise affecting 'At Home' day. Of all the stations open in September, the one which most closely rivalled and at times bettered Biggin Hill for crowd numbers, Finningley, now faced local competition for public attendance from the nearby Doncaster Racecourse. One of the course's annual fixtures is the St Leger. Hitherto, this had not presented a problem as the St Leger Festival had always been held on a Saturday in mid-September, which is a puzzle as to how it had not interfered before now. In 1973, the St Leger was to go ahead on 15 September, then on 14 September 1974.

This posed a problem as RAF Finningley sits less than 10 miles away. A significant cut in attendance was certain. The Jockey Club was not particularly concerned if the RAF display clashed, yet the RAF were. Finningley was attracting an attendance of 250,000 each year. The undersecretary of state for the RAF, Sir Antony Lambton, contacted the senior steward of the Jockey Club, Major-General Sir Randle Feilden, to see if the St Leger could be held on an alternative date. He explained the practice of holding the 'At Home' displays at a selected number of RAF stations on the Saturday preceding Battle of Britain Sunday, which immediately follows the actual anniversary date, 15 September, or on that date itself if it coincided. This meant close planning and coordination between all the stations taking part. The programme was integrated and organised as a single overall event; it would naturally be undesirable for both events to clash given the close proximity.

With no give from the Jockey Club, the only option was to move the Finningley display to an alternative date—if necessary, re-scheduled to 8 September, while the other stations went ahead, as tradition dictated. This would mean organising a second 'At Home' day albeit for just this one station. Sir Antony maintained that to do this would, on this occasion, reduce the usual high standard of the flying display here, which could very well impact on public support. As the St Leger always took place on four days culminating on the second Saturday in September, the two had clashed previously in 1963 and 1968, when there does not seem to have been any concern.

The Jockey Club, by moving to the 15th, were occupying the third Saturday. After 1974, the next clash would not occur until 1985. In 1973, the St Leger had been moved for reasons that were not publicised as such. There was therefore the possibility that the race could be re-scheduled again between 1974 and 1985. With such importance placed by the Finningley display, it attracted such a large gate; the air staff clearly would wish to offer the best possible programme of events.

The RAF wanted the Jockey Club to work with them to come to an agreeable arrangement to avoid any possible future clashes. The senior steward sent a list of future St Leger dates, revealing more clashes in 1978 and 1979. A meeting was arranged for 10 May 1973. With the one clear factor being the likelihood of the racecourse event landing on Battle of Britain Saturday randomly through the years ahead. Therefore, the solid format of the 'At Home' day was going to have to compromise.

In 1973, the idea of introducing an alternative or additional day was not popular. The expectation was that a much greater demand on resources would be inevitable, being further into summer. However, the example of the locally arranged air days held

These two Harriers do not represent a display team or formation; one is the solo performer, the other is the spare. They are departing Leuchars for either another display commitment or home, 14 September 1974. The practice of deploying a spare in case of technical faults has been a long-standing practice. (*eLaReF*)

The traditional Leuchars Lightning and Phantom formation display teams, 14 September 1974. (*eLaReF*)

Fouga Magisters of the Belgian Air Force, Diables Rouge—another European aerobatics team that became a regular visitor, seen over Leuchars, 14 September 1974. (*eLaReF*)

Clear-up at the end of the day as RN and RAF personnel make a start on dismantling barriers after the 1974 Leuchars display. The day would not end for the station personnel until the 'Fod Plod' (Foreign Object Damage Patrol) takes place. This is the slow traipse down the runway by all, including the CO, looking for anything that can be hoovered up by an engine. (*eLaReF*)

by the Navy, the USAF and those of other RAF stations provided some evidence of the expedient of spreading the effort through the summer. This now worked well for the St Mawgan IAD. The nearby naval air station at Culdrose followed a similar format, usually picking the last Wednesday in July.

It is perhaps because the other service events and the local RAF air days were seen as lacking the prestige, resources, and significance afforded those associated with the set-in-stone week in September. The acting undersecretary of state (air), Mr A. D. Harvey, suggested that when his boss met with Sir Randle Feilden, he should tell him that due to the demand on resources it would not be possible to stage a separate 'At Home' day at Finningley. Also, that there was no other suitable location in the region that could stage the event instead, not without altering its whole character and size. If that failed to get the Jockey Club to budge, a final compromise suggestion should be proposed. While the RAF would make alterations by moving the Finningley display to alternate dates in 1973 and 1974, they would hope that the Jockey Club would reciprocate by choosing an alternate date in later years as there was greater flexibility in the racing calendar 'and we would hope that they could so arrange their affairs that a clash would not arise again, or at least not more frequently than say once every ten years.'

Following the meeting between the undersecretary and Sir Randle on 10 May, the upshot was that while the St Leger could not be re-scheduled in 1973–74, future dates would be looked at. It transpired in the conversation that the RAF might serve the Jockey Club with, by way of a favour, some reconnaissance flights to conduct aerial surveys of the major racecourses across the United Kingdom. The request was passed to the RAF from the undersecretary. The belief of course was that this favour would be instrumental in getting the Jockey Club to reconsider their dates for 1978 and 1979. Otherwise, Sir Randolph explained that with some 950 racing fixtures to organise each year there was little room for manoeuvre, therefore severely limiting the choice of dates.

Sir Randolph did say that they would review the dates for 1978 (16 September) and 1979 (15 September) in order to try and leave these free for Finningley. Also, the club were made aware that the RAF were able to supply the club with aerial photos of the courses at Epsom, Ascot, and Doncaster. A later letter in June that year from Sir Randolph asserted that he had given no such undertaking in his meeting with Sir Lambert, permanent undersecretary (air), that they could alter the dates of the St Leger in 1978 and 1979 but said 'that you never know whether the Doncaster Corporation might not once again ask for the St Leger to be run on a Wednesday as it used to be.' As it transpired, the Finningley display, held on 8 September 1973, was as impressive as any previous one and in fact benefited by finding a window in the calendar of the various Training Command aerobatics teams and Strike Command solo displays that were rationed among the six other stations the following week. Again, reflecting upon calls for several displays to be spread through summer, culminating in September, allowed all to benefit from the chance of a greater availability of aircraft.

The year 1974 brought a significant reduction in the number of Training Command aerobatics teams; this included a new display team flying old aircraft, which had its public debut in 1973. The Dragons or Red Dragons, from 4 FTS based at Valley, flew a display with four Hunters in the gloss red and white of the command's latest paint scheme—essentially a series of formation flying drill manoeuvres, various tight formation turns, and climbs. It was to have run on into 1974 with its repertoire expanding into a full-formation aerobatics sequence. They displayed over Finningley and Leuchars in 1973.

In 1974, fuel restrictions and the rationalisation of the overall training programme put the kybosh on such plans. The oil crisis began in October 1973 when the OPEC nations imposed an embargo against those countries perceived as supporting Israel in the Yom Kippur conflict. By March 1974, the price of oil had quadrupled. The embargo was lifted that month, but the damage had been done, and economic measures were unavoidable, at least in the short term. This meant a very radical change to display policy.

Air Marshal Sir Neville Stack, AOC-in-C Training Command, proposed that from 1975, a sole extra team (to the Red Arrows) would be placed on a more formal footing. He based this on there being no more give in the training system that could provide sufficient capacity to form any additional 'unestablished' teams. £80,000 was also required to keep the one team running, which Sir Neville was keen to maintain for all the usual reasons, aid to recruiting, bolstering British prestige abroad and improving the climate for defence sales.

The one additional JP team formed in 1974 was drawn from No. 3 FTS based at RAF Leeming. The Swords were a popular substitute for the Red Arrows and were seen to provide a lead-in training unit for future Red Arrows pilots, but what truly gave a shot in the arm to the future of aerobatics teams was royal interest. The commandant of RAF Cranwell had received a letter from the private secretary to the queen. Sir Michael Charteris wrote that her majesty hoped very much that it may prove possible to re-form the Poachers (the Jet Provost team at the RAF College). This may be regarded as good an endorsement as one could imagine, but it was not to have a great deal of impact. The air member for personnel, Air Marshal Sir Neil Cameron, was not confident that the conditions existed to allow for another formal RAF aerobatics team to be established.

The AMSO, Sir Anthony Heward, himself a former Finningley station commander, was concerned at the loss of expected savings in terms of add backs such as this one, and DUS(AIR) had also expressed doubts about the idea. The chairman of the Participation Committee concurred. Instead, the Swords were discontinued in 1975 and the Poachers resumed. Despite the fuel restrictions of 1974, the Harrier OCU, as was invariably the case, found itself heavily committed with flying displays. They provided a tactical demonstration by four aircraft and a solo VSTOL demonstration for General Gerhardt Limberg, chief of staff of the Luftwaffe, during a visit in September. The same displays were flown respectively at St Athan and Finningley on 14 and 21 September while Flt Lts Jennings and Marshal flew full solo displays each at Biggin Hill and Leuchars.

Farnborough was back this year with the largest international line-up so far accrediting the event with the title 'Farnborough International'. Four SAAB J-37 Viggens, new in service, were deployed from F7 Wing of the Royal Swedish Air Force. The USAF sent the SR-71 Blackbird and the US Army sent a Blackhawk close support

Left: Diamond 16 Flypast over Leuchars, 15 September 1973. 43 Sqn Phantoms lead, with the navy's 892 Sqn Phantoms on the flanks while 23 Sqn Lightnings fill the slot. Robert Prest, author of *F-4 Phantom: A Pilot's Story,* is flying one of the 43 Sqn aircraft that he described in his book.

Below: The Poachers during display rehearsal. The team were the last of a variety of Jet Provost-equipped aerobatic teams, finally disbanding at the end of 1976. (*AHB*)

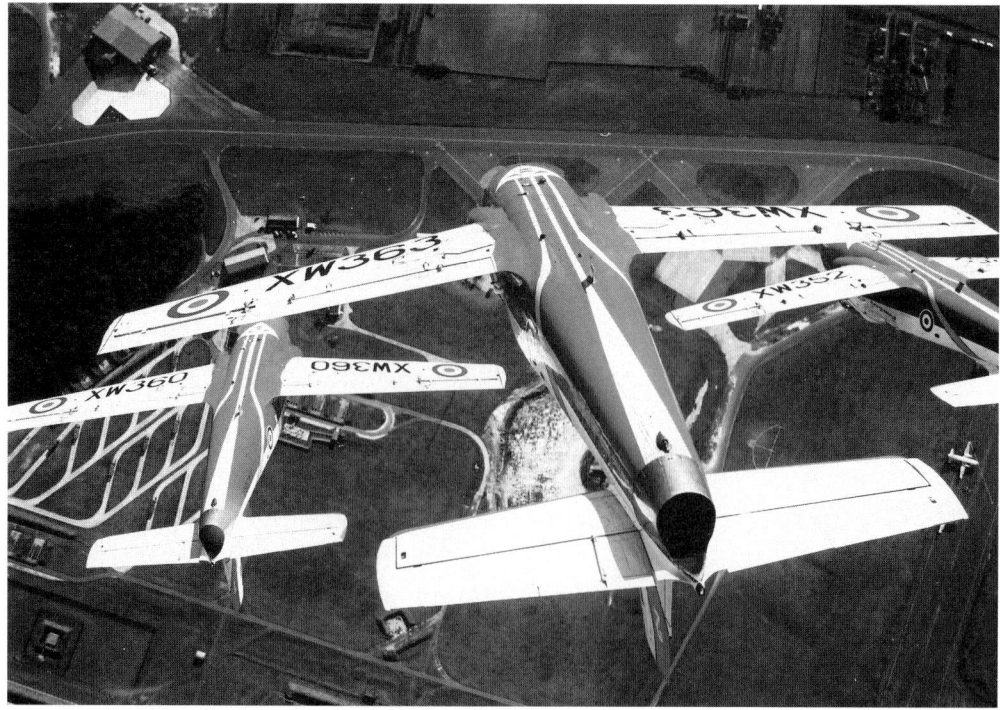

helicopter, which crashed on the first day, Sunday 1 September. As Farnborough had its public days on 6th, 7th, and 8th of the month, Finningley's alternate date was pushed back to the 21st.

The RAF'S special contribution to Farnborough was a tactical demonstration by fresh out of the box Jaguars, four from 6 Sqn alongside eight Harriers from 1 Sqn. The four RAF 'At Homes', taking place following Farnborough, presented the Jaguar for the first time, appearing either solo or as part of similar set pieces.

After the fuel crisis of 1973–74, a further reduction in the size of the RAF was on its way following a change of government. Just four stations were approved to host Battle of Britain displays in 1974—Biggin Hill, Finningley, Leuchars, and St Athan. All four were picked to maintain regional representation, covering the entire UK, which consequently placed those living in far-away locations outside any reasonable travelling distance.

The selection of four again for 1975 was again due to fuel shortages and consequent cuts following reduced manpower. For 1976, the air force board had originally approved an increase to five 'At Home' stations but with no further increase in the now established form for providing aircraft displays, even the maximum use of all that was available and with priority afforded to the big four, a good deal of stretch was evident.

The year 1975 was comparatively thin, with no Farnborough or Greenham Common and all four remaining 'At Homes' back on a single day. The year was also marred by tragedy; despite a recent policy change, two solo Harrier pilots were approved. One, Flt Lt Stephen Beckley, following a display at RNAS Yeovilton on 6 September, was killed when the ejector seat operated as he dismounted from the cockpit. There was no order to ground all Harriers pending investigation. The remaining pilot, Flt Lt Marshal, flew two solos at Biggin and Finningley two weeks later, while 1 Squadron took part in an extensive set piece also at Finningley, with aircraft borrowed from the OCU. The form since 1971 moved toward appointing typically one official solo display pilot/crew per type regarding Strike Command fast jets. Yet there were quite few types now with the RAF mostly transitioned from a strategic to a tactical force— Lightning, Jaguar, Phantom, Buccaneer, Harrier, and an occasional Hunter. The same limitations were not applied to larger aircraft or training types. Therefore, impressive fast jet solos, despite the variety, were at a premium.

There were, in 1975–6, three formal aerobatics teams: The Red Arrows, the Poachers, and a synchronised aerobatics team of two Bulldog primary trainers known as the Bulldogs; there was still also a helicopter team, the Gazelles, flying four Westland Aerospatiale Gazelles—someone thought long and hard about naming the last two. In addition, there was the now institutionalised Battle of Britain Memorial Flight and free fall team, the Falcons. Solo helicopter displays continued to be rather more hit and miss or *ad hoc* such as SAR demonstrations. Displays by aircraft and crews outside the established line up were only permitted for major events. The board also accepted that an extra special effort would need to be made in 1977 for the royal silver jubilee display.

Thereafter, the RAF would face a difficult task in maintaining its position in the public eye. All the previous defence reviews and the inevitable resulting defence cuts had reduced the RAF to what was described as the 'minimum size', which said

Pumas in action, again demonstrating the role of aircraft of what was then the RAF's 38 Group, Air Support Command, this time over Finningley, 20 September 1975. (*John Fisher*)

everything. No spare capacity was available from training and operational tasking. This left, in the eyes of the Air Force Board, very little scope for presenting the RAF to the public. In 1976, the pressure was on Support Command, which included all flying training units, to pick up the slack. It was the last year that a Jet Provost aerobatics team flew. The Poachers and the Gazelles both folded at the end of the year. So, for the especially busy silver jubilee year, only the Red Arrows were available in terms of teams.

It was also to be the last year that Biggin Hill would hold an RAF-organised 'At Home'. The previous year, the AFB called upon the Participation Committee to take a more determined look for an alternative to Biggin Hill but also to examine in detail the financial implications of these events.

It was considered too late to find an alternative for 1977; Biggin Hill was, as of December 1975, already in the preliminary planning stages for September 1976. The following year, all effort was concentrated on the royal silver jubilee, with all three services staging flagship events—the army chose the garrison at Senelager in Germany; the navy chose Spithead; and the RAF chose a location suitable but not necessarily a nationwide familiar name: Finningley. This meant that the Battle of Britain display would have a change of format and date for 1977. The navy hosted HM Queen Elizabeth II first, in June, being the senior service. The army came next on 7 July, then last but by certainly no means least, the RAF was on 29 July.

Above: The year 1976 marked the bicentenary of the declaration of American independence. These three F-111s from the 20th TFW, seen over Leuchars, toured all four RAF 'At Home' stations, 4 September. (*eLaReF*)

Right: Three F-111Es of the 20th TFW USAF conduct their demonstration over Greenham Common in July 1976, also marking the bicentenary of the US Declaration of Independence.

Left: Cover for the 1977 queen's silver jubilee royal review of the RAF. The same programme was issued for the public silver jubilee air show the following day when a more comprehensive and extensive flying programme was flown. (*Author's Collection*)

Below: Close-up of a section of the silver jubilee flypast. (*The National Archives*)

Right: The full list of what was at the queen's silver jubilee, 29–30 July 1977, as advertised in the local press. (*The National Archives*)

Below: During the proceedings on the review day, Mr Fred Mulley, defence secretary, appeared to be overcome with the pace of the dynamic flying display. In fact, this Dunkirk veteran had been up all night in London overseeing the final touches of the jubilee. The queen and Prince Philip took it all in their stride. (*The National Archives*)

THE Queen and Prince Philip were clearly fascinated. Their eyes riveted skywards, watching the R A F's magnificent Red Arrows aerobatic team. But what was Defence Secretary Fred Mulley doing during the Silver Jubilee review of the R A F at Finningley, near Doncaster? He is pictured in the kind of pose — or is it repose? — that politicians often adopt. It looks distinctly like he's been caught napping . . . Z-Z-Z-Z-Z-ZOOM!

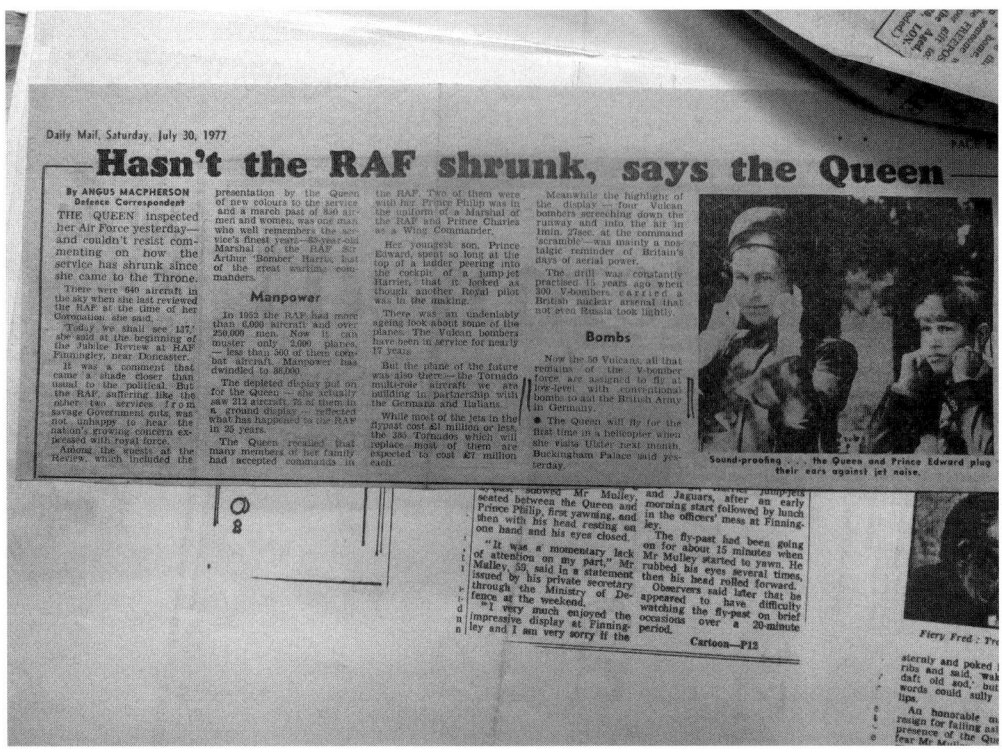

Above: The government constantly defends yet further defence cuts as fat trimming to concentrate on capability; indeed, *The Daily Mail* reported HM's observation regarding the size of the RAF in 1977. (*The National Archives*)

Left: This supplement detailing the flying programme appeared in all of the local papers. (*The National Archives*)

The following day, 30 July, the general public were invited onto the station for the official royal silver jubilee RAF display. The event attracted the Royal Australian Air Force, who brought along an F-111C which flew a dramatic solo display sequence, such as never permitted by USAF examples, certainly not this side of the pond. The display finale included a rare demonstration of fuel dump and torching, creating an enormous flame that followed the jet like a giant Bunsen burner.

There was a solo demonstration by the pre-production Panavia Tornado, still widely being referred to as the MRCA. The Tornado had flown at IAT Greenham Common a couple of weeks earlier, meaning this was likely the second public display in the UK outside Farnborough. The first non-trade show appearance was probably at Greenham Common in June. Many RAF stations held open days through the season; the comparison of official Battle of Britain displays to independent open days had now reached an inverse proportion. Come September, just two venues were available to officially celebrate the few—Leuchars and St Athan—on 10 September, a week early due to NATO exercises. The weather did not do much to help this year, after having been kind to other events through the summer. Finally, for the first time, there were no Battle of Britain displays in in England due to the time taken to select a replacement for Biggin Hill and the use of Finningley to host the RAF's silver jubilee salute to the queen.

The impression, growing since the late 1950s, that the prominence of the Battle of Britain was flagging led to a further review on top of the search for a Biggin Hill replacement. Staff studies that had been ongoing since 1976 were soon completed on the future of Battle of Britain 'At Home' days. Three main aims of the participation programme were to keep the air force in the public eye to maintain the support for the service and a sympathetic interest in air force activities, both at home and abroad. The staging of displays at RAF stations had proved to be highly successful over the years in sustaining each of the aforementioned aims.

The entertainment value and dramatic impact were such that they attracted huge audiences and were making a most favourable impression. Furthermore, the RAF is on display in the environment in which they have their *raison d'être*. Staff studies had by 1977 reached a format as to how to proceed with the Battle of Britain 'At Home' days.

Maintaining support and a sympathetic public view of the RAF together with encouraging young people to wander into the local career information office were all believed to be best served by 'live' displays on RAF stations. The impact of demonstrations by the higher performance military aircraft was duly noted. Individual displays by operational aircraft were restricted; the operating costs were by far away the highest of all. Economies and continued commitments over the years had come to suggestions of displaying certain aircraft only under certain circumstances. The principle for demonstrating front-line aircraft in 1977 was that they could only be permitted if the aim was to support defence sales interests. As one senior officer remarked, as far as principles were concerned, this was a poor one. Whatever the pressures, Battle of Britain 'At Home' days were to stay based on equitable geographical locations. A small number of large displays was to be the aim rather than the considered alternative, which was to hold a larger number of smaller displays.

Seen here over Boscombe Down during the TVS-sponsored fiftieth anniversary of the Battle of Britain air show in June 1990 is an RAAF, 6 Sqn, F-111C demonstrating its unique fuel dump and torch as a finale to its display. This same demonstration was performed at the Finningley royal silver jubilee in July 1977; I do not believe this has been seen in the UK at any other time. (*Adrian Balch*)

Perhaps only the second appearance of a Panavia Tornado, outside of Farnborough, running past at high speed, seen at Finningley, July 1977. (*Air Historical Branch*)

Even if it is just a flypast, rehearsals are required. These three Vulcans represent each operational squadron of the Scampton Wing; they are seen here on 27 July 1977, practising alone, for their walk on part in the queen's silver jubilee review and air show over Finningley. (*Adrian Balch*)

More silver jubilee-assigned Vulcans, this time from the Waddington Wing—four aircraft altogether conduct a quick reaction scramble. Spot the Harrier GR3 in the bottom left. This aircraft is one of six from 3 Sqn deployed to present a tactical role demonstration. (*Air Historical Branch*)

The silver jubilee flypast was essentially divided into separate formations, each representing an operational group or command. This is the 11 Group formation (air defence), comprising two Lightnings, two Victor Tankers (forming the stem), four Phantoms, and three Canberras (representing ECM and Target Facilities). A Shackleton AEW2 aircraft not in shot brought up the rear. (*Air Historical Branch*)

The latter would doubtless engender good local relations. Just as in 1946, the air staff of 1977 seemed to have a change of heart regarding the Battle of Britain, after the growing doubts about public sympathy during the intervening years. Yet as the RAF's principal battle honour, it should not be forsaken for quantity. The 'At Homes' held in conjunction with Wings Appeal each September was the most appropriate way to continue to commemorate such an historic campaign and as such was well established in the public mind. The ability of RAF stations to hold regular open days separately, without detriment to their operational or training tasks, was limited. The standing Battle of Britain 'At Home' commitment allowed each station involved to build up expertise in holding the event and set a precedence for developing a routine with local authorities such as councils and police. Charity was not the foremost reason for such events, but it was an important one; there was unlikely to be an increase in returns through reliance on more local open days held on a more unpredictable basis.

On the negative side, major NATO exercises seemed to be more prevalent around September. This naturally impacted on the availability of front-line aircraft and manpower then there was the SBAC show at Farnborough, which continued to be very well supported by the RAF. Up until 1976, save for the circumstances occasionally affecting Finningley, all the 'At Homes' continued to be held as a single nationwide event.

The AFB took this into consideration along with the demand on resources by having more than two large events held on the same date. In future, no more than two 'At Homes' would be held on Battle of Britain Saturday while two more would be held the Saturday before. This was seen as still in keeping with tradition as it framed Battle of Britain week and Wings Appeal. One suggestion was to have four stations earmarked but only two should hold 'At Homes' each year. This was rejected as was the further idea of dropping the replacement for Biggin Hill and instead simply sticking with the three remaining established stations, while increasing the level of flying participation at open days in the south and south-east.

The now biennial International Air Tattoo held at Greenham Common was identified as worthy of equal or greater priority for participation. The success of IAT prompted a suggestion that a single station in the south of England might also be used to stage a comprehensive 'At Home' day every other year as an alternative to the IAT, when it was not on. The organisers of the IAT were keen for the RAF to support the tattoo as a Battle of Britain event, even though it was held mid-summer. The impact of the display at Biggin Hill in terms of the growing disruption, affecting personnel from other stations including those based at Biggin, could no longer be explained satisfactorily. Simply not being an RAF controlled airfield equalled unsuitable.

The air member for personnel, responsible for overseeing and overhauling the whole endeavour of RAF public event participation, rejected the idea of blending a service Battle of Britain display with the Greenham Common IAT because Greenham was not an active RAF airfield either and the IAT was held in July. The RAF presence on the ground and in the air would not be significantly prominent.

The support from the RAF to the tattoo was paid for by the RAF Benevolent Fund, but the RAF's preferred way forward, for reasons of principal, was the traditional approach, which was to continue with four Battle of Britain 'At Homes' each September. As for IAT, the RAF Benevolent Fund, every other year, would request significant RAF support for which they were never denied. Now the short-term

Harrier XV759, originally issued as GR1, seen here upgraded to GR3 standard and still with the OCU, taxiing at Greenham Common, July 1977. The SNEB rocket pods indicate participation in a tactical role demonstration this time. (*Chris England*)

task was to find a new Biggin Hill, another station which could take up the cudgels where the iconic former fighter station left off. The working party, set up by the CPC chairman, reported back in October 1977.

They had considered no fewer than sixteen active RAF airfields as a replacement for Biggin Hill. Twelve of those were, for a variety of reasons, discarded as clearly unsuitable. The shortlist included Abingdon, Odiham, Wattisham, and Wyton. Each was therefore looked at in closer detail. Abingdon had much to recommend it, sitting further away than Biggin Hill, but not too far from London. Apart from having been an 'At Home' station on and off into the early 1970s, the base also had the potential to attract an even larger crowd than Biggin had in the last few years. It was central, meaning TV stations in London, Southampton, Bristol, and Birmingham were all sufficiently close. As well as holding Battle of Britain displays previously, it was the venue for the RAF's official golden jubilee review by HM Queen Elizabeth II in June 1968. It also had drawbacks. The station had changed roles since 1973, when it last hosted an 'At Home'. Abingdon was listed surplus to requirements following the 1974 Defence Review.

As the review took a big bite out of air transport at the time, Abingdon as a 38 Group, Air Support Command asset, was not for the chop. However, a rethink resulted in it becoming a home for the deep maintenance, repair, modification, and air testing of the new Jaguar Force. Shortly thereafter, the new Hawk advanced trainers also utilised the cavernous purpose-built Beverley maintenance hangar. In time, other aircraft were included and the heavy demand on manpower that the long job description might imply was not misplaced.

Thus, Abingdon's new role could make it difficult to provide the necessary facilities for an 'At Home' day without disrupting the station's primary task. There would also need to be an arrangement to detach personnel from other RAF stations to cope—the very problem that helped bring about Biggin Hill's demise in this regard. However, adjacent airspace restrictions were not expected to cause any trouble, and the necessary clearances would be easier to obtain than for Odiham. Yet for all the advantages, Abingdon hardly qualified as an active airfield in the sense that somewhere like Wattisham was. Additional staff would also need to be brought in to augment Air Traffic Control and airfield support services. Adequate parking was calculated for 14,000 cars. This assumed that the east–west runway would be used as the display line rather than the much longer north–south strip, which would be better utilised for parking. Additional space for parking was expected to be negotiated with local landowners.

Hangar space was described as inadequate, which was rather counter intuitive given the number of hangars at Abingdon. Accommodation for deployed personnel and others was also limited. Odiham, located in Hampshire further south, was situated in an area otherwise not possessed of a noticeable RAF presence. This station would be a more sugar-coated pill for those who had become attached to Biggin Hill for their annual September pilgrimage to pay homage to the few. Odiham was assessed to have good road access up to the last few miles where local access roads were considered poor and with no local bus service. On this latter point, it was expected that a special service for the day could be laid on if required.

A rare performance from a French Navy Etendard IV is completed with the brake chute deployed on landing. This was the occasion of the long hot summer of 1976, and the final RAF organised 'At Home' at Biggin Hill. (*Rob Finch*)

Another glimpse of the ultimate Biggin Hill, RAF Battle of Britain display, 4 September 1976. 4 FTS Gnat and Bulldog in a corner of the Static Park. (*Rob Finch*)

Odiham's airspace sits close to controlled airspace for civil air traffic, but gaining the requisite airspace block or necessary clearance was not thought to present a serious problem as precedent already existed with nearby Farnborough. However, Odiham lacked 'organic approach control'; they did not have the facilities for precision approach, but again, Farnborough was operationally linked and could provide this service.

This would be a necessity as flying displays would otherwise be severely curtailed by any worsening or forecast bad weather. As far as experience was concerned, Odiham was the venue for HM Queen Elizabeth's coronation review of the RAF in June 1953. Yet while this suggested a similar history to Abingdon for hosting a prestigious royal event, it was not particularly relevant as it was some time ago. Odiham had little recent experience of holding open days and 'At Homes'. The hangar space was adequate, as were other airfield facilities. RAF Odiham in 1977, as in the present, was a helicopter base with plenty of operational flying and at the time heavily committed to supporting operations in Northern Ireland, Belize, and ACE. Resident were 33 and 230 Squadrons operating Pumas and 72 Squadron with Wessex, all based here alongside 240 OCU with both types.

This did not stand in the way of the station becoming an 'At Home' venue, but like several stations, it was also committed to various NATO exercises each September. There were also concerns that student training on the OCU could be disrupted, though this did not seem to be a problem at Finningley, the largest flying training station in the UK.

What was harder to reconcile given the political climate of the times was that there were specific security considerations in the case of Odiham. The station's involvement in the Northern Ireland situation, the likelihood that the Hampshire base may present an overly tempting target to the IRA, could not be ignored.

One more drawback was the biannual SBAC show across the road at Farnborough. This impacted on Odiham, when it was held every other September, due to the air traffic circuit overlap, so any confliction of interest and overstretch would need to be avoided. All this paled though after a recent survey by the security branch, commissioned by the working party, advised that as well as inadequate local access roads, car parking was deemed to be likewise. This then left two more; first, Wattisham, near Ipswich, was home to two squadrons of F-4 Phantom interceptors. This station had that one thing going for it that the Participation Committee put a good deal of store by—it was a front-line operational station, like Leuchars. It was considered close enough to London. On the other hand, the location itself was thought to be poor and still a few miles away from London. The catchment area was also poor, access roads were not too good, and space for car parking was limited. The standards the working party set themselves were very demanding indeed. Wattisham had held Battle of Britain 'At Homes' previously, most recently 1972. Space for visiting aircraft was also considered not good enough, but again, the station's role was seen as 'amenable to "At Home" days with adequate hangarage available and no airspace restrictions'. Finally, Wyton, in Cambridgeshire, had excellent road access and facilities but sat perhaps too far north, which may not attract a sizeable attendance from London and the Home Counties.

Nevertheless, it had a reasonable catchment area of its own, which did infringe on the Finningley patch slightly. On the downside, being just inside East Anglia, the area had quite a few operational RAF and USAF stations surrounding it. So from a PR point of view, the location was less than ideal insofar as reaching an area of the population relatively remote from military aviation activity.

Yet the major drawbacks of Wyton were the sensitive nature of a part of the station's task and the effect that an air show could have on the operational posture, for which reasons HQ Strike Command stated that Wyton should not be considered. There was also concern about conflicting interests with the operational activities of the nearby USAF bases. Of the four stations short listed, Abingdon was chosen to line up with Finningley, Leuchars, and St Athan; from here on, they became the four permanent official locations. Change, in part, had been forced by the number of times Finningley, now attracting the largest crowd, had to move to an alternative date to avoid the St Leger.

The further purpose was to spread the resources, manpower, and opportunities far more evenly. Opinions of the rest of the air staff were broadly in agreement with only one concern—that the stations selected might have more of an operational flavour about them, Leuchars notwithstanding. The selected stations earned their bread and butter in flying training and aircraft maintenance roles. The attraction of the operational element was straightforward; they usually had the added feature of front-line assets.

Static display at Leuchars, 2 September 1978. (*The National Archives*)

By the end of the 1970s, F-100s were very rarely seen; this is an example from the Royal Danish Air Force over Abingdon, 15 September 1979. (*Air Historical Branch*)

Captain Hans Van Der Werth of the KLU lifts off Finningley's runway to start what was the final display by the Dutch F-104 in the UK, 8 September 1979. The jet for all the world appears to be smiling as the shark's mouth is just about discernible. (*Shaun Connor*)

To seek airfields with interesting home-based stuff was understandable, even though it departed from the original aspiration and general purpose but certainly made sense. Alas, the demands of geography and demographics dictated otherwise. There was also an expected underspend of resources forecast for the period 1978–79. This was used to increase the number of contacts with the public. Regarding the latter suggestion, the AMP had intended to find the right kind of balance between the spread of four Battle of Britain 'At Homes' as a reasonable compromise between public engagement, encouraging recruitment, and maintaining service prestige and access to resources to support it.

Accepting the size of the British mainland alone, huge areas of the country inevitably remained untouched by the revised effort to try and represent the regions, while the media over the years had lost the interest they once had. Another plan for the underspend was to look again at increasing the number of 'At Homes' from four to five or even six, if only temporarily. This would reach a more comprehensive demographic, then later returning to just four principal events when the additional available resources had dried up. There were the local open days/air days that mostly fell outside the catchment areas of the big four. Any additional resources could be used to support them. Kinloss, Shawbury, St Mawgan, and at least one East Anglia station were considered locations that could draw on untapped resources. The open days were always viewed as augmentation to the Battle of Britain four rather than alternatives.

Another option for the underspend was to ease the principle that front-line aircraft should only display at venues where there was a defence sale possibility. The AMP would further investigate the possibility of providing additional financial and material support to those stations conducting such open days during 1978, but outside the scope of the Battle of Britain celebrations. The year 1979 carried some significance for the now established institution better known as the Red Arrows. The team flew their last public display equipped with the Folland Gnat. The last display was flown over Abingdon on Saturday, 15 September. The following month, the team received their first BAE Hawk T1. They have flown this aircraft ever since.

10

1980–90

The year 1980 marked the fortieth anniversary of the Battle of Britain. It was going to be marked by just three open stations—Abingdon on 13 September with Finningley and Coltishall on 20th. The latter being the only front-line station among the three was picked to provide some depth to the occasion and not see the date marked with just the other two. Leuchars and St Athan were both off the menu but not before each were reviewed as their suitability was now being questioned.

At the end of 1979, the AMP, Air Marshal Sir John Gingell, outlined his proposals for commemorating and celebrating the fortieth anniversary of the Battle of Britain and, in addition, the sixtieth anniversary of the founding of the RAF College Cranwell. As far as the former was concerned, the more formal thanksgiving end of the anniversary was perhaps much easier to embroider to a suitable degree. This was the service at Westminster Abbey on Sunday 21 September. Sir John recommended that a royal guest be invited to attend, reflecting on the thirtieth anniversary when nothing out of the ordinary had been done. Going further back to the twenty-fifth anniversary, following the church service that year, the queen and Prince Philip watched a flypast from the roof terrace adjacent to the defence council suite.

This plus the publication of an anniversary booklet were along the lines of what Sir John suggested on the pure ceremonial side. The Battle of Britain Pilots' Association were planning an additional public function. As far as the Battle of Britain 'At Homes' were concerned, he recommended the same effort and pattern of flying displays, which had been established during the 1970s, be continued but with an enhanced level of participation by the Battle of Britain Memorial Flight.

The format for a full display by the BBMF was the same in 1980 as it is today—the Lancaster accompanied by a single Spitfire and a Hurricane in a formation flypast. The three aircraft then departed to the hold while one of the fighters returned to fly a solo display followed by the next and finally the Lancaster alone, which the fighters then returned to form on for a final formation flypast. By September 1980, it was expected that the BBMF would have available the Lancaster together with four Spitfires and two Hurricanes. For this year, Sir John proposed that all available, serviceable BBMF aircraft should mount a flypast over each of the official 'At Home' stations, at about 500 feet. In addition, the BBMF should be accompanied by representative aircraft of their 1980 descendants—a Vulcan, a Lightning, and a Phantom. The flypast together with suitable commentary would form either the finale or opening item at each of the stations with the Red Arrows, in their debut display season equipped with the BAE Hawk, displaying at the opposite end of the flying display. The set of four stations would have to run one short; St Athan in Wales would be undergoing runway re-surfacing, there being no suitable alternative in the south-west.

Of the likely contenders, Brawdy was ruled out due to it being poorly served by road and heavily committed through the summer in support of the re-opening of RAF Chivenor in Devonshire. Both stations were to occupy similar roles as advanced tactical training units with Hawks and Hunters, forecast to expand from here due to the now imminent arrival in service of the Panavia Tornado. That Brawdy was dismissed on the grounds of a poor road layout was curious as both under Fleet Air Arm and RAF incumbency over the years, public air days had been held here numerous times and would continue to in the decade ahead. Sir John did say that 'extra support would be given to other events in the area throughout the season'. Further compounding the lack of venues was the absence of Leuchars from the line-up.

In 1979, Leuchars was omitted due to its runway being re-surfaced. In 1980, the ASM building programme (the construction of hardened aircraft shelters) and Exercise Teamwork 80 (North Atlantic Maritime Exercise) were the two principal reasons for why the sole Scottish 'At Home' location was for the second year running unavailable.

The CAS, Sir Michael Beetham, was concerned about the impact on public relations if this left just Abingdon and Finningley, both in England, to welcome the public on board to celebrate the fortieth anniversary. What was of greater concern was how Leuchars' extensive exercise programme could best be ensured not to prejudice the holding of further 'At Homes'. Exercise Teamwork was the biggest cause of the problem. Indeed, if Exercise Teamwork 80 was not on, it was feasible that Leuchars could have held a display as usual, albeit 'with great difficulty'. The ASM programme specifically precluded the use of the southern taxiway that was normally used for display aircraft movements. This then had the knock-on effect of reducing the usual space for spectators on the north side of the airfield, also limiting space for static aircraft. It would also impede the usual access route for vehicles and disrupt the standing car parking arrangements, all on the north side of the main runway.

Exercise Teamwork was just one of several major NATO exercises taking place in or around September each year. The dates were fixed two years ahead; this was seen as presenting an opportunity to plan future 'At Home' days around such commitments so that Leuchars and other stations would have a window available.

If this did not work, Headquarters Strike Command were to be instructed to ensure that other units took on teamwork commitments during the requisite Thursday to Sunday period that specifically needed to be set aside. Apart from this, the ASM programme would be in full construction swing at Leuchars during the next two years at least, therefore more likely to be a deciding factor during 1981 and 1982. The matter of addressing the RAF

College's sixtieth anniversary was easier to put together. The RAFC's big day was to be celebrated on 2 February with a formal mess dinner to which HRH Prince of Wales had been invited but could not attend due to commitments abroad.

A founder's church service would take place the following morning. As for the much wider public effort, there were several RAF stations holding open days as was now usual. The independent stations were almost invariably front line and able to cobble together plenty of off-piste stuff taking advantage of the home-based assets. Where they fared not quite as well was in assistance from the top brass as they were a slightly lesser priority, therefore they could not take for granted all or most of the available surplus.

Tragedy struck on 7 February, when Buccaneer XV345, from 15 Sqn based at Laarbruch in Germany, disintegrated over the Nevada Desert while taking part in the red flag exercise. The crew, Sqn Ldr Ken Tait and Flt Lt Charles Ruston, were both killed.

Typically, they were operating at cactus-clipping low level, which was very much their natural habitat. The cause was a crack in the main spar. If a force between 5 and 6 *g* was sustained, then there was every chance the main spar would break off and fail. As a result, the entire Buccaneer Force was grounded. This was a serious matter for the wider defence interests. The Buccaneers formed a third of the RAF Germany Tactical Strike Force and the anti-shipping role in the UK as well as rapid reinforcement.

The RAF's residual number of suitable Hawker Hunter jets was brought to the fore as an interim supplement. The situation nevertheless had to be resolved fast, not for the purposes of display flying you will understand but for defence of the realm purposes. Whatever the depth of American/NATO assets otherwise, this predicament presented an interesting development to the Kremlin and a nightmare to NATO defence planners.

As far as the immediate future and the fortieth anniversary of the Battle of Britain were concerned, the absence now of the Buccaneer from the public forum this year was to be redressed. The RAF chose to fill the gap, likewise, with a Hunter.

No. 234 Squadron, one of two units forming 1 Tactical Weapons Unit based at RAF Brawdy in Pembrokeshire, stepped up. Hunters were quite rare now but were prevalent this year. The FRADU (fleet requirements and air directions unit) continued, albeit in their final year, to run an aerobatics team of four Hunter GA11s, the Blue Herons, who seemed to manage a quite full diary through the summer. What was conspicuously absent in 1980 was overseas participation. Only in terms of flying, the US Air Force and other air arms were as prominent as usual in the static parks but not in the air. Overall, 1980 was quite lacklustre, considering the occasion, relative to recent times.

Prominent at Farnborough this year were the Royal Navy's new Sea Harriers. The RAF turned up with a thin selection—the Red Arrows, BBMF, and a solo Spitfire, Hurricane, and Lancaster. Although not yet in RAF hands, there were two prototype Tornado variants, but UK military hardware this year was overshadowed by the international stuff. The USAF sported the F-111F, F-15B, and F-16, while Sweden, France, and Italy presented respectively Viggen, Mirage 2000 (prototype), and MB339. From McDonnell Douglas, there was also a prototype F-18 Hornet. While the allied air arms were scarce elsewhere, they (or certainly the manufacturers) were prominent at the trade show.

The culmination of events in September brought good weather to Abingdon, while the following week, Coltishall and Finningley both sat under low cloud through much of the day, which further ensured the fortieth anniversary ended up being marked with a 'phut' rather than a 'bang'. Abingdon and Coltishall both planned combined aerial engagements and Land Battle set pieces, the larger and more protracted of which was organised for Coltishall. Despite the poor weather, at least eight of the home-based Jaguars got airborne to be intercepted by four Phantoms from Wattisham while a clutch of Pumas air-landed and evacuated troops, so perhaps not such a let-down after all.

Finally, the weather did not prevent each of the big three seeing the Tornado ADV prototype put through its paces. One proposal from a member of the public that got placed on the agenda for consideration was to have a 'Battle of Britain' public holiday formally recognised. The idea was suggested in November. The patriotic soul sent his letter to the prime minister, Margaret Thatcher, who in turn passed it on to the Department of Employment. They approached the Ministry of Defence for their view. The letter writer had suggested that the May Day Bank Holiday be abolished and instead a 'Battle of Britain Bank Weekend' be instituted instead. The letter writer did not clarify whether they expected the Monday following Battle of Britain weekend as the day of the public holiday.

The MOD response, and doubtless carrying representation of the RAF, was to explain that while the Battle of Britain continued to be commemorated each year, the ministry's official position was that it would be invidious to select any one of the victories gained by the Royal Navy, the army, and the Royal Air Force in the Second World War for perpetual commemoration in the form of a national bank holiday.

The year 1981 began with a review on the operational viability of the Red Arrows. The AFB had considered a war role for the BAE Hawk back in 1979. Out of the 175 aircraft the RAF had ordered, eighty-nine were assigned to the tactical weapons units. These aircraft were to have a limited air defence and offensive support capability and that thirty-six aircraft should be assigned to the UK's local air defence role.

The Red Arrows, having recently re-equipped with the Hawk, had no operational role. Now the AFB were looking at giving them a war role. The year 1981 was another year for significant defence cuts and quite severe, the RAF had to accommodate several cuts, two Canberra squadrons disbanded but at the same time the Tornado was being delivered. The Tornado had its debut public outing in 1981, with RAF crews at the helm. Overall, fixed-wing aircraft display participation was reduced by 10 per cent from the previous year. This was accounted for as the result of a 30 per cent reduction imposed on flying display participation.

The impact of this was minimised by trimming the level of RAF flying at major displays to allow some support at minor displays, which would have nothing otherwise. A wide geographical spread was maintained as a result. As there were relatively greater financial pressures during 1981, the Central Participation Committee were not about to reclaim the 30 per cent loss in contributions to public displays but advised the AFB that any further reduction in display resources would seriously damage the service's positive exposure to the public, resulting in damage to recruitment and the public image.

This argument was accepted and all remained convinced of the 'need for display flying to let the taxpayer see the aircraft he has paid for and to remind him that this country has a potent air force, but we recognise the need for economies in the display area as much as anywhere else'.

The 1981 review of participation had, in pursuit of economy, reduced the Red Arrows display to twelve minutes from about seventeen. It was determined that this had a positive effect by sharpening and enhancing the impact of the team's display. Therefore, by 1982, commanders-in-chief were to impose a reduction in the display durations for individual aircraft, the belief being that this would similarly enhance the effectiveness of most of them.

AOC-in-C Support Command was to be invited to examine the implications of a further cut in the Red Arrows' programme to about ten minutes. There were to be reductions in transport flying and so the support for the official teams would need 'skilful and imaginative planning'. Further economic choices were being planned, which would likely have a noticeable impact. Flying by RAF aircraft at the service's own stations was to be limited in future to the order of a maximum of two hours out of any flying programme. This it was believed would not significantly degrade the RAF's exposure to the public and would contribute to savings in fuel consumption.

Emphasis was placed on RAF-organised events in 1981. Altogether, fifteen RAF stations held open days with eleven families' days and station fêtes. All were well supported by RAF resources in addition to the four 'At Homes'. Altogether, 763 bids for RAF participation were received for 1981; of these, 273 were honoured. A sizeable amount of flying was approved early on, some of which had to be withdrawn beforehand, including twelve individual displays by Canberras and five by Shackleton aircraft all due to operational reasons. Then, midway through the display season, the Phantom solo display pilot was injured in a non-related incident. It was not considered economic to train a replacement, and in the face of reduced fuel allocations, Strike Command did not wish to substitute another aircraft type to make up the three remaining Phantom display commitments. UK-based aircraft also flew at eighteen events in Europe and two more in the USA and Canada with flypasts/displays by Nimrod and Vulcan on Exercise Ranger.

About fourteen static aircraft were provided from more Ranger participants. RAF Germany were relatively heavily engaged contributing to thirty-nine displays in West Germany and just two events elsewhere in Holland and Gibraltar, this effort compared with sixteen in 1980.

The public were reported not to have noticed the cuts in 1981 despite the flying effort having been significantly reduced. This was credited to the careful management of the number of events which were no fewer than in 1980 but the number of displays was certainly reduced.

Comparable Individual Display Aircraft Figures (Battle of Britain 'At Homes' and Queen's Birthday Flypast Not Included)

Strike Command

	1980	1981	1982
Harrier	10	7	6
Hawk	10	4	9
Jaguar	20	14	6
Hunter	10	7	-

Lightning	9	7	-
Phantom	6	3	9
Nimrod	8	7	2
Shackleton	12	5	2
Vulcan	15	9	6
Canberra	4	-	-
Tornado	-	-	7

Support Command

	1980	1981	1982
Jet Provost	10	7	16
Hawk	16	10	16
Vintage Pair	42	43	unk

The year 1982 brought a shift in the balance between aircraft from Support and Strike Commands. The latter was to limit the number of high-performance aircraft as the emphasis this year was to move away from fast jets.

The service still had four UK-based professional bands that were in high demand. There was also the Queen's Colour Squadron and the two police dog display teams, both assigned to the Royal Tournament at Earl's Court in 1982, which likewise remained fully committed through the year.

There was a standard format of priority allocation of resources generally. Priority 1 was events organised by the other services and the USAF. Priority 2 was for service charities, such as RAFA, SSAFA, and RAF Benevolent Fund. Then Priority 3 was for local authorities and other private bodies. The US Air Force had suspended open days on the continent this year in response to terrorist concerns, essentially in West Germany. The Baader-Meinhof Gang, the more specific terrorist threat to American bases here, had succeeded in planting 500 lb of explosives in a car parked outside HQ AAFCE, located in the middle of Ramstein airbase.

Earlier in the year, the Falkland Islands were invaded, and virtually the entire RAF Harrier Force together with all the Sea Harriers that the Royal Navy could muster made for the South Atlantic. The Falklands War is the last decisive military action that was fought single-handed by HM Forces and resulting in victory.

The opposition, Argentina, was likewise a single national and military entity. The campaign ended with the Argentine surrender on 14 June. This was as concise a military operation as anyone had any right to expect and was recognised by the RAF with a flypast of various aircraft that were involved either directly or indirectly and set-piece demonstrations at each display in September.

This year's Battle of Britain showcase saw Finningley and Leuchars go first on 4 September, a week earlier than would be the case due to Farnborough occupying the next weekend. Abingdon and St Athan were allocated 18 September, the Saturday preceding Battle of Britain Sunday. The alternate date was 25 September, but it was objected to on the grounds of shortening day light at Finningley and work services (continued work on HAS shelters) at Leuchars.

NATO contributions were thin compared with 1981. The Royal Netherlands Air Force displayed one of their NF-5A Freedom Fighters and the Grasshoppers helicopter display team. The USAF managed their standard flypasts—an F-111 and C-5A Galaxy over Abingdon and St Athan in the south. The RAF presence at Farnborough this year received a boost—9 Squadron, newly equipped with Tornados, put together a demonstration involving a formation routine. This was a worthy effort from 9 Squadron given the workload to achieve operational effectiveness as the first front-line Tornado Squadron.

By early 1983, the Tornado GR1 was rolling off the production line, and a rare concession regarding display policy—two GR1 crews, one from the TWCU and one from 9 Squadron—were approved to work up a solo display sequence. There was a point here in so far as the RAF was keen to dispel many rumours that continued to circulate about the Tonka's manoeuvrability not to mention general criticism. Too many eggs in one basket was a more sympathetic observation followed by 'not truly multi-role anyway'. However, agility and how crucial it would be when the ADV became available was a concern the RAF wanted to assuage. So perhaps it would settle some of the negative comments if everyone got to see how the chunkier bomber version could roll about with some add on extras.

Therefore, the 9 Squadron Tornado display flew with wing stores and drop tanks in order to demonstrate just how robust and agile the new addition to the front line was; the TWCU crew flew a clean wing aircraft. Alas, immediate comparisons were not available to those members of the public who were particularly keen to offer a personal judgement, as even the 'At Homes' were rationed to one or the other.

At the Paris Air Salon earlier in the year, a mock-up of a proposed airframe design for a 'Future European Fighter Aircraft' appeared among the indoor exhibits; 1983 also witnessed the official return to the display circuit of the Buccaneer. The Lightning had also returned to the display circuit following the fallow year that was 1982. Flt Lt Mike Thompson, the Lightning display pilot, having won the IAT Embassy Trophy for the best judged aerobatics display by an individual high performance single or twin-engine jet at Greenham Common in July, lost his life when flying an impromptu short display off Scarborough on 26 August. One RAF aircraft expected to be retired from the air show circuit at the end of 1981 and then at the end of 1982, soldiered on through 1983. The Vulcan still flew on in semi-retirement as an IFR tanker with 50 Squadron.

The early proposal was to run Vulcans on as a supplement to the Victors, but the scheme was short-lived. The new VC-10 K, one of which also flew at some displays, was by now ready to step up to the plate providing strategic air-to-air refuelling, thus also allowing the start of the rundown of the Victor K Force. After the 1981 cuts had taken effect, the years ahead actually brought the promise of a slight increase in the pure military front line of the RAF. The Falklands War may have had some influence here. The growth of the Tornado fleet—first the strike variant followed by the interceptor—meant an expansion of fast jet training and an increase in the inventory of both Strike Command and RAF Germany. Despite growing contractorisation, numbers of RAF personnel began to increase likewise.

In October 1984, the first production models of the Tornado F2 were flown into RAF Coningsby presaging the start of crew conversion. The F2 was not a definitive mark and was in fact quite useless as an all-weather fighter. The Foxhunter airborne intercept radar was not yet available and so a concrete lump was fitted inside the nose cone simply for weight distribution and balance.

The year 1984 followed the 1983 form of flying a clean wing-configured Tornado display from the TWCU, now assigned the operational reserve identity of 45 Squadron, and a heavy wing display from 27 Squadron based at Marham. The last of the Vulcans were withdrawn in early 1984. However, due to the aircraft's unique public popularity and dramatic impact at air shows, a single aircraft, XL426, was maintained in airworthy condition simply to continue being put through its paces on the display circuit. Selected aircrew took on the task. Displays by Vulcans in service were much more prevalent, but the RAF in the interests of public relations were willing to follow a hunch that this was a well-advised step. The delta-winged bringer of Armageddon continued to bring a fearful ear-splitting roar, providing many an air show punter some bonus opportunities to see and hear the Vulcan again.

The 'Vulcan howl' was a characteristic description referring to the jet's eerie strained roar brought on by a combination of aircraft attitude, throttle setting, and manoeuvre. Likewise, the Hawker Hunter created a strange wind-like rush of noise, earning the nickname the 'Blue Note'. The Vulcan's two stablemates, the Valiant and Victor, while equally prominent on the display circuit in their heyday, never had anything like the same impact on the public mindset. The Victor continued in service as a strategic reconnaissance platform but its adaptation as a tanker gave it a lease of life extending many years longer than the time spent as a bomber. In the latter role, the Victor was in very high demand and likely explains why in later years was far less prevalent at air shows; when seen, it was usually to flypast trailing hose with chasing fighters. Yet for all its sterling longevity and service, the Victor simply did not retain the same resonance with the public, and certainly no one in or out of the RAF felt the inclination to keep one airworthy.

The other venerable attention getter, the Lightning, having met with tragedy in August 1983, was back in 1984 with Flt Lt John Aldington of 11 Squadron in the hotseat.

Approved solo displays by operational aircraft were now almost always assigned to the OCUs in Strike Command, having a more settled flying programme with a line-up of instructor-qualified staff to pick and choose from.

Farnborough 1984 presented an essentially international line-up of military hardware; this year included USAFE-operated F-15C and F-16A, and from France came the Mirage F1 and prototype Mirage 2000 and 4000. There was a final chance to see a late entry rival contender to the F-16 and F-18—the F-20 Tigershark. This energetic lightweight fighter came from the Northrop stable; this was the first and last time it was bounced about the skies over Farnborough and it was phenomenal, but due to relaxed competition for overseas sales, the main aim of the cheap but value for money F-20 could not compete with the already established F-16.

There was a similar attempt at the overseas market made by Dassault. They demonstrated their Mirage IIING, a development of the original Mirage; it had canards and upgraded avionics but shared the same power plant as the Mirage F1. Like the F-20, it failed to find any worthwhile sales interest.

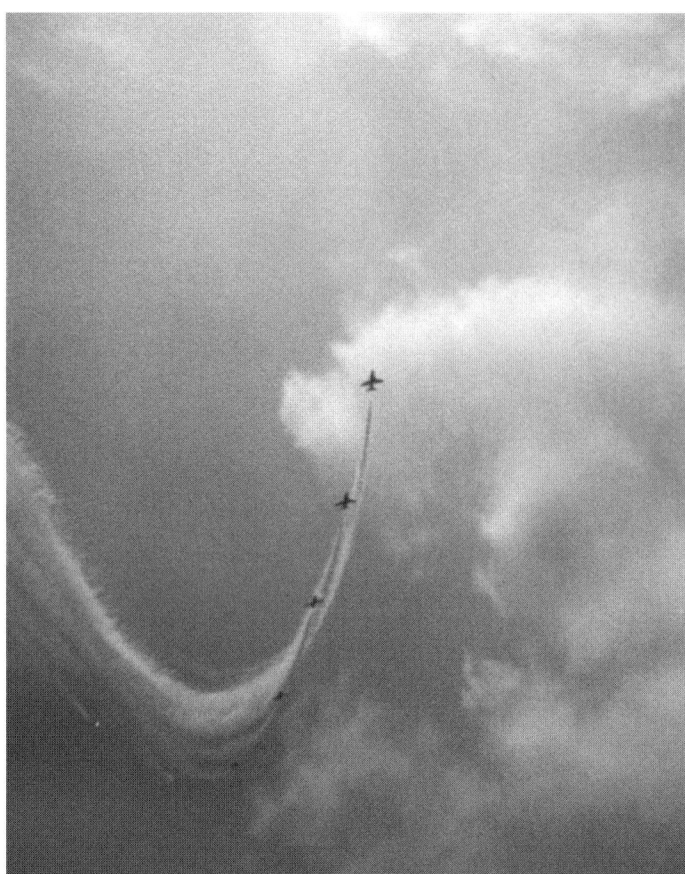

Left: The Red Arrows in 1984, Church Fenton. (*Author's Collection*)

Below: The Falcons free fall team line up for the ceremonial part of their display, the flypast by the transport/mount, in this case a C-130. Abingdon, 15 September 1984. (*AHB*)

From Italy came the AMX Centaur. Another one off was the A&AEE-operated SEPECAT 'flyby wire' Jaguar with its extended leading-edge faring. From the UK came the 27 Sqn Tornado and an RN 899 Sqn Sea Harrier. This was, relative to today, still the golden era of Farnborough.

The 1985 display season would not continue in quite the same vain as the previous ones. Fuel limitations were again imposed, this time severely and quite noticeably limiting the RAF's ability to allocate aircraft for public events. This resulted in media and public criticism of the RAF and its weakest ever showing. Much of the reductions came late on, and some events planned as late as June were already advertising a level of RAF participation that had to be withdrawn.

The weather across the season this year was the opposite of 1984—largely blustery and unpredictable, with few settled calm days that did not help. Nevertheless, the AFB Standing Committee reported that every effort had been made to utilise what there was to the very best advantage, but the loss of so many of the service's more interesting and impressive aircraft—essentially those provided by Strike Command—made the task of putting together worthwhile displays difficult. Their report concluded that a reasonable display effort had been achieved, but with some negative impact on PR and recruitment along the way.

Strike Command allowed something of a novelty display to run through the summer—a unique presentation of the then and now, presenting the latest addition to the RAF inventory, the pristine new Tornado ADV, or as it was at the time, the interim mark, the F2. The new fighter flew a synchronised aerobatics sequence with a Spitfire

The year 1985 brought a restriction in the level of RAF participation in air shows; the 'At Homes' received additional support from other NATO air arms, including the Belgian Mirage V seen here at Finningley, otherwise a very rare visitor other than at the International Air Tattoo. (*John Fisher*)

PRXIX from the Battle of Britain Memorial Flight. Allocated to only a handful of events which as expected included the first International Air Tattoo to be held at RAF Fairford, the four 'At Homes' and one or two other significantly prominent events. To avoid looking lacklustre, the embargo on other fast jet displays was partially lifted, allowing Harrier and Jaguar solo demonstrations in time for September. To remedy further shortcomings, a fair response was secured from the USAF and other NATO air forces, particularly Belgium and Holland. There was the occasional performance handling demonstration by other front-line aircraft—notably the previous year's F-4 demo crew flew such a routine at Leuchars, but as the table below shows, it was not counted officially.

RAF Public Display Comparisons
(Excluding Figures for Battle of Britain 'At Homes')

Strike Command

	1984	1985
Harrier	14	1
Hawk	9	NIL
Jaguar	5	1
Phantom	9	NIL
Tornado	10 (Tornado GR1)	1 (Tornado F2)
Nimrod	4	1
Shackleton	3	NIL
Lightning	10	NIL*
Buccaneer	8	NIL
Vulcan	10	10
Tornado F2/Spitfire	NIL	6
TOTALS	82	21

Support Command

Jet Provost	9	8
Hawk	10	8
Jetstream	2	NIL
TOTALS	21	16

Helicopters

Wessex/Sea King SAR	40	28
Gazelle	10	7
Puma/Chinook	7	NIL
Northern Ireland Wessex	4	NIL
TOTALS	61	35

The reduction in Strike Command displays in 1985 did not just stretch to fast jets, but also to rotary-wing types, Pumas, Chinooks, and the Northern Ireland Wessex were not available either. Demonstrations of Search and Rescue techniques were permitted by the SAR crews such was the level of curtailment. Support Command provided a reduced number of individual displays by the Gazelle.

The ten displays by the Vulcan were authorised by HQ Strike Command, what you might call active retirement. The RAF's predicted public demand for their latest out of service icon was not misplaced.

Bids from air show organisers were significantly more than the number of appearances that could be permitted. With Strike Command's permission, the Vulcan flew sometimes more than one display in a sortie and as many single flypasts as could be squeezed in, whenever they could be carried out as part of an already planned mission. The idea of the Tornado F2/Spitfire combination display was more of an original concept; it proved to be very popular, having started out as a kind of afterthought.

It was especially welcome given the restrictions on the front line and was also roundly well received. The poor summer weather brought five cancelled displays by the Red Arrows, but with no major incidents, the team still managed to honour seventy-four display bookings at seventy events across the UK and thirteen displays at twelve events overseas. The fuel restrictions were negotiated by using road transport as much as possible, thus reducing the amount of use of one of 38 Group's C-130 Hercules transport aircraft, themselves busy this year with the demands of aid relief to Ethiopia. The Red Arrows display sequence had expanded since 1981, leaving scope for a further fuel-saving measure; this was achieved by reducing the display sequence from eighteen to fourteen minutes. The high workload, even given the circumstances of 1985, testified to their high popularity. The team took in a wide and varied number of both military and civilian events, including fifteen mid-week seaside displays. The one display type that really gets hammered by even moderately inclement weather are free fall teams.

The RAF's Falcons free fall team sustained fifteen cancellations due to poor weather but still managed to jump at seventy-one public displays. The Falcons' other Achilles' heel was the amount that was charged for their displays. This resulted in them being withdrawn from twenty-seven other events consequently.

The Battle of Britain Memorial Flight completed a similar number of displays to the other permanent display teams with some variance, due to the fluid nature of their selection of display formats ranging from solos to all available aircraft. The total added up to fifty for the Lancaster, seventy-two for the Hurricane, and eighty-two for the Spitfire. In all, ninety-nine events were attended by one or more of the aircraft. Twenty displays were cancelled due to weather. After the Falcons, the BBMF are the most susceptible to weather conditions and the most affected by serviceability problems; six further displays were cancelled as a result. Another full-time RAF operated display team of the day was the Vintage Pair representing the RAF's first operational jet types—Meteor and Vampire. The two mounts were T-Bird (trainer variants)—a T Mk 7 and a T Mk 11 respectively. The VP completed forty-seven displays in 1985 at thirty-nine events, seven of these involved the Vampire alone. Six of their calendar

The manoeuvre executed by the Red Arrows, the 'Boomerang', in this picture, from Finningley, *c.* September 1985, was banned in the wake of the Ramstein disaster. (*John Fisher*)

dates had to be cancelled due to weather and three due to maintenance problems including the Rhine Army Summer Show. Attendance figures for the Battle of Britain 'At Homes' was quite contrasting accepting each was to accommodate a comparable region of the UK, the disparity in levels of attendance did not reflect the level of effort put into each. The figures for 1984 and 1985 are as follows:

	1984	1985
RAF Abingdon	35,000	37,000
RAF St Athan	60,000	23,000
RAF Finningley	80,000	90,000
RAF Leuchars	29,000	27,000

The steep contrast in the attendance levels at St Athan were due to the poor weather. The queen's official birthday flypast is normally mounted by operational aircraft, sometimes with the Red Arrows. This year, the latter alone filled the slot on 15 June, as another economic measure.

The Red Arrows also conducted a flypast over the Royal Tournament preview parade on Horse Guards Parade on 7 July. Ordinarily in previous years, as in the years since, the RAF Participation Committee has always been able to authorise a limited number of displays overseas by individual aircraft in both Europe and North America. This year, the need to conserve fuel meant nothing outside the full-time display teams had ventured abroad. The consequences of this impacted on flexible arrangements organised in 1984 for overseas displays. However, the committee were able to arrange for aircraft on operational and training visits on the continent to provide static displays at sixteen European events. Similarly, VC-10 and Victor aircraft were able to attend air shows across North America at Cleveland, Shearwater, Point Mugu, and Norton Air Force Base along with a single flypast by a VC-10 at the Toronto International Air Display.

The dedicated display teams, not being subject to the same restrictions as the solo aircraft from the operational and training units, participated in displays overseas in Denmark, Holland, West Germany, France, Portugal, Belgium, Switzerland, Morocco, and Gibraltar. The Red Arrows took in Gibraltar and Morocco in the same detachment. In return, RAF open and 'At Home' days in the UK, among other events, were quite well attended by overseas air arms.

The Moroccan royal family witnessed the team at Rabat and presented them with what was described as an impressive memento of the occasion. Earlier, they flew two displays at Bex in Switzerland. The Falcons displayed overseas at Aalborg, Leeuwarden, Gatow, Mönchengladbach, Rouen, and Gibraltar. That year also marked a couple of fortieth anniversaries—the liberation of the Channel Islands, Operation Manna (the aid relief flown by the RAF in support of the people of Holland), and VE and VJ Days. The three services were well-represented in the Channel Islands, including the three full time RAF teams. To celebrate Operation Manna, the RAF flew three C-130s and the Lancaster, the latter a symbol of the aircraft involved in 1945. The Red Arrows, ever in demand, flew two displays during the Manna celebrations. Feedback from the Dutch people was most positive.

What has always been less advertised is the effort made by overseas units, essentially RAF Germany. RAFG had in the past seen aerobatic teams drawn from command units during the 1950s and 1960s to represent the RAF at events on the continent without drawing on the home-based teams. During 1985, as with Strike Command, the usual authorised level of public flying was severely curtailed. RAFG decided to reduce the amount of overall flying hours associated with public appearances rather than reduce the number of events they were invited to participate in. This decision was taken early on, but either way, fewer events were attended as a result with formation flying of any kind suspended along with any displays by RAFG Phantoms. This alone resulted in a significant drop in display flying hours.

Despite the loss of hours, displays by Jaguar, Harrier, Tornado, Chinook, and Puma aircraft met a similar number of engagements as in previous years. Static displays were also authorised where possible in order to redress the balance with low flying time. Requests for RAF Germany displays were received from 116 organisers compared with the slightly lesser 104 in 1984. Respectively, they were able to meet seventy requests in 1985 and sixty-seven in 1984. As with the UK, there were disappointments because of weather or even unavailability of aircraft.

By the end of the summer, RAFG had attended sixty-two events. In 1984, they had met all sixty-seven agreed events. Costs were successfully driven down in 1985. As well as the FRG, aircraft from RAFG attended displays in France, Belgium, the Netherlands, Switzerland, and Austria.

The air staff in Germany placed surprisingly significant store by displays. They particularly felt public relations in Germany and neighbouring countries needed working on to maintain good relations and to counter the activities of environmental, political, and other anti-military organisations. These elements were said to be less in evidence in 1985, but they had successfully exerted pressure at local government level to prevent displays taking place. Despite this, a quite full and varied display season was achieved with appreciable benefits. RAF Germany also had a police dog display team, which together with the UK team completed eighty-seven displays at fifty-one events.

Finally, the Queen's Colour Squadron (QCS) were heavily committed to the Royal Tournament. With 1986 approaching, HQSTC were unable to provide any firm advice as to what aircraft they would be able to make available. In order to plan some way ahead, some assumptions were made based on a degree of optimism that some of what was lost in 1985 would be recovered but would not reach pre-1985 levels. There was a desire though to try and regain some of the lost ground of 1985. The target was to aim for, but not exceed, the original proposed level of participation for 1986. The Participation Committee were optimistic that Strike Command would at least be able to make at least one Tornado and a TWU Hawk available. From Support Command, forty SAR helicopter displays were offered.

Comparison of RAF Participation (excluding RAFG) in UK and Overseas Events, 1982–1985

1982   UK: 147   Overseas: 26
1983   UK: 142   Overseas: 26
1984   UK: 149   Overseas: 26
1985   UK: 154   Overseas: 14

The 1986 ground display teams did not change much from previous years, being comprised of two police dog display teams, the Queen's Colour Squadron, four UK-based bands, and the band of Royal Air Force Germany. As this was a lead year for the RAF at the Royal Tournament, both police dog teams could expect to be engaged along with the QCS; also, a full calendar for all the bands was anticipated. Once again, the CPC recommended that priority of asset allocation should be given to events in the UK.

Overseas participation would follow its own priority arrangements; first would be the support of RAFG events and those of NATO arms. Subject to the availability of aircraft, the committee also recommended a small increase in the number of aircraft made available for overseas displays to try and improve upon the essentially static only approach in 1985. RAFG, however, were to continue to try and support overseas events, which the UK-based units could not be made available for. The RAF had since the early post-war period operated a set of priorities for allocating aircraft and other assets to all manner of events. This had shifted according to the type of requests and the level of prestige placed on each. The four-grade priority basis followed a simple category breakdown:

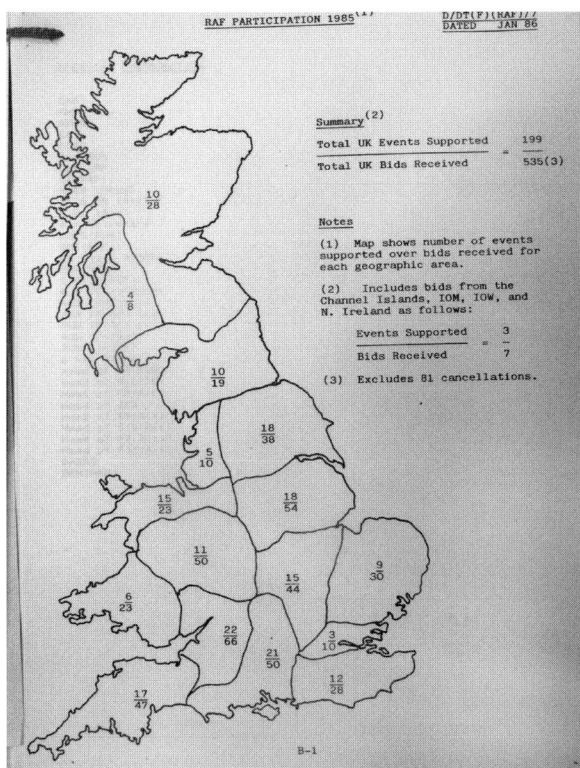

Chart reflecting number of requests for display participation made across the UK by region compared with those honoured by the RAF in 1985. This year, service participation was substantially curtailed compared with previous years. (*TNA*)

Priority 1: Battle of Britain 'At Home' Days and other RAF Open Days.

Priority 2: Events organised by the other Armed Services and the USAF.

Priority 3: Events organised by the RAF Benevolent Fund, RAFA, SSAFA and other service charities.

Priority 4: Events organised by local authorities and other public bodies.

By rights, the above order of priority should place Farnborough as a priority 4 event, Greenham Common and Fairford as priority 3, while the RAF open days outside the official 'At Home' category should have received equal status. This may well have been honoured but did not always appear so. The contributions to Farnborough and especially the International Air Tattoo were very well served given their priority status.

The approach to catering for the major non-service-organised events was very much the same as for the service ones—to try and achieve as even a geographical spread as possible, at the same time gaining the best likely return on publicity and recruitment. There was always the chance that the non-service air display could potentially yield better publicity or indeed turn a negative into a positive—better than might be expected of a service event.

If this was the case, where two such events clashed, or any other conflict of interest arose over the order of priorities, this would be considered on a case-by-case basis. For this reason, the growing number of local councils arranging seaside events—such as Eastbourne, Bournemouth, and Southend—could almost always expect the standard fare, like the Red Arrows and BBMF. The logic was that seaside shows were the very occasions when a large chunk of not particularly aviation-minded folk would be in attendance, and this presented the ideal opportunity to bring the RAF to their attention.

With early indications of a lifting of the 1985 fuel restrictions, Strike Command was approached to make more aircraft available, if possible. Certainly, the committee did not want 1986 to fall below the thread bare level of 1985.

This meant a less discerning approach; if a command offered anything by way of a display team or an individual aircraft for either events in the UK or overseas, then it was not to be refused. Offers of displays by SAR helicopters and the light Gazelle utility choppers were to be accepted as well. Any 1 Group helicopter displays should be pursued as well, these being quite rare given the operational demands. The police dog teams and QCS should likewise be made fully available subject to overriding ceremonial and service commitments. RAFG should also continue to ensure an RAF presence at European events, where possible.

There was a nominal charge levied for RAF displays, which was not usually at the forefront of anyone's considerations. This was known as 'no loss costs' and applied to both civilian and service organisers alike. The MOD was required to recover these costs. Therefore in 1986, a 15 per cent increase/surcharge was approved; this applied to the ground display teams also. There was also increasing evidence that these charges were acting as a disincentive to display organisers. Following the allocation of RAF display items for the 1986 season, some twenty-four requests for participation were withdrawn because the charges were considered too high. In some instances, this was in favour of cheaper displays or displays by aircraft of the other armed services, at no cost. No figures are available, but several requests by organisers were not pursued thereafter on the grounds of cost. The ability of the other services to provide displays on more favourable terms was naturally of concern.

As a result of these imbalances, a working party was put together to monitor the comparisons through 1987 to try and establish a more equitable charging policy. Pending the outcome of the review, the CPC hoped to obtain clearance to hold the 1987 charges at 1986 levels. Hopefully, this would allay any further deterioration in display requests. RAFG made little changes to their 1986 effort; the programme included authorised solo displays by Tornado, Harrier, Puma, and Chinook at various events throughout Europe. They excluded the Phantom from the line-up once again, the concern being airframe limitations and fatigue life. This may seem surprising as Strike Command continued to approve displays by their Phantoms and mostly drawing on the units based at Leuchars. It could be argued that the Germany-based jets spent a greater amount of flying conducted at low-level consequently placing greater demand on airframe life.

RAFG did allow their Phantoms and Jaguars to appear at various events as static items wherever they could be coordinated with planned operational and training visits. As in the UK, most requests for RAFG aircraft were received before the display season and were assessed for PR value as well as safety and display organisation. Whether static or flying, the allocation of assets was largely concentrated in West Germany and the area of 2 ATAF (such as Belgium and Netherlands). This yielded some worthwhile returns; approximately 1.2 million people attended continental air

RAF overseas organised events have been just as popular with visitors abroad. This is the NATO twentieth anniversary open day at RAF Wildenrath, 15 June 1969. 18 Sqn Wessex in the background with some of the static aircraft, a Belgian F-104 from the 10th Wing at Kleine Brogel and an F-84F from the Royal Netherlands Air Force's 314 Sqn 'Redskins' based at Eindhoven. The latter were just months away from re-equipping with the NF-5A Freedom Fighter. Also seen is a Hunter FR10 from 4 Sqn. (*Frank Klassens and Johan 'Hans' Engels*)

shows in 1986. RAFG received 131 requests for aircraft and honoured seventy-eight flying requests and fifty-five static. Two solo displays by the Harrier were cancelled because of safety concerns and a further two for technical ones.

The year did not pass without tragedy as yet another Harrier was lost with the pilot, Flt Lt B. D. Weatherley of 4 Squadron, at Chievres on 28 June. During the thrust vectoring stage of the display, the nose was depressed too far; the aircraft was nose-down perpendicular and still stationary when the pilot ejected along an approximate horizontal trajectory, so his chute opened as he hit the ground.

Despite the tragedy, RAFG reported a successful year, unlike the UK commands they had continued through 1985 business as usual and again into 1986. There was some disappointment that the Red Arrows could not perform more than once at the Hanover air show and on a non-public display as well. Participation on the public days was not possible due to the team's preparation for a tour of the Far East. Environmental and anti-military groups continued to turn up at air shows, particularly on the continent, but caused minimal disruption. The public relations side was an unmitigated success indeed, especially in areas used for low flying training.

RAFG Display Contributions in 1986

	Flying Displays	Static Displays
Tornado	22	6
Harrier	25	7
Puma	16	14
Chinook	13	10
Phantom	nil	8

Jaguar	nil	6
Pembroke	nil	2
Chipmunk	2	nil

The following year, 1987, would also see an attempt to maintain a similar level of displays by individual aircraft types following the surge in 1986. Since 1980, these had very much remained constant apart from the significant drops in 1985. The following figures represent the total number of all flying displays completed through the decade prior to 1987:

1980	1981	1982	1983	1984	1985	1986
163	169	167	165	160	72	184

The figures shown above for 1982 were unexpectedly high as that year several aircraft usually represented as solos on the display circuit were absent; Lightning, Hunter, Jaguar, and Buccaneer were all left waiting in the 'wings', so to speak. Public relations and recruitment, it was reported, benefited significantly from the reversal of the 1985 restrictions and much of the damage to the service's public image had been restored. It was therefore recommended that the 1986 display season be used as a foundation for the following year and, if possible, that additional participation by the RAF's most advanced aircraft be employed to best reflect the modern image of the RAF. There had been until May, the Vintage Pair, Meteor and a Vampire, each of which were lost in a tragic accident while displaying over Mildenhall. The team had completed just three displays before the accident. They had been tasked with fifty through the season.

Afterwards, many air show organisers wrote to the CPC to express their sympathy and condolences. To compensate for the loss of the team, a small number of additional displays of aircraft from Strike and Support Commands were authorised. The question of replacing the Vintage Pair was considered but dropped on the alters of manpower and financial concerns. The AMP, Air Marshal Sir Anthony Skingsley, invited the board to endorse these recommendations. He also urged that the continuation of the Vulcan display be looked at beyond 1987. A review on the Vulcan being continued would be conducted before the jet was due to go into its winter maintenance period. Even though the Red Arrows had been absent mid-season in 1986, this had seemingly little impact as the variety of fast jet solos available ensured a most improved and successful year. At the joint services day at Leconfield, for example, the number of enquiries made about RAF service, in particular aircrew, had doubled over the previous year to 540.

This was attributed, at least in part, to what were described as the excellent flying displays provided here by the Red Arrows and the Tornado F2. In-house recommendations were that a similar mix of aircraft should be available again with emphasis on the new stuff, a good example being the Tornado F2/F3 and, if possible, additional displays should be approved, where judged appropriate and beneficial.

RAF UK-Based Commands' Individual Display Resources Made Available (Excluding Allocations to Battle of Britain 'At Homes' and Farnborough), 1986–1987

Strike Command

	1986	1987	variation
Harrier	13	23	+10
Hawk	9	10	+1
Jaguar	13	nil	-13
Phantom	9	10	+1
Tornado GR1	9	14	+5
Tornado F2/F3	9	10	+1
Nimrod	6	6	nil
Shackleton	2	10	+8
Vulcan	10	10	nil
Lightning	9	10	+1
Buccaneer	6	10	+4
Hercules	4	6	+2
Tornado F2/Spitfire	nil	nil	nil

Support Command

Jet Provost	12	20	+8
Jetstream	10	10	nil
Hawk	12	20	+8
Bulldog	10	15	+5

Strike Command Rotary Wing

Chinook	4	6	+2
Puma	4	6	+2
SAR	40	41	+1

Support Command Rotary Wing

Gazelle	12	20	+8

A solo Hunter T7 was made available from 237 OCU as an additional item for the 1986 'At Homes'.

The overall tally of Lightning solo displays in 1987, according to the local ORB, claims a total of twenty-two displays were complete; seven of these were full, meaning inclusive of vertical aerobatic manoeuvres, eleven were rolling, and four flat. The latter are so-called as they consist of essentially horizontal (flat) manoeuvres due to low and heavy cloud.

Strike Command originally offered a solo Jaguar display for 1987 and had got as far as planning for twenty-three public displays, all of which were cancelled early on due to difficulties in making the necessary resources available; this problem persisted into 1988. Extra display flying hours were made available for the Shackleton, as can be seen in the previous table, even though the committee recommended no change from the 1986 effort. The Vulcan displays allocated remained under review.

The three official display teams—the Red Arrows, BBMF, and the Falcons—now felt like a permanent fixture. However, the long-term costing for 1987 placed the Red Arrows specifically under the spotlight as a savings measure; this was successfully resisted. Support Command offered the CPC no fewer than 100 public displays by the Red Arrows in 1987, which they readily accepted under the circumstances. They would also start public appearances a bit earlier, from about the beginning of May. The weather in 1987 was dreadful; most of the UK displays were affected by anything from blustery rain to low cloud and fog. A few did well—RAF St Mawgan in Cornwall usually had their fingers crossed for the weather, and this year they got cloudless skies, in complete contrast to many others.

It was also a significant year as it marked the retirement (effectively as of April 1988) of one of the most iconic post-war RAF aircraft, which was entirely British-built from its pitot tube to its jet pipe. The English Electric Lightning, the RAF's first truly supersonic aircraft, was seeing out its final calendar year before handing over to the Tornado F3 (the definitive fighter variant, as opposed to the interim and partly ineffective F2), which conversely made its debut on the air show circuit when kicking off over a cloudy Fairford that July.

Due to the re-equipment phase in progress, Strike Command, 11 Group, had three different all- weather interceptors in the front line. Aside from the Lightning and the Tornado F3, there was the F-4 Phantom; this year, 74 Sqn were chosen to provide the solo F-4 Phantom. This likely was regarded as an opportunity to show off the unique variant operated by the 'Tigers', who since the Falklands War had been reformed to fill a gap left by F-4s deployed, permanently to the South Atlantic.

The most readily available fighter to equip the reformed the chosen squadron, the Tigers, was boiled down to a surplus of unused J variants originally intended for the US Navy. Fifteen of these aircraft had been bought second-hand, meaning one previous careful owner. The 'J' was quite different from the 'K' and 'M' in UK service since 1968. The ex-US Navy Js were powered by the American General Electric J79 turbojet, as opposed to the Rolls Royce Spey high-velocity turbofans of the K and M.

The latter were shorter, fatter engines, which required a slight widening of the intake. More powerful, they had an efficacious affect at lower level while the longer, more-slender J79s provided better performance at altitude.

The differences were relative but the choice of the J to represent the Phantom on the show circuit in '87 provided the enthusiast specifically, with a chance to see a very rare version of the F-4 put through its paces in British skies. The Lightning being on its swansong was scheduled to meet the usual calendar of display dates.

The chosen mount was a Mk 3 of 5 Squadron flown by Flt Lt John Fynes. While nothing out of the ordinary for everywhere else, the Lightning's homestead RAF Binbrook had its own open day planned. Billed unofficially as the 'Last, Last Lightning Show', Binbrook featured on local television during the week preceding the open day on 22 August. The station commander, Grp Capt. John Spencer, himself led a formation of eleven Lightings drawn from 5 and 11 Squadrons. On the big day, as might have been predicted, following a fair start weather wise, the rain clouds gathered and by about mid-morning the rain was battering down like stair rods. The open day proved to be a greater public attraction than the RAF anticipated, the Lightning's reputation was more uniquely significant than the air staff had banked on. Parking, both on the airfield and off, was packed.

The Binbrook open day office had planned to expect an attendance of 25,000 visitors and 6,000 vehicles; instead, they received 40,000. What contingency plans were in place were not expected to be relied upon, but they certainly were. At each car park, including those organised as overflow reserves in fields off the station and some walk away, RAF personnel were deployed. Still in an era where 'Best Blues' was the uniform dress code for any public event, airmen stood soaked but cheerfully on duty, their uniforms turning from air force to navy blue with the rain, while rivulets of water ran off the peaks of their caps. Despite the effort to accommodate the unexpected traffic, many vehicles were not able to reach the station because of the volume of congestion clogging up all the local lanes, leaving many disappointed. It was not a wash-out; even though the weather lifted only slightly at about 1 p.m., Flt Lt Fynes still got airborne to put the Lightning through its paces and a largely full display at that given the temporary full but high cloud base.

Soon after, the formation got aloft in unforgettable style. The eleven Lightnings followed one another in singles off the runway, once airborne each jet turned right and disappeared into a dark grey mix of rain and cloud. By about the stage where the third aircraft was retracting its undercarriage, the first was streaking over the airfield toward the crowd line shrouded in bursts of exposed moisture and reheat ablaze before nosing up to a near vertical attitude to rocket into a clear patch over the station. This continued until the eleventh Lightning disappeared into the overhead cumulus. The formation returned in diamond nine for two flypasts in improving weather prompting the commentator, Mike Whitehouse (a former Red Arrows team manager) to warn the punters to get their cameras and VCRs at the ready for the second pass, following which he informed all, 'that's it, if you did not have your camera ready, forgot to put film in or take the lens cap off, you've missed it!'. That was indeed the last chance to record a diamond nine formation of Lightnings. There were eleven; two had split, each to come racing down the crowd line in full afterburner, creating more grey shapes of evaporating moisture. It was not the last time Lightnings would display in public, but it was the last time so many would be seen in the air together.

Flt Lt Fynes' first official display of the year was at Colmar in France finishing on 19 September at Finningley and Leuchars. As soon as he returned to Binbrook, the two aircraft that he had used, XP741 and XR716, were withdrawn from service. With the display season for 1987 over, the public continued to show an interest in what was,

With a suitably dramatic setting, a Lightning F6 pulls up hard across the crowd line at the Binbrook open day, 22 August 1987, held to mark the last year of the type's operational service. (*John Fisher*)

Another glimpse of the Buccaneer being put through its paces, Binbrook, 22 August 1987. (*Author's Collection*)

The last Lightning solo, with pilot Flt Lt John Fynes, races past, Binbrook 22 August 1987. (*Author's Collection*)

Binbrook's last Lightning show, 22 August 1987, as one aircraft gets airborne one or two in front returns at full tilt over the crowd line—worth getting soaked for the experience. (*John Fisher*)

alongside the Vulcan, the most charismatic post-war aircraft to be operated by the RAF. The station ORB also noted afterwards 'a few personalities in the close vicinity of the airfield who continue to complain about the noise at every opportunity'. A particular feature of most of the major RAF displays this year, not seen for a while, were the simulated airfield attacks by aircraft of No. 1 Group, Tornados, Harriers and Buccaneers—another example of how operational commitments sometimes found a window to allow extra commitment along the lines of a more operational nature.

Another expected feature that failed to show was the Harrier GR5 in the hands of a BAE pilot. All four flagship displays suffered from poor weather, especially Finningley which had the largest flying display composed, a possible record of at least fifty-two items, other than positioning movements. A rare fly through by the SR-71 was billed but aborted because of the weather. The day here started off fine but low cloud gradually crept in to make flying virtually impossible.

The year 1988 ending in an even number presaged another Farnborough year and heralded a surprise or two, quite apart from the efforts of the RAF. Two words had entered the vocabulary of the English language—Glasnost and Perestroika. Their English meaning, openness and reconstruction/reform, would strike terror into the hearts of all warmongers. Cold War relations between west and east had thawed substantially following the appointment of Mikhail Gorbachev as Soviet president three years earlier, and we were, quite unbelievably for the era, witnessing the invitation to Farnborough of two Soviet MiG-29 Fulcrums. With media interest being what it is, images of the Russian jets being escorted by Tornado F3s from 5 Squadron, based at RAF Coningsby, were seen across the world's press.

This, however, was one of the lighter moments of 1988 as far as air shows were concerned. Otherwise, three incidents, two involving the RAF, brought the whole business of display flying under scrutiny, specifically involving high-performance military aircraft in close proximity to the public. The first had a relatively benign outcome. Sqn Ldr Pete Collins of the Red Arrows was forced to eject while getting airborne for a practice sortie from RAF Scampton. He suffered back injuries, but he survived to fly again. The incident was followed by the most tragic so far recorded in the western hemisphere. The Italian Air Force aerobatics team, Il Frecce Tricolori miscalculated while performing a particular manoeuvre, resulting in carnage and tragedy on a never-before-seen scale. The team were performing their sequence before the crowd of spectators over the USAF Air Base at Ramstein in Germany.

Two of the MB339 advanced trainers collided and the debris caught a third aircraft; this resulted in loss of control and a consequent crash into the spectators' enclosure. In all, seventy people were killed, many from the resultant burst of kerosene that ignited and engulfed all like a napalm bomb. The reaction was unparalleled; this was the first time the media and public reaction took a truly questioning view of air shows.

Unlike Farnborough in 1952 or Syerston in 1958 or any other early post-war air show crash, this was not reported as another tragic accident with nothing more to say. The calls to ban air shows got underway, but to be fair, there was balance provided in the press. Some made outrageous and glib comparisons with gladiatorial deaths in the Colosseum, and some nations' governments reacted by imposing bans.

The Lightning's replacement, the Panavia Tornado F3, makes its debut the same year at Abingdon, 12 September. (*Author's Collection*)

Changing times—the very first appearance at UK air show of a frontline Soviet fighter, the MiG-29 Fulcrum, was at Farnborough in 1988. This one is seen at 1990 SBAC show. (*Author's Collection*)

Denmark and West Germany placed an immediate embargo on all displays by military aircraft. This was also taken up by the USAF based in Germany, which stopped hosting air shows on air bases in the Federal Republic. The Red Arrows made concessions too—a manoeuvre called the Boomerang, which involved two of their aircraft converging toward the crowd line requiring one pilot to aim to miss the other. This part of the sequence was removed.

Were it not bad enough, during rehearsals for the Abingdon 'At Home', the Phantom display crew were both killed when their aircraft failed to complete a looping manoeuvre, hitting the airfield. I have written comprehensively about this incident in the book *Northern Q*. Flt Lts Chris Lackman (pilot) and Jack Thompson (navigator) were both killed. They and their aircraft came from 228 OCU, based at Leuchars.

This sad incident rounded off the year—would things ever be the same again? Early in 1989, the air staff placed their overall public relations policy under review. They had the incidents from 1988 to mull over and how it impacted on the future of military display flying. Also, the significance of the Battle of Britain changed as younger people—making up the larger chunk of the population—were not alive during the war, much less took part.

The RAF PR report for the period 1987–88, however, claimed that the service's efforts had become increasingly positive rather than reactive. Three new initiatives had been introduced; one was a mobile exhibition devoted to low flying in rural areas, which went down rather well and attracted a substantial degree of interest, favourable at that; secondly, the CAS, now Sir Peter Harding, had approved the publication of an RAF broadsheet and a pilot edition was expected toward the end of the year; and thirdly, there was to be a survey of public attitudes to the RAF. Two points drew some interest—the first found that the public generally understood the need for low-level flying although there was a sense that the RAF was indifferent to public concerns. A further rather more concerning point, but not too surprising, revealed the depth of public ignorance about air power.

The report was a prompt for the RAF to tackle such concerns about public perceptions. The future of the Battle of Britain 'At Home' Days was under review as well. AOC-in-C Support Command had informed the assistant chief of the air staff that changes would be needed in the procedures governing the 'At Home' Days particularly. Air Marshal Sir John Sutton believed the 'At Homes' needed to be given more recognition. He also advised that if contractorisation at RAF Finningley went ahead, as was being planned for various support services, then the station could no longer be 'At Home'. Air Chief Marshal Sir Patrick Hine, AOC-in-C Strike Command, had been consulted with a view to selecting an alternative station within his command as a replacement should Sutton's concerns about Finningley turn out to be the case. Hine was unable to offer a suitable alternative. The imminent plan to outsource a substantial degree of services, currently provided by RAF personnel, had prompted the preparation of a draft paper and then submitted to the Participation Committee by the AMP and ACAS. The commanders in chief had given their responses.

Among the various recommendations were proposals to change the emphasis on the formal tasking of four 'At Home' stations each September to a more flexible

Phantom low fast pass over Coningsby, 11 June 1988. The crew—Flt Lts Chris Lackman and Jack Thompson—were killed during a practice display over Abingdon later in the year. (*Author's Collection*)

Occasionally, the RAF fielded an additional Tornado GR1 display. At a time when just one pilot/crew represented each fast jet type, the second solo GR1, seen here from 27 Sqn, was to demonstrate the type's manoeuvrability with wing pylon attachments; this countered early press reports about lack of agility. Finningley, 17 September 1988. (*Author's Collection*)

Strike Command Hawk solo, 151 Sqn taxiing out for his slot, Finningley, 17 September 1988. (*Author's Collection*)

C-130 Hercules completes the Khe Sanh approach at Finningley, 17 September 1988. (*Author*)

arrangement. The suggestion had been made earlier, which was to allow more stations to open to the public in accordance with local circumstances. This was very much the form that had taken shape over the previous two decades. As it turned out, the contracting out at Finningley had slipped to 1991 before it would take effect and so Finningley could hold 'At Homes' in 1989 and 1990 before any further review of the current arrangements would be necessary. It was also objected by some air staff opinions that contractorisation did not necessarily mean an RAF station could not hold an 'At Home'. Instead, that resources needed to be clearly identified regarding requirements for the purpose of staging such an event. The upshot was that the current arrangement was sound enough and the 'At Homes' offered good value for money; they were a tried and tested formula and should be retained subject to an examination of the costs involved. Sir Peter Harding was happy for the current four stations to continue officially representing the RAF's great moment, publicly, in 1989 and 1990. Thereafter, depending on contractorisation plans, thinking specifically of Finningley, three or four RAF stations would continue to be 'At Home' during Battle of Britain week. Other stations would continue to be allowed to stage public air/open days at the respective station commander's discretion to suit local conditions and circumstances. A paper setting out the way ahead was to be prepared for the committee to consider inside the next twelve months.

The Red Arrows' 'Goose' manoeuvre seen at Finningley 1988. Those with a keen eye for detail will note the team are down to seven aircraft following an incident earlier in the year. (*John Fisher*)

11
Post-Cold War Change of Direction

That there have been air shows, such as they are understood, at all has always very much depended on there being a substantial degree of military air power, for both military and civilian-organised events alike, because air arms always provided the real showstoppers. By nature of design and intent, as has been noted in the preceding chapters, they own the more impressive and interesting aircraft and, as has also been revealed, the likes of the RAF have invariably, been oversubscribed with requests.

One of the Red Arrow's former PR officers, Sqn Ldr Tony Cunnane, some years ago, spoke to me while I researched an earlier project about the era of the Cold War. He had also been involved with organising the Finningley Battle of Britain display back in 1960. When we spoke, about 1999, about what up until then had been the loss of many of the RAF open days, Tony observed that the Cold War presented the near ideal conditions to allow the various NATO air arms to make the effort they did toward air shows.

The Cold War resulted in a better-funded defence industry and output, coupled with an air force and other air arms that stood ready but were not placed on a war footing. Nor were they committed to too many long-term operational deployments. In other words, they were a static force but with no war to fight, only to stand ready for one. This situation therefore facilitated the by-product of display flying.

The nature of HM Forces in the 1990s and 2000s was expeditionary; in the 1950s–1980s, the emphasis was on the defence of Europe resulting in this static but ready in-depth posture. This therefore placed most units and assets in Britain or Germany. The latter was considered a 'home posting' by the army, and although the RAF had a smaller representation on the continent, it still amounted to about 16 per cent of overall strength in the 1980s. It is impossible to truly quantify the level of expenditure on defence by NATO countries during the Cold War. It is difficult to find an appropriate comparison to see whether the resources for defence were higher than they might otherwise have been during the continued 'ready' posture of the period from 1949 to 1991. A former CAS, Sir Richard Johns believes, like many others, that the NATO defence posture through the Cold War was sufficient for any unchallenged peacetime state. The Cold War was certainly approached by all, save the USA, with a bare minimum top line. On 9 November 1989, the ebb and flow of both the NATO and Warsaw Pact states of readiness jarred suddenly as something happened that had never crossed anyone's mind before.

The residents of both East and West Berlin, epicentre of the Cold War, set about pulling the edifice, the very symbol of the Cold War, down. The Berlin Wall was about to disappear, some bits of it to private homes as souvenirs and some into museums and certain other public buildings for historic posterity. The dismantling of the wall by citizens of both Berlins surely risked being crushed with gun fire, certainly initially, from the East German Guards, and with almost equal certainty, with West Germans involved, retaliation from the allied military personnel on the other side. If they, as would likely been the case, opened fire on the East German Guards and therefore, unavoidably, upon Soviet troops present, the big day we had lived in fear of at the back of our minds would have arrived. Since the USSR detonated their first atomic bomb, the world had lived under this sword of Damocles. The actions of the Berliners, Glasnost or not, was extremely foolhardy. Yet with Eric Honecker, the East German leader, having resigned (he had been forced out), and having been replaced by the reformer Egon Krenz, circumstances were much different. When a television broadcast announced that people could cross back and forth either side of the Berlin Wall without fear of 'Sanction', that is just what happened. This was the start of a train of rather bloodier events in the months and years ahead, but it did mean an end to the hostile standoff between east and west in short order. Quite simply, that was that—a single display of people power brought an end to the Cold War.

What did all this have to do with air displays? A lot. There were two outcomes from the situation. On the upside, enthusiasts in western Europe could look forward to seeing Soviet/Warsaw Pact hardware, in the flesh, at NATO bases. On the downside, the trend from here on would be cuts, cuts, and more cuts. As defence budgets contracted so would follow the inevitable reduction in the military presence at air shows. Before much in the way of change could take place, 1989 gave way to 1990 and the RAF were some ways along the road of preparing for a big year ahead. Planning was already underway for the forthcoming fiftieth anniversary of the Battle of Britain.

Glossy aviation magazines were reporting on the prospect of a substantial flypast down the mall and over Buckingham Palace where the RAF were also to be on full public view for the anniversary parade before HM Queen Elizabeth II. Some 166 aircraft, including four RN Sea Harriers, would compose the flypast in two essential sections. Had the weather not played ball, a second attempt to mount the flypast was planned to overfly Finningley the following weekend.

The year 1990 was a real milestone, and post-Cold War impact or not, the Battle of Britain was going to be marked in style. As well as the events in September, other RAF stations—Brawdy, Chivenor, Coningsby, Cosford, Manston, St Mawgan, and Swanton Morley—all held open days through the summer, and each attached themselves to the fiftieth anniversary, highlighting this significant moment in history. Overshadowing the preparations was the looming outcome of the deepest defence review since the

A significant sign of the ending Cold War and a presentation well outside the realms of possibility just three years previously—taking its place in the static display at Abingdon 1990, a Mikoyan MiG-21 presented by the Czechoslovakian Air Force to mark the fiftieth anniversary of the Battle of Britain, a gift from a prominent contributor to the campaign. Another sign of the times, the information board already describes the previous owners as the Czech & Slovak AF. (*Author*)

The Red Arrows at the Biggin Hill Air Fair, June 1989, celebrating their twenty-fifth display season, with a Chinook providing a backdrop to the proceedings. The team leader, Sqn Ldr Tim Miller, is stood at centre. (*Peter March*)

Right: Marking the fiftieth anniversary of the Battle of Britain, the four official 'At Homes' permitted by the Air Force Board received the highest priority for assistance with resources; the four respective programme covers each give a taste of what the punter should expect. Abingdon, as the specific 'flagship' event, has this conveyed through its strikingly reflective cover. The USAF aeros team, the Thunderbirds, had been withdrawn due to Operation Granby, Desert Shield, and Storm, but it was too late to remove them from the artwork. (*Author*)

Below: The solo display Tornado F3 for 1990, seen here on the home turf, Coningsby, for that station's open day, 16 June 1990. (*Author's Collection*)

'Black Mike'—a familiar airframe to the enthusiast community, parked up here at Coningsby, 16 June 1990. This aircraft was the last airworthy F-4K Phantom II and continued to be flown until its final airborne public appearance at the Leuchars 'At Home' in September. After years on show at Leuchars as a static exhibit, it is now a museum piece. (*Author's Collection*)

end of Suez. The review, titled Options for Change, was already rumoured to ring the death knell for three operational aircraft—the Buccaneer, the Phantom, and the Shackleton, meaning this year was going to be unforgettable. The USAF were the first to truly break the ice; the USAF European Command celebrated at Mildenhall with the US Air Fete. This was the first of the large military air shows on the calendar and presented two modern day examples of air-to-air warfare.

One set piece each came from the navy and the RAF. The navy launched two Sea Harriers to intercept two FRADU Hunters under control from a Sea King AEW, culminating in a tail-chasing dogfight. The RAF set piece consisted of two 29 Squadron Tornado F3s scrambled to intercept four Hawks of 2 TWU, Chivenor, with a (by then very rare appearance) Victor tanker and E-3A, the latter provided by 1 Squadron of the NATO AEW Force based at Geilenkirchen. The RAF team rounded off their sequence with an airfield beat up with the two Tornados overtaking the Hawks before pulling into a vertical climb out of sight; the four Hawks in finger four formation appeared at first to try and follow before executing a turn in formation, off stage.

The next major pivotal event, there not being an IAT this year, was the official Battle of Britain fiftieth anniversary air show held at the A&AEE aerodrome at Boscombe Down—QinetiQ as they are known today. This two-day extravaganza took place on 9 and 10 June and was organised by the same team responsible for the air tattoos. Very much like the Fairford set-up, a heavy wealth of overseas military types as well as from the RAF filled the programme. The air defence component and control body, 11 Group of Strike Command, permitted a formation display team of four Phantoms from 56 Squadron; they followed the Battle of Britain set piece enactment each day. This was in keeping with the theme by presenting an example of the present-day RAF air defence force.

The fiftieth anniversary of the Battle of Britain was celebrated in quite some style in 1990. The entire fighter inventory of the BBMF is seen here rehearsing for the honour of leading the largest RAF flypast since the queen's coronation. (*Peter March*)

15 September most conveniently fell on a Saturday in 1990, and the weather was near perfect. This one of two Tornado GR1 solo aircraft rounding off the display with a steep climb in full reheat over Abingdon. (*Author's Collection*)

More Tornado GR1s in a Diamond 16 formation, one of eight such formations making up one half of the total in the Battle of Britain fiftieth anniversary flypast. Given the variation in aircraft performance, the larger fast jet section arrived ahead over Abingdon out of sequence with the pass over Buckingham Palace, which saw the slower half pass over head first. (*Author's Collection*)

The final two Tonkas in the flypast over Abingdon, both from 13 Sqn, accompanying two VC-10 Tankers (101 Sqn) led by a VC-10C (10 Sqn). (*Author's Collection*)

A week later, 229 OCU/65 Sqn had the honour of mounting the queen's birthday flypast, operating from the homestead Coningsby on 16 June. Eighteen Tornados streamed off, over flew the station, headed to London, and returned to Coningsby to flypast again then run in, break and stream land.

For Farnborough, No. 1 Squadron mustered as many of its brand-new Harrier GR5s as could be made available—nine in all. In addition, especially for Farnborough this year, was a reprisal of the Tornado/Spitfire duo display, last seen in 1985, then with the interim F2, this time with the definitive F3. Oddly this was not seen anywhere else this year—not even the open day at their homestead, Coningsby. There were more examples of the hatchet being buried between east and west at Farnborough with demonstrations by a MiG-29 Fulcrum and an SU-27 Flanker—could enthusiasts expect this to become the new norm?

The number of individual demonstrations made available from the RAF this year was as extensive as it had ever been since the end of the 1970s.

Farnborough 1990 marked the Battle of Britain's fiftieth anniversary celebrations with this combined display of a Spitfire and a modern Panavia Tornado F3. This format was started in 1985 and has continued, on and off usually for special anniversary occasions, since. (*Author's Collection*)

On 22 September, the celebrations continued at Finningley and Leuchars with full RAF participation again. With the impact of 'options for change', it was expected this would be the final F-4 Phantom solo display to be authorised as these venerable Vietnam-era fighters were to be pensioned off; however, they stayed on long enough to allow one more in 1992. (*Author's Collection*)

Final flourish as Flt Lts Steve Howard and Nige Marks rocket into a vertical departure—a party trick beloved of many RAF fast jet display jockeys. (*Author's Collection*)

Strike Command Solo Displays, 1990

Tornado F3 from 65 Sqn/229 OCU Coningsby
Tornado GR1 from 45 Sqn/TWCU Honington
Tornado GR1 from 27 Sqn Marham
Phantom FGR2 from 64 Sqn/228 OCU Leuchars
Buccaneer S2 from 237 OCU Lossiemouth
Jaguar GR1A from 226 OCU Lossiemouth
Harrier GR5 from 233 OCU Wittering
Hawk T1A from 234 Sqn/1 TWU Brawdy
Canberra TT18 from 100 Sqn Wyton
Four Nimrod MR2 individual crews, each from 120, 201 and 206 Sqns Kinloss and
a fourth from 42 Sqn St Mawgan
Shackleton AEW2 from 8 Sqn Lossiemouth
VC-10 from 10 Sqn Brize Norton
VC-10K from 241 OCU Brize Norton
C-130K from Lyneham

Support Command Solo Displays, 1990

Hawk T1 from 4 FTS Valley
Jet Provost T5 from 6 FTS Finningley
Tucano T1 from CFS Cranwell
Jetstream T1 from 6 FTS Finningley
Bulldog T1 from various UAS's

Add to all this the regular teams—the Red Arrows, BBMF, and the Falcons—together with the various one-off formations, and various photo passes from a 1 PRU Canberra PR9; this was a vintage year. The seventieth anniversary of the first Hendon Pageant was marked as well but was certainly overshadowed by the Battle of Britain celebrations.

To crown the lot, the centrepiece was the fiftieth anniversary flypast down the mall, then over Abingdon. The backdrop to all the preparations from July onwards was Saddam Hussein's invasion of Kuwait. Saddam claimed Kuwait was a component part of Iraq and was only separated during British imperial rule; it is likely Kuwait's oil fields also had some influence on his view. It is likely the Iraqi president did not expect the international response. Operation Desert Shield was already underway before the culmination of celebrations in September. Even with the deployment of eighteen Jaguars and an even larger number of Tornado GR1s and a squadron of Tornado F3s, supported by all the C-130s, VC-10s, Tristars and Victors that could be mustered, the arrangements for the flypast and other events remained intact. Nothing was allowed to intervene, alter, or curtail this or anything else, save that the contributing units had to be juggled.

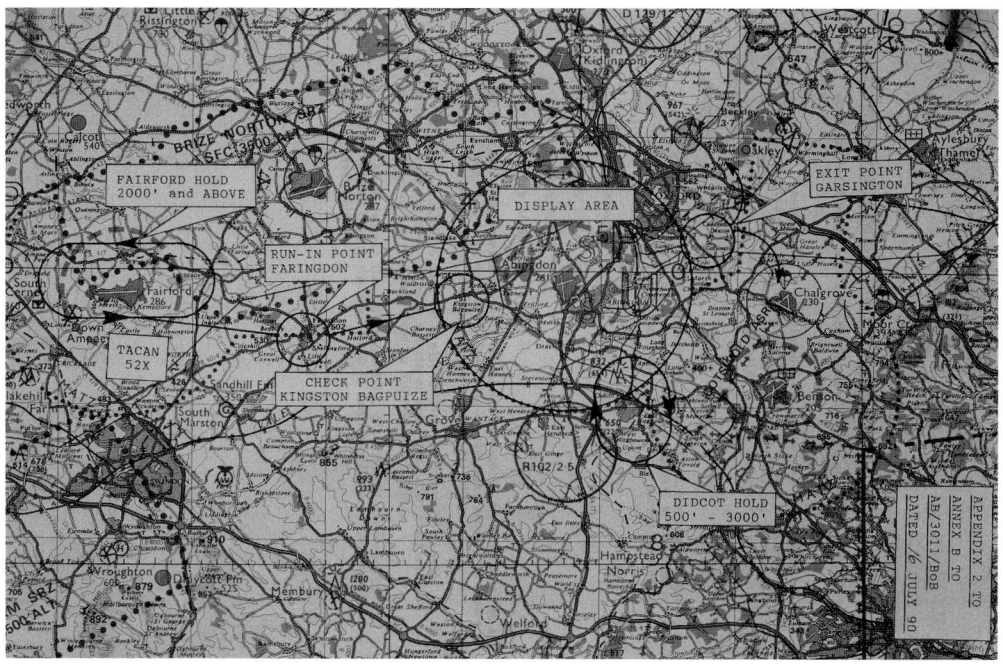

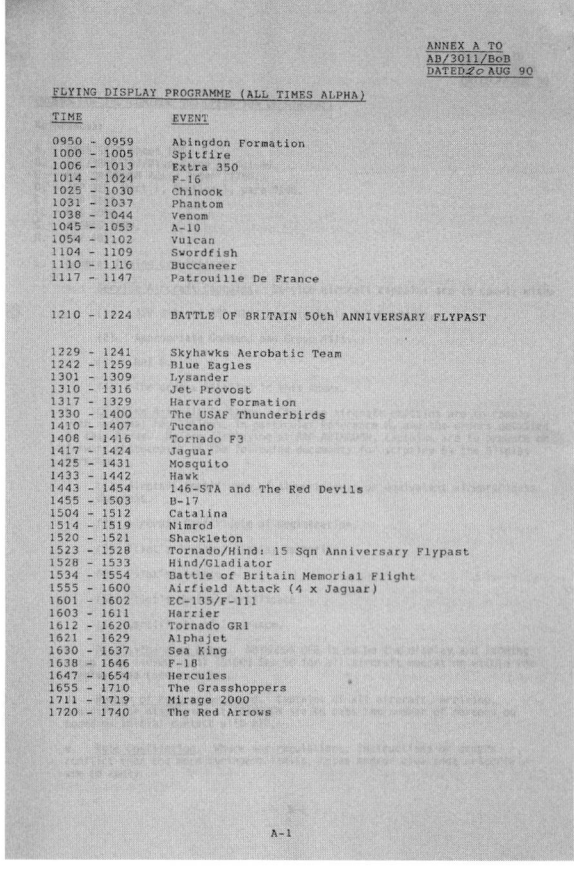

ANNEX A TO
AB/3011/BoB
DATED 20 AUG 90

FLYING DISPLAY PROGRAMME (ALL TIMES ALPHA)

TIME	EVENT
0950 – 0959	Abingdon Formation
1000 – 1005	Spitfire
1006 – 1013	Extra 350
1014 – 1024	F-16
1025 – 1030	Chinook
1031 – 1037	Phantom
1038 – 1044	Venom
1045 – 1053	A-10
1054 – 1102	Vulcan
1104 – 1109	Swordfish
1110 – 1116	Buccaneer
1117 – 1147	Patrouille De France
1210 – 1224	BATTLE OF BRITAIN 50th ANNIVERSARY FLYPAST
1229 – 1241	Skyhawks Aerobatic Team
1242 – 1259	Blue Eagles
1301 – 1309	Lysander
1310 – 1316	Jet Provost
1317 – 1329	Harvard Formation
1330 – 1400	The USAF Thunderbirds
1410 – 1407	Tucano
1408 – 1416	Tornado F3
1417 – 1424	Jaguar
1425 – 1431	Mosquito
1433 – 1442	Hawk
1443 – 1454	146-STA and The Red Devils
1455 – 1503	B-17
1504 – 1512	Catalina
1514 – 1519	Nimrod
1520 – 1521	Shackleton
1523 – 1528	Tornado/Hind: 15 Sqn Anniversary Flypast
1528 – 1533	Hind/Gladiator
1534 – 1554	Battle of Britain Memorial Flight
1555 – 1600	Airfield Attack (4 x Jaguar)
1601 – 1602	EC-135/F-111
1603 – 1611	Harrier
1612 – 1620	Tornado GR1
1621 – 1629	Alphajet
1630 – 1637	Sea King
1638 – 1646	F-18
1647 – 1654	Hercules
1655 – 1710	The Grasshoppers
1711 – 1719	Mirage 2000
1720 – 1740	The Red Arrows

A-1

Above: Map showing holding patterns, run in, and exit points for the Abingdon 'At Home' day, 15 September 1990. All naturally had to be coordinated with all surrounding civilian and military air traffic agencies. (*TNA, Via Hugh Alexander*)

Left: Abingdon's provisional flying programme for 1990 'At Home'. The impact of the invasion of Kuwait prompted some revision, including the withdrawal of the much-anticipated USAF Thunderbirds aerobatics team. (*TNA, Via Hugh Alexander*)

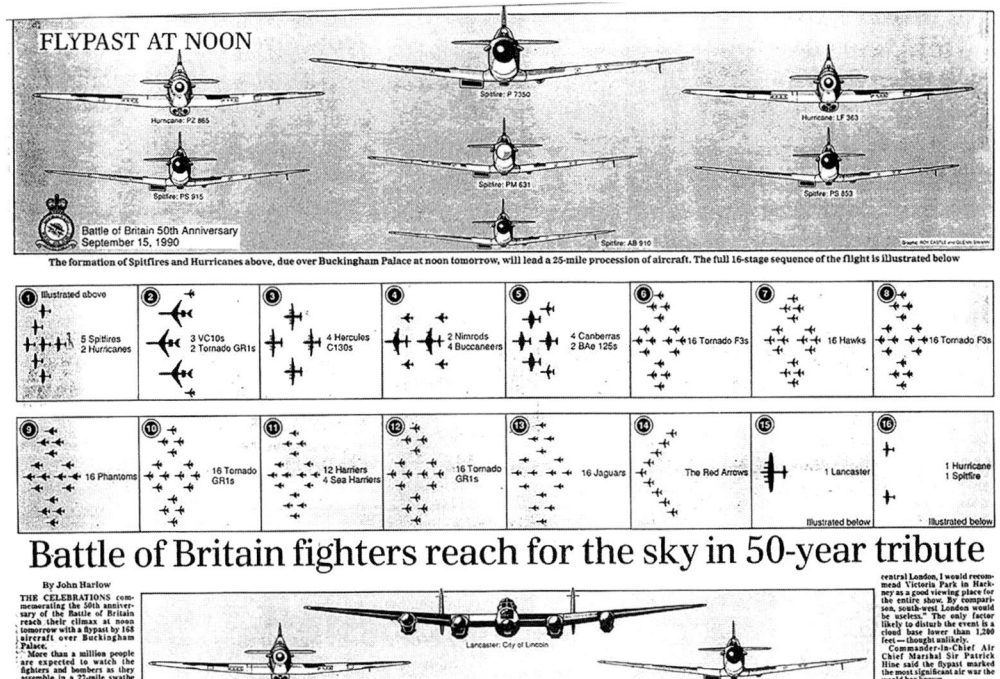

Battle of Britain fighters reach for the sky in 50-year tribute

The flypast plan in full. Despite the operational commitments and imposed cuts circling the project, it still went ahead, in full. (*TNA, Via Hugh Alexander*)

The first section of the Battle of Britain's fiftieth anniversary flypast arrives as the second section flies over RAF Abingdon, VC-10s with Tornado GR1 outriggers from 13 Sqn followed by C-130Ks in diamond followed by Buccaneers in a vic formation with a Nimrod. (*Author*)

Abingdon 1990, two of eight Diamond 16 formations; the lead is made of Tornado GR1s, following a consignment of Jaguars. (*Author*)

Abingdon 1990 flightline—'Classic Jet' de Havilland Venom in Suez stripes. In background, Belgian AF Alpha Jets, solo and spare. Also seen is an early Shorts Tucano. (*Author*)

Against the backdrop of the international crisis and the cuts imposed by Options for Change guaranteed through the CFE (Conventional Forces in Europe Treaty), the full programme of celebrations went ahead. As many Spitfires and Hurricanes as could be found in an airworthy condition, from the BBMF and various private operators, brought historical context and, on top of the celebrations, the end of an era of global military stand-off. It all seemed perfect but marred slightly toward the end by the burgeoning situation in the Middle East. Still, it all went ahead in a manner that no one had any right to expect. From here, it was downhill all the way; the afterparty hangover was not severe at first, but the future was not going to be bright.

A total of thirty-two Tornado GR1s and sixteen Jaguars in the middle—less than half of the fast section of the milestone Battle of Britain's fiftieth anniversary flypast. (*Author*)

The air defence element—first formation of 16 Tornado F3s followed by sixteen F-4 Phantoms. (*Author*)

Sixteen Tornado F3s up close. The Battle of Britain's fiftieth anniversary flypast is likely the largest to have flown over an air show and is the largest mounted by the RAF since the coronation; we will never see the RAF mount such a spectacle ever again. (*Author*)

Patrouille de France bending over Abingdon, 15 September 1990. (*Author*)

Eight diamond 16 formations of Tornados F3s/GR1s, Phantoms, Jaguars, Harrier GR5s, and Sea Harriers depart north-west over Abingdon. Those of an older vintage would say, as they have over the ages, 'That's when we had an Air Force!' (*Author's Collection*)

12

Air Shows, Defence Cuts, and Defence Commitments

With the fiftieth anniversary of the Battle of Britain out of the way and with an uncertain future in terms of what the long-term impact would be on the size and configuration of the future RAF, the Air Force Board had its work cut out. The CPC also faced a new task of tailoring the resources left to accommodate a new set of priorities.

The first air staff decision to have an impact at all was to bring forward, by several years, the disbandment of the Phantom and Buccaneer; the gaps in role and capability would be plugged by existing Tornados of both variants accordingly. The Phantom was the first scheduled to go in 1993; this meant no new crews would be required for conversion after 1990.

Therefore, the OCU shut down in January 1991, meaning no more F-4 solos. The plan for service events in 1991 had not really changed from 1990. Initially, Abingdon and St Athan were both pencilled in for 14 September. This arrangement had clearly been arrived at well back in 1990 but were still published in the public domain after it was announced that Abingdon was due to close. Abingdon was to be relinquished by the RAF and handed over to units of the army returning from Germany.

The Abingdon display was cancelled around January, even though all seemed so certain it would continue. A VHS recording of the 1990 edition was produced; Sean Maffett narrating on the video can be heard explaining that the traffic problems encountered that year and in previous ones were expected to be fully resolved in time for 1991. All roads leading to the station in 1990 were at a standstill. The rather more pedestrian open day at Cosford was instead upgraded from being just an open day to official 'At Home' status to replace Abingdon. St Athan was to continue but the AFB had concluded that the imposition of tradition had run its course. St Athan would continue as an 'At Home', but selected stations would be able to choose the date for opening that would best suit regarding weather, annual training, and exercise programmes.

St Athan elected to re-schedule for the end of June in the hope of meeting better weather conditions. This left Finningley and Leuchars as the only two still in line to welcome the public over the threshold in September. The station open days cracked on with all the usual venues except RAF Coningsby, which was heavily engaged during Operation Granby up until the based Tornados returned in the spring, leaving little scope for staging the air day. During the summer, the solo Harrier GR5 met with disaster when an electrical fire forced the pilot to head back to Wittering during a display on 29 July. The Harrier GR5 fleet was grounded pending further investigation, which lasted from 30 July to 16 September by which time the display pilot was out of currency and so was discontinued for the rest of the year. IAT was held as a biannual event for the last time; when it returned in 1993, it would continue as an annual show. The 1991 IAT had coincided with the hosting of the NATO Tiger meet, which involved a representative gathering of NATO fighter squadrons with the tiger as their crest; therefore, the international Tiger Squadrons were this year's IAT special theme. No. 74 Squadron were this year's hosts and while there was no RAF Phantom solo, 74 Sqn put up a formation of four aircraft each day of the tattoo, much the same way 56 did at Boscombe the year previous.

The visiting aircraft from the Tiger squadrons were entered into a competition for the best tiger art design. The extra special and unprecedented feature of the two remaining September displays, at Finningley and Leuchars, was the quite unexpected debut, at a UK (and in all probability, Western) air show, by the air force of the USSR. The plan was for a full display at both stations by either one of the Red Air Force's premier aerobatics teams. The options were the Blue Swifts (Mig 29 Fulcrums) or the Russian Knights (SU27/30 Flankers); the latter was chosen.

The team were to arrive at Scampton shortly before the event; this would be their principal operating base during their UK visit. For the big day, they would pre-position up at Leuchars. The trip was very nearly scuppered because of an attempted coup in Moscow on 19 August to overthrow the architect of Perestroika and Glasnost, Mikhail Gorbachev. This was broadcast on regular news bulletins, just like the Gulf War. The moment was hairy but short-lived, helped along by Gorbachev's eventual successor, Boris Yeltsin, who famously stood atop a tank and delivered a public address, condemning the coup. The whole matter was over by 22 August. RAF organisers of the Finningley 'At Home' when interviewed for local television reported how they felt their own unbelievable good luck in attracting the Russian Knights was over as well; thanks to Boris Yeltsin, the deployment was back on again. Doubtless there would have been some aviation enthusiasts who would have thought, briefly, that the Russian coup leaders were about to reset the Cold War and rewind things back just the way they were.

The aerobatics team visited Finningley on the Friday before the air show to fly a rehearsal. One more highlight for the Finningley crowd was the organising of a protracted set piece as a tribute to the recent liberation of Kuwait. Four of Leuchars' Tornados—together with four GR1s, two Buccaneers, and a Tristar K1—put on a grand display of modern aerial warfare condensed and squeezed inside a small radius centred on the main runway with a low upper ceiling so the punters could see what was going on. Meanwhile up in Fife, further Tornados were made available to form the traditional Battle of Britain four. The weather at both stations was fine; at Finningley, it was particularly warm and dry for the time of year.

The Russian Knights, 21 September 1991, over Finningley. Their appearance over an RAF station on such an occasion marked a truly defining moment that the Cold War was over. (*Alec Blyth*)

The following year brought a surprise return of the Phantom solo. This was, however, the final fling. The crew came from 74 Squadron but had two aircraft assigned with the markings of both the last remaining units displayed. This meant the 74 Sqn fin with a 56 Squadron marking below the forward cockpit. The honour of being the ultimate F-4 display crew went to Flt Lts Archie Liggett and Mark 'Manners' Mainwaring; the latter, now a group captain, commentates at RIAT alongside publisher and chief commentator Ben Dunnell. The crews of both squadrons had the honour of providing the 1992 queen's birthday flypast, and just as in 1990, the Coningsby open day coincided, so for maximum publicity the sixteen-strong formation operated from here.

A reflection of the early 1960s was visible in that all the participating Phantoms had coloured fins—black with yellow/black tessellating triangles along the fin tip for 74's aircraft and red with red/white chequers for 56. Eight from each and good weather saw the F-4 bow out in style.

Farnborough returned to claim its September slot with a growing number of Eastern Block aircraft among Western types now becoming quite routine. The Russian Air Force turned up in force here with SU-24, SU-35, MiG-31, and MiG-29s. The SBAC show remained quite some spectacle, but all the heavy metal came from overseas, The Royal Swedish Air Force brought the Viggen again while SAAB showed its replacement, the JAS 39 Gripen. The RAF provided a solo Tornado F3, this time from 25 Sqn with a black and silver fin—the squadron's colours—and a Harrier.

The Soviet Air Force were up at Leuchars a week later where a Soviet Air Force SU-27 was seen among the highlights, but the weather was not at its best this time. The same was true for Finningley, where the star attraction was the US Navy Blue Angels.

The year 1992 brought the last Phantom solo display, from 74 Sqn carrying 56 Sqn markings to represent the last two operational units. The crew were Sqn Ldr Archie Liggett and Flt Lt Mark 'Manners' Mainwaring; the latter is now a group captain and commentates at the Fairford RIAT. (*Adrian Balch*)

The weather was a repeat of 1967—low cloud and mist that refused to move. Despite this, both stations attempted to do their best. At Leuchars, the Flanker flew a tight demonstration while the home-based Tornado F3s from 111 Squadron conducted a series of low passes, again reflecting the circumstances affecting 74 Squadron's Lightnings here in 1966. Down south at Finningley, the Blue Angels also bent over backwards to avoid disappointment even if they could only manage their flat show.

From an operational perspective, while shrinking, the RAF was getting busier. After intense action in the Gulf in 1991, they were now being dragged into operations over the former Yugoslavia while simultaneously contributing to both northern and southern no-fly zones being enforced over Iraq.

The year 1993 was the RAF's seventy-fifth birthday, again reviewed by the queen this time at Marham, where a still sizeable representation of aircraft was forgathered. The flypast included a formation of Phantoms getting airborne for the last time publicly. Tornados dominated on the airfield, representing each squadron. Unlike the fiftieth anniversary in 1968, there was no public day to follow.

Another finale for another iconic aircraft, the RAF's Cold War legacy bomber, the Buccaneer was to receive a gold clock and pension. Just as with the Phantom, a big party for the Buccaneer was at least planned to take place at Coningsby's open day. This again took in the queen's official birthday parade and Trooping the Colour. While the weather on the day in 1992 was outstanding, 1993 was different. Coningsby's open day fell on the queen's official birthday once again. This year, a diamond 16 formation of Buccaneers was to fly down the Mall and then over Coningsby. The Buccaneers were operating from RAF Manston this time, where a total of twenty-two aircraft were gathered. When the formation, spares, and whippers-in were airborne,

'Tanker and Chicks'—Four Tornado F3s from 111 and 43 Sqns, break away from the Tristar inflight refuelling station before commencing their 'Gulf Salute Flypast', an extensive tactical role demonstration, also involving Buccaneers and Tornado GR1s, paying tribute to the recent liberation of Kuwait, seen over Finningley, 21 September 1991. (*John Higgins*)

the weather behaved until the flypast over the Mall was complete. Thereafter, the weather deteriorated and the planned flypast, followed by a demonstration airfield attack, at Coningsby had to be abandoned while the formation instead returned home to Lossiemouth. Finningley and Leuchars were both blessed with better weather this year with the Buccaneer displaying at both. Two display crews, Flt Lts Glenn Mason and Ian Donnelly from 12 Sqn and Flt Lts Neil Benson and Gary Davies from 208 Sqn, were made available to ensure the Buccaneer appeared at as many events in the aircraft's final year of operations. The final swansong, flown by Mason and Donnelly, was over Cranfield on 19 September, accurately advertised as the 'final public appearance' on the programme cover, the Cranfield display was organised by the home-based aeronautical college.

With the Buccaneer now withdrawn, the RAF's once extensive inventory of high-performance jets was reduced to three essential operational types—Tornado, Jaguar, and Harrier. The former existed as two essential designs to meet two completely different roles. Both variants, F3 and GR1, along with the Jaguar and Harrier GR7, now covered all offensive/defensive and tactical reconnaissance roles. In three years, the RAF'S core front line of thirty squadrons was now down to twenty-one.

Further, the Nimrod maritime ASW force shed a squadron reducing from four to three. The Priority 1 status applied seemingly in practice now to IAT Fairford, that is they got everything from the RAF. The still four official 'At Homes' now included Cosford and St Athan in June and, keeping the faith still, Finningley and Leuchars in September. If anything, from an enthusiasts' point of view, the 1990s were surprisingly something of a golden age. To live up to any kind of expectations, the more prominent air shows now needed and managed to attract an equal or sometimes larger contribution of resources from NATO air arms. Coupled with the newly liberated East European countries,

Another curtain finale, the Buccaneer was due to receive its gold clock and pension by the end of March 1994, so 1993 was the last opportunity to demonstrate the last wholly British jet bomber in service, from 12 Sqn here landing at RNAS Yeovilton. (*Adrian Balch*)

Buccaneer high speed run at Finningley, 18 September 1993; seven months later, the aircraft would be retired from service. (*John Fisher*)

including Russia, this disguised the very skinny resources of the RAF with a deep pool of overseas resources, which could all but be guaranteed. A further benefit of so many resources now expected from abroad was the reduced demand on the RAF meaning the impact on operational commitments was minimal. This was just as well as operational tasking was developing along a different direction to that of the Cold War.

UK-based units now spent more time overseas, meeting long-term policing of Iraq and the Balkans. There was no review of defence requirements as a result. Furthermore, as far as displays were concerned, the attraction of exotic overseas aircraft displays brought added risk. Display authorisation regarding some of the former Warsaw Pact countries needed closer scrutiny.

At the Fairford IAT in 1993, a particularly impressive array of foreign air arms from either side of the old Iron Curtain descended on this small corner of Gloucestershire. They included a pair of Jordanian F-18 Hornets and a new display team from what was now the Russian Federation. The new team consisted of two MiG-29s in a bright yellow and blue paint scheme. The two jets flew a similar close mirror/synchronised sequence to that of many similar pairs. They collided in mid-air, both pilots ejected, and both came down safely and the twisted remains of their still burning charges fell within the airfield confines. The two pilots seemed no more shaken than if they had just blown a tyre on a country road. Seen standing on the grass, cigarette in one hand and free hand in pocket, they were duly admitted to hospital, as per routine, twenty minutes later. One RAF officer described them as 'cool as a cucumber'.

Another RAF officer on duty at the Hradec Kralove air show in the Czech Republic, the weekend prior, witnessed the Russian team's display and thought 'That looks bloody sporting'. It is rumoured that during the subsequent accident investigation, a former Red Arrows pilot placed a same scale overlay of RAE Farnborough over Fairford using the same display datum (the centre point of a display area, usually halfway along the crowd line). It made for an interesting eye-opener. Had the accident happened over Farnborough, given this airfield's smaller size, the outcome would have been quite different. In 1993, the RAF still sanctioned a healthy number of open days, as had become customary through the summer. This practice was about to lose some of the more established regulars as Chivenor, Brawdy, and Coningsby all opened their gates to the public for the last time in 1993. The former two were due to be relinquished by the RAF in the next couple of years, the latter to focus on the more intense deployments due to the growing demands for overseas operations of one form or another, further exacerbated by the ongoing climate of cuts.

The year 1994 brought another fiftieth anniversary, this time D-Day. The centre focus for the air element was a mass flypast of RAF and other current aircraft from the air arms, which took part in the campaign.

The government meanwhile pursued further cuts through the announcement of 'Front Line First'. This was a follow-up review from 'Options for Change'. A short-notice announcement revealed the disbandment of 23 Squadron based at RAF Leeming in North Yorkshire. This squadron's loss was unexpected; it had not been detailed in the previous review and was implemented ahead of the next. Front Line First brought more bad news—Finningley and Scampton (now home of the Red Arrows) were to close. The streamlining concluded that Scampton would simply be abandoned. The Red Arrows, now to move to Cranwell, could still use the airfield to rehearse over.

This arrangement was necessary as Cranwell's circuit was too busy, which in turn questioned the logic of moving the Red Arrows here. Eventually, by 2001, the Red Arrows returned to Scampton after much of the station infrastructure had either been sold off, such as married quarters, or left to go to seed. Finningley's closure ironically might have been guessed at; a lot of new building work had recently been completed and the station was the busiest it had ever been. The resident No. 6 Flying Training School had been at Finningley since 1970 and provided elementary to advanced training for every aircrew position and lead-in training for multi-engine pilots. They had recently been joined by 100 Squadron of Strike Command operating Hawks in the Air Defence Target Facilities role. Further, Finningley was the home base for the Headquarters of the two SAR squadrons—22 and 202. The purpose behind the decision to close Finningley was not that the units themselves faced disbandment or that the base was in anyway underused.

The government simply want to sell off real estate. This has been pursued by governments of either hue at every opportunity, squeezing retained units onto fewer airfields freeing up others for closure, sale, or transfer to elements of the army returning from Germany. This seems to be an irresistible craving affecting parliamentarians and their bean-counting overseers. Following on from 1990, the closure of entire RAF stations on account of the savings in operating costs has continued regardless of the country's economic state and security concerns.

Finningley was certainly a plum target given its size. The units in question would be split and sent to other stations where space could be found, on the face of it no capability loss but a return to the exchequer. No. 100 Sqn went to Leeming (Air Defence); the Jetstreams and Dominies had no other home, so they were assigned to Cranwell while the Tucanos headed for Linton-on-Ouse, with the SAR Sea Kings and 6 FTS Hawks to Valley. Finningley held a fantastic last Battle of Britain display on 17 September 1994, sharing a large chunk of the flying programme with Leuchars, as had become quite a tradition. A mooted plan to hold a final hurrah in 1995 was shelved and instead the Battle of Britain office staff at Finningley were given permission to bag up everything and head to another station in the region.

There not being a lot to choose from, not so much because of a lack of stations, but available road and rail services and the distances from substantial population centres. As with the exercise conducted by the Central Participation Committee to find an alternative to Biggin Hill eighteen years earlier, the hunt was on to find a suitable alternative.

The gate figures at Finningley each year were a factor affording the South Yorkshire base the reputation for the presenting the largest one-day military air show in the UK, possibly Europe. A small shortlist was narrowed to Leeming and Waddington. Leeming, which was further north, was perhaps more accessible being on the A1. It also had the added frisson of the undeniably popular noisy fast jets being *in situ*. Waddington was more central nationally, and with more space, it was the picked station but with a slight change to the traditional format.

A regular feature of the Finningley displays in later years was the 'Balboa'—essentially quartets of each type flown by the resident 6 Flying Training School; here Dominies lead Jetstreams then Jet Provosts. (*Author's Collection*)

The dry weather at Finningley, 21 September 1991, is evident by the yellowing grass. 6 FTS JP crews mount up for their part in the station flypast. (*Alec Blyth*)

The effective move of Finningley to Waddington included a reschedule from September to the first weekend of July and an expansion from a one-day event to two days. The time normally spent reviewing the recent event and planning for the next was instead disrupted by the time spent transferring the Finningley Battle of Britain office staff, headed by Sqn Ldr (retired) Paul Byram, across to their new set-up at Waddington. The amount of effort devoted to putting together a 'double' display—using essentially the same 'At Home' format, with a sparser catchment area and a station full of personnel, many of which would be on their 'first rodeo'—would render anything achieved worth a round of applause.

Another change was the title—Battle of Britain 'At Home' day was not dismissed altogether, but the more descriptive 'Waddington International Air Show' was preferred.

The dates chosen were 1 and 2 July. It was perhaps no coincidence that this was approximate to the weekend of the very first Hendon Pageant exactly seventy-five years before. Bearing in mind this was still an inaugural first attempt and shaky weather over the weekend, it was not too bad. The display content did not set any new standards but under the circumstances attracted some impressive overseas participants—the Russian 'Test Pilots' aerobatics team with their two Sukhoi SU-27/30 Fighters and a rare chance to see a USAF F-117 Night Hawk stealth attack aircraft likely for the first time in the UK.

The 'At Home' day at St Athan was held for the last time on 24 June. Continued outsourcing of all aircraft maintenance functions were heading toward rendering St Athan an all-civilianised MOD maintenance facility, with the RAF presence no longer significant.

Contracting out of aircraft maintenance services reduced the once-copious number of RAF personnel below the point where further displays on the same scale could continue to be held. As 1995 was another significant anniversary (VE/VJ Day), a significant effort was made by the IAT operating company, RAFBFE. Since the end of the Cold War, IAT more than any other had wielded clout to attract, each year, a heavy Eastern European contingent. That year brought aerobatics teams from the Czech Republic and Poland along with a MiG-29 from Slovakia, now a wholly separate country having separated from the Czech Republic. Flying on each of the two days extended now to at least eight hours, with some aircraft alternating with each other between each of the days, so congested was the programmed amount of flying to coordinate.

Another milestone anniversary marking seventy-five years since the first Hendon Pageant was recognised at Fairford this year. The good folks at the RAFBFE put on a theatrical display reminiscent of the era where an Avro 504K and other aircraft of a similar vintage flew a slow racetrack pattern to bomb a pretend fort, just like the good old days.

The RAF, as was now the form, placed all its resources at the disposal of the IAT team. This year included additional contributions, including four Harriers from 3 Squadron (still based in Germany) to fly a tactical demonstration and internationally, a variety of aircraft, including Luftwaffe Tornados, USAF F-15s, and RAF Hawks to fly missing man formations to draw a line under the half a century since 1945. A finale set piece was complete with a red smoke victory sign flown by two of the Red Arrows through which a Spitfire, Mustang, and (again in the spirit of reconciliation) a ME 109 flew a 'Vic' formation, finishing with an upward bomb burst manoeuvre. Gathered on the main runway below, and facing the punters, were aircraft representative of every allied air arm directly involved in the war in Europe. They sat static with engines running while various military helicopters hovered just above.

Alas, 1995 did not escape without tragedy striking. Toward the end of the display season, a Nimrod MR2 from 120 Squadron based at Kinloss stalled during a climb over the Great Canadian Lake, Toronto. As the aircraft hit the water, the fuselage ruptured and all seven on board were killed.

Leuchars, now hosted the sole surviving, in all respects, traditional Battle of Britain 'At Home' day, as per the original 1945 format. That year, on 16 September, a first was chalked up—displays by the Luftwaffe. The German contribution included a colourful Alpha Jet, almost indistinguishable from the Belgian one also flying and, bringing back old memories of the recent Cold War for Leuchars, an F-4 Phantom.

A final display of its kind, hitherto a regular feature at Leuchars, was a rehearsed formation display by one of the resident fighter squadrons. These volunteer supplementary displays had become increasingly rare along with set-piece role demonstrations, all subject to operational availability outside of the official display commitment for the year. This time being the turn of 43 Squadron, with five of their Tornado F3s, the finale to the home team's effort was spectacular enough as each of four F3s raced down the runway before pulling skyward with the fifth aircraft reciprocating from the opposite end.

RAF allocation of resources for displays was very much set into the routine now until 2005, save for the additional provisions directed to take part in the Fairford tattoo each year. Farnborough could no longer draw anything like the level of RAF assets, which it managed only as recently as 1990. The two supposedly comparably prestigious occasions have since 2000 diverged further down different paths.

Fairford was also becoming, in part, something of a trade show as well but has always been prioritised by the RAF, while Farnborough has increasingly been either sidelined or the latter's organisers have placed less store by service participation.

Each year, IAT has a theme or two; for 1996, it was the advent of the jet engine. This brought some privately operated classic jets and a return of the missing man formations like 1995. Two RAF aircraft, which were routinely on the display circuit, were absent this year—the Nimrod, pending the outcome of the AAIB initial findings following the crash in Canada the previous year, and the Tornado F3. A lack of available personnel meant no spare capacity to train a display crew.

Neither of these suspensions were permanent and so the overall picture remained very much as it was the previous year.

The defence secretary, Michael Portillo, sent the Red Arrows on an overseas flag-waving tour promoting business, meaning they missed the second Waddington International Air Show where the hole was filled by a team of Hawker Hunters from a civilian company called Jet Heritage. Ex-military jets were now becoming more of a regular feature in the hands of civilian owners with more money than Midas. This was a sign of things to come, so the weight of opinion concurred.

The German air force and navy, not universally known in quite the same way as the RAF or other NATO air arms for any kind of demonstration flying, especially since the Ramstein disaster, were out in force this year. There were solo demos by a Tornado, a F-4, and, because of reunification, a MiG-29. The latter came from a handful of jets inherited by the Federal Luftwaffe following the disbandment of the *Luftstreitkrafte der Nationalen Voksarmee* (Air Forces of the National People's Army). The Germans also had a C-160 Transall display to see the RAF C-130K. The *Bundes Marineflieger* supplied their own Tornado crew from MGF 2 the last naval air unit to operate them.

That German military aircraft were seen at all on the European air show circuit was down to a simple legal wording, stating that the flying sequence demonstrated officially was not a display. They were demonstrations of operational tactical manoeuvres and pretty raunchy it all was. This declared status kept any hard-nosed troublemakers at bay, for now at least. While making this clear at the 1996 Fairford event, Sean Maffett (the voice of RIAT) concluded, in an upbeat tone, following the 'tactical sequence' flown by the *Marineflieger* Tornado, 'I think that was a very good not a display'.

The IAT's *pièce de résistance* this year was as many serviceable Harriers as 1 Squadron could muster for a spectacular role demonstration, and another first was achieved—a demonstration by an Ukrainian SU-27 Flanker. Such a sight was beyond the limit of possibility just seven or more years earlier when this very aircraft was the potential adversary of RAF Phantom and Tornado fighter crews. Farnborough was held in September 1996, a week before Leuchars, and the dominance of British military prowess emphasised by heavy RAF and sometimes RN participation was now a distant memory. Instead, ahead of the curve, the Royal Swedish Air Force already had in service their own fourth-generation fighter, the JAS39C Gripen; they sent over three, one to fly, one to sit in the static, and a spare for the former.

The US Navy, nowhere near as common as the USAF in European circles, provided a couple of F-18 Hornets while the continued good relations with Russia were maintained with another strong showing of new enormous twin-engine fighters, with unparalleled handling and manoeuvrability. 1996 saw IAT officially become RIAT as the RAFBFE display at Fairford had received royal prerogative.

As 1997 approached, the only RAF-organised air shows were three 'At Homes'—Cosford, Waddington, and Leuchars—and the last locally organised station air day continued at St Mawgan, but this year would be the penultimate for the St Mawgan holidaymakers' special. We also saw the return of the RAF Tornado F3 solo, this time in the hands of Flt Lts Peter Hackett and Al Taylor from Leeming-based 25 Squadron. The year began with a flypast of three F3s from 111 Squadron as part of a memorial service for Sir Frank Whittle, the British inventor of the jet engine.

Waddington 1997 attracted its best international showing so far, the White Albatrosses from the Slovakian AF, the Swiss AF's Patrouille Suisse, with their six F-5E Tigers and the Royal Jordanian Falcons. Overseas participation was quite substantial this year. The F-16, now the standard tactical fighter of most of Europe's air forces, had become as commonplace at UK air shows as RAF front-line types. Usually, displays by F-16s have been provided by Belgium and Holland; this time, Denmark and Norway sent over their representative F-16 solo performers. From other allied air arms came a USAF B-1B, a MiG-29, again from Slovakia, and the return of the French Air Force 'Voltige Victor' display team, flying a pair of Mirage F1s. RIAT was officially RIAT this time around, and RAFBFE had put together the largest flying programme on record at about sixty items, squeezed into over eight hours each day and blessed with perfect weather, the weekend was incomparable. This time, the Ukrainians returned with an aerobatics team of six MiG-29s, a Lockheed F-104S from Italy, and an F-100 Super Sabre from Tracor Systems; a mock air battle from the RAF involving four 111 Sqn Tornado F3s and four Hawks from 100 Sqn all rounded off the day with more unique and protracted flypasts.

Also, in their final season, the Silver Swallows from the Irish Air Corps with four Fouga Magisters flew over mainland UK for what was the first time. The Silver Swallows returned to the UK in September, this time destined for Leuchars. The demonstration by home-based Tornados and Leeming Hawks was on the cards for Leuchars as well until operational commitments got in the way. The Hawks could not make it, and someone believed this rendered the Tornado involvement pointless. This may well be, but to cancel the latter half as well is where the point was missed. After the initial concerns about contraction, the status of military air shows and the RAF's contributions were far more robust than any had a right to expect. The RAF effort was, overall, at its most constrained in history, but it was well balanced and with fewer events, better resourced and spaced across the summer, as had previously been argued, allowing the most to be made of what there was.

The year 1998 was the RAF's eightieth birthday, and they were therefore the host service at the Royal Tournament. Once again, the noticeable celebrations to mark the occasion were organised by the RAFBE at Fairford. No fewer than twenty-three Tornado aircraft were sent by various units from across Strike Command. The RIAT people also introduced large screens this year positioned slightly back from the crowd line and showing a mix of livestreamed images alternated with archive footage from across the preceding eighty years.

After years of seeing the RAF twisting and turning to avoid clashing with the SBAC at Farnborough, this year, the crucial public weekend was allowed to overlap with the sole remaining RAF display in September at Leuchars. The demands of meeting both events in terms of service resources no longer posed the dilemma it once did. Demands on training also removed the familiar Hawk solo. From the RAF's point of view, 1998 was another year that ended in the publication of another 'government review'. Defence reviews were now regularly being labelled with reassuring nicknames, all the better to mask the true intent. The Strategic Defence Review had a more impartial ring to it than the previous two, but there were some really spun titles to come. However, they all amounted to one thing—cuts.

The losses to the RAF this time included two Tornado squadrons. Yet while Chancellor Gordon Brown's axe was still being sharpened, the long-awaited Eurofighter had reached another stage in development; we might expect to see more of it in public. As the Farnborough show coincided with Leuchars, the latter was expected to benefit from the first ever appearance of the new fighter, making the trip up north from Hampshire on the Saturday. Alas, the dreaded serviceability reasons intervened this time. Farnborough was held in September for the last time; by 2000, the SBAC 'extravaganza' was moved to July, the week following RIAT. The theory was that going back-to-back would allow the two to share aircraft.

The year 1999 brought a climax to the conflict in the Balkans. The war was to culminate in Kosovo; this placed a heavy demand on NATO, which ended up on a war footing in the region. Although the campaign lasted little more than a couple of months, most military air shows across Europe were cancelled, some in anticipation.

The USAF air fête at Mildenhall bit the dust early on. Established in 1976, the 'Hall' had established a reputation as the largest 'militarily organised air show in Europe' and continued as an annual event with no misses until now. The impact of the war meant the end of the St Mawgan International Air Day. Like many this year, plans were well in hand when the decision was taken to cancel. The date picked was 11 August, significant as this was the day there would be a total eclipse of the sun. Given St Mawgan's vantage point, the eclipse would have been seen quite clearly from this far deep into Cornwall. The station air day office marketed the day as 'the eclipse air show'. This in part contributed to the cancellation, on top of the lack of medical personnel, which was the key reason for nearly all cancellations. The Devon and Cornwall Police were concerned about the success of the day with the added attraction of attending an air show. The snarling traffic jams alone were going to be a nightmare, with or without a big-ticket event thrown into the mix.

Since the end of the Cold War, the level of RAF staff at St Mawgan had dropped considerably, making the air day difficult to keep running, just as had been the case with Biggin Hill. The predicted impact of operational commitments over the Balkans compelled the RAF to cancel the Leuchars display.

This made September 1999 the first since 1945 when not a single RAF base opened to the public. The navy's two regular air days at Culdrose and Yeovilton were further casualties, with personnel from both bases being deployed.

Curious was the survival of Waddington and Cosford and no reduction in the level of RAF flying, which this year included a Canberra from 39 Squadron painted in the same pale blue scheme as the original prototype to celebrate the fiftieth anniversary of its maiden test flight. Also unaffected was Fairford. RIAT was held here for the last time before moving briefly to RAF Cottesmore. When the world's 'officially' largest air show returned to Fairford in 2002, things would be different.

Having seen its final air day in 1998, and with the turn of the century approaching, the wonder was how St Mawgan would return after 1999, especially with some of the dramatic and nonsense predictions afoot. Another negative regarding military public engagement, flare, and panache, the Royal Tournament this year was reported to be the last. The reason was insufficient resources and personnel. Bearing in mind, the government were now well into implementing the 'Strategic Defence Review'; this did bring more personnel reductions, for all the review's positive tone about readiness and ability.

The year 2000 otherwise brought a return to business as usual. While this year's special anniversary was the sixtieth anniversary of the Battle of Britain, we were not going to see anything along the lines of the 160+ aircraft flypast over London or over any RAF stations as we did in 1990, but having missed the fiftieth anniversary appearance they had planned for Abingdon, the USAF Thunderbirds did keep their date this time with the Waddington air show, albeit on the Saturday only; anyone turning up on Sunday could see them leaving. A similar enactment to one at Boscombe Down's fiftieth anniversary show, with all the Spitfires and Hurricanes that could be mustered, was planned for RIAT.

Held at Cottesmore this year, RIAT was marred by low cloud; a lot of aircraft were reduced to taxiing down the runway in place of their flying slots then back to the flight line. There was more than a tinge of disappointment especially as the weather over Fairford was reported to be ideal. Mildenhall Air Fête returned but was also hampered by poor weather. The RAF's last remaining Battle of Britain display, at Leuchars, was blessed with good weather and no fewer than eight NATO Air Forces were represented at least once each in the flying programme; as for the RAF, everything available turned up. The station put together, for the first time in some years, an air combat set piece involving four of the home-based Tornados, four Hawks, and a very rarely seen VC-10 tanker. Like the Victor before it, the VC-10 soldiered on in service long after the RAF had withdrawn it from any flying display commitments.

A surprise item was included—a short run through followed by a couple of tight turns then a vertical departure heralded the future, courtesy of prototype Eurofighter Typhoon DA-02. You can see DA-02 today in the Century of Flight Hall at the RAF museum near Hendon, suspended from the ceiling. After 1999, Leuchars very nearly did not happen, three years on the trot, which might have finished it off earlier. After the Kosovan crisis initially brought an early cancellation, September 2000 brought fuel refinery blockades and go-slow protests by haulage company drivers on several main roads and motorways. The week leading up to the day was characterised by long queues of cars at seemingly every garage forecourt. Yet the sixtieth anniversary of the Battle of Britain 'At Home' day happened, presenting the largest military air show of the year. The fuel shortage forced a short-notice decision to press ahead. The regular commentator at Leuchars, Roger Hoefling, remarked on the unexpected high attendance, wondering where everyone got their fuel from. The next year was expected to be something of an anti-climax with the Battle of Britain's sixtieth anniversary out of the way, but there were some nice surprises, two of them centred on RAF Valley in Anglesey.

First, the Hawk solo display was resumed after a two-year absence, with the pilot and jet both being based at Valley. The station itself was to hold an open day on 18 August, as a one off, to mark its own sixtieth birthday. This was the first open day here since 1994. Seven years had taken its toll on planning experience, with long moribund queues of traffic on base, entering this time rather than leaving.

The military contributions were limited compared with previous events here. The weather contrasted severely with 1994, and a billed appearance by the Typhoon prototype failed to materialise. The RAF's third remaining official 'At Home' at Cosford seemed to endure but it contrasted considerably with the other two remaining regulars. This year, however, the Cosford air show office benefited from the cancellation of the air show at BAE Warton. The French Air Force sent their package to Cosford instead, which included a pair of Jaguars, 'Raffin Mike', and a solo Mirage

2000; the Belgian F-16 was also diverted here as a result. Yet the real marvel was the appearance of an ex-Navy Cold War warrior, resurrected after years of restoration—a Sea Vixen.

Privately operated ex-military aircraft under the broad heading 'Classic or Cold War Jets' were a growth industry. The RAF's now flagship event at Waddington pulled off a significant coup in terms of overseas participation this year, from beyond NATO came the Israeli Air Force. They confirmed late on that they would send over three F-15I Ra'ams (Eagles), one to fly a most energetic tactical display with various wing stores. Two displays were flown, both on the Sunday. The first was a practice demo, before the public, due to the required display authorisation still outstanding on the Saturday. RIAT took place at Cottesmore for the second and final time in July 2001. A display by a German Air Force MiG-29 was curtailed on safety grounds but at least this year the weather was outstanding.

The Leuchars 'At Home' was scheduled for Saturday 15 September. As such, Leuchars followed the first week of the conference season, which, as always, started with the TUC. With just four days to go, preparations were well in hand, then at lunchtime on the Tuesday, the world was turned upside down. The age of rolling broadcast news was now with us and now delivered the most dramatic and tragic 'breaking news' yet.

This time, the phrase 'the world would never be the same again' certainly applied by mid-afternoon. What unfolded that day had a seismic impact on the future, another day to rank with the destruction of the Berlin Wall or the assassination of JFK.

The world looked on through the medium of television and twenty-four-hour rolling news to see hijacked airliners, in real time, flown deliberately into the World Trade Centre buildings. As the minutes and then hours passed, New York became an apocalyptic vision. No weapons of mass destruction were utilised, and there was no vast invading army—just two hijacked commercial jets.

The UK prime minister, Tony Blair, was at the TUC conference when Bill Morris, TUC president, was seen tapping the PM on the shoulder to alert him to the situation now reorienting the future of western foreign and defence policy. Some 2,000 miles away, the US president, George Bush Jnr, was attending a primary school where he was being entertained by the school choir; once appraised of events, he placed his country on a war footing in response. In the UK as with everywhere across the civilised world, the British government acted with the suspension of all transatlantic flights. In the USA, all commercial air travel was suspended.

The idea of gathering masses of people in one location is one of the routine practices that governments all over the globe have, to varying degrees, refused to allow the perpetrators of 9/11 and their ilk to put an end to.

A considered and planned response and the long-term consequences were going to unfold over time to come. As for the immediate implications, having the public congregate in their thousands on an operational British military airbase, under the new security climate, needed an instant decision. The Leuchars air show was facing a crisis review for the third year in succession. As with the previous two years when Kosovo and the fuel crisis placed a yes or no question over proceedings, the same was happening now, at very short notice. The question of whether the display should still be held, given the stage reached, would not have been beyond cancellation. Yet just what was the immediate security threat? Was 9/11 the firing shot of an imminent mass terrorist invasion of the West? The understanding of the security situation and how it affected Leuchars has not been released into the public domain. However, the decision taken by the Leuchars station commander, certainly in touch with the AFB, was certainly to go ahead.

Would it be overly frivolous or insensitive? Just what kind of public impact, good or bad, would arise, and was it dangerous to carry on regardless? It was most likely to be met with criticism and favour no matter what they did. A simple bold gesture—'the terrorists will not prevail'—might prevail over the public mood; the bold was accompanied with appropriately reflective sentiment. During the afternoon, Leuchars' now long-standing commentator, Roger Hoefling, called for a minute's silence, signalled by a whistle over the Tannoy.

As expected, what was a quite substantial USAF contribution this year had been cancelled and the long-term impact on military-hosted air shows was set in motion. Surprisingly, RAF events retained the more traditional approach, allowing on-airfield parking, which has been abandoned almost everywhere else. With immediate effect, initially under review, the USAFE Mildenhall Air Fête was cancelled for 2002 and would not return despite rumours up to 2005 that it might. That it did not was in part attributed to the lack of remaining experience at staging such a major proposition; everyone involved with the last air fête in 2001 had moved on by 2005.

Another quite inadequate proposition was a much scaled-down open day for invited guests. Mildenhall was the last USAF-organised air show in Europe, like the RAF open days; these had been widespread up to the early 1990s. Most disappeared during the early post-Cold War period. Reduced force levels and fewer active bases meant the inevitable reduced scope or even the need to engage the public and build a rapport. This was especially at the core of American thinking as their bases stood on foreign soil; regardless of the efficacy and justification, the need to be good neighbours was the aim of the exercise.

The increased operational tempo, which has never stopped since, has not helped as a heavier demand on resources has continued. One can argue, following 9/11, that the war on terror would see a reversal in military spending cuts. Curiously, any reversal to the now perennial rounds of defence cuts does not appear to have been regarded as an advantage.

In 2002, RIAT moved back to the home turf—the USAF base at Fairford, which was active as a standby forward-operating base as opposed to a fully active one, but no less a USAF base. Now access to tens of thousands of people over one weekend each year under the new security climate meant a radical change from the preceding years.

Previously all the way back in 1999, the Thamesdown shuttlebus from Swindon would decanter the punters, so travelling along a small road leading through Kempsford, they would then descend through an open (and unmanned) emergency access gate, walk about 20 yards or so, then meet a couple of RIAT volunteers, perhaps with a trestle table selling tickets and programmes. Fast forward to 2002 and onwards, the bus has to be parked up on site but in a zone isolated from the designated public area; from here, everyone forms a queue at the relevant entry marquee, with different colours for different zones.

Here the ponderous security checks take place—x-ray machines, hand-held scanners, swarms of private security operatives, and RAF personnel to conduct bag searches and wield the scanners. Afterwards, you will meet a friendly face to get your ticket checked. In 2002, they could still be purchased on site on the day. The impact of international terrorism has prompted similar arrangements at many public events—such as at Ascot, Farnborough, and Twickenham—all to now resemble, to varying degrees, airport security for international departures.

Following on from the Twin Towers tragedy of 2001 with US/UK armed forces having been engaged from one Middle East conflict to the next, one might have expected a strengthened military position as a result. Instead, the state of the UK's standing defence posture, especially air power, has continued to decline. In March 2003, the long-advertised incursion into Iraq got underway. Unlike the Kosovo crisis of 1999 and despite the protraction of this operation, with a heavier level of UK involvement, the proposed number of military-supported air shows remained unaffected. This time, only the now established display at RAF Cosford was cancelled, perhaps prematurely, based on the expectation that, as in 1999, resources would be sparse.

The focus for celebration in 2003 was the centenary of the first manned flight. Nothing out of the ordinary was concocted for such an auspicious anniversary, but the RAF authorised a second Hawk solo display for perhaps the first time since 1994 and a rather *ad hoc* flypast of tankers and Tornados over Waddington, which by 2003 was very much out of the ordinary other than at RIAT. A final display from a venerable fighter, once operated by the RAF & RN, was provided by the Luftwaffe at Leuchars in September where the Scots got to see the last display by an F-4 Phantom. The following year, the Luftwaffe shortly followed by the *Marineflieger* suspended public displays by high-performance aircraft; in the case of the latter, they were about to lose their last tactical air wing as part of the German government's restructuring of the *Bundeswehr*.

The sixtieth anniversary of D-Day was in 2004. This was largely celebrated in the centre of Hyde Park. A stage show and as many remaining war veterans as could be mustered were there for what was perhaps the last large gathering of Second World War veterans. From here, future milestones would naturally see fewer veterans with the passage of time.

From an aviation point of view, there was nothing to match the fantastic salute to the wartime generation at Fairford back in 1995. What was more to the fore this year was the inaugural public appearance of the Eurofighter Typhoon in RAF hands. There was not a fully choreographed aerobatics demonstration, but pilots from the operational and evaluation and operational conversion units flew examples of the 'T-Bird' (an in-service colloquial term referring to a two-seat trainer variant of a single-seat operational aircraft)—T1s—at a small number of priority one events. The demonstrations followed a series of tight turns culminating in a steep departure, all very reminiscent, for some, of the early displays by the English Electric Lightning, some forty-five years earlier, if somewhat restrained.

The navy provided a Sea Harrier, now facing retirement, from 899 NAS. The aircraft assigned to display duties specifically was dressed in a gloss indigo paint scheme with a gloss-white underside and high visibility markings, known as the 'Admiral's Barge' scheme. The return of the set-piece display at this year's Leuchars air show provided something of a post-Cold War renaissance, suggesting things could be looking up again. Such set pieces involving several aircraft from various operational units were considered outside the scope of assigned display aircraft.

The year 2004 was further encouraging as the return to public display flying by the Boeing Vertol Chinook surprised some after several years out of the public eye; it has proved arguably one of the more popular display items since. The promising start to the year did not last; in July the government announced the results of the latest defence review; this one had been given an unwieldy title: 'Delivering Security in a Changing World'. At the time, British forces—essentially the army and the RAF—had significant deployments on going in both Iraq, Afghanistan, Saudi Arabia, and Turkey, the latter two locations to support the no fly zones, the former to contribute to military policing actions.

On top of this, the new review proposed a range of cuts to operational units, essentially air and naval units but the army was to be streamlined through a reduction in infantry and armour along with a radical reorganisation of the regimental system. This was defended by some as a much-needed modernisation to drag the army kicking and screaming into the twenty-first century.

The 2015 Chinook display crew. The Chinook was initially introduced to the display circuit in about 1982; in the 1990s, it was removed from display flying but returned in 2004, since when it has been a regular feature. As chopper displays go, this one really is scintillating. (*Air Historical Branch*)

The navy were already expected to lose the Sea Harrier rather than see it upgraded (too costly), the RAF was to lose some of the Nimrod fleet, the entire Jaguar force, and another squadron of Tornado air defence fighters, all with the corresponding personnel losses further compounded by more civilianisation and contractorisation.

The Jaguar had been through a quite extensive upgrade programme including a more advance avionics suite and cockpit changes. This included the introduction of HOTAS (hands on throttle and stick) controls and, in some cases, uprated new engines. It came as no surprise then, given the MOD's craving for irony in every decision, to learn that all the Jaguars were to go. This aircraft was now at its best—an asset the MOD had so recently spent a lot of taxpayers' loot on. The RAF would share its remaining Harrier fleet with the navy, requiring both RAF and naval personnel to be carrier deployable, although this was already in train following the Sea Harrier cancellation.

The RAF bore the brunt of the cuts—7,000 personnel lost while 1,500 went from the RN and just 1,000 from the army. The number of future Nimrod MRA4 aircraft was to be further reduced (originally twenty-one) from eighteen to sixteen; these cuts reached quite deep into the RAF's flexibility and depth of capability.

The following year, 2005, brought only a couple of changes to the display commitment. The RAF suspended displays by the existing Nimrod MR2s; fatigue restrictions on the airframe limited their use, therefore display flying was excluded, as with the RAF Phantoms based in Germany in the 1980s.

On the plus side, the Typhoon was presented this year with a far more comprehensive display sequence flown by the first officially designated display pilot, Flt Lt Matt Elliott, an instructor on 29 Reserve Squadron. Following the sixtieth anniversary of D-Day, the same marker for VE/VJ Day was to be officially observed in 2005.

It was also the last year that the RAF were able to present an inventory of its still extensive front line, with an allocated solo display pilot/crew per type. Again, the two Tornado variants were represented as different aircraft, meaning those higher priority events—RIAT/RAF 'At Homes'—got to see both the GR4 and F3 being put through their paces. Despite the Jaguar being destined for the scrapyard courtesy of the recent round of cuts, 41 Sqn (based at Coltishall) were able to operate a final solo display. Joining the Jaguar, the Sea Harrier was also being withdrawn, but the Navy Board gave permission for a formation demonstration by a quartet of Sea Harriers from 801 NAS, assigned to the priority 1 air shows and the two remaining naval air days. The fleet now faced the future sharing the RAF's fleet of Harrier GR7s and 9s.

The Jaguar and Harrier had most of their airframes re-engined, in each case delivering a significant increase in thrust resulting in some interestingly enhanced performance from the aerobatics point of view; each now included more in the way of vertical and looping manoeuvres, weather-permitting. The connoisseurs of the country's second most popular spectator sport could also look forward to the opportunity to compare two Hawk solos again with one each from Strike and Personnel and Training Commands.

Away from the service events, Eastbourne's seafront air show this year drew an impressive line up together with some RIAT-style fare from overseas including a French Mirage 2000 and from the USAF, quite unbelievably, a B-1B Lancer. The weather behaved.

The year 2005 was the most prolific year for RAF/RN displays since 1990. The Nimrod was not forgotten entirely either, with a single robust flypast being made on each day of the Waddington air show thanks to unexpected availability at the time. What was not at all expected was that this would be the last year that a solo Tornado F3 display would be seen.

It was being reported in some aviation magazines that the RAF was reviewing display policy again. Of this, there could be no doubt. The level of overseas commitments coupled with material cuts to operational assets and personnel now left little room for manoeuvre. Up to the present, the impact of the 2004 review was unfolding quickly by the start of 2006. Two squadrons of Jaguars remained at Coltishall. By the end of the year, the station was abandoned, and the last Jaguar equipped unit had left for Coningsby to spend the last few months before disbandment. The cuts were presented as an improvement in effectiveness—'leaner and meaner' or 'less means more'.

Through 2006, the impact of the 2004 'defence review' continued to be implemented. The RAF display line up was reduced accordingly, the Jaguar while still operational had been seen in RAF hands for the last time, the Jaguar bowed out with scarcely a public footnote unlike the effort to mark the retirement of the Lightning, Phantom, and Buccaneer. The Tornado F3 was more of a surprise, still very much the RAF's principal all-weather fighter. The F3 solo was withdrawn for 2006 due to operational commitments and a lack of sufficient ground crew. The Typhoon was now the most prominent fast jet from the RAF available to the air show scene.

By 2006, the amount of effort the RAF could commit to public displays was subject to further review. For many, this image from Leuchars, 9 September, may now represent the tail end of a golden age in air shows, with Tornados participating in a set-piece airfield attack. (*Air Historical Branch*)

The other two on the circuit this year, the Harrier GR7A and the Tornado GR4, were both in high demand operationally, essentially in the Middle East. Bowing out after about fifty-five years of continuous service was the English Electric Canberra. Represented by the last operational version, the PR9, this version alone was forty-five years old. There were probably about three or four serviceable airframes and yet a most impressive semi-aerobatics sequence was flown at a small number of locations culminating in RIAT. After this final curtain call, the PR9 retired at the end of July. After a rather lacklustre year for the RAF's flagship Waddington International Air Show, the year finished on a high note as the sole remaining homage to 'the few' at Leuchars went ahead a week earlier than tradition would expect, on 9 September. On reflection, this Leuchars show was something of a last hurrah in terms of substance. At the start of July, everything but the proverbial kitchen sink seemed to have been thrown at Leuchars; the home-based units provided a heavier contribution than had been seen for many years.

Solo F3 displays might be suspended, but the station's own squadrons all made an extraordinary effort reminiscent of a much earlier era. Ten of the Base's F3s got airborne to form a diamond nine formation with the single aircraft to act as a 'whipper in' to keep a choreographer's eye on the formation that swooped around two times, to the theme from *Braveheart* (the formation was identified as Braveheart formation), before returning to beat up the airfield in one large 'V' made up of three smaller 'V' formations. Reheat was used in abundance, while later on, four more F3s from 111 Squadron got airborne to defend the airfield and, uncharacteristically for dedicated interceptors, demonstrated strafing runs followed by high-speed low bombing runs by four GR4s of 617 'Dambusters' Squadron.

From overseas, Belgian and Dutch F-16s, a Czech Gripen, and a Polish MiG-29 were put through their paces while the MiG and Typhoon flew twice to make up for one or two cancelled aircraft that could not get airborne due to the weather at airfields in the south of England—quite the opposite of the fair skies over north-east Fife on this occasion.

It had already been notified that in 2007, Leuchars, for that year, would not be 'At Home' due to airfield works to prepare for the forecast arrival of what would eventually be three operational squadrons of Typhoons. Much would be radically different. Seemingly, the air staff had directed the Events Team (formerly the Central Participation Committee) toward a new format for 2007, central to which was a move toward far fewer jet solos. Instead, the still healthy inventory of front-line types would be represented on the air show circuit, at priority one events, and they would all appear on stage together in a single set-piece 'role demonstration'. This was not a new approach but was significant in that it was a scheduled display item and more so because it represented the bulk of what the RAF felt able to place before the public this year.

Initially, the plan was to run two such teams:

Team A: 2 × Tornado F3s; 2 × Tornado GR4s; 2 × Hawk T1/1As; 1 × C-130J; 1 × Chinook HC2; and 1 × E-3D Sentry.

Team B: 2 × Typhoon F2s; 2 × Harrier GR7/7As; 2 × Hawk T1/1As; 1 × C-130J; 1 × Chinook HC2; and 1 × E-3D.

It was not clear whether both teams would be made available simultaneously or would alternate at events running for two or more days—for example, RIAT,

Waddington, or Biggin Hill. The latter here was the civilian-run but highly prestigious air fair and was now included as a priority-one event by the RAF events team. Before the summer arrived, Team B was dropped while the form for the first team was to draw on operational units as available; there was to be no set demonstration crew as was necessary with aerobatics displays of any description.

The cost in terms of fuel and personnel hours, to meet the level of training for an assortment of FJ solo aerobatics sequences and rehearsals, made the role demo, with its much lower rate of lead up training and much lower number of calendar appointments—a far more viable alternative. Among the hitherto regular individual displays removed (forever) were the Tornado F3, Tornado GR4, Harrier, C-130J, and Jetstream T1. This left largely Personnel and Training Command aircraft to meet to fill the solos gaps—Tutor T1, Tucano and Hawk.

A rather less successful and rather cringeworthy innovation was created to try and shore up the downward slide—the 'Spirit of Adventure'. This idea was as mawkish as it sounds. It also represented an unnecessary diversion of funds to try and reach out to the growing number of Brits who now lived in parts of the country which, following the years of base closures, were several counties away from the nearest RAF station.

A small number of what were essentially former RAF airfields were identified to host a 'Spirit of Adventure'. This was in effect a small but essentially RAF air display. The airfields picked to host these pocket air displays included the old aerodromes at Abingdon in Oxfordshire, Woodvale near Manchester, and a suitable location at Kinross in East Central Scotland. On the plus side, each venue would be open on two consecutive days and the 'role demo' would be the jewel in the crown at each together with all the surviving approved service displays. This was perhaps possible because the ensemble was so scaled back on 2005.

The compact if impressive flying was one thing, the presentation was almost certainly what killed off the concept. It was deliberately engineered, with all due respect, for a 'tabloid' intellect. The funfair, fantasy escapism, and interactive flavour of the whole deal said it all. At the only Spirit of Adventure to take place, Abingdon (or to use the location's new name, Dalton Barracks) in May, the crowd line was marked at regular intervals with living room-sized television flatscreens in much the same way as the speaker system. On here, a hammy-acted scenario with all the camp nonsense of a *Flash Gordon* space romp was played out, with IMAX sound effects. This then moved to the real world as the storyline dovetailed with the live action over head and dramatic incidental music, just like a real Hollywood blockbuster.

It was an expensive way of trying to appeal to the bedroom computer game culture. The second day of the Abingdon Spirit of Adventure was cancelled due to weather—a claim the RAF were entitled to make as certainly as the cloud base did not really break which then turned to heavy rain from the middle of the afternoon. However, the word on the street was the gate on the first day was dismal. The remaining planned Spirits of Adventure bit the dust in short order and were discreetly swept under the carpet. A *bona fide* enthusiast queried why the RAF did not just pour the resources into the existing three 'At Home's and RIAT. A more worrying development, if only due to its unprecedented nature, the 2007 Waddington had to cancel the second day, 1 July, following an overnight torrential down pour. The latter part of June had already brought heavy rain and flooding across various parts of the country with some tragic consequences. On the morning of Sunday, the air show director, Paul Byram, took a bold decision and cancelled the show due to the number of waterlogged areas on the airfield. This presented too great a risk to a large gathering, some of which were already through the gates.

The following year marked the ninetieth anniversary of the founding of the RAF. The light blue contribution to the public arena in 2008 was very much the same as in 2007 but with one or two additions, one being the return of the 1985 format of the latest fighter in a coordinated display with a Supermarine Spitfire from the BBMF. This was reintroduced as a one off to mark the RAF's ninetieth anniversary, this time with the Typhoon in place of the Tornado. Also, a display sequence for the King Air was introduced, an unusual choice but probably due to the desire to regain some variety, but at low cost. Events team officer Sqn Ldr Andy Pawsey, who was very much behind the creation of the 2007 role demonstration, managed to get his project accepted again for this year. Andy had wanted to show the RAF off at its best and subsequently believed his role demo was the way to go rather than a farrago of individual aerobatics displays, as though military aircraft existed primarily for this reason, which was perhaps rather presumptuous. That said, what turned out to be a most impressive solo-aerobatics display by a 45 (R) Squadron King Air was most welcome and so well executed that the crew for 2008 won the Wright Jubilee Trophy. It was flown by Flt Lt Leon Creese, a C-130 Hercules captain, even though this usually went to instructors of the Hawk and Tucano. An aircraft of the size and design of the King Air, a derived executive communications type, was not supposed to pick up such awards.

The role demo was back again but with a slight configuration change from 2007, yet the biggest news event of 2008 was the return to life of an airworthy Vulcan. Although privately operated, the Vulcan to the Skies Trust (the private venture responsible for restoring Vulcan XH558 to airworthy condition) had managed to get Vulcan B2, XH558, back in the air on 18 October 2008. The venerable icon returned, post-retirement, many years after indeed, to grace the skies and be displayed at as many events as could be attended.

Being the RAF's ninetieth birthday, a suitable venue was chosen to officially mark the occasion—RAF Fairford. Operational commitments were still at a high tempo after the relative static posture of the Cold War when assets sat ready on standby and available in relative abundance. Continuous long-term deployments on a war footing and drawn from a rapidly shrinking pool of manpower and airframes was the lot of the RAF of the early twenty-first century. The date chosen for HM Queen Elizabeth II to review the RAF at ninety years young was Friday 11 July.

The same problem affected RIAT this year as had beset Waddington the previous year; a monsoon passed over Fairford through much of Friday. People still thronged the airfield, even though (or because) the usual onsite pre- and post-event viewing enclosures remained shut.

The queen reviewed the proceedings while a sopping wet grey shroud provided the aerial stage for a flypast by formations of Typhoons, Tornado GR4s, F3s, Harriers, Hawks, Pumas, Merlins, Sea King, Chinook, Tristar, E-3D, Sentinel, C-17, VC-10

Tanker, Dominies, King Airs, Tutors, Tucanos, BAE 125s, Squirrels, Iroquois', BBMF, and the Red Arrows—eighty-seven aircraft altogether flew past during a relative lull in the weather. The finale was a special display flown by four Typhoons of 11 Squadron complete with bomb burst manoeuvre over the parade. At the very least, forty officers' ceremonial swords needed urgent repair to remove rust. Unusually, none of the ceremonial flying was to be repeated on either of the two air show days as had been the case with the silver jubilee flypast over Finningley all the way back in 1977.

It did not matter anyway as with Waddington the previous year, continuous heavy rainfall in the preceding days ensured nothing else flew either. A water-logged airfield and surrounding car parks turned into quagmires forcing both days to be cancelled. RAFCTE's post-9/11 policy, since the return to Fairford in 2002 of placing all public parking off site, had to be revised as this was a contributory reason to the cancellations. A lot more use of the new hard standings and dispersals to park aircraft had been a biproduct of the changes but this had to be reviewed again in light of 2008.

A compromise allowing a degree of on airfield parking was accepted, but the security concerns coupled with the likelihood of excessive traffic brought another unprecedented change and a not too welcome one. From 2009, RIAT would be entry via advanced ticket sales only. Advanced ticket sales would gain interest while sat in the bank account, and in the unlikely event of another cancellation and refunds being unavoidable, the outlay would have a lesser impact. Situations such as that encountered in 2007 at Waddington and again in 2008 at Fairford could not become too regular an occurrence. The Leuchars Battle of Britain display returned after a hiatus imposed by the runway resurfacing and other development work presaging the arrival of the confirmed Typhoon Wing.

The year 2009 brought the most lightweight showing by the RAF in the public arena perhaps on record. The operational demands now of Afghanistan, particularly the Helmand Province, had since 2006 placed a particularly heavy toll on the Harriers of both the RAF and RN. The Tornado GR4 was now selected to deploy aircraft to Kabul in place of the returning Harriers while winding down the detachment of Tornado GR4s in Iraq as part of Operation Southern Watch. This naturally placed a heavy demand on airframe usage, especially in such an extreme climate, not to mention the turnaround of air and ground crews. The Tornado F3 had been severely reduced in numbers, again due to the offset of the cost of maintaining any size of force on a war footing. The cost was recovered through unit disbandment. A new phrase had by now entered military jargon; 'capability holiday' referred to the unfilled gaps between aircraft retired from service and the eventual arrival of their planned successor.

The overall demands on men and machine meant that the Role Demo of the past two years would be suspended. Money is now a bigger obstacle to overcome than ever before, especially with the additional matter of display insurance and indemnity. There has been something of a misperception that legal and financial obligations have been complicated by the introduction of PFI owned aircraft in RAF service. The rules governing the use of rented aircraft in RAF colours do not necessarily prohibit their use for display purposes, but the rules are different. If the MOD/RAF own an aeroplane involved in an incident while involved in a public display, the liability is straightforward enough.

If, however, the same thing happens involving an aircraft operated under a PFI arrangement, then an indemnity clause can be agreed prior to any risks being taken. Either way, the RAF would be out of pocket if something went wrong. The impact of the culmination of operational commitments and a very much reduced force was quite evident at the 2009 flagship Waddington air show, good weather blessed the weekend, but an already weak flying display was further blighted by the fact that the civilian Vulcan crew were not in possession of a valid display authorisation and, as a result, had to sit in the static park all weekend, while the sole representation of the RAF's front line was a single Typhoon.

There still existed the feeling that the presence of overseas military aircraft was something of a distraction from what were events intended to sell the RAF. Yet as the RAF had concluded, long ago, that such events could not rely on purely RAF fare, were, proven right; the list of allied aircraft this year at Waddington was slender.

By September, the RAF operated a single squadron of Tornado F3s based at Leuchars, which this year presented, without doubt, the best of the three events still sponsored by the RAF. Good weather blessed Leuchars again, which benefited, in contrast to Waddington, by being well attended by other NATO arms.

The year 2010 marked the seventieth anniversary of the Battle of Britain; it was also an election year and the economic circumstances meant there was to be a Strategic Defence and Security Review. With no understanding of the kind of mindset driving the dreaded SDSR, the word on the street was the cuts would be deep, but if an educated guess was to carry any weight at all, nobody would have put a bet on the Harrier Force being in receipt of the proverbial P45. The review's remit determined that the RAF would be able to afford a front-line force of just two manned high-performance aircraft types. There was no mention on the actual numbers or the ability of the picked two airframes, but the government defended the cuts as driven by practical military concerns, rather than a pure exercise in financial retrenchment.

Regardless of the worrying situation, the RAF were determined to mark the seventieth with an increased level of participation at their own and other displays. The Supermarine Spitfire and Eurofighter Typhoon dual aerobatics display was reprised as part of the tribute; there was also a substantial increase in the level of participation by aircraft of 1 Group.

The Harrier was back in the form of a performance handling demonstration rather than a full aerobatics sequence. Another new and impressive addition or rather return to the display circuit and, perhaps even more of a shock under the circumstances, was a tactical demonstration made up of two Tornado GR4s from the OCU aka 15 Squadron.

The first of the official RAF events was at Cosford, mindful of the seventieth anniversary, they had put together a protracted homage to the Battle of Britain, like with previous significant Battle of Britain anniversaries, Cosford's show planned as large a gathering of Spitfires and Hurricanes they could. Alas, this fantastic tribute was curtailed due to deteriorating weather, but the taxpayer visiting Cosford did get to see a Harrier airborne again and while the hard to believe, a pair of Tornado GR4s, which flew a quite substantial and robust sequence of manoeuvres based around providing top cover, show of force, and various weapon delivery profiles.

Waddington had redeemed itself following a rather paltry show the year before with a tribute to the ninetieth anniversary of the first Hendon Air Pageant. They also brought back the very popular Turkish aerobatics team, the Turkish Stars, for what was their last appearance in the UK—perhaps not quite the same now without their 1996 manic commentator when they first pitched up at Fairford, but the formation of Crimson and White F-5s put on an impressive display once again.

The Leuchars Battle of Britain office again put together the largest representation of the RAF inventory in their flying programme. With the forthcoming review, there was almost a sense of 'live for the moment'. The Scottish show put together a 'past, present, future' flypast represented by a Spitfire, a current Tornado F3, and a Typhoon. In addition, 6 Squadron officially reformed during the day with a ceremony in front of the station's listed Second World War control tower. An interesting new civilian-run outfit from Sweden, the Swedish Air Force Historic Flight, turned up with a first—a display by a SAAB J-29 Tunnan, 'the Barrel'.

Furthermore, in these pre-Shoreham days, a UK-based civilian-operated team of four Hawker Hunters 'Team Viper' (the moniker 'Team Viper' originated from the team's original mount, Strikemasters, powered by Rolls Royce Viper engines) made for a truly impressive day for the hardcore enthusiast, and the weather cooperated as well. To round it all off, a flypast/high-speed pass by a home-based Tornado and a new Typhoon represented the handing over of the air defence baton to the latter from the former as the outgoing jet pulled skywards and raced to the heavens while the new boy shot ahead over Balmullo Quarry, a famous Leuchars landmark.

It might as well have been an epitaph to the ghost of the past. The SDSR loomed a month away; it had commenced as soon as the new Conservative-led coalition, with the Liberal Democrats, had agreed the new cabinet seating plan. The review lasted through that summer, and the upshot was announced on 19 October—aviation wise, some jaw-dropping shocks were forthcoming. Newspapers had carried editorials, armchair expert critiques, and some quite outrageous predictions, never without a political slant. The chief mischief makers were not necessarily left-wing pacifists as the knives were out to see the RAF dismembered. To be fair, the knives had been out ever since the Soviet Union collapsed and stopped testing UK airspace routinely. There has been heavy use of air power since the First Gulf War, which, in turn, led to no-fly zone enforcements over Iraq. Following from this, the Balkans conflict culminated in Kosovo. Next came the Second Gulf War leading to CAS/BAI, reconnaissance, and show of force missions over Afghanistan and Iraq. All of this has placed a heavier demand on military air power than at any time since the Second World War, as far as the RAF is concerned. Despite the increased tempo of air operations, the RAF and the rest of HM forces have been left with less to do it all with.

War funding in the UK was still confined to the defence budget. War footings should mean direct Treasury spending, though it certainly did not appear to be the case. So, with money ever tightening, representative voices of the two more senior arms fiercely defended their corner while pointing an accusatory finger at the junior partner—outrageous comments as far back as 2006 were being voiced.

The Battle of Britain Memorial Flight, the centrepiece of RAF Heritage, formed at RAF Biggin Hill in 1957. They moved from there to Coltishall and, for at least the last forty-five years, have been at Coningsby, they continue to this day as a living/flying tribute to the 'Few' and to all who served in the RAF during the Second World War. (*Peter March*)

The principal argument was that the junior service had lost its *raison d'être* after the strategic role was transferred to the Royal Navy's Polaris fleet; since then, the RAF was no longer justified as an independent arm.

Interestingly, it would appear no other countries seemed to place their own air forces on trial by media in quite the same way. The critics claimed the RAF's remit be subsumed into the other two arms as appropriate. Perhaps just another attempt to be original, or old fashioned, in any case, radical—another bright idea to fall at the first hurdle.

13

Changing Culture

Among the SDSR cuts was the loss of more air bases. The review determined that the RAF would only need three operational air bases in future, meaning essentially for fast jet combat aircraft. There were seven such bases which lived up to this criterion in October 2010—Kinloss, Lossiemouth, Leuchars, Coningsby, Marham, Cottesmore, and Wittering. Kinloss, Wittering, and Cottesmore were already facing likely closure as RAF stations specifically; following the decision to withdraw the Harrier and cancel the Nimrod MRA4, the latter had finally been reduced to an order for twenty-one to fourteen, then to nine before SDSR then wielded the axe.

This left the remaining four to fight it out. Marham sits near Sandringham; almost certainly, the proximity of the royal estate would have some influence on the decisions taken. Lossiemouth had been slated to receive the yet-to-leave-the-traps F-35B. This did not seem to reassure the good people of the Lossiemouth area who immediately took to the streets marching to the RAF station's main entrance to demand it remain open. Attempting to placate the already tense political situation in the area, the government played out this part of the SDSR review in public. This began by drawing attention, before the end of 2010, to the possibility that Leuchars might close instead. The first half of 2011 meant waiting for the next planning round to the SDSR as this would determine which base was for the chop. The last operational Tornado F3 squadron, 111, disbanded at Leuchars in April, handing over the now resumed testing by Russia of Britain's QRA (which has been routinely scrambled to intercept both Russian military aircraft and suspected hijacked airlines over the last ten years or so) to 6 Sqn's Typhoons.

On 18 July, Dr Liam Fox, defence secretary, announced the winners and losers. Leuchars was to become home to the Royal Scots Dragoon Guards, 2nd REME, and a Provost company that was returning from Germany. What was not made clear was the long-term future of the airfield.

No comment was made regarding the now very long-standing Battle of Britain 'At Home' day. Many hoped, perhaps unrealistically, that a way would be found to keep one of the largest public attractions north of the border running on.

Indeed, Gerald Howarth, defence minister, suggested as much, but that there might not be a way. Meanwhile, the CAS, Sir Stephen Dalton, confirmed that there would at least be three more 'At Homes' at Leuchars, indicating a lengthy period before the units moved up to Lossiemouth once the squadrons already there disbanded or left. As for the display scene in 2011, the USAF Thunderbirds returned to Waddington. The RAF provision was little different to 2010 save there were no Harriers or the Tornado F3. The Typhoon solo was absent as well on account of the next conflict that the British government assigned the RAF—this time to assist the Arab Spring uprising in Libya. The operational commitment taken on by the still small number of Typhoons meant the Typhoon display, while held off temporarily, was after all cancelled.

At the Leuchars 'At Home' in 2011, there was a sense of slow contraction; this year's edition was a shadow of the previous year. Still, four of 6 Sqn's Typhoons did manage to get airborne in a stream launch into a vertical climb beneath a grey but very high ceiling overhead Leuchars. They returned for a series of flypasts to round off what was probably the smallest flying programme here since the early 1950s.

Tragedy struck earlier in the year when Flt Lt John Egging, one of the pilots with the Red Arrows, was tragically killed when forced to try and eject while entering the circuit to land over Bournemouth following a display over the sea front. Not long after, on 8 November, a second member of the team, Flt Lt Sean Cunningham, was lost when the ejector seat he was in activated without any deliberate attempt to activate it. The year ended therefore on a sad note.

The year 2012 brought a thinner line up of air shows generally due to the demand for resources to serve the Olympics in London. Some regular events—Yeovilton, RIAT, and Farnborough—were all re-scheduled to slightly earlier dates than usual. The air day at RNAS Culdrose was cancelled instead of rescheduling by a few weeks. These changes became unavoidable, in part due to the heavy demand for military personnel to provide security at the games at short notice. This might not have been such a problem, but the contracted security company turned up with insufficient staff.

The year 2012 saw another rare first; the Republic of Korea's air force sent over their answer to the Red Arrows. The RAF Waddington air show office and the Fairford RIAT team both played host to the RoKAF aerobatics team, the Black Eagles. Just to confuse matters regarding the team's name, the aircraft they flew were nine KAI T-50 Golden Eagles. The Golden Eagle was a light-weight version of the F-16, probably the most powerfully engined and complex fast jet intended primarily as an advanced trainer. It was a mark of how limited Farnborough was becoming that the South Korean team only got to send a single aircraft here during their UK tour. The year 2012 also marked the end of the line for three more RAF displays—the GR4 tac demo wound up at the end of 2012 and the Hawk T1 solo aerobatics displays were discontinued, as was the impressive King Air display.

Leuchars 2012 was to be the penultimate event, but this had not yet been determined absolutely and in fact false hopes were kindled when 1 Squadron reformed here on the Eurofighter Typhoon during the summer, with the official reformation of the unit during the 'At Home' day, which fell on 15 September.

Was it a good omen? Both 1 and 6 Squadrons played a significant part as four of 6 Squadron's Typhoons got airborne to open the flying with a formation flypast across the display axis and over the 1 Squadron reformation ceremony; later, both units launched eleven more Typhoons, the last two off the runway rotating into the vertical. Also, the 2012 event was billed as the official diamond jubilee air show. This then was, supposedly, to all intents and purposes the equivalent of the silver jubilee spectacular held at Finningley in 1977. Such an auspicious occasion may well have given rise to speculation that the RAF were not moving after all as it must be wholly unprecedented for an RAF squadron to form/reform at a station already slated for closure.

The rundown of Leuchars was, by comparison, a drawn out and unusual process. All rumours and expectations within the aviation enthusiasts' community that Leuchars might just be reprieved were doused when the newly appointed station commander, Air Commodore Gerry Mayhew, was described as the man who would hand Leuchars over to the army. The 2013 'At Home' day was scheduled to take place on 7 September 2013. With the army due to move in by March 2015, no public mention was made about the future of the air show until the early evening of Friday 6 September, on the local news, stating this would be the last. The announcement attracted criticism of the government by the SNP recalling that in 2011, Sir Stephen Dalton had confirmed three more would take place; they discounted the 2011 display as this announcement was made in the week that edition of the air show was held.

The ambiguity was not clarified at the time, but the day after the 2013 display, *The Sunday Post* and other Scottish papers carried the weight of feeling from further up the chain. *The Sunday Post* recorded:

> With the attraction looking set to move to RAF Lossiemouth, northeast Fife MSP Roderick Campbell said the Coalition had broken its promise to keep the air show at Leuchars for the next three years.
>
> … It is disappointing that the air show's history is ending more prematurely than expected. While the end is always nigh, the guarantee from the Scottish Office, and the RAF, in 2011 that the air show would remain at Leuchars for the next three years has clearly not come to pass … we shouldn't be surprised by the cack-handedness of the UK Government in relation to this decision, however. From staff cuts to how many personnel will move in, and when, this is simply just another broken coalition promise.

The Sunday Post's expectation that the air show would naturally move to Lossiemouth, with the squadrons, was to prove overly optimistic yet not unfounded. There were indications in Moray that such a transition would be welcome, and along with the announcement about the air show, Andrew Murrison, defence minister, in his announcement did say the option of RAF Lossiemouth holding a similar event in the future was under consideration.

The year 2013 marked the seventieth anniversary of the Dambusters' raid. Leuchars made an effort to mark this. With squadrons standing down well ahead of re-equipment, it was somewhat lucky that 617 Sqn was still operational, allowing a

Last knockings for the RAF Leuchars Battle of Britain 'At Home' Day, this image shows two of the homestead's Tiffies formating on a Waddington-based 8 Sqn E-3D Sentry AEW 1 on 7 September 2013. (*eLaReF*)

flypast of a Tornado GR4 with the BBMF Lancaster. Finally, the GR4 returned down the airfield with a 1 Squadron Typhoon to provide 'the finale'—the oldest squadron with the latest aircraft and the most junior with the next airframe to be pensioned off, if a good deal earlier than planned.

As the punters started toward the exits, the PA system played a reflective closing instrumental piece by Jon and Vangelis. Thus, the end of the last official RAF Battle of Britain 'At Home' day was played out in a strangely fitting style. The RAF shortly after confirmed that they were commencing a comprehensive review of their public participation policy.

As 2014 approached, just Cosford and Waddington were to open their gates that year, in June and July. September was now free of any significant effort by the RAF in the display arena, whether connected with the Battle of Britain or anything else. The overall allocation of resources to represent the RAF in 2014 was desperately threadbare. There were the now established display teams—RAFAT, Red Arrows, BBMF, and the Falcons. Operationally, there was a single Typhoon and the Chinook heavy helicopter; the only other two types being put through their paces were the two light trainers, Tutor and Tucano. What was missing stood out—Tornado GR4 and the Hawk T2 (a trainer, but an impressive aircraft) and anything from the transport inventory. The latter had something more interesting to present to the public now with the introduction into service of the most impressive A-400 Atlas. The A-400 has quite unbelievable aerial handling for such a large heavy aircraft, yet it has virtually been wholly absent from the air display circuit except for demonstration crews from airbus, who have always been confined to throwing the beast around over Fairford and Farnborough. Apart from the limitations applied to the existing inventory, the RAF in 2014 operated a less than full spectrum fleet; after 2010, there were no maritime patrol aircraft. We were living in a different era compared with just ten years earlier.

The Tornado GR4 was approaching accelerated retirement while conducting non-stop overseas deployments, concentrating on the day job with fewer airframes ensuring that in its twilight years, the 'Tonka' very much stayed out of the limelight. The punchy and more powerful replacement for the Hawk T1, the T2, was allowed out the following year, 2015, since then training has demanded every available airframe.

This was far from a comprehensive presentation, but matters now are different, even with a much smaller air force. Everything else was stretched by either operational demand or increased maintenance requirements, often brought on by the former, especially where older types were concerned. It was announced shortly before the 2014 Waddington air show that runway resurfacing and other airfield works services would begin shortly after. The expected length of time involved precluded the possibility of the air show taking place in 2015.

It took a fraction of a second before the enthusiast websites were speculating that 2014 would be the last. In this case, the doom-mongers were right. A later announcement claimed that 2016 was out of the question due to the work overrunning. At the time, the RAF were about to reveal the conclusions of the comprehensive review of their display policy.

With Leuchars to become essentially an army barracks by early 2015, the enthusiasts were proved right about Waddington. Security fears had suddenly become a problem, so the decision was taken to make the 2014 Waddington air show the last. It is logical they would have come to the conclusions they did, but it is strange that the same security considerations had not troubled the RAF before. The station could no longer host any public gatherings with the highly controversial Reaper/Protector squadrons based here as well as all other RAF ISTAR aircraft and operations. This left Cosford as the sole station to host a wholly RAF-organised air show. There was something to look forward to briefly as 2015 brought a fresh addition to the display scene—a tactical display, this time by a pair of Hawk T2 aircraft.

As it was the seventy-fifth anniversary of the Battle of Britain, the occasional appearance of the Typhoon/Spitfire duo made another return, this time with the Typhoon in the sea green and tan top surface and duck egg blue underside camouflage widely in use in 1940. The Hawks might have been placed on a more permanent footing, but despite their impressive display sequence, the team were discontinued as the window in the training schedule closed again.

Much of the gap left by the heavily reduced presence of RAF aircraft on the air show circuit was now being filled by the growing number of ex-military high-performance aircraft pensioned off by various air arms and now in the hands of skilled enthusiasts with extensive overdraft facilities. Over the years, we have seen Hunters and earlier types in increasing numbers.

In the UK, the relevant authorities have not proved keen to encourage such enterprise no matter what the professional qualifications and currency of those involved. As far back as the early 1990s, attempts were made and repeatedly thwarted to get an English Electric/BAE Lightning aloft; no matter how exact the efforts to meet the CAA's strict parameters, the entire exercise was a non-flyer so to speak.

One amusing observation about the CAA's aversion to the Lightning, in particular being returned to flying condition, finds its way back to the RAF and the government not wanting the air force's current inventory upstaged by a fighter that became operational in 1960 with superior airframe/engine performance. Alas, the CAA have determined the Lightning and others too 'complex' and that is it. If there is one mindset British officialdom has absorbed from the USA, it is the risk-aversion culture brought about by how easy it is for anyone to take legal proceedings against anyone flying such a machine at an air show should it all go very wrong. By contrast, Sweden and Norway are two countries that probably do not spring to mind when one thinks of any country where one might find some well-funded enthusiasts maintaining high-performance ex-military aircraft for display purposes. Yet each have an historic flight; the former has the most robust stable full of former high-performance jet types, including Viggen, Draken, Lansen, and Hunter.

The two most potent UK-based exceptions to the CAA's rules on flying 'complex' aircraft in public, particularly with regards to aerobatics, are the Sea Vixen and the Vulcan. The latter lasted until 2015, following which the aircraft could not fly on due to the airframe being simply time-expired, with no further technical support. The Vulcan had, save for some occasional hairy technical issues, enjoyed an incident-free short return from retirement and the crews that flew XH558 executed some hair-raising manoeuvres along the way. The aircraft appeared to climb vertically off the runway at Fairford in its final year.

In August, another pivotal crash resulted in several innocent deaths. Were it not for the nature of the incident, it might have warranted news coverage for just a few days. Former Harrier pilot, Andy Hill, got airborne from Shoreham airport in a Hunter T7, an aircraft very much associated with air displays, particularly in the hands of RAF squadrons in its 1950s and 1960s heyday. In this less constrained era, aerobatics teams flew formation aerobatics with the single-seat fighter version of the Hunter, as many as eighteen aircraft strong.

Hill, in good weather conditions, flew the T7 through an individual aerobatics sequence and was descending from the top of a loop when something went wrong. The aircraft flew toward the ground and given the fact that Shoreham airport is particularly small, not to mentioned bordered on two sides by significant infrastructure and houses and to the north by a dual carriage way and a tall church on rising ground, the incident that unfolded might have been different elsewhere. Much of the manoeuvring as well as positioning of the aircraft took place well outside the confines of the airfield, this is not uncommon. Yet how much did this contribute to the Shoreham crash?

Remembering the outcome of the MiG crash at Fairford in 1993, Hill's aircraft appeared to descend along an almost perpendicular trajectory before sharply pulling out; by this time, it was clear that all was lost but the Hunter still had a way to go to cross over the airfield's boundary again. With insufficient momentum and power, the aircraft came down on the dual carriageway, just shy of the airfield boundary.

The result was that Hill miraculously survived and was pulled from the wreckage; the tragedy was the resultant death of eleven innocent bystanders—all men, and not one attended the air show; instead, they were each going about their business travelling on the carriageway.

This placed air shows, in the UK specifically, back under the spotlight. This time, the reaction would be harder to mollify or reason with. The findings determined that Hill entered the loop at 200 feet instead of the minimum 500 feet and at an entry speed of 310 knots instead of 350. Cleared of manslaughter, the response was understandable. The relatives of the deceased would never understand the verdict, but an immediate embargo was placed on high-performance aerobatics by any privately operated ex-military jets over mainland UK. The rules since have been relaxed sufficiently to allow straight-wing aircraft within the category to fly aerobatics before public gatherings again; swept-winged types may perform the less complicated manoeuvres covered by performance handling displays. This now means that the UK has probably the most restrictive rules on display flying within Europe.

Hunters still fly in the UK operated for military training purposes by HHA (Hawker Hunter Aviation), based at RAF Scampton. Now, this venerable and iconic British-built fighter and a symbol of RAF Cold War operations remains active on the air show circuit only overseas, in the hands of the Dutch and Swedish Air Force historic flights.

In 2016, the navy ran two air days to the RAF's one, which is slightly odd. The fleet's efforts in the air show arena had logically always been overshadowed by those of the RAF, even back in the era when the navy fielded a quite substantial carrier-based tactical air force, requiring more airfields to support the fleet. In 2016, the Naval Air Day at Culdrose sat in a bank of endless sea mist and low cloud which annihilated the flying programme. Early in 2017, plans were already underway for that year's Culdrose display. Before the spring, it was cancelled, the given reason being operational commitments conncctcd with trials of the pristine HMS *Queen Elizabeth*.

Held very much in the same vein as the onetime RAF St Mawgan International Air Day, Culdrose staged its open day mid-week in July, for the same reasons, to accrue as big an attendance as possible from holiday makers. Since then, the sole remaining naval air day, at Yeovilton, has been re-billed as the 'Royal Naval International Air Day'. This re-badging makes quite clear that this is it; there would be no other fleet air arm display venues. The year 2017 was due to be the first of the (planned to be annual) Scampton Air Shows; the outcomes of this event are addressed in the next chapter. With Culdrose now cancelled for what were transient reasons but almost certainly permanent, the scope of activity was further reduced. Put together with the loss of the RAF's Waddington and Leuchars air shows, 2017 took another step toward the irreducible minimum.

The year 2018 marked the RAF's 100th birthday. They would not be able to mark the centenary in quite the same way as the fiftieth Battle of Britain anniversary, but as far as the official flypast over London was concerned, they would have a good try. Some 100 years of unbroken service as the world's oldest continuously serving independent air arm has celebrated its centenary. The intervening years have seen the RAF confront threats from all manner of foe abroad and, to be frank, threats to its very existence from within—the political establishment, the navy, the army, and a not always sympathetic media. There has always been at least some tongue in cheek

An attempt to salvage the discontinued RAF Waddington International Air Show resulted in the decision by RAFCTE (organisers of RIAT) to stage what was to be a new regular event at nearby RAF Scampton; just one edition of this air show has taken place so far, in September 2017. The SWAFHF Saab Draken here remained static following the post-Shoreham UK ban on privately operated high-performance ex-military aircraft aerobating at such events. (*Author's Collection*)

More of the Swedish Air Force Historic Flight's assets at Scampton, Viggen (nearest camera), and Tunnan, to the left. (*Author's Collection*)

Also, from SWAFHF, and perhaps the only time ever in the UK, the Saab J-32 Lansen, a real old banger but real monster of a fighter of its generation. (*Author's Collection*)

The Hawk T1 continues to be operated by the Red Arrows, its bread-and-butter role has since transferred to the meatier, more able T2 variant seen here, static, at Biggin Hill, August 2017. The T2 had only one serious outing on the flying display circuit, as tactical pair in 2015. (*Author's Collection*)

comments about the 'one-hundred-year experiment' meeting its demise before the century marker was reached.

References to the one-hundred-year experiment was more of a flippant reaction to calls for the RAF to be disbanded. This is particularly true during the 2010 SDSR review; when the centenary was only eight years away, many serving and retired senior navy and army officers expressed such concerns, or rather hopes, in some broadsheet papers that the RAF would be disbanded as no longer sufficiently relevant to justify an independent air force.

The world's first independent air force, alas, appears to have passed this first significant hurdle. There are negatives and positives to note from 2018; to start, the use of RAF Cosford to host the sole RAF display was overall a success, but it does not change the fact that this airfield is not the most suitable. Its limitations are avoided elsewhere, as was determined so by the air staff all the way back in 1961.

Despite this, there is much here to enhance the visit for enthusiast and family day out alike. There is the Aerospace Museum, which is big for sure; it consumes a lot of hangar space as annexes to the main museum, which is in a purpose-built complex. Contained within, as the centre piece attraction, is a Cold War exhibition complete with film shows, journals, papers, magazines, and other general artefacts from the era.

Yet more in favour of Cosford is the continued accommodation of on airfield parking, which is perhaps the best way to see an air show, certainly as a family. The ability to use the car, camper van, or people carrier as a base camp and viewing position allows forays around the rest of the 'show ground'. It is as close to ideal as possible and a feature of many air shows before 9/11. On-field parking was never relinquished by either Leuchars or Waddington to the last. Among the reservations, Cosford's airfield is frankly too small. The one and only runway is a paltry 3,698 feet (1,127 metres) in length.

To draw an unfavourable comparison, RNAS Yeovilton has a secondary runway with a length of, 4,800 feet (1,463 metres) while the main runway is a more realistic 7,579 feet (2,310 metres). As such, the naval air day, not faced with any such significant marker as the 100th anniversary of the service, was able to put on an even more impressive display of current aircraft on the ground as well as in the air. Furthermore, the navy are still able to organise their, albeit now much reduced, unique finale assault demonstration.

The former also has insufficient hard standings and dispersals. The credibility of the flying previously mustered here always fell short of the breadth of content achieved elsewhere. Thus, where it counts, Cosford has always suffered unavoidable shortcomings.

In the service's 100th anniversary year, much of what should have made up the static display—Tornados, Typhoons, A400M, A330, and aircraft of all denominations from across NATO—were absent simply because of the lack of space. Instead, too many current aircraft were represented, as always, with fibreglass mock-ups. The flying having been similarly restricted in the past has increasingly, with the aid of nearby RAF Shawbury, been able to attract a wider range of more impressive hardware from overseas, and in this auspicious year, Cosford managed to push the boat out.

The RAF has so little capacity and depth now that to mount anything like the event they wanted the 100th anniversary parade along the mall to Buckingham Palace to be, they had to beg steal and borrow. RAF police personnel paraded amid the blue hats with their white ones; this stood out. While recruits were used to line the mall and make up the numbers as seen here. However, they did all concerned proud, as the parade was nothing short of marvellous. (*Author's Collection*)

Flypasts by a Tornado GR4 and formations of various trainers together with the A400M and as many privately operated aircraft from the past as could be gathered to take part. From allied air arms to the fore and very welcome came the Polish Air Force (MiG 29), Belgium (F-16), and France (Rafale). The Polish MiG flew together with a Hurricane—a fitting tribute to the Polish contribution to the war, conspicuously so during the Battle of Britain when Poland provided the largest contingent of volunteers from outside the UK to Fighter Command.

As for the RAF's wider celebrations for its centenary, by present-day standards, a supreme effort was made—the flypast down the mall and over Buckingham Palace consisted of 100 aircraft, the more remarkable contingent being a '100' formation made up of twenty-two Eurofighter Typhoons, formations of Tucanos, Hawk T1s and T2s, and a seven-ship formation of Tornado GR4s; each of the large transports and ISTAR aircraft were seen, as well as the A330 trailing chicks and the E3-D with a pair of Typhoons.

It may not have been on the same scale as either the silver jubilee flypast in 1977 or the Battle of Britain's fiftieth in 1990, but it was certainly a genuine effort. The peak of the presentation at air shows was reserved for that special weekend in July, Fairford. The latter, a long time ago, became the one that attracts the senior management of the RAF. At Cosford, you are likely to bump into a vendor selling inflatable Red Arrows; at Fairford, you are more likely to bump into the chief of the air staff and his way to the VIP enclosure. With three full public days but with a juggling act to perform regarding aircraft availability, Fairford in 2018 was to stage the '100' flypast again, on the Friday only.

Foreign air arms were very much out in force to celebrate the RAF's centenary at Fairford, including the Mirage 2000D pair aerobatics team, Couteau Delta. (*Author's Collection*)

Taken the same day, this is the USAF F-35A solo display. At one time, the RAF made by far the greater effort toward this endeavour, it will be interesting to see if they will be able to allocate an RAF F-35B solo display in the future. (*Author's Collection*)

A first glimpse, having just arrived at RAF Marham—three brand new F-35B Lightning II strike fighters. (*Author's Collection*)

A '100' formation flown by twenty-two Eurofighter Typhoons. (*Author's Collection*)

The service's centenary flypast over the mall while not as big as the Battle of Britain's fiftieth in 1990; it was 100-aircraft strong and included this last chance to see, before retirement, a formation of seven Tornados. (*Author's Collection*)

RIAT pulled the stops out to mark the occasion. Here, a USAF F-35A formates with a P-51 Mustang and a Spitfire XVI. (*Author's Collection*)

Not quite same as the 100 formation down the mall, planned for the Friday only at Fairford before the weather intervened. However, this Typhoon nine-ship formation flew past on the Saturday and Sunday. (*Author's Collection*)

The RAF answer to the USAF Heritage Flypast, consisting of an F-35B from 617 Sqn with a Tornado GR4 from 41 Sqn flanking the older aircraft this time, the BBMF's Avro Lancaster. (*Author's Collection*)

The Battle of Britain Memorial Flight put together this formation for the 2018 edition of RIAT, consisting of two Hurricanes, three Spitfires, a Dakota, and the venerable Lancaster. (*Author's Collection*)

Weather did not permit, but a nine-ship of Typhoons managed in better conditions on the next two days. On the Sunday, a distant oscillating thunder could be detected as the nine returned overhead from crowd rear at near contrail height. The brand-new acquisition for the front line—the Lockheed Martin F-35B Lightning II—made its debut here at Fairford in 2017. This time, it was present in the hands of an RAF pilot and as this year also marked the seventy-fifth anniversary of the Dambusters' raid, an aircraft from the recently reformed 617 Squadron.

The new machine flew in formation with a Lancaster and a Tornado GR4. Fairford's reputation received a boost this year; they showcased one of the largest and most varied gatherings of air arms from around the globe. Next came Farnborough, running back-to-back with Fairford/RIAT since 2000. In March 2019, the organisers of the Farnborough SBAC Air show announced that the two public remaining days (there used to be three) over the weekend would be cancelled, permanently. In 2008, the Farnborough show billed the ninetieth birthday of 111 Squadron as part of that year's highlights as they were still operational at the time with the Tornado F3. Would the RAF, as there is precedence, allow a special anniversary appearance? No one had any right to expect the pterodactyl loop recreated, not with twenty-two Tornados for certain, but one might have expected the possibility of more than a single F3 to sit in the static park. Again, this could all be indicative of the far greater logistics problems facing the RAF.

To represent 111 in the skies over Farnborough, a single privately operated Hawker Hunter T7, in the colour scheme of the legendary Black Arrows aerobatics team, did the honours.

2018 brought the final public appearances of the Panavia Tornado along with a last chance to see the 'Tonka' make an old-fashioned vertical departure. (*Author's Collection*)

The Farnborough show held at the end of July 2018 was memorable for all the wrong reasons, and the event organiser's Facebook page was filled with negative comments. First, and perhaps not necessarily the fault of the SBAC, the RAF presentation, thin at Farnborough, for some years, was unbelievable. That is in the sense that the best-known air show in the UK, and longest continuously running, was in this year of all years, seemingly, dismissed by the RAF in the immediate shadow of what was done for RIAT.

The lacklustre approach to Farnborough had been getting more and more so, arguably since the move from September to July. The Red Arrows' self-imposed ban on anything but flypasts over Farnborough post-Shoreham was not compensated for at all. This essentially could be due, once again, to the growing level of infrastructure surrounding Farnborough. The airfield size would not present a problem were it not for this, thus, 'the team' would only conduct a single flypast.

Following suit, the BBMF likewise made for a simple flypast. Quite what the expected public reaction to this embargo would be seems not to have concerned anyone. Both display teams operated from the field, which may have saved fuel but added nothing to expectations.

Aerobatics were not prohibited, but there was nothing from the RAF; this was a supreme irony as the two military jets that were individually displayed came from far afield. The United States Air Force sent an F-16 from their Pacific Air Command. Of all likely military contributors, this had to be one of the least likely, yet their F-16 put on a scintillating display twice on each of the two public days—twice, it is imagined, to fill the huge gap left by the absence of anything else interesting.

The second and most ironic contribution came from the Spanish Navy—a solo demonstration by a Harrier concentrating, as always, on the puffer jet's thrust-vectoring party trick and, in turn, presenting another spoonful of irony.

Reflections of the past and the Hendon pageants—a Tiger Moth, Avro Tutor, and a Hawker Fury, all lined up for close quarter inspection—at Fairford, 13 July 2018. (*Author's Collection*)

The Hawker Fury up close, the leading interceptor fighter at the start of the 1930s, wearing the markings of 43 Squadron, in post-war years, famous for its contribution to the air show scene. (*Author's Collection*)

The famous 'Fighting Cock' crest of 43 Sqn. (*Author's Collection*)

Before the first RAF display, two protagonists of the First World War; the nearest camera is a Royal Aircraft Factory's B.E.2e and further back, a Sopwith Camel. (*Author's Collection*)

The appointed solo Typhoon for the 2018 display season wore the 'RAF 100' fin decor, as other aircraft assigned to appear in public, here at Fairford, 13 July 2018. (*Author's Collection*)

The F-16 has become as likely a participant at UK air shows as any RAF fast jet display now. This one is from the most regular UK attendee, the Belgian Air Force. (*Author's Collection*)

The Harrier, a unique and remarkable British invention, was prematurely retired following the conclusions of the SDSR. This aircraft is still serving with the US Marine Corps and the Spanish Navy, but now regarded as beyond the means of the British defence budget.

Otherwise, save for a small number of commercial new types being put through their paces, the bulk of the four hours or so of flying was made up of vintage but interesting and mostly ex-commercial aircraft, war vintage tail draggers, and entertaining civilian aerobatics teams with high-performance light competition aeros types.

This unlikely line up was a poor whimper for what was once the stage for the cutting edge of both commercial and military aviation in the UK. Farnborough was, in an earlier golden age, heavily supported by all the UK armed services, providing it with an edge, with impressive role demonstrations, aerobatics, and flypasts that used to darken the sky overhead.

By 2018, the organisers had managed to minimise the public days to an emaciated shadow of what was less than twenty years before still an impressive date in the aviation calendar. Farnborough's response to heavy public criticism was to cancel the two remaining public days, announcing on Tuesday, March 5, 2019, that it would be ending the bi-annual public weekend.

Declining attendances, popularity and a move to place a "renewed focus on engaging young people" were cited as the reasons behind the move.

Farnborough no longer managed to cling onto booked participating aircraft, aimed at market sales each year, long enough to be around for the public days to make the general public's visit worth the eye-watering ticket prices. Again, Farnborough is another location where on-field parking was not a problem before 9/11. Since then, all public parking is off field or far enough away to ensure you will have to leave your car behind. You can then take the bus or walk, if you are feeling fit, with all your worldly possessions; next it is the queue for ponderous security checks.

Again, one cannot pour opprobrium over the organisers for this, as extensive security checks have become prevalent everywhere.

In a way, one can see where the ticket costs go, but after all, this is supposed to be the public's chance to peer through the International Aviation Shop window and catch a glimpse of things to come. Farnborough's loss of sheen is not unique and very much seems to have suffered from a variety of circumstances beyond the organisers control.

Also, one cannot expect the same menu to be available week in week out through the summer, display flying hours are rationed, always have been. However, in such a commemorative year, Farnborough could have been better supported, even if dates had to slide about a bit.

That the SBAC could not wield sufficient clout is perhaps a sign that this once pinnacle event on the calendar will, given the developing structures surrounding the airfield, have to move. If a suitable alternative can be found and more importantly the will, enthusiasm, and dare I say, money, it could be for the better. The year was rounded off with the Duxford September Air Show, the only other public event to welcome the F-35B, and again accompanied by its immediate soon to be pensioned predecessor, the Tonka.

The very last curtain call—the Tonka's final appearance of all in 2018, departing here over Duxford in September. (*Author's Collection*)

The Pakistan Air Force made their own poignant contribution to mark the RAF's centenary at RIAT, depicting the founding father, Lord Trenchard himself. (*Author's Collection*)

14
Future of RAF Air Displays

Of the twelve RAF stations that opened their gates to the public on 18 September 1965 to celebrate the twenty-fifth anniversary of the Battle of Britain, only one remains that can truly be described as an RAF primary flying station to use the present-day vernacular.

Abingdon is now Dalton Barracks; the post-war air traffic control tower has been demolished and likely used as aggregate to prop up the widening of the M4. RAF Acklington in Northumberland is now HMP Acklington. Biggin Hill is now wholly civilianised; the RAF's officer and aircrew selection centre moved in the early 1990s.

The last active RAF squadrons left Colerne by January 1968. In 1985, the married quarters were sold for civilian development. Bristol UAS and the ATC still use the airfield, but the army's 21 Signal Regiment are the primary residents.

Coltishall is a solar farm and a prison, but general aviation still uses the runway. Cottesmore is an army barracks, the airfield out of use. Finningley is Robin Hood Airport. Leuchars is still an active RAF airfield, but the station is now home to units of the British Army. St Athan is MOD St Athan, the maintenance role having been entirely contractorised. St Mawgan still has a small RAF presence—the escape and evade training centre—but the airfield is Newquay Airport, Ternhill, another home for the army. Waddington remains the only primary light blue flying station.

Today apart from the post-Cold War irony of burgeoning operational commitments, civilian personnel now fulfil the essential day-to-day functions of many remaining military bases, not just those of the RAF. Consequently, they have no obligation to give up free time to support any kind of service event. The cutback in serving personnel was so acute that for the 100th anniversary march down the mall, many of those on parade, particularly to line the route, were trainees—that is they are not yet effective. The marchpast was almost half and half bands and marching ranks, which had a handful of conspicuous RAF police in their white hats—something I do not believe I have ever seen before.

Otherwise, the parade was spectacular which was the aim and still placed more RAF personnel in one spot than has been seen since 15 September 1990. Also, the availability of aircraft from a much smaller pool and a reduced variety of types meant the effort was worthy of applause. Today, the RAF, considering it is now at its smallest size in history, makes, in relative terms, the smallest available surplus of assets available for public displays of any kind. There is of course a different climate under which such activities go ahead now.

As far as staging air shows for public benefit goes, this has become more of a problem of recent years. The provision of accommodation for visiting personnel from NATO and other overseas air arms now extends beyond the days of finding accommodation available within the confines of military bases. Tim Prince, co-founder of the (Royal) International Air Tattoo together with Paul Bowen when organising their very first IAT in 1971, at North Weald, had attracted the Patrouille de France. When the team turned up, they were told they would be billeted in a billet, literally. The response was that they would not 'billet' their dogs in such a place. With minds freshly focused, more agreeable digs were soon found elsewhere with bellhops and room service. Back in the good old days, these problems did not appear to be quite so problematic. In recent times, the setting of dates for the Waddington air show was governed by the availability of student accommodation at Lincoln University.

As soon as the summer recess began, the dates for the air show could be set. Such a narrow field with so little flexibility does not help provide a sufficient window of opportunity to attract much in the way of visitors from overseas given the complexities of display flying—hours used, rest times, and other display bookings.

Patrouille de France, *c.* 1971. Overseas military flying displays were also rather racier in the old days. The team seen here over an unidentified airfield with Fouga Magisters. They used the Magisters from 1964 to 1980 before converting to the Alpha Jet. (*Tony Hawes*)

The years 2006 and 2009 were especially lean for the Waddington air show office, especially the latter when RAF participation was particularly light. Security concerns are the modern age phenomena. Again, the irony is that the age of espionage and the knife-edge tension of the Cold War presented relatively little to worry about. In fact, the presence of the odd Soviet bloc spy at an RAF 'At Home' was tacitly welcomed just to let the buggers see what they were up against. The security threat today is another matter entirely, whether it is radical anti-war demonstrators objecting to drones or terrorism.

They both existed in one form or another during the Cold War as well, and at times were quite prevalent, but neither seemed to cause much anxiety. The lack of action from the IRA could be related to the simple logic that all UK military air shows were almost certain to have US military personnel and aircraft in attendance. The effect this would have upon the IRA was the risk of inflicting death and injury on US personnel or aircraft. This could have a most undesirable impact on Irish sympathies across the pond. Concerns, under the present climate, having seen the Waddington air show cancelled, were addressed by the RAF with the aid of the local MP, the RAFCTE, and the *Lincolnshire Echo*. Demands for an air show in Lincolnshire had to be heeded. Having arrived at conclusions to their comprehensive review on the very subject, the RAF was happy to 'support' another air show somewhere in the region but were not keen to provide one of their own directly.

This was very much the outcome following the demise of Leuchars; the resolution in that case was to assign Priority 1 status to the civilian-run Ayr, sea front air show at Troon, on the west coast of Scotland. If the idea of moving the Leuchars air show to Lossiemouth was ever seriously considered, it was vetoed. Whether, as some commentators and critics observed, transport links and catchment area or other concerns were the reason was never publicly declared. To compensate for the loss of Waddington, all interested parties agreed that with some work on the station infrastructure and airfield, RAF Scampton would be as good a replacement venue as any for what was confused with a straightforward transfer of the Waddington air show. Many enthusiasts prematurely expected this to become the RIAT of the north; after all, RAFCTE had agreed to run the event.

The reality was the organisers were not really looking to organise either. Exactly what the fundamental aim was, is difficult to pin down. However, the decision to hold an air show at Scampton very much created some confusion that the RAF would be running the show. Wing Commander Mike Harrop, Scampton station commander, told the local papers that he would welcome an air show.

'This is one of the things that happened recently that's made me think that someone is looking at Scampton and saying, 'I've got an idea for what Scampton can do in the future.'

The first thing to be made clear was that there would be no air show in 2016 due to the amount of airfield service work that needed doing. At the time, Scampton was home to several units, the best known, by far, being the Red Arrows.

Among the others was the RAF'S principal Air Defence Ground Environment operations centre. On the civilian side, HHA (Hawker Hunter Aviation) operated a handful of Hunters and a smattering of various ex-Cold War jets. Their primary purpose was to provide DCAT (dissimilar air combat training) and other air defence training profiles. HHA rent themselves out to various air forces and other air arms.

Scampton's history could not be more legendary, even alongside Biggin Hill. Scampton is the base from which as many, not even interested in aviation, will know, the Dambusters (617 Sqn) flew their raid on the Ruhr dams—Eder, Mohne, and Sorpe—destroying the first two and damaging the third.

There is a hangar now designated as a museum and the plot of land where Wing Commander Guy Gibson's famous pet black Labrador, the one with the contentious name, is buried. In the final scene of the 1955 film *The Dambusters*, where Michael Redgrave's Barnes Wallis is talking to Richard Todd's Guy Gibson, a black dog can be seen over Gibson's shoulder crossing the grass in the distance. All present at the time deny that any dogs were present during filming, and when questioned, no one else had seen a dog anywhere on the station during that day of filming.

Further to the station's history, it continued its Bomber Command role into the cold-war era, with Lincolns, Canberras, and finally Vulcans. A number of 'At Homes' were held here into the 1950s.

Through from 1958 to 1982, Vulcans operated from Scampton carrying the primary, then from 1969, standby nuclear deterrent. To take the V bombers, the runway had to be extended in the late 1950s. The extension pushed so far to the east of the airfield that the A15 had to be re-routed into a bulging bend and back in again. Much of the station itself and at least one of the C-type hangars is in a desperate state of disrepair. The dates for the air show were set for 9 and 10 September 2017.

Scheduled for the weekend prior to Battle of Britain week, it was near enough to this important point in the calendar, and expectations were high. Were we about to see the return of a great tradition, the return of a major RAF, or rather RAF-supported, air show in September?

The organisers (RAFCTE) released something of a mission statement, stating that this was going to be a family show. This can be read all kinds of ways, but to specifically advertise an air show as family friendly is often a euphemism saying not to expect RIAT.

As the spring arrived and as is the norm in this age of instant access to the planning progress of such events via the internet, expectations were not fired up initially. The Scampton air show displayed on the official website constant updates to the flying and static; at first, people put the slow start down to a simple question of early days. RAFCTE did try to replicate RIAT in one sense as the layout was almost the same as for Fairford, with colour-coded service stations—a good idea actually, providing extensive catering outlets with both open and sheltered seating areas.

The static display turned out to be quite well supported; it benefited from the presence of a Canadian F-18 Hornet with a Viggen, Draken, and Lansen from the Swedish Air Force Historic Flight. Ordinarily, the Swedes would have been flying their wares, but post-Shoreham, restrictions would prevent any aerobatics specifically. The HHA's own interesting collection of Cold War relics, including a former Polish AF SU-22 and a Luftwaffe F-4 Phantom, were front and centre, but again, unavailable for flying. This was, indeed, a different matter.

Again, this was made up of what has become known as filler, not to be disparaging, but civilian aerobatics teams and vintage aircraft are all part of the general mix. Yet all depends upon what is expected. In this case, the impression was still that it would lean toward a predominantly military showcase, given the profile of the organiser and the host.

Instead, save for the Typhoon, the Belgian F-16, and a familiar French advanced trainer, an Alpha Jet, along with the Red Arrows, on home turf, the rest of the day was filled with pleasing displays by light and old aircraft.

An oil spill response Boeing 727 from Doncaster Airport (Finningley) owned by 2Excel Aviation Ltd was a late addition, and an impressive demonstration by the crew gave some variety and body to the event, but not quite enough. Off-field parking was the order of the day again, for which the East of England Showground was utilised—no doubt for a small consideration, but at least it was nearby. The station's desperate state was evident; the officers' mess was boarded up and surrounded by building-site metal barriers. Originally, this was to become a hotel, yet tentative plans announced recently seek to build a massive edifice as a tribute to the Red Arrows with a 550-acre commemorative park for the RAF and the Dambusters along with a 65-acre filming and gaming studio.

A rather early finish time—between 4 to 4.30 p.m.—raised an eyebrow or two as well. The official programme was published, confidently advertising the dates for the 2018 edition.

The immediate response from RAFCTE was to bill Scampton 2017 as a runaway success. It was not; it did not get the same pasting as Farnborough 2018, but while the magazine reviews were more accommodating, the reflex comments from those who take the trouble to personally convey their appraisals were clearly disappointed. Unofficial comments online tried to be helpful, suggesting the traditional Battle of Britain weekend or perhaps the old Waddington slot at the end of June to early July, should be looked at for 2018. Nothing else was communicated for a while as the announced dates remained provisional.

September remains a busy month for air shows across Europe. In Belgium, usually on the dates provisionally picked for Scampton, there is either Sanicole or the Belgian Air Force Days. Usually, Battle of Britain weekend now or the week after is booked by the Czech Air Force for their NATO air days at Ostrava each year. This may very well have been a problem from the outset together with the accommodation factor. RAFCTE were relying on the University of Lincoln to help with accommodating the bulk of the participants, just as the RAF did for Waddington. Yet on top of this, the gate takings at Scampton (another ticket in advance-only set up) were poor, so no one could make their minds up, at short notice, whether to head out on the day.

The tickets were regarded as pricey for what there was. RAFCTE failed to explain the still provisional status of the selected dates. Eventually, after a prolonged period of silence, just before Christmas, the cancellation of the 2018 air show was announced. Even though they had attracted 50,000 visitors over the weekend, they had made a loss. Andy Armstrong, the Scampton air show chief executive officer, said he was proud of what had been achieved. He further said, 'post-event there remains a lot to reflect on, and areas where we would like to improve'. The organiser's newfound refrain from updating their public website continued into 2018, having claimed the ambition to avoid 2018 but hold an event in 2019. Eventually, there was more

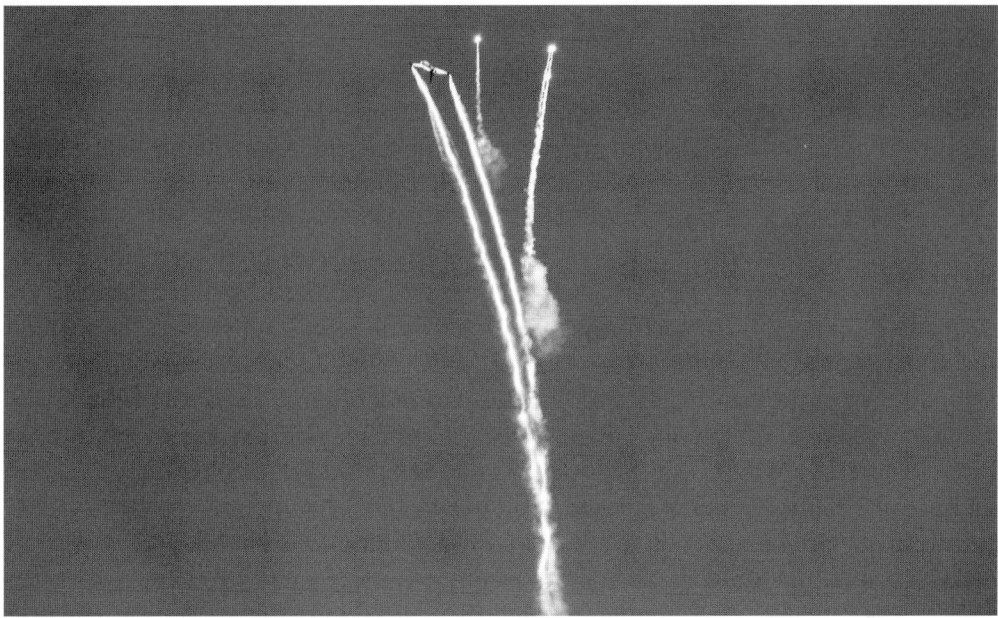

Belgian F-16 dispersing flares—an impressive but sometimes controversial element of display flying activity.

Patrouille de France over Volkel again, completing their own roll back manoeuvre toward rather than along the crowd line. The premier French team are regular visitors to the UK. (*Author's Collection*)

bad news for the idea of a Scampton air show—the government announced further defence cuts, meaning Scampton along with RAF Linton-on-Ouse were to shut.

Further, the air show director, Paul Sall, the last to oversee the Waddington air show, had resigned. The day-to-day management of service sponsored events had, since the 1990s, largely become the province of retired RAF officers. Paul had served for twenty-two years beforehand and had overseen Scampton despite it being a RAFCTE operation. This gem was released late in July 2018 shortly after the pending Scampton closure was announced. The ambition to hold the air show again needed clarification; there was none.

The closure notice was not due to take effect until 2022. This kind of long lead-in time allowed the Leuchars air show, for example, to continue for a couple more years. Meanwhile, the air show held at Scampton was neither in nor out, with no confirmation one way or the other. This situation lingered on with no final notice and the local papers referred to Scampton as Lincoln's air show and the successor to Waddington. Since 2019, however, it has become clear that the Scampton air show was stillborn.

In 2019, as well as the Eurofighter Typhoon, the F-35 had entered service, slowly, yet surely, growing in numbers. The RAF managed to make a 617 Squadron jet available to fly a couple of circuits over Yeovilton and Fairford, though not to Cosford for some reason. The RAF and RN are still getting to grips with the F-35 to make it fully carrier deployable and in such lean times.

As for the future, the globe has been thrown into chaos by COVID-19. As a result, large indoor and many outdoor events have been cancelled. The arrival of a vaccine at the end of 2020 seemed to presage the end of the scourge. However, a mixture of reluctance to be vaccinated, demands to divert vaccines elsewhere, and the emergence of new strains have all conspired to disrupt a more orderly process. As 2021 came and went, there was some return to a degree of normal activity. That said, the principal military events to have been held this year—such as Cosford, Yeovilton, and RIAT—were cancelled for a second time. The long-term future has never been less clear since the war. So, dare I say, in December 2021, here's to the next 100 years of the RAF on display.

Above left: The classic Spitfire, the very sight that would have shaken awake many a Luftwaffe air gunners as they had few seconds to react before the hail of lead. Biggin Hill, August 2017. (*Author's Collection*)

Above right: The situation with warbirds today after the effort by various dedicated groups means that in 2019, as many as sixteen Spitfires could be flown in formation as seen here over Duxford's September air show that year. (*Author's Collection*)

The Red Arrows' palm break manoeuvre. This image was taken on Saturday, 14 July 2018—the second public day of the Fairford RIAT. (*Author's Collection*)

15
Memories

The following anecdotes and short stories are collected from people involved in air shows from either a professional, enthusiast, or simple onlooker.

Nick Wilcock (Former RAF Pilot, Buccaneer, Phantom, and VC-10)

Ah yes, St Athan Battle of Britain, in the summer of 1976. What a great time that was!

3 September 1976, 40 min LL Nav around Wales in Hunter F6A XK149. I'd expected to be allocated a pristine FGA9 for the static display, but some idiot put it U/S with a radar ranging fault, so I had to take a really grubby jet instead. The flight was great, culminating in a 480KIAS arrival at idle thrust and a little below 250 feet, to create a glorious blue note!

The Hunter display pilot arrived a little later in his jet from Brawdy. But when they parked his aircraft in the hangar, someone thought that the black and yellow handle marked 'Canopy Jettison' was a handbrake. It wasn't … and it did! So, he flew my old jet the next day instead and I was free to wander about to enjoy myself.

Flew back on Monday the 6th in 20 minutes. Then an SAP trip later in the day in FGA9 XK137. But that was the day the music died for me; as I pulled the throttle through the gate to HP Off and timed the run down, I realised that I'd never fly a single seat Hunter ever again as I was posted to Buccs—waddapissa!

46 years ago, nearly, and yet it feels like yesterday!

John Houlston (Gliding Instructor)

A few recollections from those with a particular interest, professional or amateur, from over the years, some light-hearted, some not so:

Back in the '90s(?) RIAT was moved to Boscombe Down while they resurfaced the runway at Fairford. During the display, a couple of Tornados took off to intercept a pair of Russian aircraft which had flown nonstop from Russia and lead them to Boscombe from the North Sea. Eventually these two Russian aircraft arrived on the approach. I can't remember exactly what they were, but one was a smallish twin like a regional jet, the other was a MiG-29 (or similar). The MiG was flying echelon starboard to the airliner who was lined up in the centre line. This put the MiG heading between the runway and the crowd line which was much closer in those days. The commentator started to mutter questions about what this guy was intending to do. He got so low that I lost sight of him behind the crowd until I heard the commentator say something like 'Oh, that's interesting'. The MiG appeared with lots of noise, going vertical and then went into a typical MiG-29 display. Absolutely amazing and it was claimed that it broke the record for the maximum distance flown to perform a display.

Steve Ward (Group Captain, Royal Australian Air Force)

Currently enjoying our biennial three-week air show, known locally as Exercise Pitch Black.

They started back when the RAAF flew Mirages, the Kiwis still had Skyhawks and USAF B-52s were commonplace.

This is year we have RAAF Hornets, Growlers and Rhinos, Wedgetail, C-17, KC-30, C-130, C-27 and PC-9 (FAC).

Joining in are USAF F16s and FA-18s, USMC F-16s and Ospreys, Indonesian F-16s, Thai Gripens, Singaporean F-15s and F-16s, Indian Su-30s, French Rafales, Malaysian A400, Canadian C-130 and assorted others.

One year included flypasts by most types of our Mindle Beach Sunset Market, culminating in a sneak, low-level high-speed pass by one of the Classic Hornets. Shock and Awe was reportedly an understatement.

Saturday was an open day at the RAAF Base with static displays only, sadly. OH&S has killed off the flying displays for now.

For or the next two weeks, we'll have two or three waves launch most days, with ops running to 2300 each night.

Large gatherings of spectators gather at the end of the runway to watch the departures and arrivals.

And it doesn't cost us spectators a cent.

Trevor Pearson (Ex-Air Traffic Control, RAF Finningley)

Finningley (1976?) Battle of Britain 'At Home' Day (remember them?). A couple of days before THE DAY, everyone was very busy as all the static and flying display aircraft were arriving using slot times for separation, etc.

The 'stars' were to be Les Diables Rouge in their Magisters transiting down from having a look see at Leuchars where they were also to display.

The FY Local Controller had a steady stream of mixed traffic arriving when, up on frequency popped Diables Rouge.

Use your imagination (think 'allo 'allo) to the following:

DR: Feeninglee, Good Moaning, Diables Rouges.

ATC: Diables Rouge Good Morning, Runway 21 QFE blah. 4 aircraft ahead, 6 aircraft following. Straight in to land please. (or words to that effect)

DR: Feeningley roger, 4 ahead, 6 following. Request 10 minewts display practisse.

ATC: Diables negative, circuit full. Report Finals for Full Stop.

DR: 'Er Roger. (then various mumbles in French)

DR: Finals with gear.

ATC: Patrouille Clear Land, surface wind blah

DR: Clear land.

Then, coming over the northern fence line.

DR: Overshooting.

and they did so, and broke into a display practice (complete with smoke) and buggered up the stream of mixed aircraft arriving.

OC Flying (watching in Local) went ape. Once Diables had finished and landed, he screamed across the runway in his Mini to confront the Flems (er Belgians). He was met, at canopy lift, by a grinning Belgian Air Force 2-star General lighting a fag.

Diables Rouge were never invited back.

Interestingly enough, Mon General had a nifty ashtray attached in the cockpit with a clip device to hold his fag!

Steve Raper (Ex-Air Traffic Controller RAF/RN)

I remember the Boscombe display very well, little did I know that within a year I would be controlling there.

Church Fenton late 70s. Crowd line marked by a piece of string on bamboo posts. About 30yds towards the runway were the stanchions holding the PA speakers. Just to our right a family were watching as we were but there was one lad, about 7 years old, who kept ducking under the string and running out to the speaker, round and back. He did this a few times until eventually RAF Police came and had a word with him and his folks. Discussion about 'oh, he's only doing boy things, and no harm', etc. Anyway, told not to do it again.

5 mins later, off the kid scoots again heading out to the speaker; parents oblivious and not caring. What they hadn't seen though was the F-4 coming in from the right in a very low and VERY fast fly-by. The kid dropped to the floor a gibbering wreck and his dad had to go and collect him. Last I saw was them leaving, dad fuming, mum nagging and the kid still trembling with distinctly urine-coloured patches down his trousers. I bet that was an interesting journey home.

John Houlston

An SU27 carried out the usual spectacular display at the Yeovilton Air Day some years ago. After it landed, I wandered round to the visitors parking area to have a look at it. I took the pilot to be a very grumpy, scruffy sort of guy in a blue overall. He borrowed a ladder and leaned it against the leading edge of the port wing. He climbed the ladder and opened a hatch in the top of the wing and started tugging angrily at whatever was inside. He pulled out what looked like small supermarket bags and threw them onto the ground. Eventually, after a lot of tugging he pulled out a coiled-up length of hose and, after throwing that on the ground he descended back down the ladder. It appeared that this hose was an adapter which enabled them to connect some vital service to the NATO system. Once the hose was finished with, he returned the hose and plastic bags the hatch and closed the lid.

He then placed the ladder under the nose wheel area and started another vigorous tug of war with something inside the nose wheel arch. It turned out to be a folded-up tarpaulin, which he refolded and replaced. I couldn't get over the fact that all of these objects were in place during his extremely energetic display with lots of negative G.

Having replaced everything, he got on board and taxied out. I set my scanner to the appropriate UHF frequencies and listened in to his various conversations with London Military. The last I heard was a frantic controller pleading with him to descend back down to the altitude to which he had been cleared.

Sadly, you don't get anything like that at the Yeovilton Air Day anymore.

Julian Treadwell (Aviation Enthusiast)

On 23 September 1988, the RAF solo display Phantom crashed during rehearsal over RAF Abingdon with the tragic loss of both crew members.

I watched the Phantom display at Duxford a week or two before the Abingdon crash and recall feeling extremely uncomfortable - the pull outs looked extremely hard to this then 24-year-old civilian whose only expertise was a decade or so of air show attendances.

Paul Wheatley (Pilot on Fixed-Wing Refresher Course on 6 FTS Standards Sqn, Based at Finningley)

I too watched the F-4 practice at Finningley the week before and was worried by what I saw during a loop. The pilot definitely appeared to push the nose up whilst inverted, without gaining height, or perhaps even descending a little. As the aircraft bottomed out, pulling a lot of G, it began wing rocking. I never flew the type but did know that this was a pre-emptor of the type departing from controlled flight.

I was very sad to hear the outcome of the BOI.

In my mind's eye I can still see that F-4 descending whilst the pilot attempted to gain altitude when it was at the top of that loop. The tragic accident occurred only a short time later, at RAF Abingdon and appeared to replicate the same error of judgement. A great shame that no-one with any clout realised what had happened and could have debriefed them. I was a mere observer and just a helicopter pilot so I would have been deemed unworthy to comment—but I wish I had been able to.

Ian McFadyen (1976 Phantom Solo Display Pilot and Station Commander, RAF Leuchars, 1985–88)

I joined No. 43 Squadron, as A Flight Commander in the autumn of 1975, flying the Phantom FG1. With a background in formation aerobatics (having flown with the Poachers aerobatic team in 1971 and 1972), I was fortunate to be selected as the No 11 Group Phantom display pilot for 1976. I was equally fortunate to have as my back-seater, a remarkable navigator by the name of Norman Browne who was later to earn a DFC in the 1991 Gulf War. The work up proceeded smoothly until, in April a Phantom lost a wing tip due to metal fatigue. All Phantoms had a wing fold capability because of the type's original design as a Carrier-born machine. This put immediate limitations on what one might do in a display, and I was forced to change the whole display. 1976 was wonderful summer for display flying with weeks of sunshine and little cloud so I was able to do a full display for most of the year. The Phantom was a great aeroplane but required some careful handling near the stall. The Americans had added an AOA gauge (Angle of Attack) which showed up clearly by a simple display near to the front canopy. This was a new device in RAF service and was quickly to become the norm on all fast-jet machines. It enabled one to work to the limit with comparative ease although fixed height/speed bands, aided by Norman Browne, was essential to ensure safe ground clearance.

At high speed at a low level, one was pushing the aircraft to its limits; on one occasion, at the USAF Bicentennial air show at RAF Mildenhall, I was completing my display with a high-speed low pass at a tad over .9 Mach when the right-hand engine suddenly quit in spectacular fashion (a very loud bang) and wound straight down to zero. I elected for an immediate landing at Mildenhall, and I was rather surprised to see smoke beside the runway as I landed. Fire engines were racing to the scene, and I was completely ignored. Fortunately, the failure was confined to the engine and jet pipe and so there was no on-board fire in the aircraft—a tribute to Rolls-Royce if not the failure! What had happened was that the entire aft section of my right Spey engine had blown out of the jet pipe and onto really dry grass immediately setting up a serious fire!

Ten years later, I was back at RAF Leuchars as the Station Commander where one of my roles was to oversee the Phantom display pilot, as the task had remained with Leuchars, in good measure due to its location of being next to the sea, although not always to the delight of golfers playing on the Old Course at St Andrews! I had written a letter apologising for the noise (and the Phantom was noisy in full reheat!) during a rehearsal when St Andrews was hosting the Amateur Open. But, as Station Commander, I had wider responsibilities, and this included the annual Battle of

Britain 'At Home' Day every September. By today's standards, the show was run on as shoestring with little professional support. Nevertheless, things normally ran very smoothly. On my second year, we had majored on publicity with some impressive results in that people turned up in large numbers.... much more so than before, and the subsequent traffic chaos did not lead to happy visitors. For my third show, we had to completely revise our thinking, working closely with the Fife Police we developed a much better traffic control system. We had a string of famous pilots visiting the show; one Friday evening the day before the Open Day, I was wandering around welcoming people when I came across Duncan Simpson. He was flying a Miles Magister in the display and wanted some practice. He invited me to join him, and I needed no second invitation. There was no intercom or radio in such pre-war machines, so everything had to be done by Aldis light from Air Traffic Control. As we were lining up on the runway, I noticed in the shadow of evening sunshine that the pilot cover was still clearly in place. This would have meant we had no airspeed indication in the cockpit and some embarrassment to the famous pilot in charge! I signalled by hands and arms that something was not right, pointing to under the left wing. Out got Duncan to rectify the situation, somewhat to the consternation of ATC! As he climbed back in, he shouted above the noise of the engine: 'Well done, Group Captain, well done!' We had a marvellous flight thereafter and we became very good friends.

David Edward Langley (Ex-Met. Officer)

Battle of Britain (at Finningley) was such a big deal that a B o B Telephone Directory was printed. We treasured the number of the 'Officer i/c Temporary Erections' [As to whether the directory was a mighty spoof, I know not, but I read it with my own eyes].

Appendix I

HQ Fighter Command Allocation of Surplus for Battle of Britain 'At Home' Day, 14 September 1957

Battle of Britain 'At Home' Day on 14 September 1957 was the first to be held following the early but substantive implementation of cuts to RAF fighter squadrons. It was also the first to be fully coordinated by Headquarters Fighter Command, all overseen and coordinated by a cell at HQFC. The surplus of resources organised through HQFC usually amounted to little more than about three-quarters of both the total flying and static surplus and in some cases no more than half the contribution, the rest being put together by the local Battle of Britain office.

Absent from the list are two or three stations that became particularly synonymous with such events, specifically Finningley, which was in the process of introducing the Vulcan into operational service, Leuchars was undergoing runway resurfacing and Abingdon alternated with nearby Benson, whose turn it was this year. There was a further event, not listed, with the airfield located on the north face of Gibraltar, as well as a static exhibit at London Heathrow Airport. However, here is the distribution of assets organised through the FCHQ coordinating cell.

Fighter Command Aircraft Allocated for Static Displays

Home Station	Aircraft Type	Allocated 'At Home' Station
Chivenor	Hunter	London Airport
Wattisham	Meteor NF 12/14	London Airport
West Raynham	Hunter	Binbrook
West Raynham	Hunter	Hemswell
West Raynham	Hunter	Honington
West Raynham	Hunter	Syerston
Odiham	Javelin	Little Rissington
Coltishall	Javelin	Lindholme
Coltishall	Javelin	Syerston
Coltishall	Javelin	Upwood

Leeming	Javelin	Kinloss
Leeming	Javelin	Valley
Leeming	Javelin	Binbrook
Leeming	Javelin	Aldergrove
Leeming	Javelin	Dishforth
Leeming	Javelin	Colerne
Stradishall	Venom	Castle Bromwich
Stradishall	Meteor T7	Hemswell
West Malling	Meteor F8	Kinloss
West Malling	Meteor F8	Lindholme
Odiham	Meteor F8	Upwood
Odiham	Meteor F8	St Eval
Stradishall	Meteor F8	Honington
Acklington	Meteor F8	Aldergrove
Middleton St George	Meteor F8	Gaydon
Middleton St George	Meteor F8	Castle Bromwich
Church Fenton	Meteor F8	Binbrook
Church Fenton	Meteor F8	Disforth
Middle Wallop	Balliol	Jurby
North Luffenham	Balliol	Ternhill
North Luffenham	Balliol	Hendon
North Luffenham	Balliol	Halton
North Luffenham	Balliol	Castle Bromwich
Odiham	Vampire T11	Jurby
Stradishall	Vampire T11	Hemswell
Biggin Hill	Vampire T11	Gaydon
Chivenor	Vampire T11	St Eval
Chivenor	Vampire T11	St Athan
North Luffenham	Vampire T11	Honington

Fighter Command Aircraft for Flying Displays

Leuchars	Hunter (Solo Aeros)	Kinloss
North Weald	Hunter (Solo Aeros)	Hendon & Andover
Wattisham	Hunter (Solo Aeros)	Dishforth & Weeton
West Raynham	Hunter (Solo Aeros)	Upwood & Honington
Waterbeach	Hunter (Solo Aeros)	Gaydon & Castle Bromwich
Waterbeach	Hunter (Solo Aeros)	Benson & Halton
Waterbeach	Hunter (Solo Aeros)	St Athan & St Eval
Waterbeach	Hunter (Solo Aeros)	Lindholme & Norton
West Raynham	Javelin (Solo Aeros)*	St Athan & St Eval
Odiham	Hunter (Solo Aeros)	Binbrook
Chivenor	Balliol (Solo Aeros)	St Athan
Wattisham	8 × Hunters (Formation)	Aldergrove, Valley & Jurby

West Malling	8 × Meteor NF12/14 (85 Sqn)	Aldergrove
West Malling	6 × Meteor NF12/14 (153 Sqn)	Horsham St Faith
West Malling	4 × Meteor NF12/14 (153 Sqn)	Kinloss
Biggin Hill	12 × Hunters (Flypast)	Hendon
North Weald	9 × Hunters aeros team	Biggin Hill & Hendon
Leuchars	4 × Hunters aeros team	Turnhouse & Kinloss
Chivenor	4 × Hunters aeros team	Chivenor & St Athan
Chivenor	6 × Hunters (Flypast)	St Eval

*Javelin solo later cancelled by Fighter Command due to crew experience and performance/handling concerns.

Bomber Command Aircraft Allocated for Static Displays

Binbrook	Canberra	Gibraltar
Binbrook	Canberra	Acklington
Binbrook	Canberra	Aldergrove
Bassingbourn	Canberra	Benson
Bassingbourn	Canberra	Biggin Hill
Bassingbourn	Canberra	Chivenor
Upwood	Canberra	Church Fenton
Upwood	Canberra	Colerne
Upwood	Canberra	Dishforth
Bassingbourn	Canberra	Leconfield
Bassingbourn	Canberra	Duxford
Bassingbourn	Canberra	Horsham St Faith
Binbrook	Canberra	Kinloss
Bassingbourn	Canberra	North Luffenham
Binbrook	Canberra	St Athan
Bassingbourn	Canberra	St Eval
Binbrook	Canberra	Syerston
Bassingbourn	Canberra	Tangmere
Binbrook	Canberra	Thornaby
Binbrook	Canberra	Turnhouse
Upwood	Canberra	Valley
Waddington	Canberra	London Airport
Marham	Valiant	Acklington
Marham	Valiant	Aldergrove
Marham	Valiant	Benson
Marham	Valiant	Biggin Hill
Marham	Valiant	Church Fenton
Marham	Valiant	Colerne
Marham	Valiant	Dishforth
Marham	Valiant	Leconfield

Wittering	Valiant	Duxford
Wittering	Valiant	Horsham St Faith
Marham	Valiant	London Airport
Wittering	Valiant	Kinloss
Wittering	Valiant	North Luffenham
Wittering	Valiant	St Athan
Wittering	Valiant	St Eval
Wittering	Valiant	Turnhouse
Wittering	Valiant	Valley

Bomber Command Aircraft Allocated for Flying Displays

Waddington	Canberra	Jurby & Weeton
Upwood	Canberra	Ternhill & Norton
Bassingbourn	Canberra	Castle Bromwich & Cosford
Binbrook	Canberra	Andover & Halton
Marham	Valiant	Hendon

Coastal Command Aircraft Allocated for Static Displays

St Eval	Shackleton	Biggin Hill
St Eval	Shackleton	St Athan

HQ 90 Signals Group Aircraft Allocated for Static Displays

Watton	Varsity	Acklington
Watton	Varsity	Biggin Hill
Watton	Varsity	Church Fenton
Watton	Varsity	Chivenor
Watton	Varsity	Duxford
Watton	Varsity	Leconfield
Watton	Varsity	Dishforth
Watton	Varsity	Andover

HQ 90 Signals Group Aircraft Allocated for Flying Displays

Watton	Canberra	Turnhouse & Bishopbriggs
Watton	Canberra	Hendon

Transport Command Aircraft Allocated for Static Displays

Abingdon	Beverley	Andover
Abingdon	Beverley	Biggin Hill
Abingdon	Beverley	Hendon
Abingdon	Beverley	Thornaby
Colerne	Hastings	Turnhouse
Colerne	Hastings	St Athan
Colerne	Hastings	Horsham St Faith
Colerne	Hastings	St Eval
Lyneham	Hastings	Chivenor
Lyneham	Hastings	North Luffenham
Dishforth	Hastings	Castle Bromwich
Dishforth	Hastings	Kinloss
HQ Transport Cmd	Hastings	London Airport

Transport Command Aircraft Allocated for Flying Displays

Dishforth	Pioneer	Bishopbriggs & Turnhouse
Dishforth	Pioneer	Acklington & Thornaby
Dishforth	Pioneer	Valley & Weeton

Flying Training Command Aircraft Allocated for Static Displays

Oakington	Vampire	Acklington
Oakington	Vampire	Duxford
Oakington	Vampire	Cosford
Oakington	Vampire	Colerne
Oakington	Vampire	Horsham St Faith
Oakington	Vampire	Lindholme
Oakington	Vampire	St Eval
Oakington	Vampire	Tangmere
Worksop	Vampire	North Luffenham
Worksop	Vampire	Binbrook
Worksop	Vampire	Dishforth
Swinderby	Vampire	Benson
Swinderby	Vampire	Castle Bromwich
Swinderby	Vampire	Church Fenton
Swinderby	Vampire	Turnhouse
Cranwell	Vampire	Biggin Hill
Cranwell	Vampire	Honington
Cranwell	Vampire	Hemswell
Cranwell	Vampire	Kinloss
Cranwell	Vampire	Thornaby
Shawbury	Vampire	Aldergrove

Shawbury	Vampire	Gaydon
Shawbury	Vampire	Jurby
Shawbury	Vampire	Upwood
Topcliffe	Vampire NF10	Jurby
Topcliffe	Vampire NF10	St Eval
Topcliffe	Vampire NF10	Aldergrove
Worksop	Meteor	Syerston
Manby	Canberra	Syerston
Manby	Canberra	Valley
Manby	Lincoln	Syerston
Manby	Valetta	Syerston
Topcliffe	Valetta T3	Aldergrove
Topcliffe	Valetta T3	Jurby
Thorney Island	Valetta	London Airport
Thorney Island	Varsity	Cosford
Thorney Island	Varsity	Hendon
Thorney Island	Varsity	Castle Bromwich
Thorney Island	Varsity	Halton
Thorney Island	Varsity	Horsham St Faith
Thorney Island	Varsity	Jurby
Thorney Island	Varsity	Kinloss
Thorney Island	Varsity	St Athan
Thorney Island	Varsity	St Eval
Thorney Island	Varsity	Aldergrove
Thorney Island	Varsity	Thornaby
Thorney Island	Varsity	Turnhouse
Shawbury	Varsity	Ternhill
Shawbury	Varsity	Valley
Topcliffe	Marathon	Ternhill
Topcliffe	Marathon	Valley
Topcliffe	Marathon	Syerston
Topcliffe	Marathon	Little Rissington
Shawbury	Chipmunk	Ternhill
Shawbury	Chipmunk	Jurby
Shawbury	Chipmunk	Kinloss
Shawbury	Chipmunk	Lindholme
Middle Wallop	Chipmunk	Binbrook
Middle Wallop	Chipmunk	Colerne
Middle Wallop	Chipmunk	Cosford
Middle Wallop	Auster Mk 7	Hendon
Middle Wallop	Auster Mk 7	Little Rissington
Middle Wallop	Auster Mk 7	Horsham St Faith
Middle Wallop	Auster Mk 7	Thornaby
Middle Wallop	Auster Mk 9	Ternhill

Middle Wallop	Auster Mk 9	Castle Bromwich
Middle Wallop	Auster Mk 9	Biggin Hill
Middle Wallop	Auster Mk 9	Halton
Hullavington	Provost T1	St Eval
Hullavington	Provost T1	St Athan
Hullavington	Provost T1	Hendon
Hullavington	Provost T1	Andover
Hullavington	Provost T1	Halton
Hullavington	Provost T1	Jurby
Feltwell	Provost T1	Biggin Hill
Feltwell	Provost T1	Castle Bromwich
Feltwell	Provost T1	Cosford
Feltwell	Provost T1	Horsham St Faith
Cranwell	Provost T1	Thornaby
Cranwell	Provost T1	Turnhouse
Cranwell	Provost T1	Colerne
Cranwell	Provost T1	Kinloss
Cranwell	Provost T1	Acklington
Little Rissington	Provost T1	Chivenor
Feltwell	Provost T1	Aldergrove
Feltwell	Provost T1	Hemswell
Feltwell	Provost T1	Gaydon
Feltwell	Provost T1	Honington
Ternhill	Provost T1	Valley
Ternhill	Provost T1	Duxford
Ternhill	Provost T1	Binbrook
Hullavington	Jet Provost	Syerston
Hullavington	Jet Provost	Biggin Hill

Flying Training Command Aircraft Allocated for Flying Displays

Little Rissington	Provost Aerobatics Team	Little Rissington & Colerne
Cranwell	Vampire Aerobatics Team	Castle Bromwich & Cosford
Oakington	Vampire Aerobatics Team	Horsham & Duxford
Worksop	Meteor Aerobatics Team	Thornaby & Acklington
Worksop	Vampire Aerobatics Team	Norton & Lindholme
Swinderby	Vampire Aerobatics Team	Syerston & Hemswell
Swinderby	Vampire Aerobatics Team	North Luffenham & Upwood
Valley	Vampire Aerobatics Team	Weeton & Ternhill (Based Shawbury)
Manby	Meteor Aerobatics Team	Leconfield & Church Fenton
Feltwell	Provost Pair Aerobatics	Horsham St Faith & Duxford
Cranwell	Vampire Solo Aerobatics	Hemswell & Binbrook
Little Rissington	Vampire Solo Aerobatics	Gaydon & Benson
Little Rissington	Hunter Solo Aerobatics	Little Rissington & Colerne

Oakington	Vampire Solo Aerobatics	Honington & Duxford
Oakington	Vampire Solo Aerobatics	Horsham St Faith
Oakington	Vampire Solo Aerobatics	Hendon & Halton
Worksop	Meteor Solo Aerobatics	Norton & Lindholme
Worksop	Vampire Solo Aerobatics	Turnhouse & Bishop Briggs (Based Turnhouse)
Worksop	Vampire Solo Aerobatics	Church Fenton & Leconfield
Swinderby	Vampire Solo Aerobatics	Syerston
Swinderby	Vampire Solo Aerobatics	Castle Bromwich & Cosford (Based Castle Bromwich)
Swinderby	Vampire Solo Aerobatics	St Eval & St Athan (Based St Eval)
Valley	Vampire Solo Aerobatics	Jurby
Manby	Meteor Solo Aerobatics	Ternhill
Manby	Meteor Solo Aerobatics	Aldergrove
Manby	Hunter Solo Aerobatics	Syerston & Ternhill (Based Syerston)
Little Rissington	Provost Solo Aerobatics	Colerne & St Athan
Cranwell	Provost Solo Aerobatics	Hemswell & Binbrook
Cranwell	Provost Solo Aerobatics	Lindholme & Dishforth
Cranwell	Provost Solo Aerobatics	Church Fenton & Leconfield
Cranwell	Provost Solo Aerobatics	North Luffenham & Upwood
Hullavington	Provost Solo Aerobatics	Chivenor & St Eval (Based Chivenor)
Hullavington	Provost Solo Aerobatics	Andover & Tangmere
Hullavington	Provost Solo Aerobatics	Jurby & Weeton (Based Jurby)
Hullavington	Provost Solo Aerobatics	Aldergrove (Based Locally)
Hullavington	Provost Solo Aerobatics	Hendon & Benson (Based Hendon)
Hullavington	Provost Solo Aerobatics	Halton (Based Halton)
Ternhill	Provost Solo Aerobatics	Castle Bromwich & Cosford
Ternhill	Provost Solo Aerobatics	Kinloss (Based Kinloss)
Ternhill	Provost Solo Aerobatics	Horsham (Based Horsham)
Feltwell	Provost Solo Aerobatics	Biggin Hill
Feltwell	Provost Solo Aerobatics	Honington & Duxford
Feltwell	Provost Solo Aerobatics	Gaydon
Feltwell	Provost Solo Aerobatics	Turnhouse & Bishopbriggs
Hullavington	Jet Provost Solo Aerobatics	Valley & Ternhill
Hullavington	Jet Provost Solo Aerobatics	Thornaby & Acklington (Based Thornaby)
Syerston	Provost Solo Aerobatics	Norton
Shawbury	Chipmunk Solo Aerobatics	Castle Bromwich & Cosford
Middle Wallop	Chipmunk Solo Aerobatics	Horsham & Honington (Based Honington)
Middle Wallop	Chipmunk Solo Aerobatics	Thornaby & Dishforth
Middle Wallop	Chipmunk Solo Aerobatics	North Luffenham & Norton (Based North Luffenham)
South Cerney	Chipmunk Solo Aerobatics	St Athan & Chivenor (Based St Athan)
South Cerney	Chipmunk Solo Aerobatics	Hendon (Based Hendon)
Little Rissington	Sycamore Flying Demo	Ternhill & Cosford
Little Rissington	S.51 Flying Demo	Syerston & North Luffenham

Home Command Aircraft Allocated for Static Displays

Langham	Mosquito	Horsham St Faith
Llanbedr	Mosquito	Thornaby
Llanbedr	Mosquito	Turnhouse
Exeter	Mosquito	Biggin Hill
Exeter	Mosquito	Castle Bromwich
Llanbedr	Mosquito	Leconfield
Woodvale	Mosquito	Jurby
Exeter	Mosquito	Hendon
Langham	Mosquito	North Luffenham
Exeter	Mosquito	Little Rissington
White Waltham	Balliol	Andover
White Waltham	Balliol	Cosford
White Waltham	Balliol	Little Rissington
White Waltham	Balliol	Lindholme
Llanbedr	Meteor F8	Colerne
Llanbedr	Meteor F8	Hemswell
Dyce	Chipmunk	Kinloss
Filton	Chipmunk	St Eval
Cambridge	Chipmunk	Upwood
Sydenham	Chipmunk	Aldergrove
Hamble	Chipmunk	Tangmere
Newton	Chipmunk	Syerston
Ushworth	Chipmunk	Dishworth
Cambridge	Chipmunk	Honington
Brough	Chipmunk	Hemswell
Castle Bromwich	Chipmunk	Gaydon

Home Command Aircraft Allocated for Flying Displays

White Waltham	Mosquito Flying Demo	Aldergrove & Jurby (Based Aldergrove)
White Waltham	Mosquito Flying Demo	Binbrook & Dishforth (Based Binbrook)
Biggin Hill	Chipmunk Formation Drill + Solo Aeros	Andover
Turnhouse	Chipmunk Formation Drill + Solo Aeros	Turnhouse
Perth	Chipmunk Formation Drill + Solo Aeros	Bishopbriggs
Dyce	Chipmunk Formation Drill + Solo Aeros	Kinloss
Kidlington	Chipmunk Formation Drill + Solo Aeros	Benson
Woodvale	Chipmunk Formation Drill + Solo Aeros	Valley
Yeadon	Chipmunk Formation Drill + Solo Aeros	Weeton
Filton	Chipmunk Formation Drill + Solo Aeros	Colerne
Brough	Chipmunk Formation Drill + Solo Aeros	Leconfield
Cambridge	Chipmunk Formation Drill + Solo Aeros	Duxford
Brough	Chipmunk Formation Drill + Solo Aeros	Church Fenton

United States Air Force Aircraft Allocated for Static Displays

Woodbridge	F-84 Thunderstreak	Gaydon
Woodbridge	F-84 Thunderstreak	Honington
Manston	F-86D Sabre	Colerne
Manston	F-86D Sabre	Duxford
Woodbridge	F-86D Sabre	Tangmere
Manston	F-86D Sabre	Hemswell
Manston	F-86D Sabre	Church Fenton
Manston	F-86D Sabre	Chivenor
Manston	F-86D Sabre	Biggin Hill
Woodbridge	F-86D Sabre	Turnhouse
Manston	F-86D Sabre	Benson
Woodbridge	F-86D Sabre	St Athan
Manston	F-86D Sabre	Horsham St Faith
Woodbridge	F-86D Sabre	North Luffenham
Woodbridge	F-86D Sabre	Valley
Manston	F-86D Sabre	Binbrook
Manston	F-86D Sabre	Aldergrove
Alconbury	B-45 Tornado	Aldergrove
Alconbury	B-45 Tornado	Valley
Sculthorpe	B-45 Tornado	Kinloss
Sculthorpe	B-45 Tornado	Upwood
Sculthorpe	B-45 Tornado	Lindholme
Sculthorpe	B-45 Tornado	Leconfield
Sculthorpe	B-66 Destroyer	Gaydon
Sculthorpe	B-66 Destroyer	Honington
Sculthorpe	KB-50	Biggin Hill
Sculthorpe	KB-50	Horsham St Faith
Sculthorpe	KB-50	St Athan
Sculthorpe	KB-29	Thornaby
Sculthorpe	KB-29	Turnhouse
Sculthorpe	KB-29	Chivenor
Sculthorpe	C-119	Hendon
Sculthorpe	C-119	Castle Bromwich
Sculthorpe	C-119	Halton
Alconbury	SA-16	Andover
Alconbury	SA-16	Jurby

United States Air Force Aircraft Allocated for Flying Displays

'Skyblazers'   4 × F-100s Formation Aerobatics Team   Biggin Hill & Hendon

Flying Display Touring Formations and Individual Aircraft

Base Station	*Aircraft & Number*
Church Fenton	6 × Hunters
Horsham St Faith	8 × Hunters
Odiham	4 × Javelins
Duxford	8 × Meteor 12/14s
Tangmere	24 × Hunters
West Malling (Deployed Chivenor)	8 × Meteor 12/14s
North Luffenham	9 × Meteor 12/14s
Wattisham	8 × Meteor 12/14s
Duxford	8 × Hunters
Odiham	6 × Hunters
Acklington	4 × Hunters
Horsham St Faith	4 × Meteor F8s
RNAS Lossiemouth	4 × Sea Hawks
RNAS Lossiemouth (Deployed Acklington)	4 × Sea Hawks
RNAS Brawdy	3 × Balliols
RNAS Brawdy	3 × Vampires
RNAS Eglington	4 × Gannets
RNAS Eglington	4 × Gannets
Boscombe Down (A&AEE)	Vulcan
RAE Farnborough	3 × Canberras
HP Radlett	2 × Victors
Vickers Wisley	N.113 (Scimitar)
Bristol Filton	Britannia
Defford	2 × Valettas
Defford	Hastings
RAE Farnborough	Valiant
West Freugh	Lincoln
A&AEE Boscombe Down	Victor
A&AEE Boscombe Down	Valiant
A&AEE Boscombe Down	DH.110 (Sea Vixen)
A&AEE Boscombe Down	DH.110 (Sea Vixen)
Waddington	Vulcan
Waddington	Vulcan
Marham	Valiant
Coningsby	3 × Canberras
Waddington	Vulcan

Home' Stations on Tour Route

ton, Lindholme, Leconfield, Thornaby, Dishforth, Church Fenton

brook, Hemswell, Horsham St Faith

gin Hill, Tangmere, Andover, Odiham

le Rissington, Gaydon, Castle Bromwich, Cosford, Ternhill, Duxford

son, Silverstone, Little Rissington, St Athan, Colerne, Andover, Tangmere

than, St Eval, Chivenor

don, Little Rissington, Colerne, Andover, Benson, Halton, Upwood, North Luffenham

gin Hill, Tangmere, Benson, Halton, Duxford, Honington

wood, North Luffenham, Syerston, Honington, Duxford

ton, Gaydon, Castle Bromwich, Ternhill, Cosford, Little Rissington, Benson, Odiham

nhouse, Bishopbriggs, Acklington

gmere, Biggin Hill, Hendon, Duxford, Honington, Horsham St Faith

nhouse, Bishopbriggs, Kinloss

hforth, Church Fenton, Norton, Lindholme, Hemswell, Binbrook, Leconfield, Thornaby,
lington

val, Chivenor, St Athan

val, Chivenor, St Athan

ey, Jurby, Aldergrove

ergrove, Jurby, Weeton

son, Halton, North Luffenham, Syerston, Norton, Weeton, Ternhill, Cosford, Castle Bromwich,
don, Little Rissington

val, Chivenor

ford, Honington, Horsham St Faith, Binbrook, Hemswell, Lindholme, Leconfield, Thornaby,
hforth, Church Fenton, Norton, Syerston, North Luffenham, Upwood, Hendon

sham, Honington, Hendon

val, Chivenor, St Athan, Colerne, Andover, Biggin Hill, Tangmere

le Bromwich, Cosford, Ternhill, Weeton, Jurby, Valley, St Athan

ford, Ternhill, Weeton, Jurby, Aldergrove, Valley

e Rissington, Castle Bromwich, Cosford, Ternhill, Norton, Syerston, North Luffenham,
ford, Halton

ton, Jurby, Aldergrove

e Rissington, Gaydon, Castle Bromwich, St Athan, Colerne, Biggin Hill, Tangmere, Andover

gmere, Biggin Hill, Andover, Benson, Colerne, St Athan, Chivenor

e Rissington, Gaydon, Castle Bromwich, Cosford, Ternhill, St Athan, Colerne

over, Tangmere, Biggin Hill, Duxford, Upwood, North Luffenham, Halton, Benson

sham St Faith, Honington, Upwood, Gaydon, Lindholme, Hemswell, Binbrook, Hendon

le Bromwich, Colerne, St Athan, Chivenor, St Eval, Andover, Tangmere, Biggin Hill, Duxford,
th Luffenham

nfield, Thornaby, Jurby, Weeton, Norton

ton, Weeton, Jurby, Valley

nfield, Thornaby, Acklington, Turnhouse, Bishopbriggs, Jurby, Weeton, Norton

Bassingbourn	3 × Canberras
Lyneham	Gannet
Lyneham	Gannet
Colerne	
Kinloss	Shackleton
Cosford, Ternhill	
St Eval	Shackleton
Kinloss	Shackleton
Kinloss	Shackleton
Duxford, Honington, Horsham St Faith,	
Watton	Comet
Sculthorpe	3 × B-45 Tornados
Wethersfield	4 × F-100 Super Sabres
Bentwaters	4 × F-84 Thunderstreaks
Wethersfield	4 × F-100 Super Sabres
Manston	4 × F-86D Sabres
Bentwaters	4 × F-84 Thunderstreaks
Manston	4 × F-86D Sabres
Sculthorpe	3 × B-45 Tornados

In addition to the 'At Home' day, Fighter Command also took on responsibility for coordinating the RAF display element of the Farnborough Airshow the week before.

RAF Participating Units at Farnborough SBAC Show, 1957

Bomber Command
3 × V bombers 'Flypast' time = 2 minutes
100 × Canberras and Valiants, to flypast at Contrail height = 14 minutes, to be conducted throughout the RAF Display segment.

Flying Training Command
Provost Aerobatics Team time = 5 minutes

Fighter Command
Formation Flypast of 27 × Javelins, from 23, 46 & 141 Squadrons and 228 OCU and 27 × Hunters, from 1, 34 and 41 Squadrons
+ Aerobatics display by 9 × Hunters of 111 Squadron (The Black Arrows) = 7 minutes.

ton, Benson, Little Rissington, St Athan, Colerne, Andover, Tangmere, Biggin Hill

lover, Tangmere, Biggin Hill, Duxford, Honington, Horsham St Faith, Upwood, Binbrook,

nswell, Syerston, Halton, Benson

le Rissington, Gaydon, Castle Bromwich, Cosford, Ternhill, Valley, St Eval, Chivenor, St Athan,

nhouse, Acklington, Thornaby, Leconfield, Binbrook, Hemswell, Lindholme, Syerston,

venor, St Athan, Colerne, Andover, Biggin Hill, Hendon, Benson

opbriggs, Jurby, Valley, Weeton, Norton, Church Fenton, Dishforth

ey, Cosford, Castle Bromwich, Gaydon, Little Rissington, Halton, North Luffenham, Upwood,

brook, Hemswell, Lindholme, Church Fenton, Leconfield, Dishforth, Thornaby, Acklington,

nhouse, Bishopbriggs, Jurby, Weeton, Norton, Castle Bromwich, Syerston, North Luffenham,

wood, Duxford, Honington

sham St Faith, Honington, Duxford, Upwood, North Luffenham, Syerston, Binbrook,

nswell, Norton, Lindholme, Church Fenton, Dishforth, Bishopbriggs, Turnhouse, Acklington,

rnaby, Leconfield

gin Hill, Tangmere, Andover, Colerne, St Athan, Castle Bromwich, Gaydon, Duxford

sham St Faith, Leconfield, Thornaby, Acklington, Norton, Hemswell

sham St Faith, Binbrook, Leconfield, Thornaby, Dishforth, Church Fenton, Lindholme,

ston, North Luffenham, Upwood

gin Hill, Tangmere

ton, Benson, St Athan, Chivenor, Castle Bromwich, Honington

ford, Honington, Horsham St Faith

gin Hill, Tangmere, Andover, Colerne, St Athan, Chivenor, Ternhill, Cosford, Castle Bromwich,

don, Little Rissington, Benson, Halton

Appendix II

Available Surplus for Twenty-Fifth Anniversary Battle of Britain
'At Homes',
18 September 1965

The two most significant anniversaries commemorating the Battle of Britain since the war have been the twenty-fifth and the fiftieth. The twenty-fifth anniversary demanded a greater juggling of resources by FCHQ than in 1957 despite involving fewer open airfields, albeit on a much smaller scale than was the case through the 1950s.

The latter still involved a large-scale number of RAF stations open to the public but spread across the summer with a far lesser impact on resources and commitments.

By the twenty-fifth anniversary, a significant contribution from overseas NATO air arms had become a regular feature.

Again, the list is not exhaustive as much reliance on participation through local arrangement was still necessary. While the number of 'At Home' stations continued to decrease every couple of years or so, the twenty-fifth anniversary of the Battle of Britain, with twelve stations open, had reached a defining high-water mark in terms of ratio; this was the last time the number of simultaneous open stations was counted in double figures.

Fighter Command Surplus for Static Displays

Home Station	Aircraft Type	Allocated 'At Home' Station
Chivenor	Hunter	Acklington
Chivenor	Hunter	Biggin Hill
Chivenor	Hunter	St Mawgan
Coltishall	Lightning	St Mawgan
Coltishall	Lightning	Waddington
Coltishall	Lightning (several)	Coltishall
Coltishall	Lightning	Cottesmore
Leuchars	Lightning	Finningley
Leuchars	Lightning (Several)	Leuchars

Leuchars	Javelin (Several)	Leuchars
Leuchars	Hunter T7	Leuchars

Fighter Command Surplus Aircraft for Flying Displays

Chivenor	Hunter (Aeros)	Acklington & Leuchars
Chivenor	Hunter (Aeros)	Finningley
Chivenor	Hunter (Aeros)	St Athan & St Mawgan
Chivenor	8 × Hunter Tac Demo	Biggin Hill
Binbrook	4 Hunter Tac Demo	Biggin Hill & Finningley
Binbrook	Meteor (Aeros)	Cottesmore
Coltishall	Lightning (Aeros)	Coltishall
Coltishall	4 × Lightning Demo	Cottesmore (deployed) & Ternhill
Coltishall	9 × Lightning Demo	Coltishall
Leconfield	Lightning (Aeros)	Finningley & Waddington
Leuchars	Lightning (Aeros)	Leuchars
Leuchars	Lightning (Aeros)	Colerne & St Mawgan
Leuchars (23 Sqn)	4 × Lightning Demo	Acklington & Leuchars
Leuchars (74 Sqn)	4 × Lightning Demo	Leuchars
Leconfield (92 Sqn)	4 × Lightning Demo	Abingdon, Colerne & St Athan
Leconfield (19 Sqn)	4 × Lightning Demo	Finningley & Waddington
Wattisham (111 Sqn)	9 × Lightning Demo	Biggin Hill
Leuchars	2 × Lightnings Scrbl/AAR	Leuchars
Leuchars	Javelin	Acklington
Leuchars	Javelin T3	Finningley
Leuchars	4 × Javelin Demo	Leuchars
Wattisham	Lightning (Aeros)	Biggin Hill & Cottesmore
Wattisham	Hunter T7 (Aeros)	Coltishall & Cottesmore

Bomber Command Surplus Allocated for Static Displays

Waddington	Vulcan	Abingdon
Waddington	Vulcan	Leuchars
Waddington	5 × Vulcans	Waddington
Finningley	Vulcan	Biggin Hill
Finningley	Vulcan	Coltishall
Honington	Victor	Coltishall
Honington	Victor	St Mawgan
Cottesmore	3 × Vulcans	Cottesmore
Cottesmore	Vulcan	St Mawgan
Wittering	Victor	Cottesmore
Wittering	Victor	Finningley

Wittering	Victor	Waddington
Finningley	3 × Vulcans	Finningley
Wyton	Victor SR	Leuchars

Bomber Command Surplus Allocated for Flying Displays

Bassingbourn	Canberra LABS	Abingdon, Biggin Hill & Coltishall
Bassingbourn	Canberra LABS	Acklington, Finningley & Leuchars
Bassingbourn	Canberra LABS	Cottesmore, Ternhill & Waddington
Bassingbourn	Canberra LABS	Colerne, St Athan & St Mawgan
Cottesmore	1 × Vulcan Demo	Cottesmore
Finningley	1 × Vulcan Demo	Finningley
Cottesmore	4 × Vulcan Scramble	Cottesmore
Scampton	4 × Vulcan Scramble	Finningley
Waddington	4 × Vulcan Scramble	Waddington

Coastal Command Surplus Allocated for Static Displays

Kinloss	Shackleton	Abingdon
Kinloss	Shackleton	Acklington
St Mawgan	Shackleton	Biggin Hill
Kinloss	Shackleton	Coltishall
Kinloss	Shackleton	Cottesmore
Kinloss	Shackleton	Leuchars
Kinloss	Shackleton	St Mawgan
Manston	Whirlwind	Biggin Hill
Coltishall	Whirlwind	Coltishall

Coastal Command Surplus Allocated for Flying Displays

Acklington	Whirlwind SAR Demo	Acklington
Coltishall	Whirlwind SAR Demo	Coltishall
Leuchars	Whirlwind SAR/Ensign Tow	Leuchars
St Mawgan	Whirlwind	St Mawgan
St Mawgan	4 × Shackletons	St Mawgan

Transport Command Surplus Allocated for Static Displays

Abingdon	2 × Beverlies	Abingdon
Lyneham	Britannia	Abingdon

Odiham	Twin Pioneer	Abingdon
Benson	Argosy	Abingdon
Northolt	Bassett	Acklington
Benson	Argosy	Biggin Hill
Thorney Island	Beverley	Biggin Hill
Lyneham	Comet	Colerne
Colerne	Hastings	Colerne
Odiham	Wessex	Colerne
Abingdon	Beverley	Colerne
Benson	Argosy	Colerne
Northolt	Valetta	Coltishall
Northolt	Devon	Coltishall
Northolt	2 × Pembrokes	St Mawgan

Transport Command Surplus Allocated for Flying Displays

Abingdon	3 × Beverlies	Abingdon
Abingdon	1 × Beverley	Colerne
Abingdon	1 × Beverley	Finningley
Benson	1 × Argosy Para Drop	Abingdon & Biggin Hill
Benson	3 × Argosies	Abingdon
Benson	3 × Argosies	Colerne
Odiham	1 × Belvedere	Colerne
Stradishall	Meteor NF (T)	Acklington
Hullavington	Valetta	Acklington

Flying Training Command Surplus Allocated for Static Displays

Cranwell	Jet Provost	Abingdon
Little Rissington	Chipmunk	Abingdon
Stradishall	Meteor NF	Acklington
Hullavington	Valetta	Acklington
Linton-on-Ouse	Vampire	Acklington
Valley	Gnat	Acklington
Acklington	Jet Provost	Acklington
Valley	Gnat	Biggin Hill
Cranwell	2 × Jet Provosts	Biggin Hill
Hullavington	Varsity	Colerne
Little Rissington	Vampire	Colerne
Little Rissington	Chipmunk	Colerne
Valley	Gnat	Colerne
Syerston	2 × Jet Provosts	Colerne

Little Rissington	Jet Provost	Colerne
Church Fenton	Jet Provost	Colerne
Little Rissington	Varsity	Colerne
Little Rissington	Gnat	Colerne
Cambridge UAS	2 × Chipmunks	Coltishall
Linton-on-Ouse	2 × Jet Provosts	Cottesmore
Valley	Gnat	Finningley
Stradishall	Varsity	Finningley
Topcliffe	Varsity	Leuchars
Linton-on-Ouse	Vampire	Leuchars
Acklington	Jet Provost	Leuchars
Valley	Gnat	St Athan
Little Rissington	Jet Provost	St Athan
Stradishall	Meteor NF	St Athan
Oakington	Varsity	St Athan
UAS of Wales	Chipmunk	St Athan
Little Rissington	2 × Jet Provosts	St Mawgan
Church Fenton	2 × Jet Provosts	Ternhill
Ternhill	Sioux	Ternhill
Ternhill	2 × Whirlwinds	Ternhill
Ternhill	Sycamore	Ternhill
Hullavington	Valetta	Ternhill
Little Rissington	Mosquito	Ternhill
Ternhill	Whirlwind	Waddington
Oakington	Varsity	Waddington
Linton-on-Ouse	Jet Provost	Waddington
Linton-on-Ouse	Vampire	Waddington
Valley	Gnat	Waddington
Notts UAS	Chipmunk	Waddington

Flying Training Command Surplus Allocated for Flying Displays

Syerston	4 × Jet Provosts Aeros team	Abingdon & Biggin Hill
Little Rissington	Gnat Solo Aerobatics	Abingdon
Oxford UAS	2 × Chipmunks Aerobatics	Abingdon
Church Fenton	Jet Provost Solo Aerobatics	Abingdon & Colerne
Little Rissington	7 × Gnats Aeros Team	Biggin Hill & Ternhill
Acklington	Jet Provost Solo Aerobatics	Acklington & Leuchars
Acklington	3 × Jet Provost Aeros Team	Acklington & Leuchars
Acklington	16 × Jet Provosts Balbo	Acklington
Linton-on-Ouse	4 × Vampires Demo	Acklington & Finningley
Valley	Gnat Solo Aerobatics	Acklington
Stradishall	Meteor Solo Aerobatics	Acklington & Leuchars

Linton-on-Ouse	Jet Provost Solo Aerobatics	Biggin Hill
Little Rissington	Mosquito	Abingdon & Colerne
Manby	4 × Jet Provosts Aeros Team	Coltishall & Cottesmore
Leeming	3 × Jet Provosts Aeros Team	Finningley & Waddington
Linton-on-Ouse	3 × Jet Provosts Aeros Team	St Athan & St Mawgan
Little Rissington	4 × Jet Provosts Aeros Team	Colerne & Ternhill
Woodvale	7 × Chipmunks Set Piece	Finningley
Liverpool UAS	2 × Chipmunks	Finningley
Ternhill	Whirlwind	Finningley
Little Rissington	Gnat Solo Aerobatics	Leuchars
Dyce	Chipmunk Solo Aerobatics	Leuchars
Valley	4 × Gnats Formation Demo	Colerne, Cottesmore, St Athan & Ternhill
Syerston	Jet Provost Solo Aerobatics	St Athan
Bristol UAS	Chipmunk/Glider	St Mawgan
Syerston	Jet Provost Solo Aerobatics	St Mawgan
Ternhill	Whirlwind	Ternhill
Ternhill	4 × Whirlwinds Set Piece	Ternhill
Syerston	Jet Provost Solo Aerobatics	Waddington
Nottingham UAS	Chipmunk Solo Aerobatics	Waddington
Ternhill	Whirlwind	Waddington

Signals Command Surplus Allocated for Static Displays

Watton	Canberra	Abingdon
Watton	Canberra	Biggin Hill
Watton	Varsity	Biggin Hill
Watton	Varsity	Cottesmore
Watton	Canberra	Finningley

Maintenance Command Surplus Allocated for Static Displays

Bicester	Valetta	Biggin Hill

Maintenance Command Surplus Allocated for Flying Displays

St Athan	Meteor	St Athan
St Athan	AOP 9	St Athan
St Athan	Vampire	St Athan

90 Signals Group

Static

Watton	Canberra	Abingdon
Watton	Varsity	Biggin Hill
Watton	Varsity	Coltishall
Watton	Varsity	Cottesmore
Watton	Canberra	Finningley

Royal Air Force Germany Surplus Allocated for Static Displays

Laarbruch	Canberra	Acklington
Wildenrath	Canberra	Coltishall
Geilenkirchen	Javelin	Coltishall
Gutersloh	Hunter	Cottesmore
Wildenrath	Canberra	Leuchars

Royal Air Force Germany Surplus Allocated for Flying Displays

Laarbruch	Canberra	Acklington
Gutersloh	Hunter FR	Biggin Hill
Bruggen	Canberra	Waddington

Royal Navy Surplus Allocated for Static Displays

Farnborough	Wessex	Abingdon
Lossiemouth	Buccaneer	Acklington
Culdrose	Whirlwind	Colerne
Yeovilton	Sea Vixen	Cottesmore
Lossiemouth	Buccaneer	Leuchars
Brawdy	Whirlwind	St Athan
Culdrose	Wasp	St Athan
Culdrose	Wessex	St Athan
Yeovilton	Sea Vixen	St Athan

Royal Navy Surplus Allocated for Flying Displays

Brawdy	5 × Hunters Aerobatics Team	St Athan & St Mawgan
Culdrose	10 × Wessex	Biggin Hill
Culdrose	3 × Hillers	Biggin Hill

Culdrose	2 × Hillers	St Mawgan
Culdrose	Wessex V (Para Drop)	St Mawgan
Lossiemouth	Buccaneer	Acklington & Leuchars
Lossiemouth	Buccaneer	Colerne & Ternhill
Lossiemouth	Buccaneer	St Athan & St Mawgan
Lossiemouth	Scimitar	Abingdon & Biggin Hill
Lossiemouth	Scimitar	Acklington & Leuchars
Lossiemouth	Scimitar	St Athan & S Mawgan

Army Air Corps Surplus for Static Displays

| Middle Wallop | Beaver | Ternhill |

Army Air Corps Surplus for Flying Displays

| 6 Flight | Beaver | Finningley |

A&AEE, RAE, ETPS, Ministry of Aviation and Aviation Companies, Static

Boscombe Down	Canberra	Abingdon
Farnborough	Hunter	Abingdon
Boscombe Down	Harvard	Acklington
Bedford	P-1127	Biggin Hill
Pershore	Canberra	Colerne
Farnborough	Hunter	Colerne
Boscombe Down	Harvard	Colerne
Bedford	Fairy FD2	Coltishall
Bedford	Meteor NF	Cottesmore
Bedford	HP-115	Cottesmore
Farnborough	Viscount	Finningley
Farnborough	Twin Pioneer	Ternhill
Boscombe Down	Harvard	Ternhill
Pershore	Canberra	Waddington
Farnborough	Hunter	Waddington

Flying

| Boscombe Down | Hunter | Abingdon & Colerne |
| Boscombe Down | Lightning | Abingdon & Colerne |

Boscombe Down	Canberra	Abingdon
Dunsfold	Dominie	Biggin Hill & Ternhill
Dunsfold	Hurricane	Abingdon & Biggin Hill
Filton	HS 125	Colerne & Cottesmore
Redhill	Stampe	Cottesmore
Shoreham	Beagle 206	Coltishall
Redhill	2 × Turbulent	Coltishall
Tibenham	Tiger Moth + Skylark	Coltishall
Staverton	Airtourer	Coltishall
Tollerton	Falco 4	Coltishall
Boscombe Down	Canberra	Finningley
UK Skydiving Ltd	Dragon Rapide (Para Drop)	Finningley
Boscombe Down	Javelin	St Athan
Holme-on-Spalding	Buccaneer	Finningley

Belgian Air Force Surplus Allocated for Static Displays

Florennes	F-84F	Leuchars
Melsbroek	C-119	Leuchars
Melsbroek	C-119	St Mawgan

Belgian Air Force Surplus Allocated for Flying Displays

Kleine Brogel	F-104		Coltishall & Cottesmore (Deployed Lakenheath)
Melsbroek	C-119	(Para Drop)	Coltishall
Florennes	F-84F	Leuchars	
Brustem	7 × Fouga Magisters Team		St Mawgan

Royal Canadian Armed Forces Surplus Allocated for Static Displays

Baden Sollingen	T-33	Abingdon
Summerside	Neptune	St Mawgan

Royal Danish Air Force Surplus Allocated for Static Displays

Aalborg	C-47	Waddington

Royal Danish Air Force Surplus Allocated for Flying Displays

Skrydstrup   5 × F-100s Demo   Acklington, Leuchars & Waddington
(Deployed Waddington)

French Air Force Surplus Allocated for Static Displays

Villacoublay	Paris	Abingdon
Orleans Bricy	Nor Atlas	Coltishall
French Army	Allouette II	Cottesmore
Villacoublay	Paris	Finningley
Orleans Bricy	Nor Atlas	St Mawgan
Dijon	Mirage III	Waddington

French Air Force Surplus Allocated for Flying Displays

Dijon	Mirage III	Waddington
Salon-de-Province	7 × Fouga Magisters Team	Biggin Hill & Coltishall

Royal Norwegian Air Force Surplus Allocated for Flying Displays

Bodo   4 × F-104s Demo   Finningley, Ternhill & Waddington (Deployed Lakenheath)

United States Air Force Surplus Allocated for Static Displays

Alconbury	T-39	Acklington
Toul	RB-66	Coltishall
Bentwaters	T-33	Coltishall
Bentwaters	2 × F-101s	Coltishall
Lakenheath	F-100	Coltishall
Alconbury	RB-66	Cottesmore
Lakenheath	F-100	Cottesmore
Bentwaters	2 × F-101s	Finningley
Lakenheath	F-100	Leuchars
Bentwaters	2 × F-101	Leuchars
Wethersfield	T-39	St Athan
Wethersfield	F-100	St Mawgan
Bentwaters	2 × F-101s	St Mawgan
Rhein Main	C-47	Ternhill
Bentwaters	F-101	Waddington

United States Air Force Surplus Allocated for Flying Displays

Lakenheath	6 × F-100s Flypast	Abingdon, Biggin Hill, Coltishall, Cottesmore & Finningley
Wethersfield	6 × F-100s Flypast	Colerne, St Athan, St Mawgan, Ternhill
Bentwaters	3 × F-101s Flypast	Abingdon, Biggin Hill, Coltishall, Cottesmore & Finningley
Bentwaters	3 × F-101s Flypast	Colerne, St Athan, St Mawgan & Ternhill
Alconbury	2 × RF-4s Flypast	Abingdon, Biggin Hill, Coltishall, Cottesmore & Finningley
Alconbury	2 × RF-4s Flypast	Colerne, St Athan, St Mawgan, Ternhill & Waddington
Rhein Main	Cessna 172 (Para Drop)	Waddington

Touring Formations and Individual Aircraft

Chivenor	4 × Hunters	Abingdon, Colerne, St Athan & St Mawgan
Chivenor	4 × Hunters	Cottesmore, Finningley, Ternhill & Waddington
Scampton	1 × Vulcan	Abingdon, Biggin Hill, Colerne, Coltishall, St Athan & St Mawgan (Deployed St Mawgan)
Scampton	1 × Vulcan	Acklington, Leuchars & Ternhill (Deployed Leuchars)
Marham	1 × Victor	Abingdon, Colerne, St Athan & St Mawgan
Marham	1 × Victor	Biggin Hill, Coltishall, Cottesmore & Ternhill
Marham	1 × Victor	Acklington, Finninglcy, Lcuchars & Waddington
Bassingbourn	3 × Canberras	Ternhill
Benson	1 × Argosy	Acklington, Cottesmore, Finningley Leuchars & Ternhill
Benson	1 × Argosy	St Athan & St Mawgan
Lyneham	1 × Comet	Abingdon, Cottesmore & Finningley
Lyneham	1 × Comet	Acklington, Leuchars & Waddington
Lyneham	1 × Comet	St Athan, St Mawgan & Ternhill
St Mawgan	1 × Shackleton	Abingdon, Biggin Hill, Coltishall, Cottesmore, Finningley & Waddington
St Mawgan	1 × Shackleton	Colerne, St Athan, St Mawgan & Ternhill
St Mawgan	1 × Shackleton	Acklington & Leuchars
Manby	3 × Canberras	Acklington, Finningley, Leuchars & Waddington
Syerston	6 × Jet Provosts	Coltishall, Cottesmore, Ternhill & Waddington
Oakington	4 × Varsities	Abingdon, Colerne, St Athan
Topcliffe	3 × Varsities	Acklington & Finningley
Stradishall	3 × Varsities	Ternhill & Waddington
Yeovilton	2 × Sea Vixens	Colerne, St Athan & St Mawgan
Yeovilton	2 × Sea Vixens	Cottesmore & Ternhill
Bedford	Comet	Coltishall, Cottesmore, Finningley & Waddington
Wisley	VC-10	Finningley & Waddington

Vintage Aircraft—Military and Civil

Static

Shuttleworth	Avro 504K	Abingdon
Abingdon	Spitfire	Abingdon
Shuttleworth	Bristol F2B	Biggin Hill
Coltishall	Spitfire	Colerne
Coltishall	Spitfire	Coltishall
Bedford	HP115	Cottesmore
St Athan	Britannia Prototype	St Athan
St Athan	P1A Lightning Prototype	St Athan
Shuttleworth	Avro 504K	Waddington
Shuttleworth	Sopwith Pup	Waddington
Waddington	Lancaster	Waddington

A Number of Stations Held Their Own Museum Collections, most of which Were Prepositioned

Biggin Hill	Flying Flea, Fiat CR42, JU88, ME 109E, ME 110, FW 190, Henschel 293, Mitsubishi Dena, Wellington, V1 & V2
Colerne	Spitfire IIa, Hawker P1052, Valetta C2, Vampire T11, Javelin FAW4, Hunter Prototype WB188, Prone Pilot Meteor, HE 162, ME 163B, Auster T7, Anson C19, Meteor F4, Hunter F2 & Canberra B2
Coltishall	Feisler Storch
Cottesmore	Spitfire F24, ME 163 & ME 262
St Athan	2 × Javelins, Victor B1, 2 × Valiants, Vampire T11, Defiant 1, JU87, Watkins Monoplane, Replica Box Kite, BE2, Bristol Scout, Sopwith Camel & Montgolfier Balloon, 5 × Hunter F1s, Hunter F4, 3 × Provost T1s, Dragonfly, Sycamore, & Canberra

Vintage Aircraft Allocated for Flying Displays

Coltishall	Spitfire PR19	Abingdon, Coltishall & Colerne
Dunsfold	Hurricane	Abingdon & Biggin Hill
Little Rissington	Mosquito	Abingdon, Biggin Hill, Colerne & Ternhill
Coltishall	Spitfire PR19	Acklington, Cottesmore & Leuchars
Shuttleworth	Avro Tutor	Biggin Hill
Shuttleworth	Bristol FB2	Biggin Hill
Shuttleworth	Hawker Hart	Biggin Hill
Shuttleworth	Swordfish	Biggin Hill
Coltishall	Spitfire	Biggin Hill
Coltishall	Hurricane	Coltishall, Cottesmore, Finningley & Waddington
Hucknall	Spitfire	Finningley & Ternhill
Redhill	Super Tiger	Leuchars
Shuttleworth	Gladiator	Ternhill

Shuttleworth	Tomtit	Ternhill
Shuttleworth	Miles Hawk	Ternhill
	Avro Anson	Ternhill
Shuttleworth	Sopwith Pup	Waddington
Elstree	Spitfire IX	Waddington